aven's Will

A Poem of Atonement

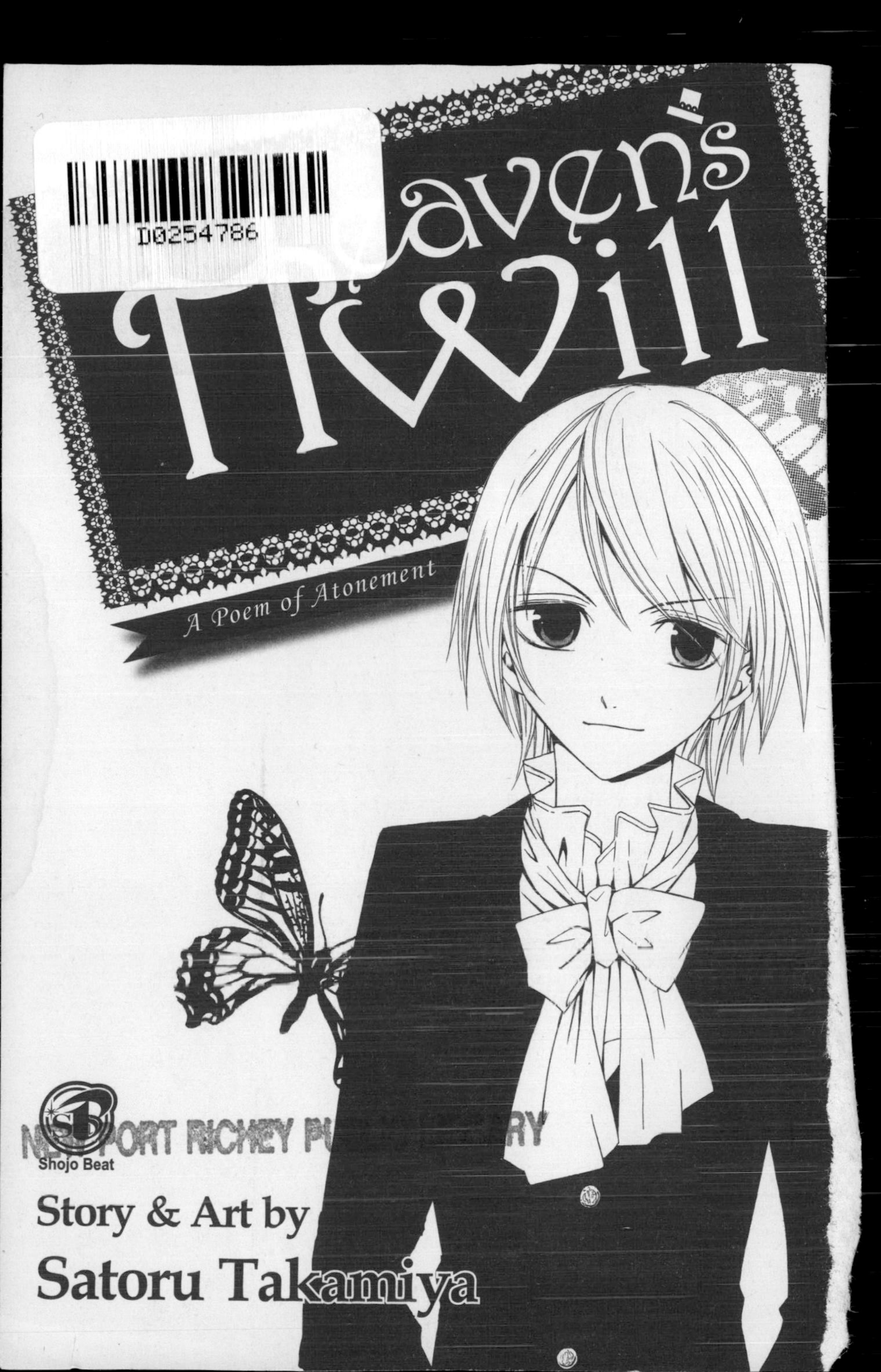

Shojo Beat

Story & Art by

Satoru Takamiya

Heaven's Will

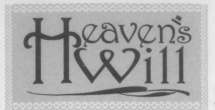

CONTENTS

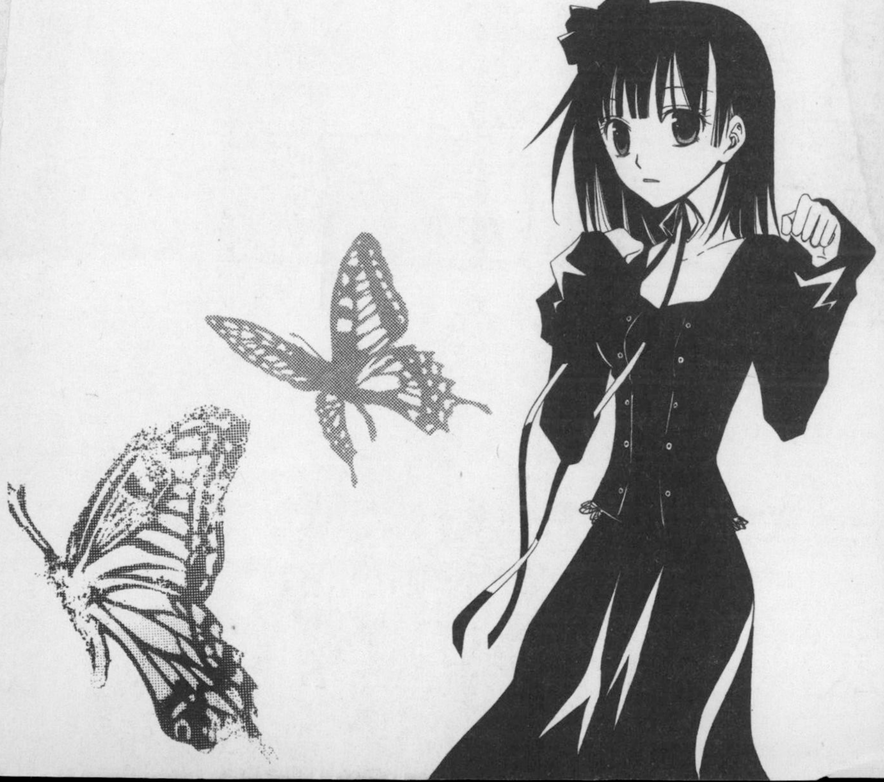

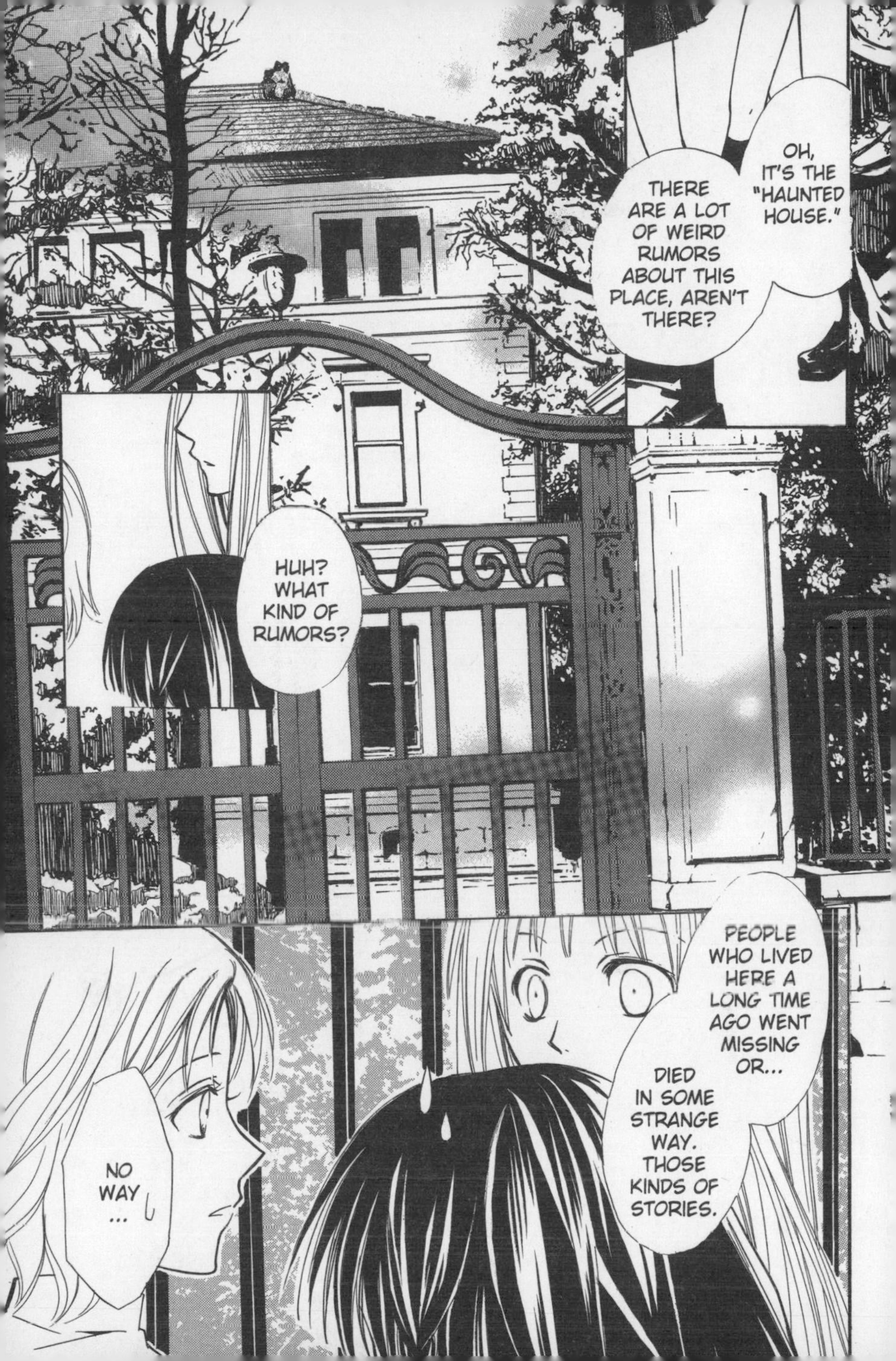
OH, IT'S THE "HAUNTED HOUSE."
THERE ARE A LOT OF WEIRD RUMORS ABOUT THIS PLACE, AREN'T THERE?
HUH? WHAT KIND OF RUMORS?
PEOPLE WHO LIVED HERE A LONG TIME AGO WENT MISSING OR...
DIED IN SOME STRANGE WAY. THOSE KINDS OF STORIES.
NO WAY...

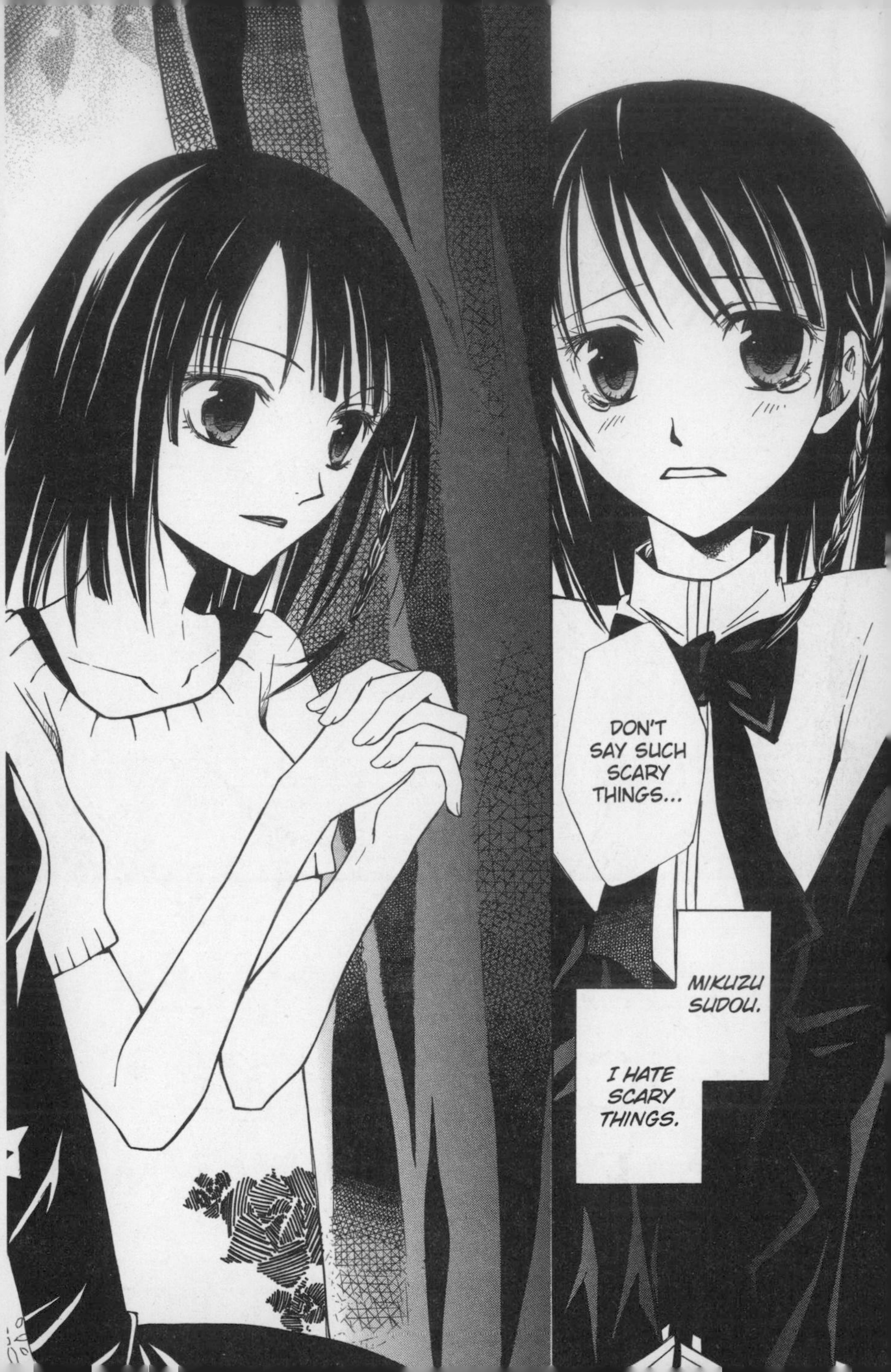
DON'T SAY SUCH SCARY THINGS...
MIKUZU SUDOU.
I HATE SCARY THINGS.

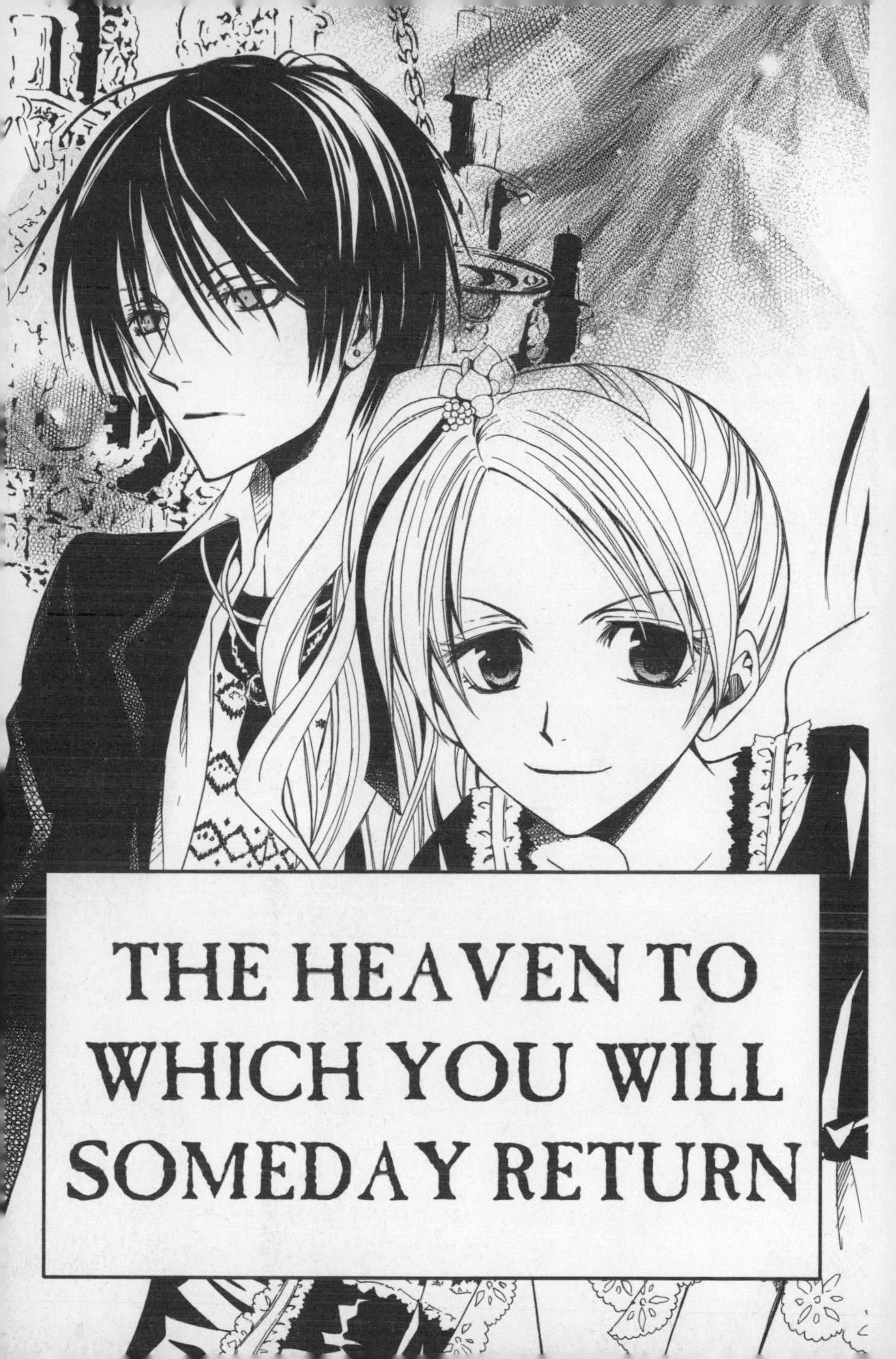
THE HEAVEN TO WHICH YOU WILL SOMEDAY RETURN

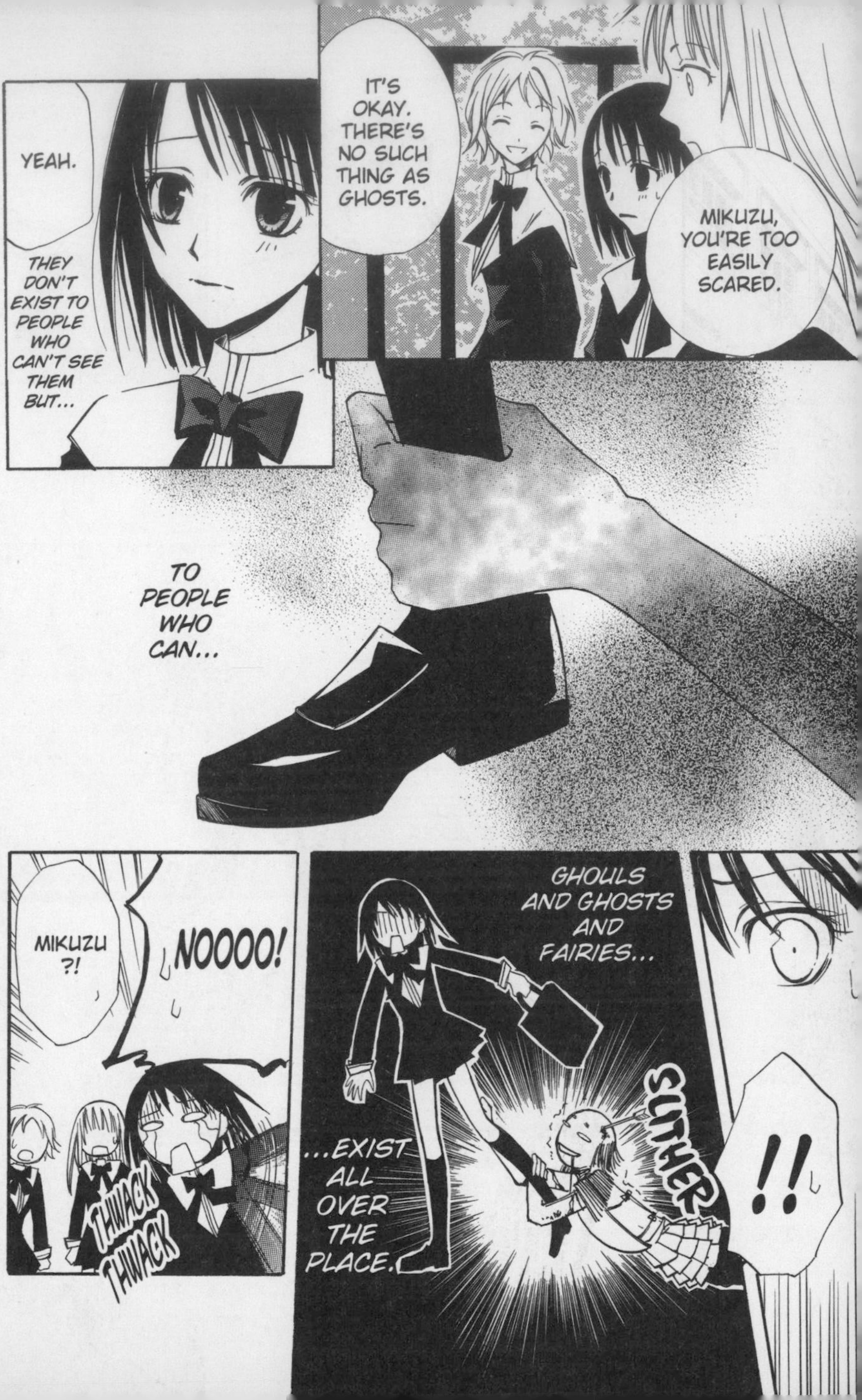
MIKUZU, YOU'RE TOO EASILY SCARED.
IT'S OKAY. THERE'S NO SUCH THING AS GHOSTS.
YEAH.
THEY DON'T EXIST TO PEOPLE WHO CAN'T SEE THEM BUT...
TO PEOPLE WHO CAN...
!!
GHOULS AND GHOSTS AND FAIRIES...
SLITHER
...EXIST ALL OVER THE PLACE.
NOOOO!
MIKUZU ?!
THWACK THWACK

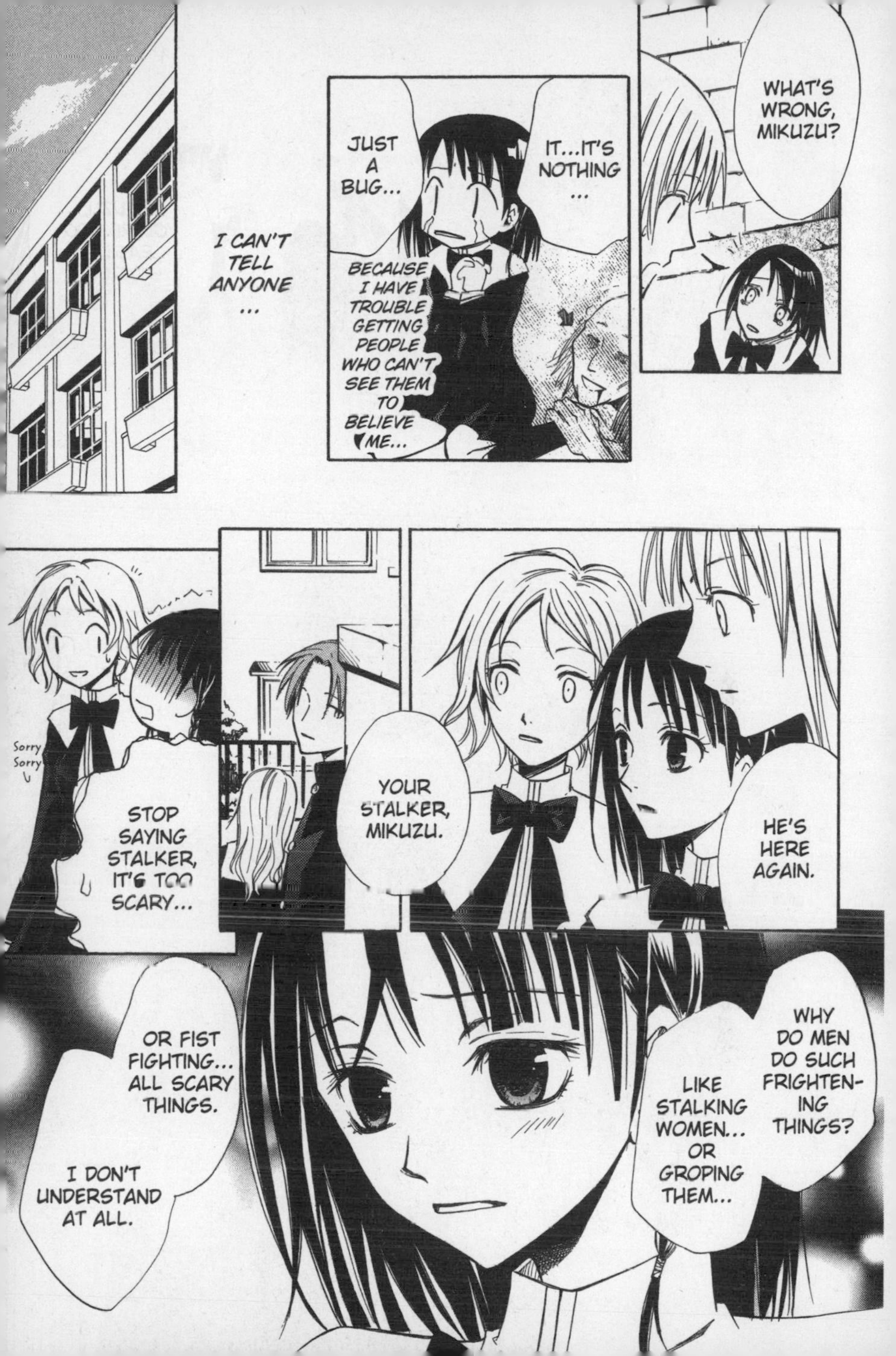
WHAT'S WRONG, MIKUZU?
IT...IT'S NOTHING ...
JUST A BUG...
BECAUSE I HAVE TROUBLE GETTING PEOPLE WHO CAN'T SEE THEM TO BELIEVE ME...
I CAN'T TELL ANYONE ...
HE'S HERE AGAIN.
YOUR STALKER, MIKUZU.
STOP SAYING STALKER, IT'S TOO SCARY...
Sorry Sorry
WHY DO MEN DO SUCH FRIGHTENING THINGS?
LIKE STALKING WOMEN... OR GROPING THEM...
OR FIST FIGHTING... ALL SCARY THINGS.
I DON'T UNDERSTAND AT ALL.

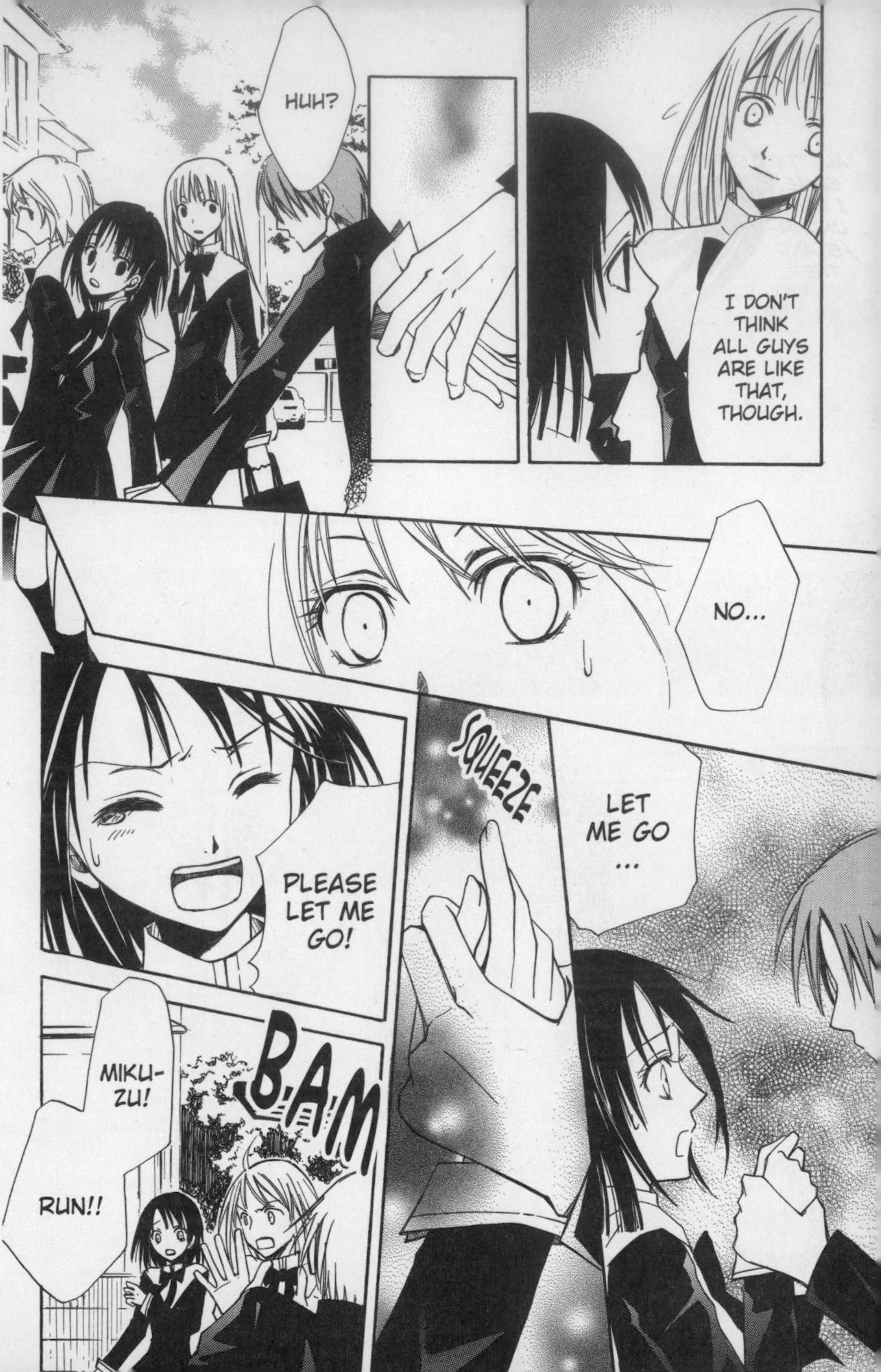
I DON'T THINK ALL GUYS ARE LIKE THAT, THOUGH.
HUH?
NO...
SQUEEZE
LET ME GO ...
PLEASE LET ME GO!
BAM
MIKU-ZU!
RUN!!

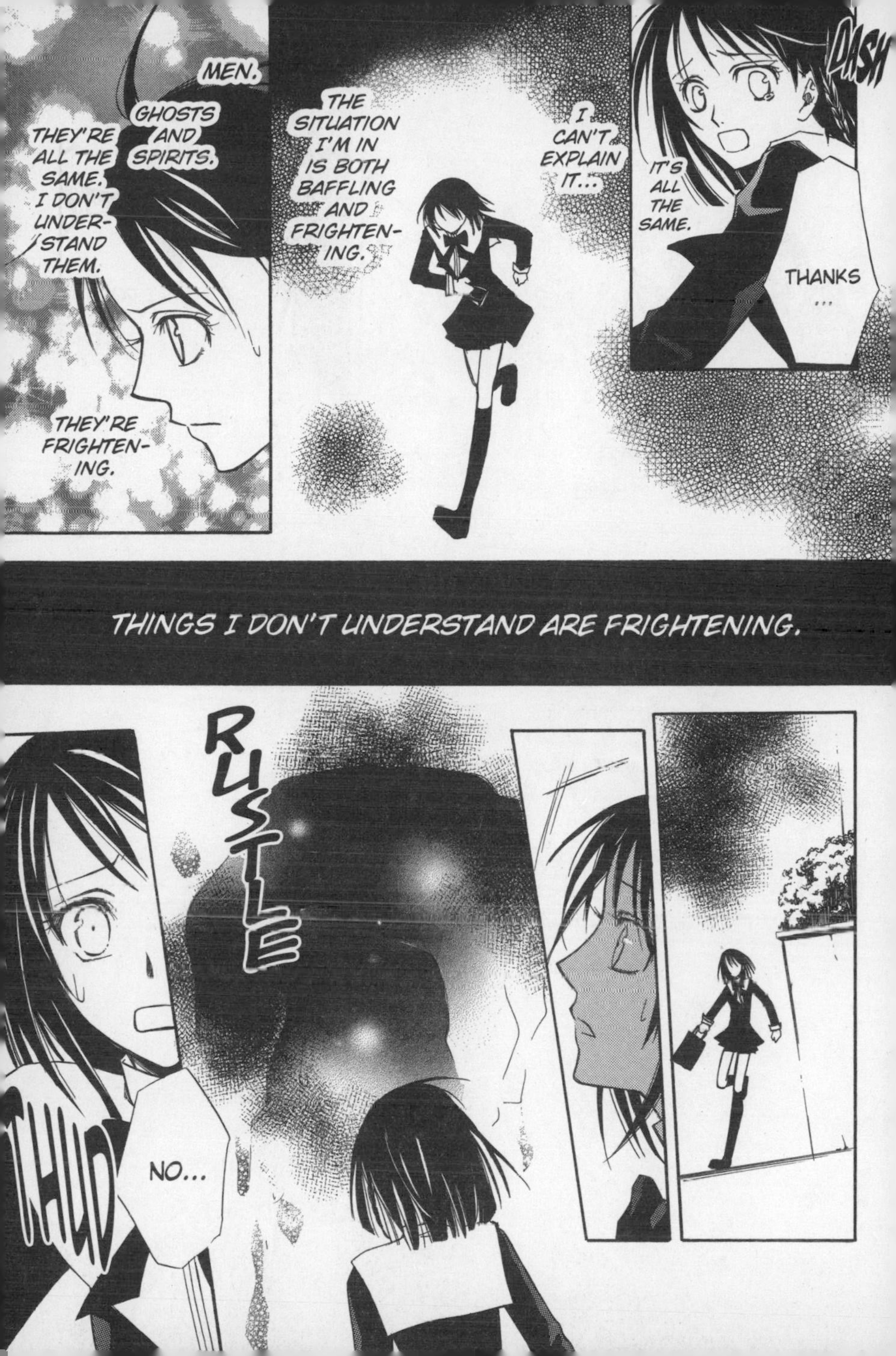
DASH
IT'S ALL THE SAME.
THANKS...
I CAN'T EXPLAIN IT...
THE SITUATION I'M IN IS BOTH BAFFLING AND FRIGHTENING.
MEN.
GHOSTS AND SPIRITS.
THEY'RE ALL THE SAME. I DON'T UNDERSTAND THEM.
THEY'RE FRIGHTENING.
THINGS I DON'T UNDERSTAND ARE FRIGHTENING.
RUSTLE
THUD
NO...

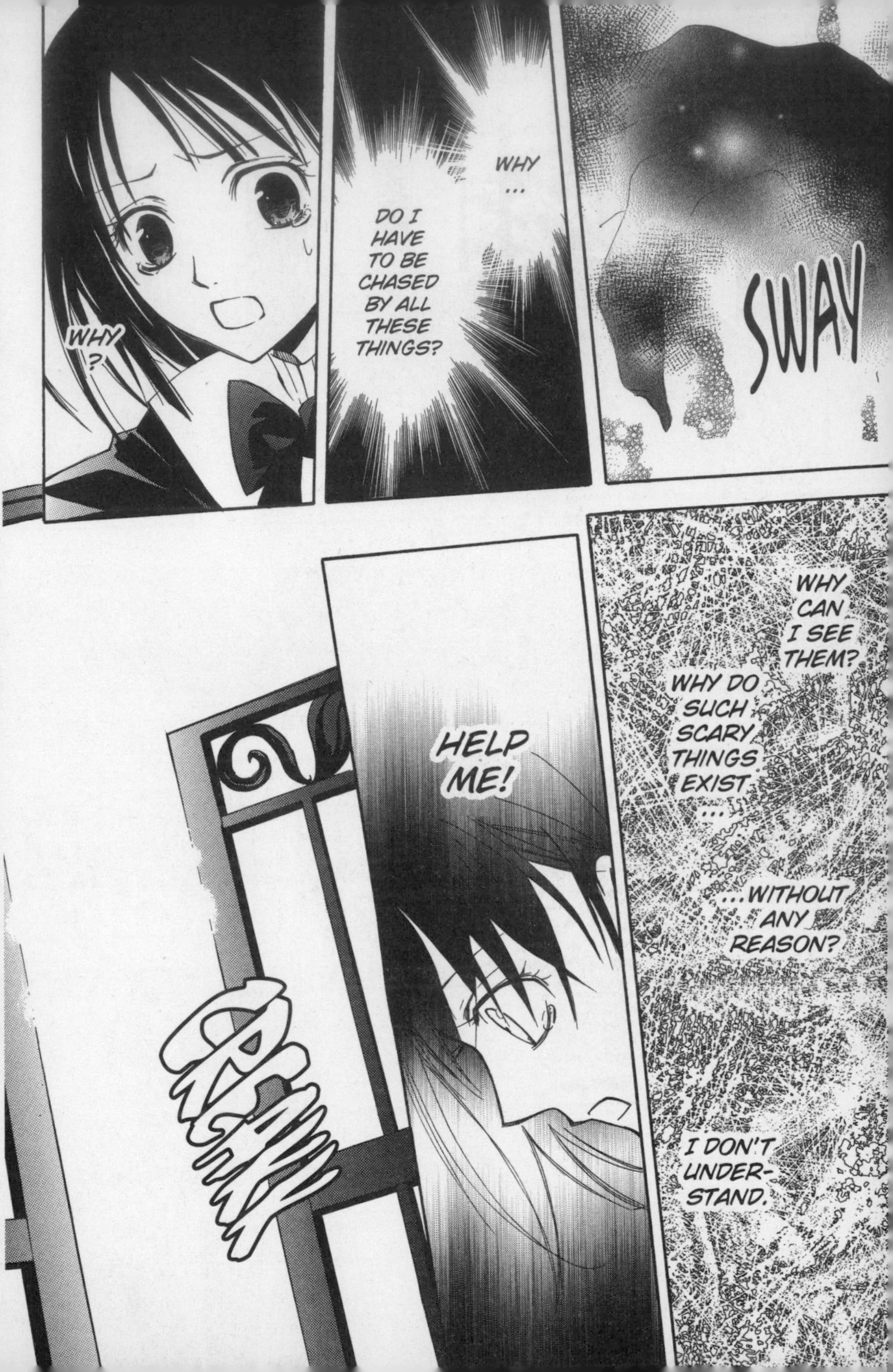
SWAY
WHY ...
DO I HAVE TO BE CHASED BY ALL THESE THINGS?
WHY?
WHY CAN I SEE THEM?
WHY DO SUCH SCARY THINGS EXIST ...
...WITHOUT ANY REASON?
I DON'T UNDER-STAND.
HELP ME!

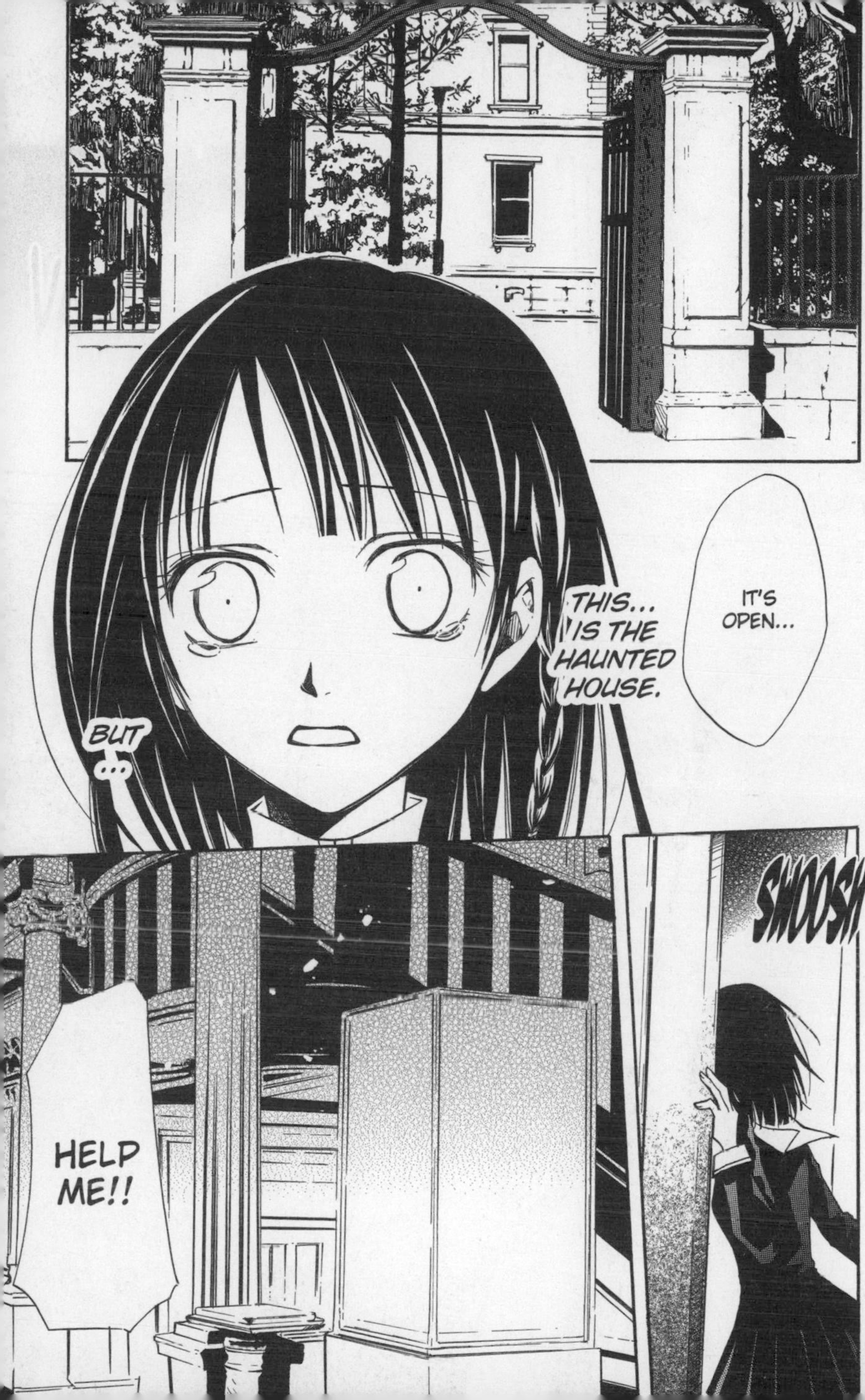
IT'S OPEN...
THIS... IS THE HAUNTED HOUSE.
BUT ...
SWOOSH
HELP ME!!

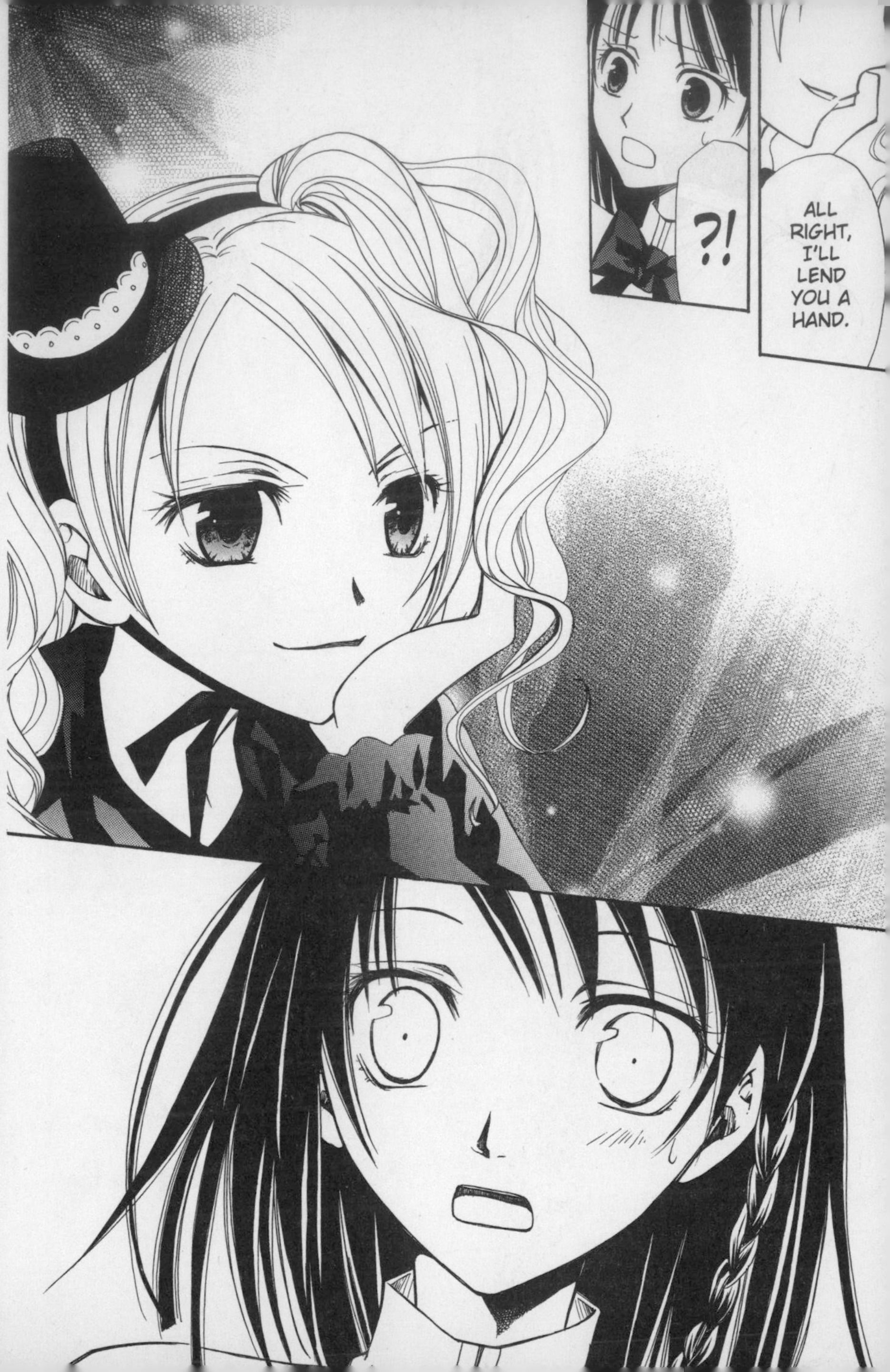
ALL RIGHT, I'LL LEND YOU A HAND.
?!

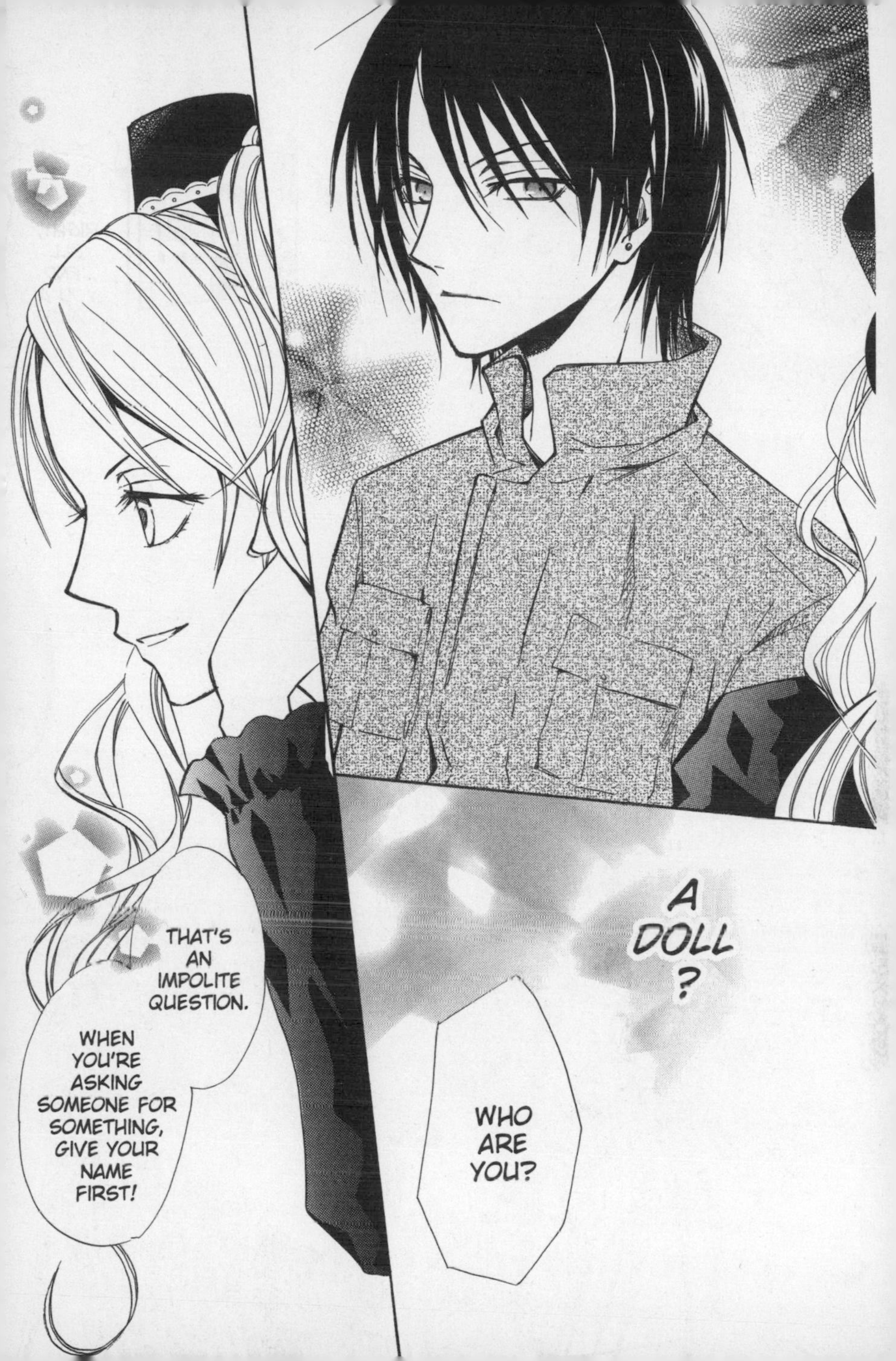
A DOLL?
WHO ARE YOU?
THAT'S AN IMPOLITE QUESTION.
WHEN YOU'RE ASKING SOMEONE FOR SOMETHING, GIVE YOUR NAME FIRST!

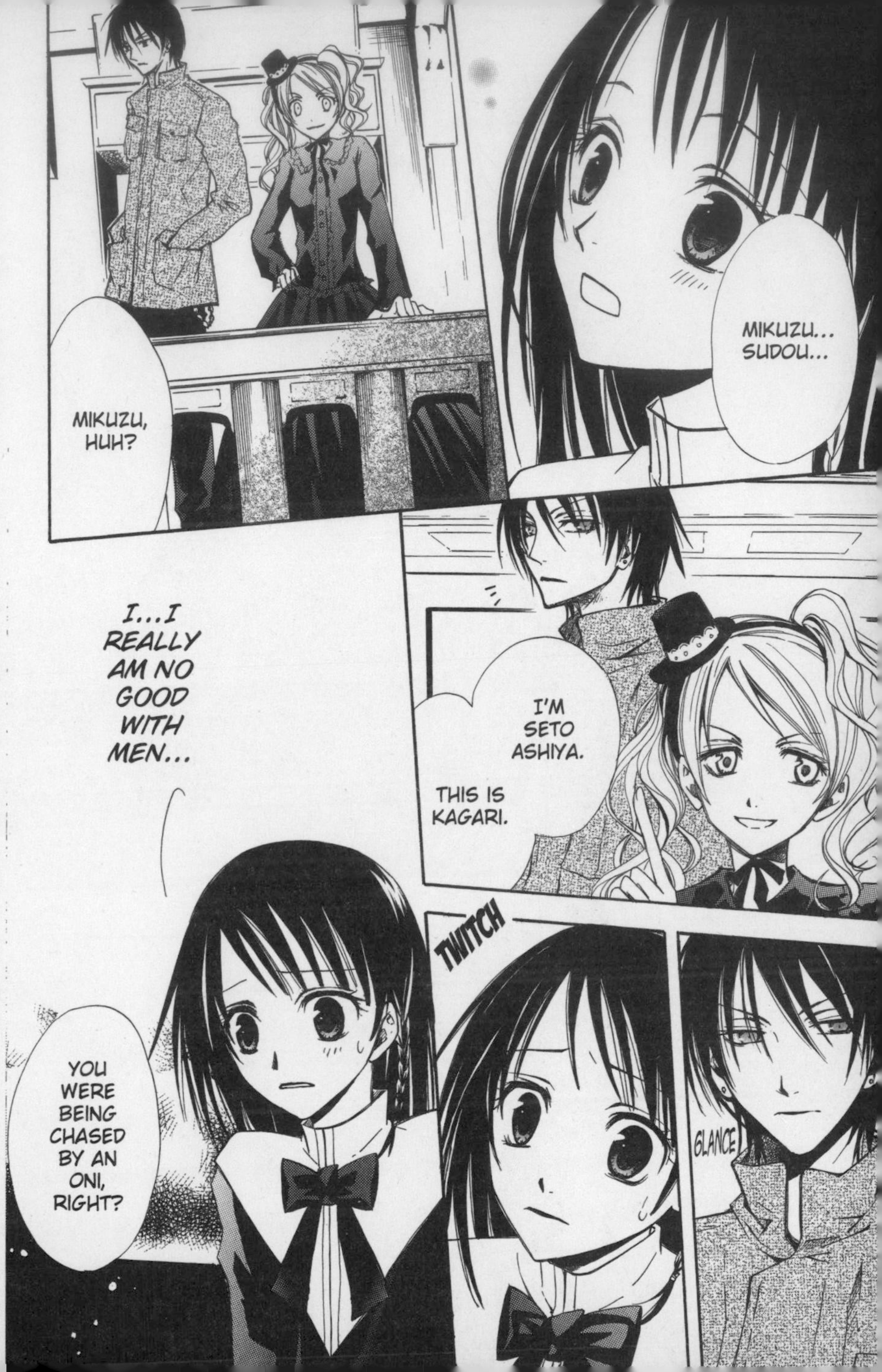
MIKUZU... SUDOU...
MIKUZU, HUH?
I'M SETO ASHIYA.
THIS IS KAGARI.
GLANCE
TWITCH
I...I REALLY AM NO GOOD WITH MEN...
YOU WERE BEING CHASED BY AN ONI, RIGHT?

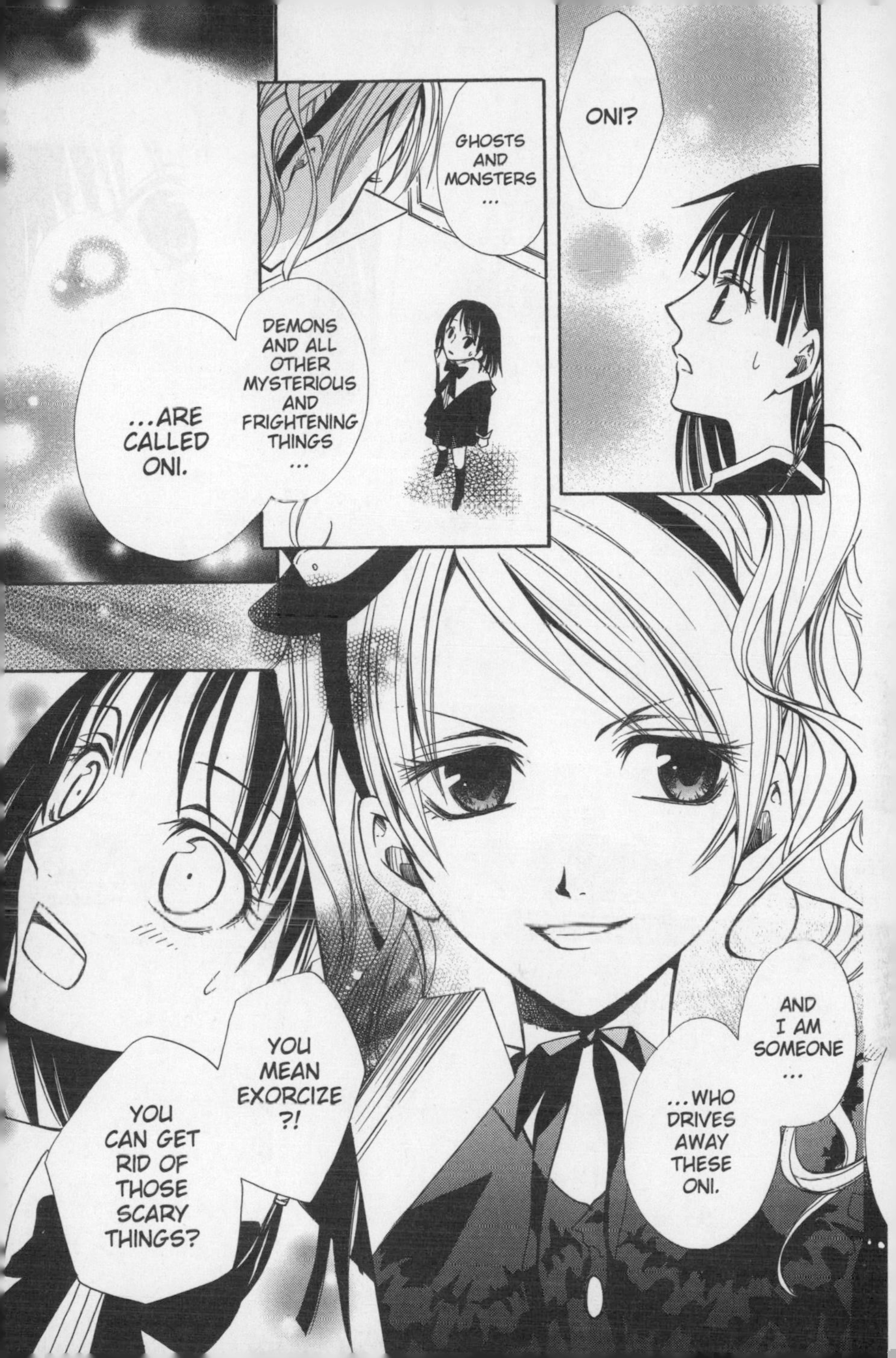
ONI?
GHOSTS AND MONSTERS ...
DEMONS AND ALL OTHER MYSTERIOUS AND FRIGHTENING THINGS ...
...ARE CALLED ONI.
AND I AM SOMEONE ...
...WHO DRIVES AWAY THESE ONI.
YOU MEAN EXORCIZE ?!
YOU CAN GET RID OF THOSE SCARY THINGS?

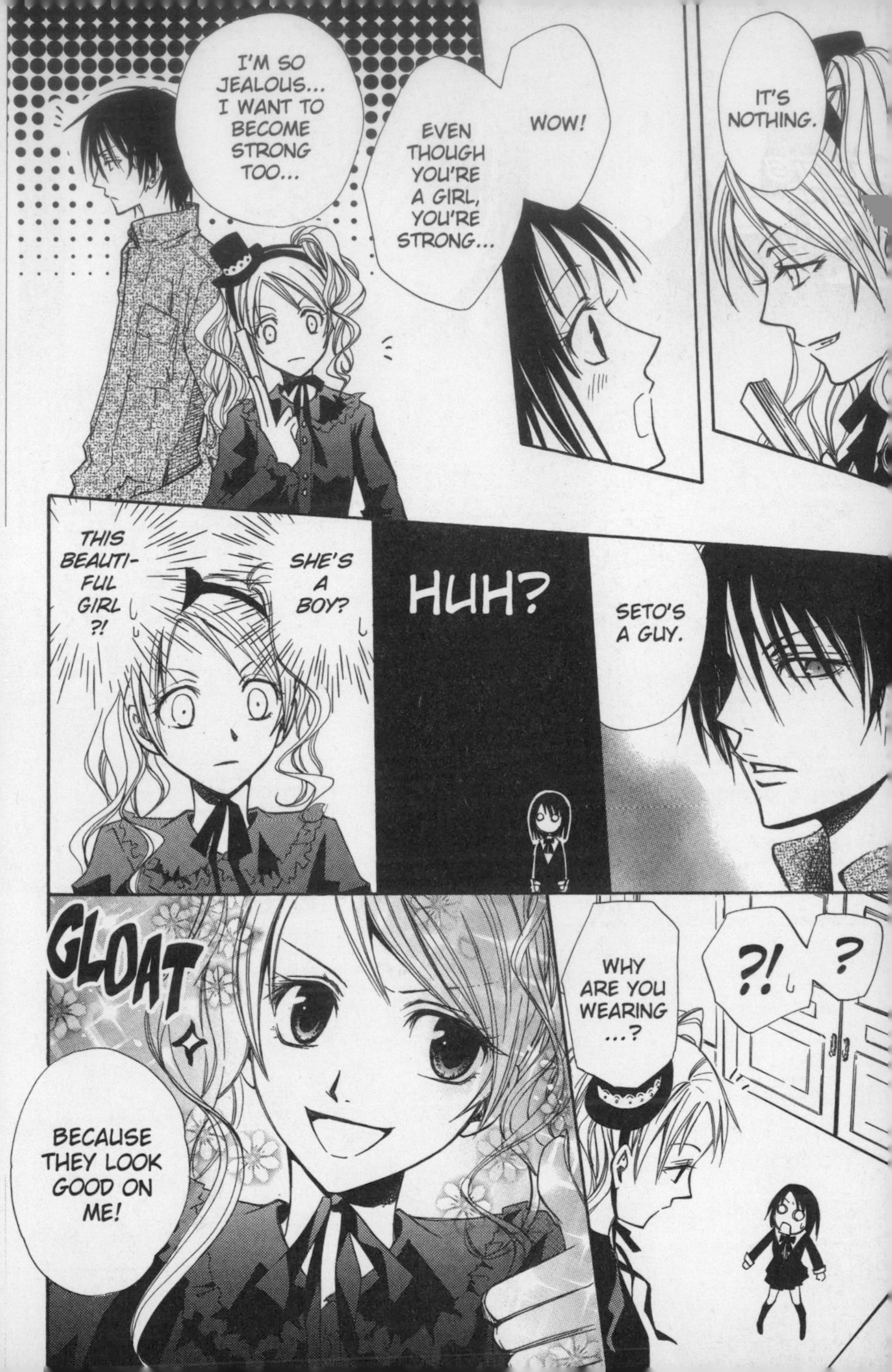
IT'S NOTHING.
WOW!
EVEN THOUGH YOU'RE A GIRL, YOU'RE STRONG...
I'M SO JEALOUS... I WANT TO BECOME STRONG TOO...
SETO'S A GUY.
HUH?
SHE'S A BOY?
THIS BEAUTI-FUL GIRL ?!
?! ?
WHY ARE YOU WEARING ...?
GLOAT
BECAUSE THEY LOOK GOOD ON ME!

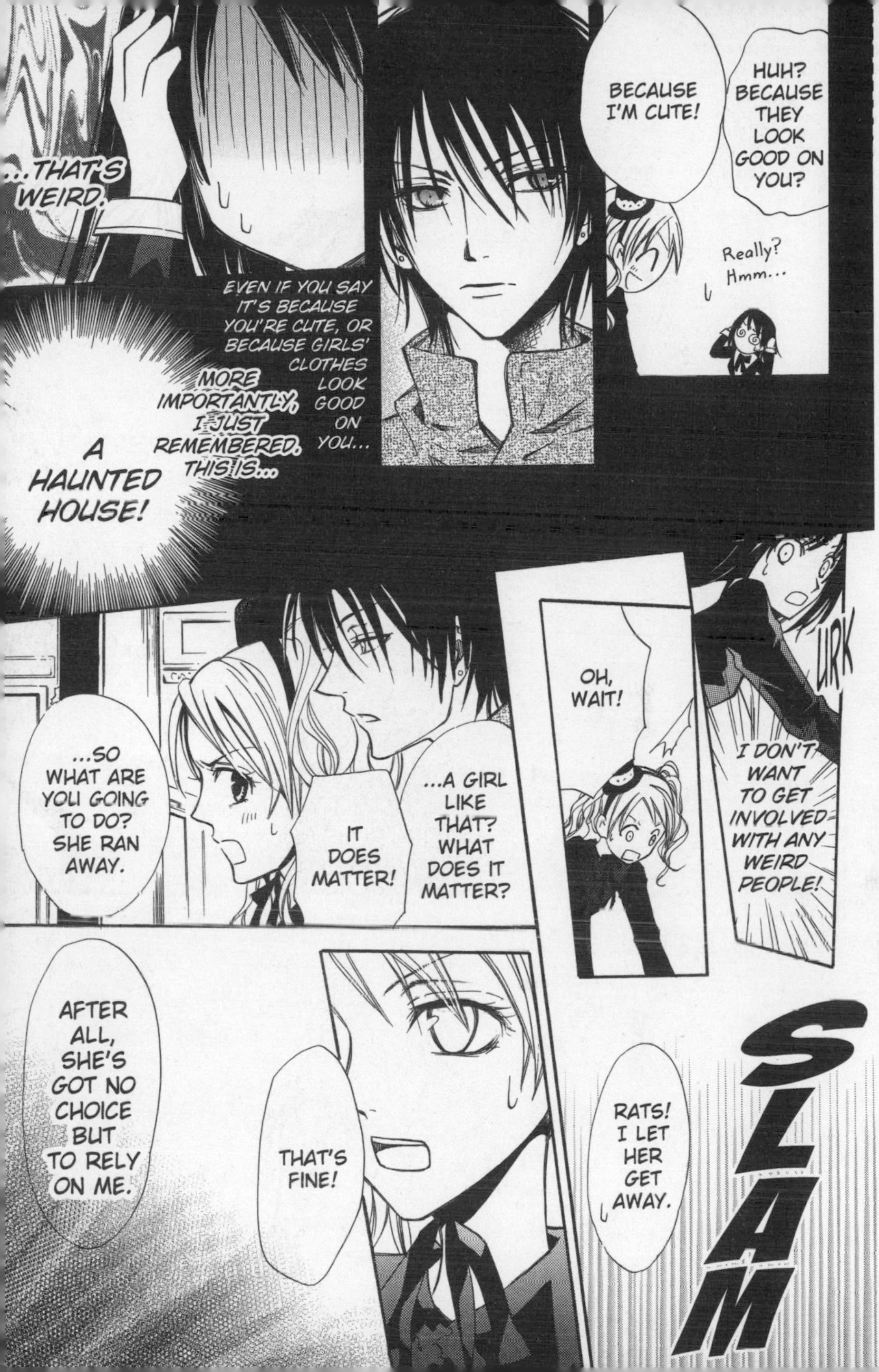
BECAUSE I'M CUTE!
HUH? BECAUSE THEY LOOK GOOD ON YOU?
Really? Hmm...
EVEN IF YOU SAY IT'S BECAUSE YOU'RE CUTE, OR BECAUSE GIRLS' CLOTHES LOOK GOOD ON YOU...
...THAT'S WEIRD.
MORE IMPORTANTLY, I JUST REMEMBERED. THIS IS...
A HAUNTED HOUSE!
URK
I DON'T WANT TO GET INVOLVED WITH ANY WEIRD PEOPLE!
OH, WAIT!
...A GIRL LIKE THAT? WHAT DOES IT MATTER?
IT DOES MATTER!
...SO WHAT ARE YOU GOING TO DO? SHE RAN AWAY.
SLAM
RATS! I LET HER GET AWAY.
THAT'S FINE!
AFTER ALL, SHE'S GOT NO CHOICE BUT TO RELY ON ME.

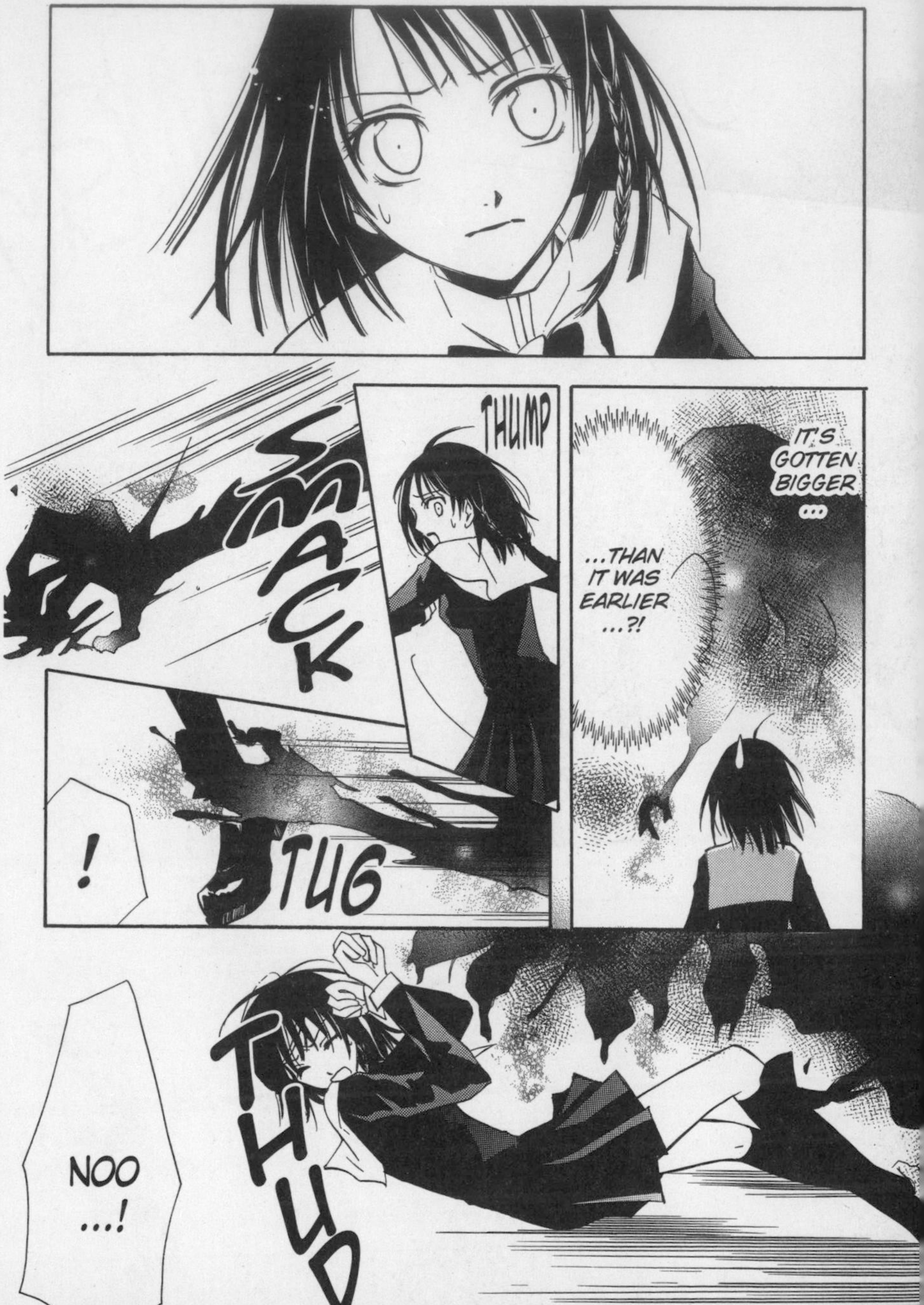
IT'S GOTTEN BIGGER ...
...THAN IT WAS EARLIER ...?!
THUMP
SMACK
TUG
!
THUD
NOO ...!

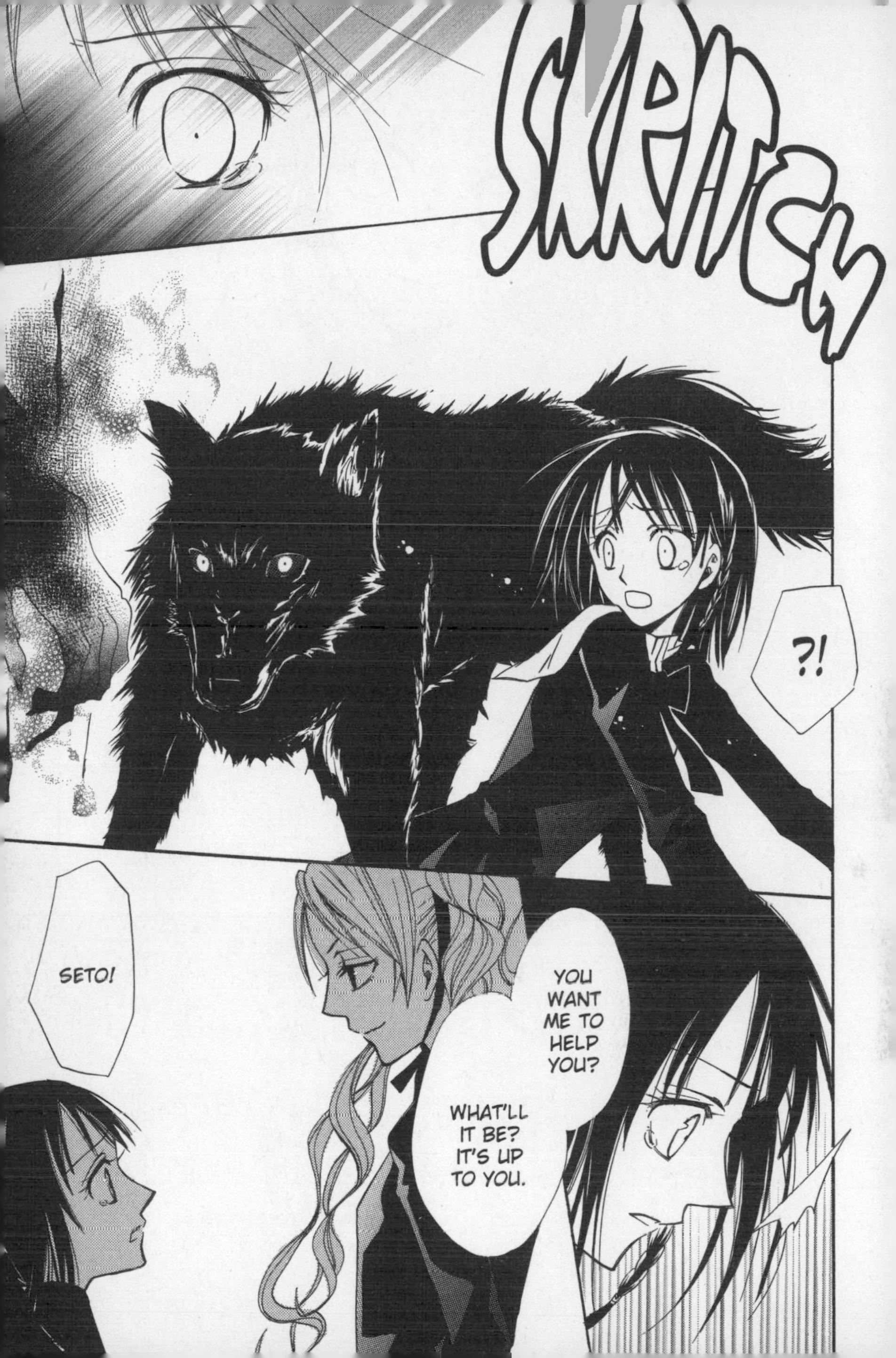
SNATCH
?!
YOU WANT ME TO HELP YOU?
WHAT'LL IT BE? IT'S UP TO YOU.
SETO!

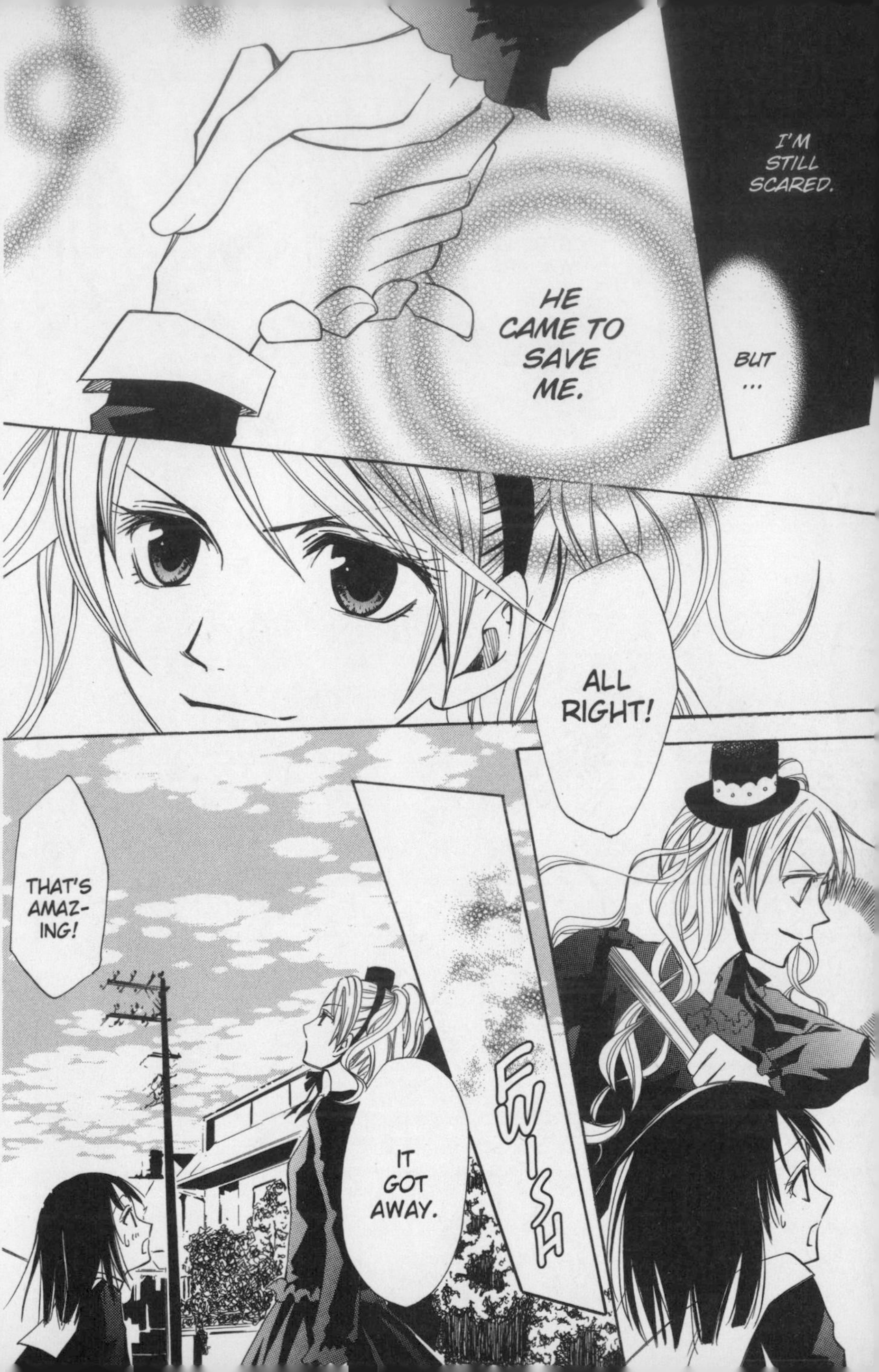
I'M STILL SCARED.
BUT ...
HE CAME TO SAVE ME.
ALL RIGHT!
FWISH
IT GOT AWAY.
THAT'S AMAZ-ING!

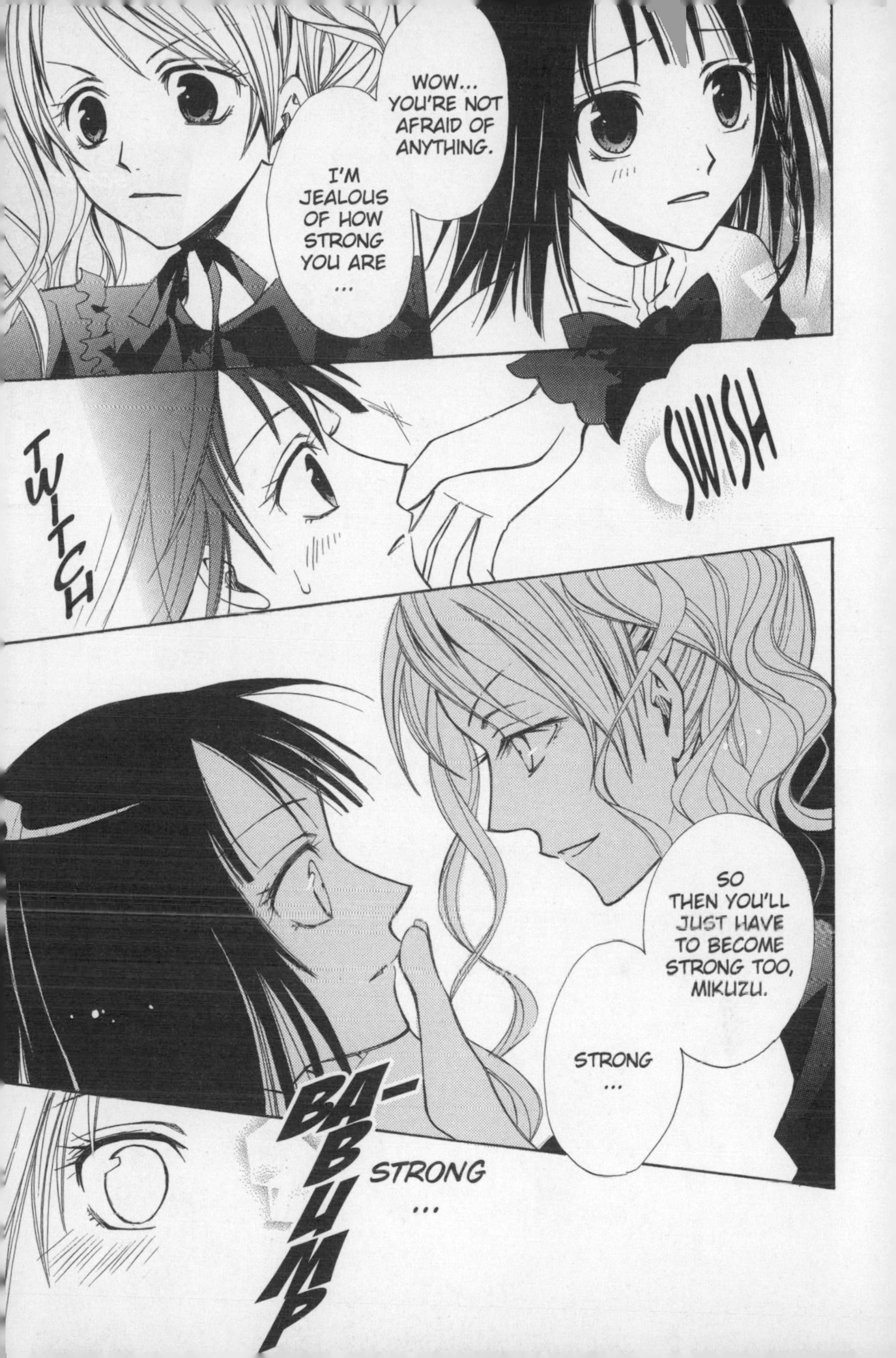

WOW... YOU'RE NOT AFRAID OF ANYTHING.
I'M JEALOUS OF HOW STRONG YOU ARE ...
SWISH
TWITCH
SO THEN YOU'LL JUST HAVE TO BECOME STRONG TOO, MIKUZU.
STRONG ...
STRONG ...
BA-BUMP

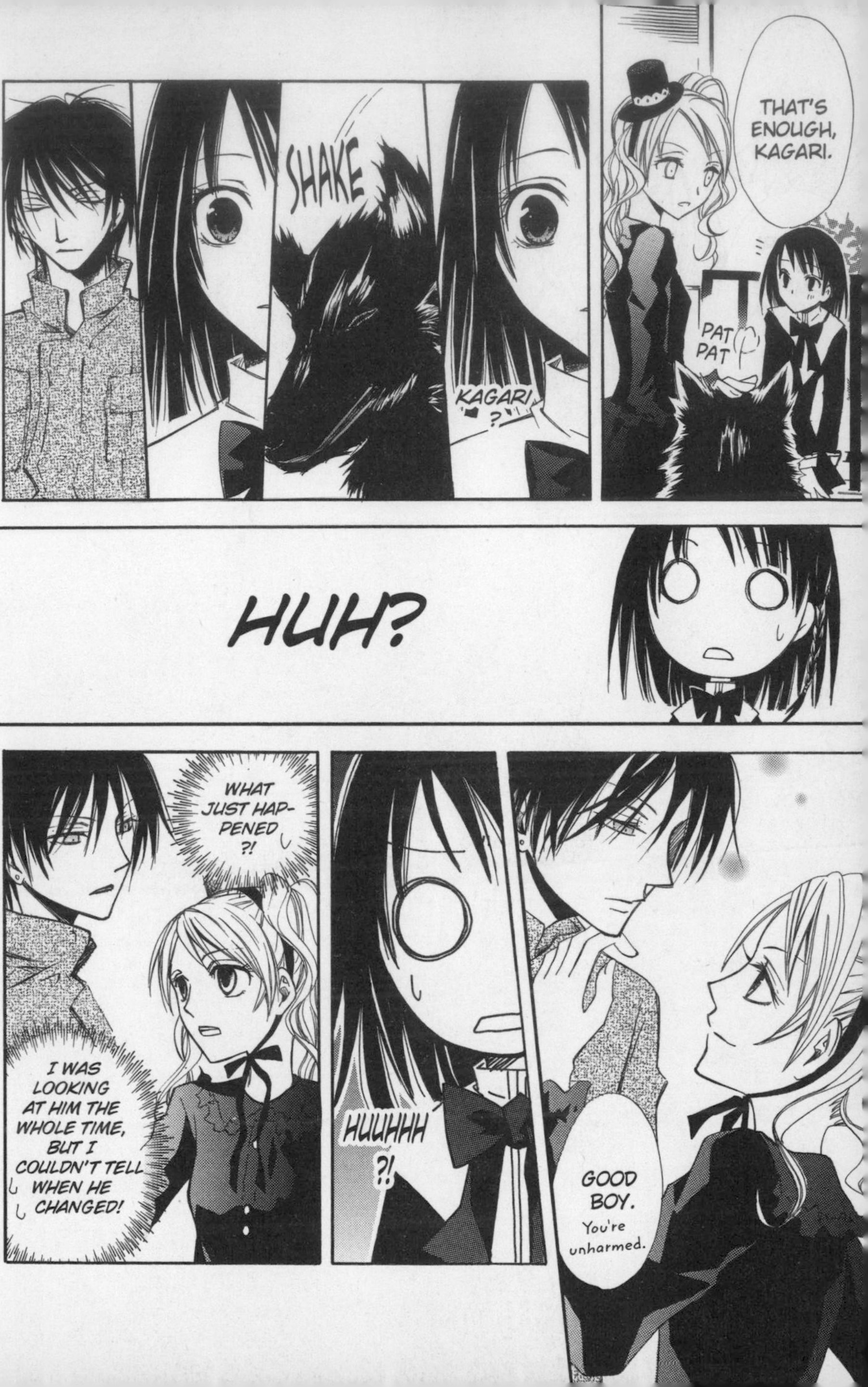
THAT'S ENOUGH, KAGARI.
PAT PAT
KAGARI ?
SHAKE
HUH?
GOOD BOY.
You're unharmed.
HUUHHH ?!
WHAT JUST HAPPENED ?!
I WAS LOOKING AT HIM THE WHOLE TIME, BUT I COULDN'T TELL WHEN HE CHANGED!

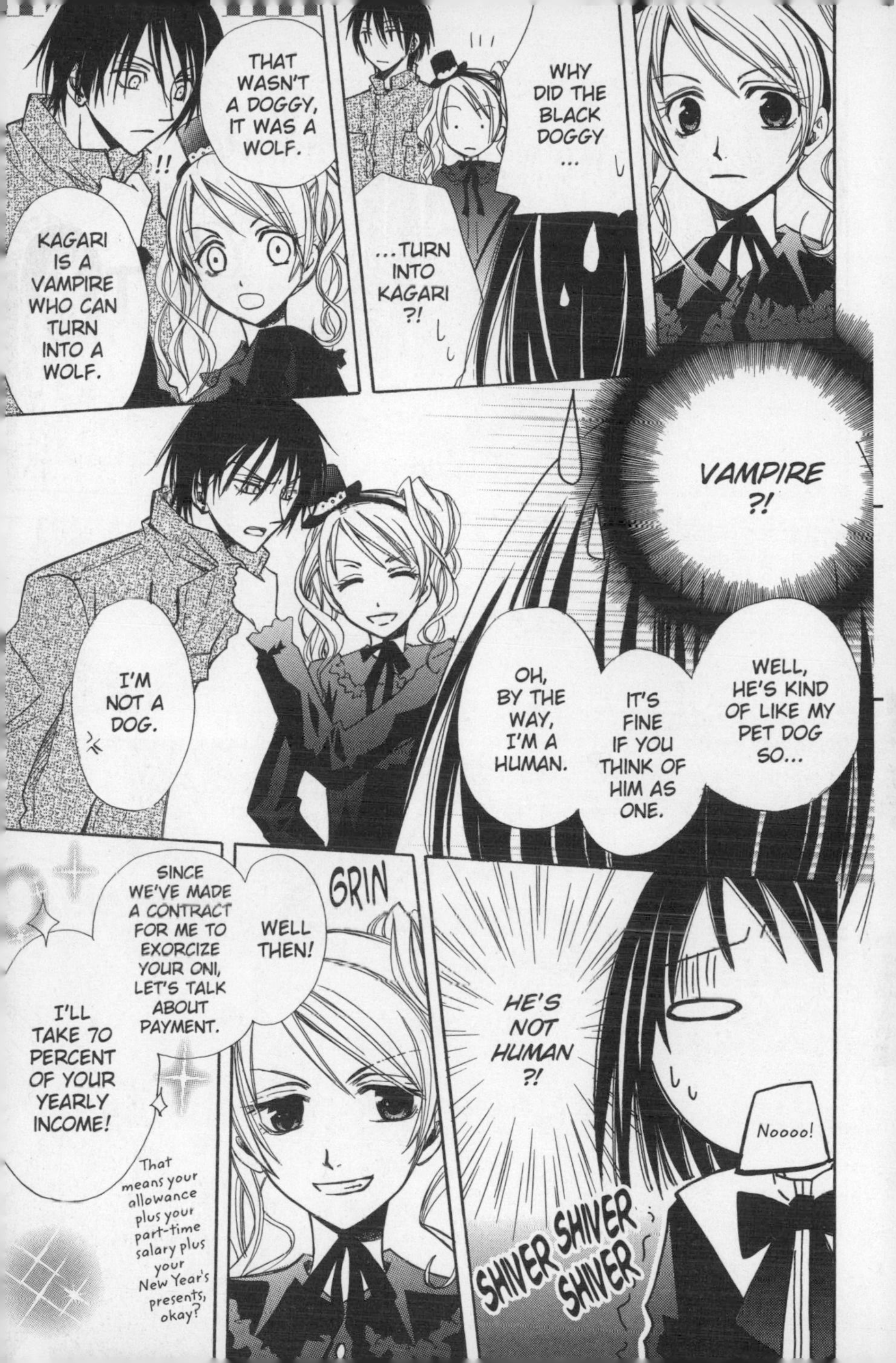
WHY DID THE BLACK DOGGY...
...TURN INTO KAGARI?!
THAT WASN'T A DOGGY, IT WAS A WOLF.
!!
KAGARI IS A VAMPIRE WHO CAN TURN INTO A WOLF.
VAMPIRE?!
WELL, HE'S KIND OF LIKE MY PET DOG SO...
IT'S FINE IF YOU THINK OF HIM AS ONE.
OH, BY THE WAY, I'M A HUMAN.
I'M NOT A DOG.
HE'S NOT HUMAN?!
Noooo!
SHIVER SHIVER SHIVER
GRIN
WELL THEN!
SINCE WE'VE MADE A CONTRACT FOR ME TO EXORCIZE YOUR ONI, LET'S TALK ABOUT PAYMENT.
I'LL TAKE 70 PERCENT OF YOUR YEARLY INCOME!
That means your allowance plus your part-time salary plus your New Year's presents, okay?

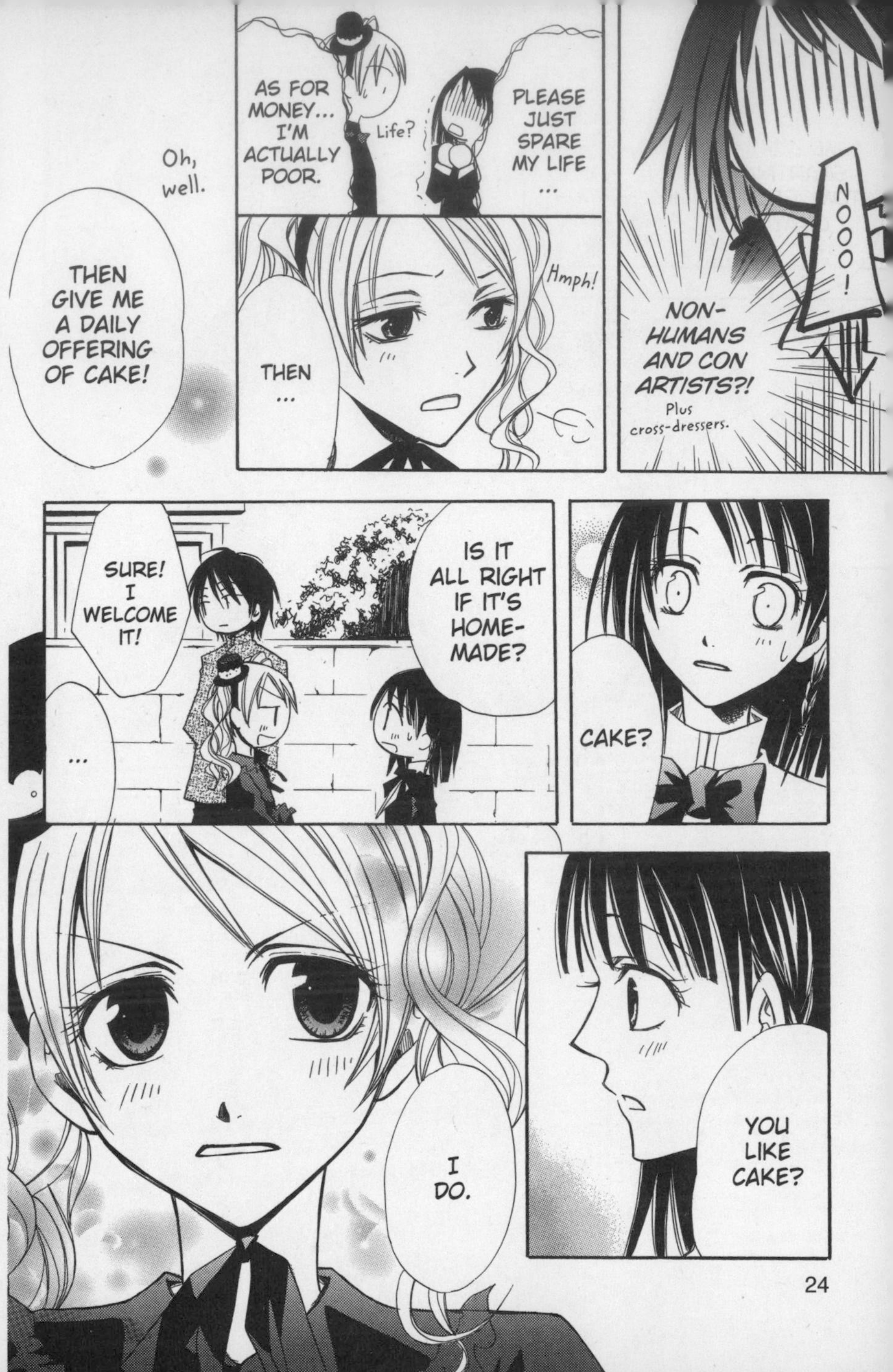
NOOO!
NON-HUMANS AND CON ARTISTS?!
Plus cross-dressers.
PLEASE JUST SPARE MY LIFE ...
Life?
AS FOR MONEY... I'M ACTUALLY POOR.
Oh, well.
Hmph!
THEN ...
THEN GIVE ME A DAILY OFFERING OF CAKE!
CAKE?
IS IT ALL RIGHT IF IT'S HOME-MADE?
SURE! I WELCOME IT!
...
YOU LIKE CAKE?
I DO.

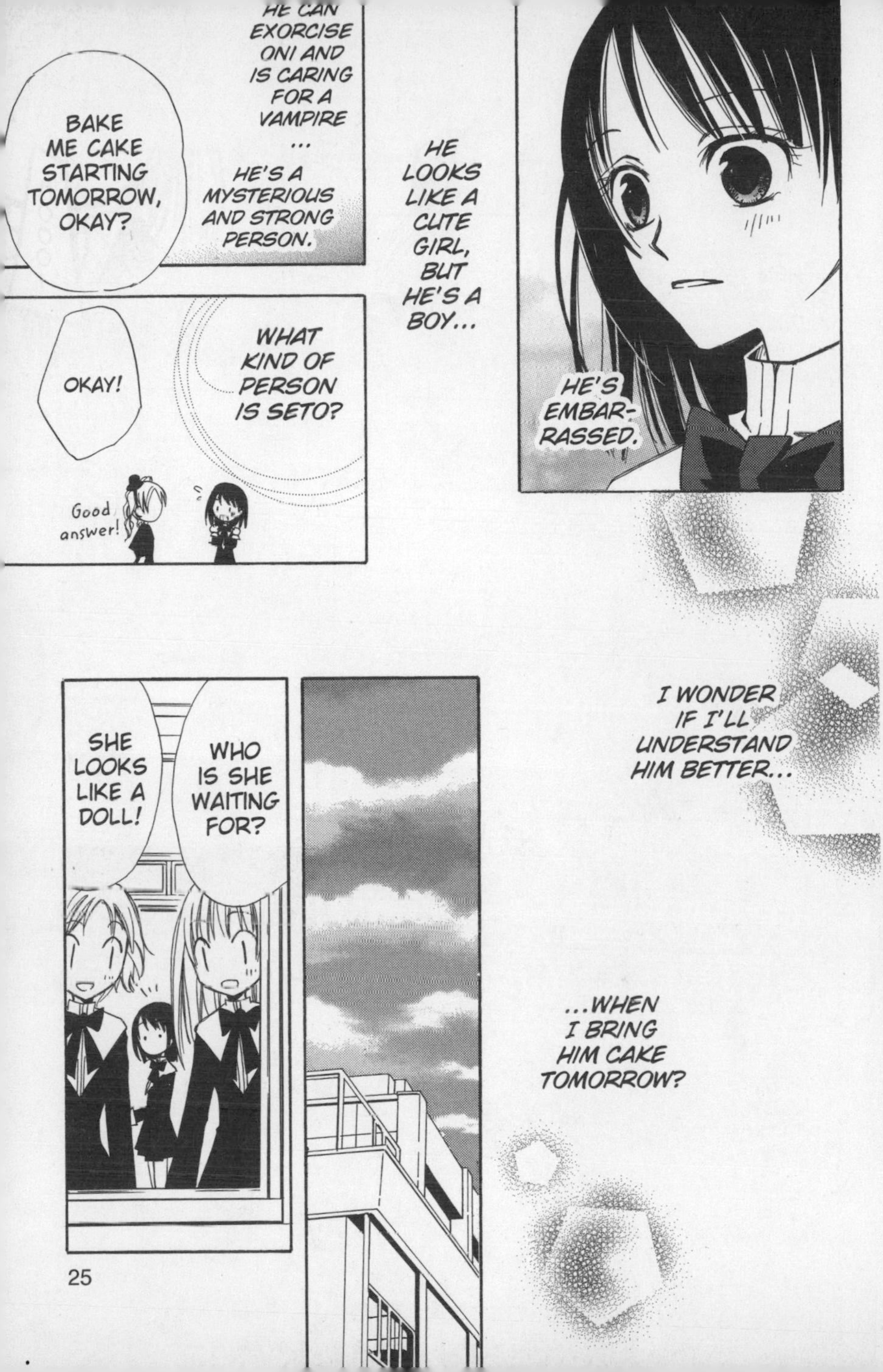

HE LOOKS LIKE A CUTE GIRL, BUT HE'S A BOY...
HE'S EMBARRASSED.
HE CAN EXORCISE ONI AND IS CARING FOR A VAMPIRE ...
HE'S A MYSTERIOUS AND STRONG PERSON.
BAKE ME CAKE STARTING TOMORROW, OKAY?
WHAT KIND OF PERSON IS SETO?
OKAY!
Good answer!
I WONDER IF I'LL UNDERSTAND HIM BETTER...
...WHEN I BRING HIM CAKE TOMORROW?
WHO IS SHE WAITING FOR?
SHE LOOKS LIKE A DOLL!

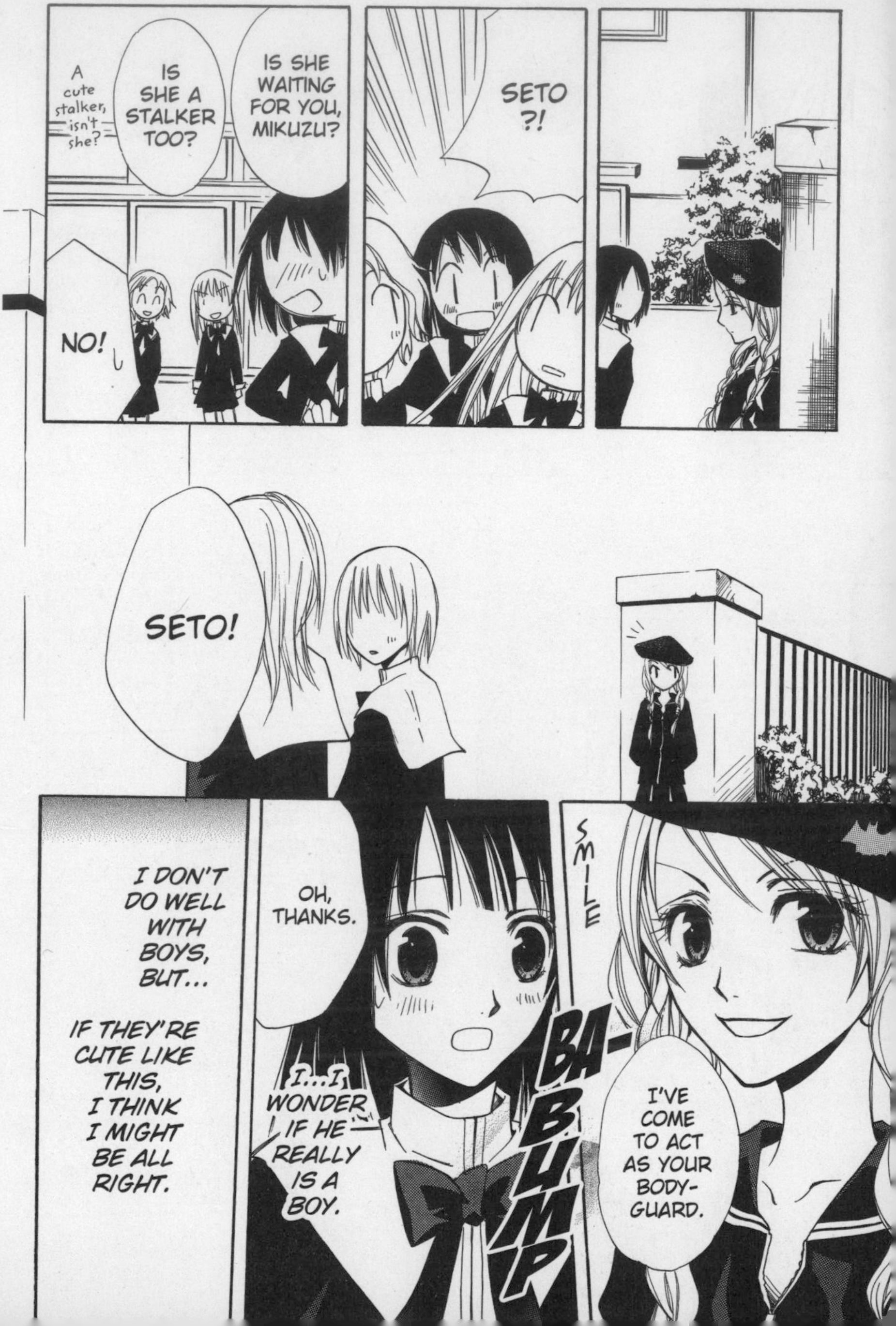
SETO ?!
IS SHE WAITING FOR YOU, MIKUZU?
IS SHE A STALKER TOO?
A cute stalker, isn't she?
NO!
SETO!
SMILE
I'VE COME TO ACT AS YOUR BODY-GUARD.
BA-BUMP
OH, THANKS.
I...I WONDER IF HE REALLY IS A BOY.
I DON'T DO WELL WITH BOYS, BUT...
IF THEY'RE CUTE LIKE THIS, I THINK I MIGHT BE ALL RIGHT.

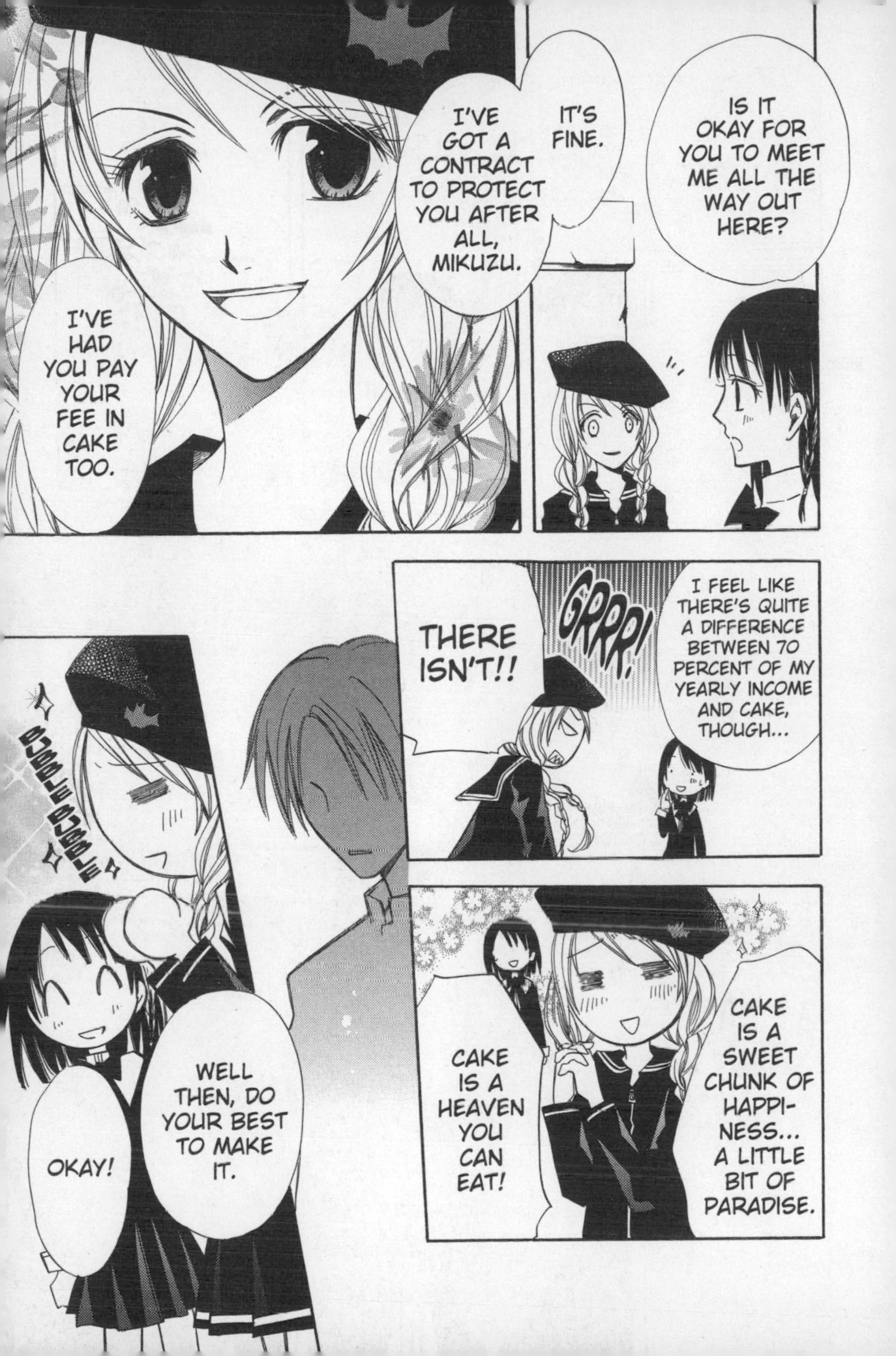
IS IT OKAY FOR YOU TO MEET ME ALL THE WAY OUT HERE?
IT'S FINE.
I'VE GOT A CONTRACT TO PROTECT YOU AFTER ALL, MIKUZU.
I'VE HAD YOU PAY YOUR FEE IN CAKE TOO.
I FEEL LIKE THERE'S QUITE A DIFFERENCE BETWEEN 70 PERCENT OF MY YEARLY INCOME AND CAKE, THOUGH...
GRRR!
THERE ISN'T!!
CAKE IS A SWEET CHUNK OF HAPPI-NESS... A LITTLE BIT OF PARADISE.
CAKE IS A HEAVEN YOU CAN EAT!
BUBBLE BUBBLE
WELL THEN, DO YOUR BEST TO MAKE IT.
OKAY!

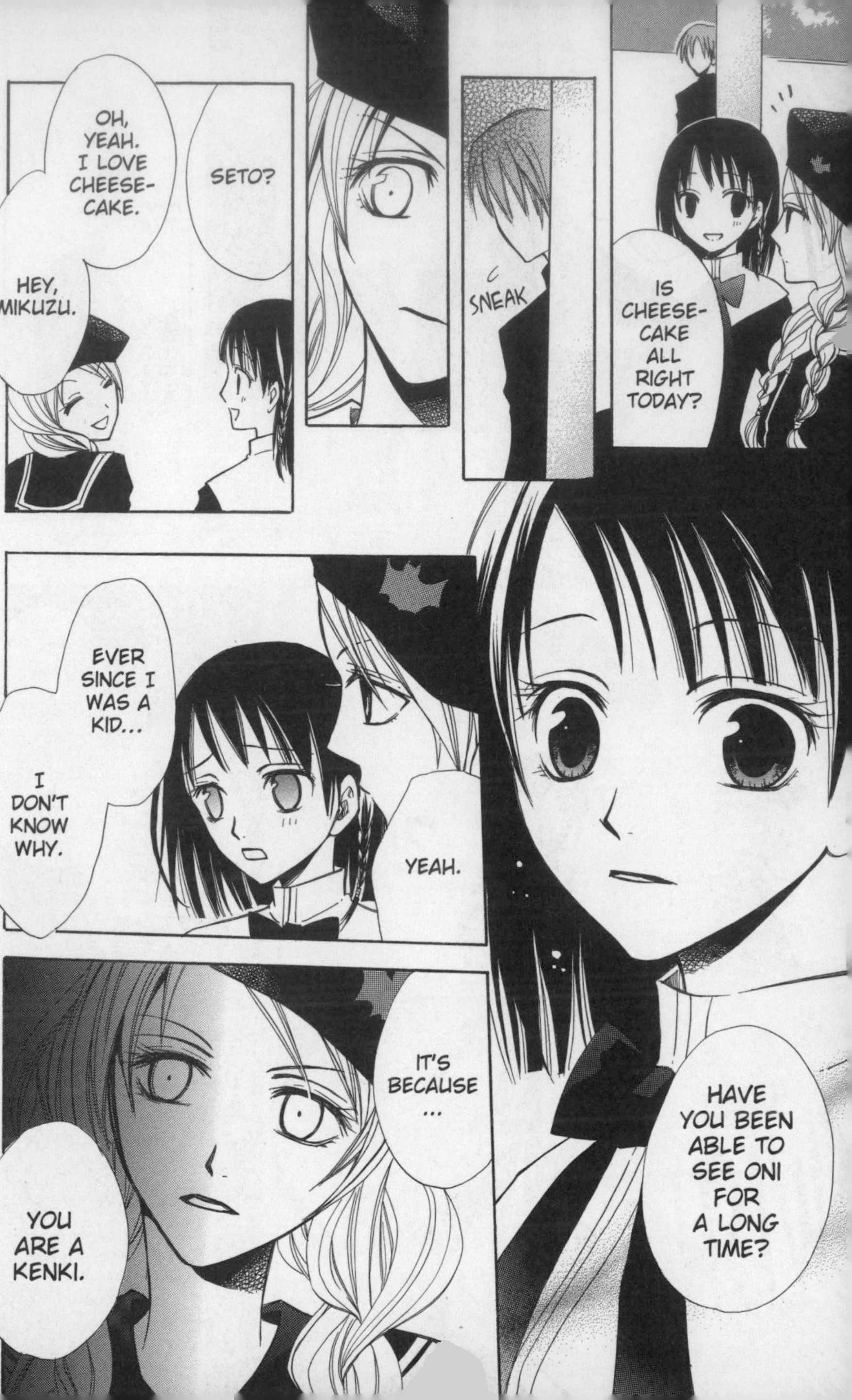

IS CHEESE-CAKE ALL RIGHT TODAY?
SNEAK
SETO?
OH, YEAH. I LOVE CHEESE-CAKE.
HEY, MIKUZU.
HAVE YOU BEEN ABLE TO SEE ONI FOR A LONG TIME?
YEAH.
EVER SINCE I WAS A KID...
I DON'T KNOW WHY.
IT'S BECAUSE ...
YOU ARE A KENKI.

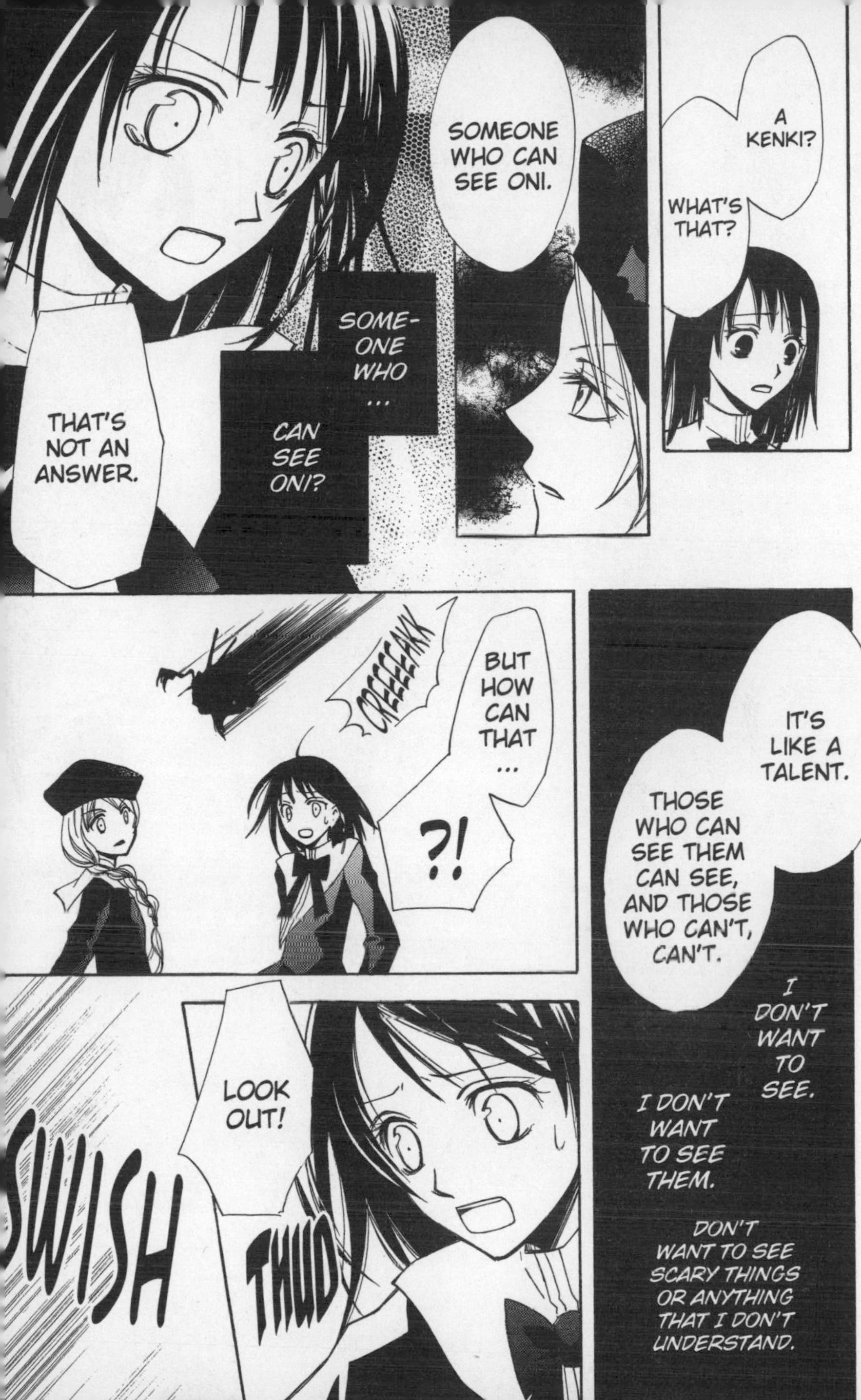
A KENKI?
WHAT'S THAT?
SOMEONE WHO CAN SEE ONI.
SOME-ONE WHO ...
CAN SEE ONI?
THAT'S NOT AN ANSWER.
IT'S LIKE A TALENT.
THOSE WHO CAN SEE THEM CAN SEE, AND THOSE WHO CAN'T, CAN'T.
I DON'T WANT TO SEE.
I DON'T WANT TO SEE THEM.
DON'T WANT TO SEE SCARY THINGS OR ANYTHING THAT I DON'T UNDERSTAND.
BUT HOW CAN THAT ...
CREEEEAKK
?!
LOOK OUT!
THUD
SWISH

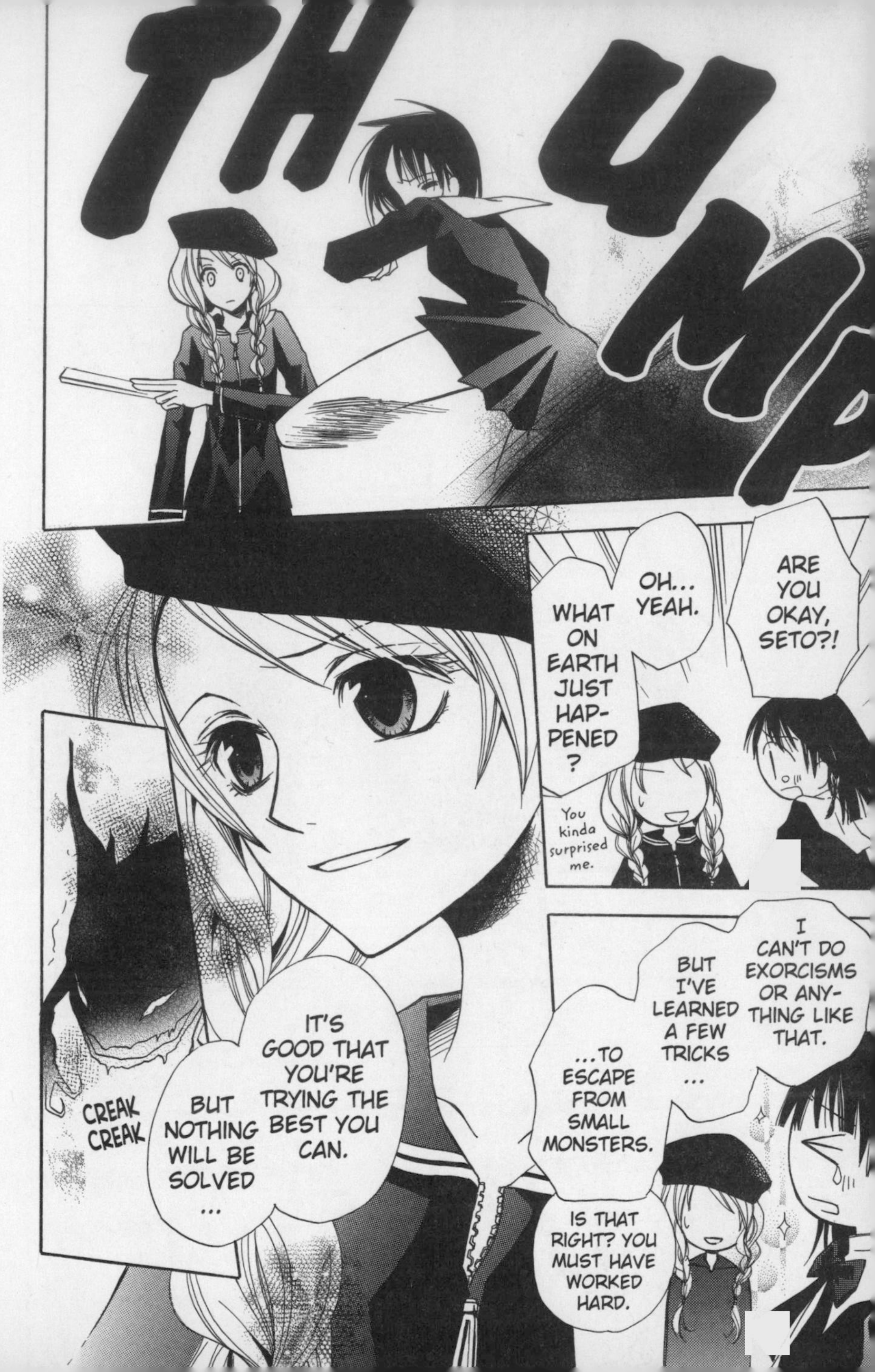
THUMP
ARE YOU OKAY, SETO?!
OH... YEAH.
WHAT ON EARTH JUST HAPPENED?
You kinda surprised me.
I CAN'T DO EXORCISMS OR ANYTHING LIKE THAT.
BUT I'VE LEARNED A FEW TRICKS...
...TO ESCAPE FROM SMALL MONSTERS.
IS THAT RIGHT? YOU MUST HAVE WORKED HARD.
IT'S GOOD THAT YOU'RE TRYING THE BEST YOU CAN.
BUT NOTHING WILL BE SOLVED...
CREAK CREAK

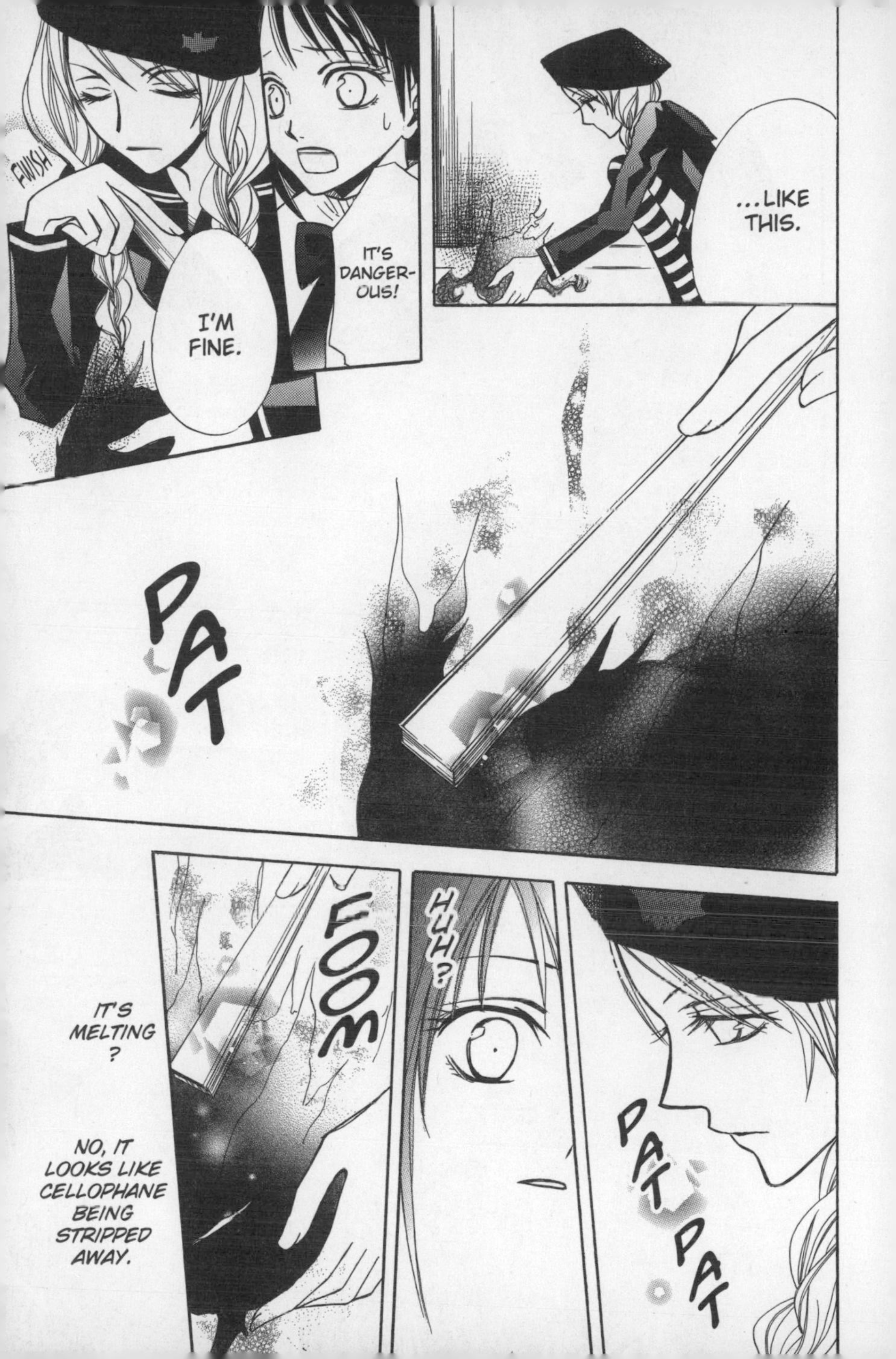
...LIKE THIS.
IT'S DANGER-OUS!
FWISH
I'M FINE.
PAT
PAT PAT
HUH?
FOOM
IT'S MELTING?
NO, IT LOOKS LIKE CELLOPHANE BEING STRIPPED AWAY.

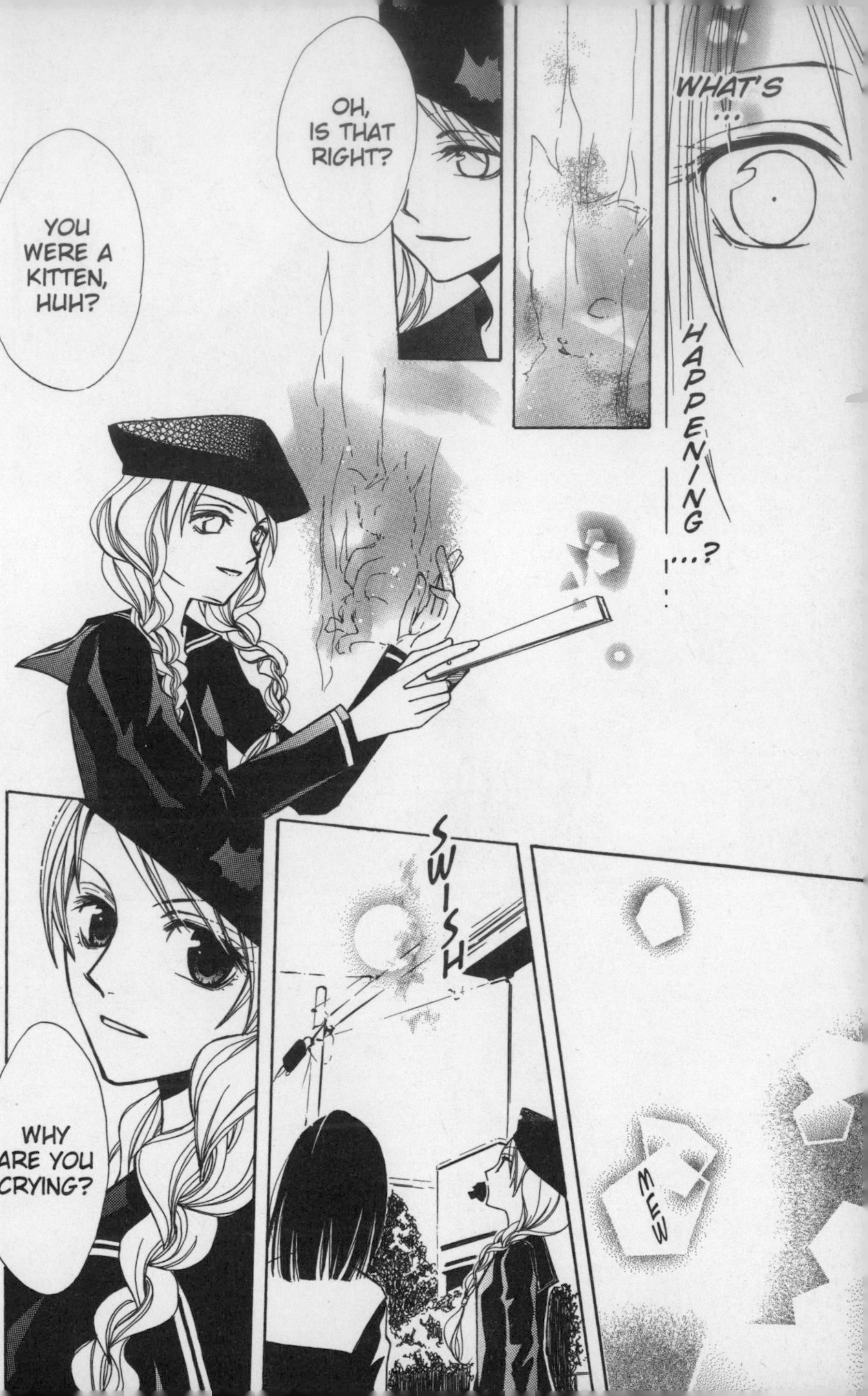
WHAT'S... HAPPENING...?
OH, IS THAT RIGHT?
YOU WERE A KITTEN, HUH?
MEW
SWISH
WHY ARE YOU CRYING?

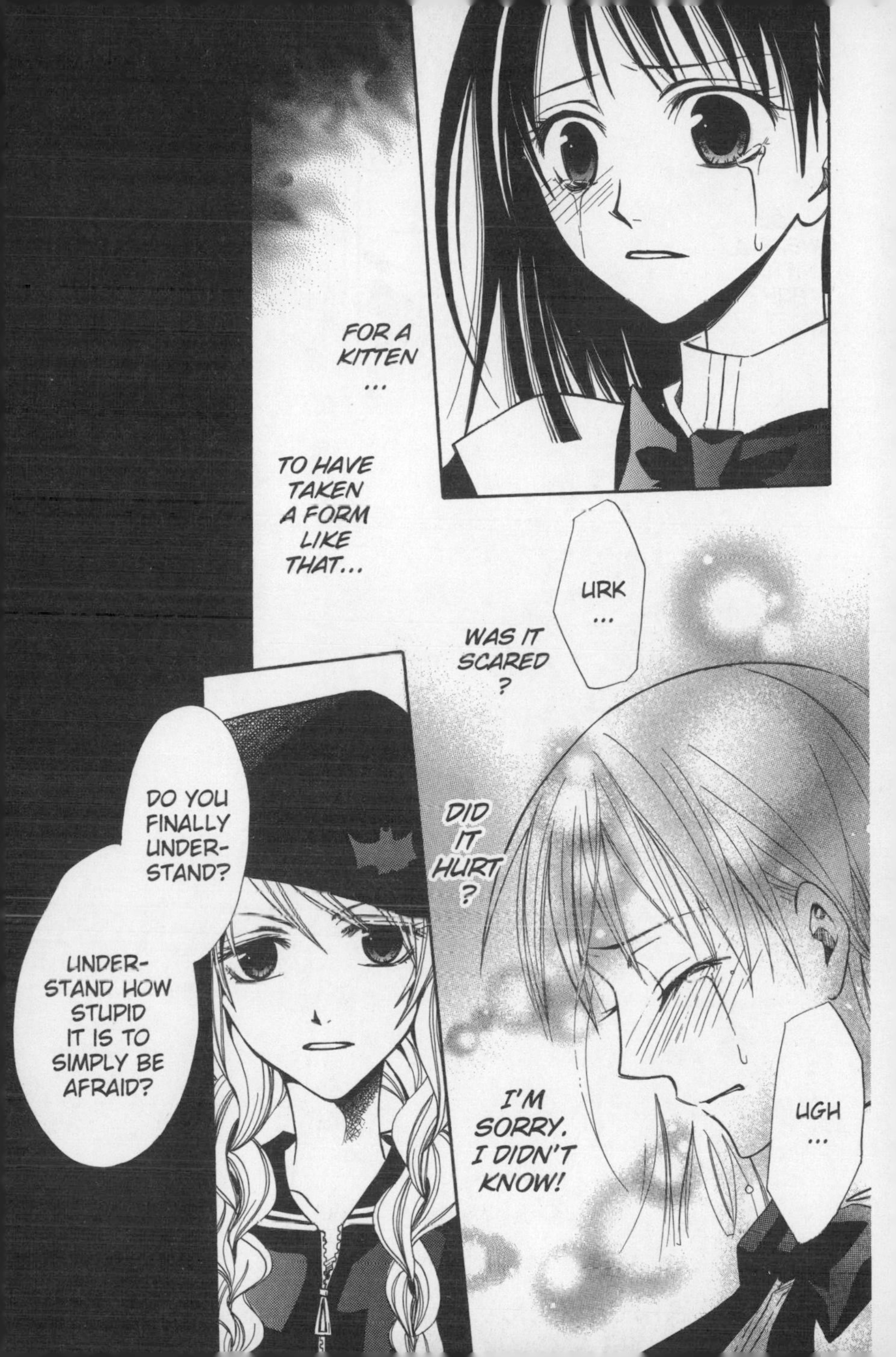
FOR A KITTEN ...
TO HAVE TAKEN A FORM LIKE THAT...
URK ...
WAS IT SCARED ?
DID IT HURT ?
UGH ...
I'M SORRY. I DIDN'T KNOW!
DO YOU FINALLY UNDER-STAND?
UNDER-STAND HOW STUPID IT IS TO SIMPLY BE AFRAID?

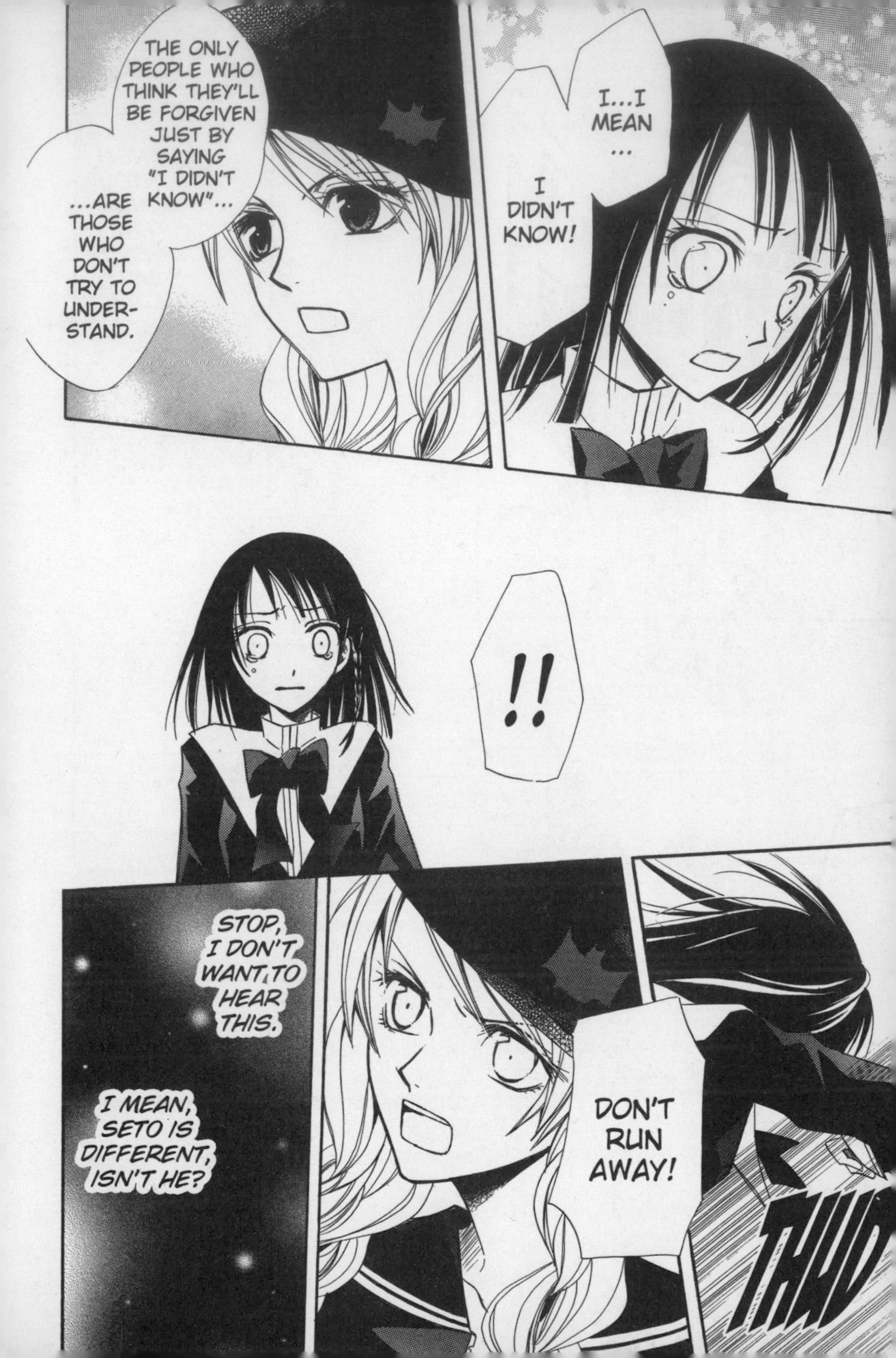
I...I MEAN ...
I DIDN'T KNOW!
THE ONLY PEOPLE WHO THINK THEY'LL BE FORGIVEN JUST BY SAYING "I DIDN'T KNOW"...
...ARE THOSE WHO DON'T TRY TO UNDER-STAND.
!!
THUD
DON'T RUN AWAY!
STOP, I DON'T WANT TO HEAR THIS.
I MEAN, SETO IS DIFFERENT, ISN'T HE?

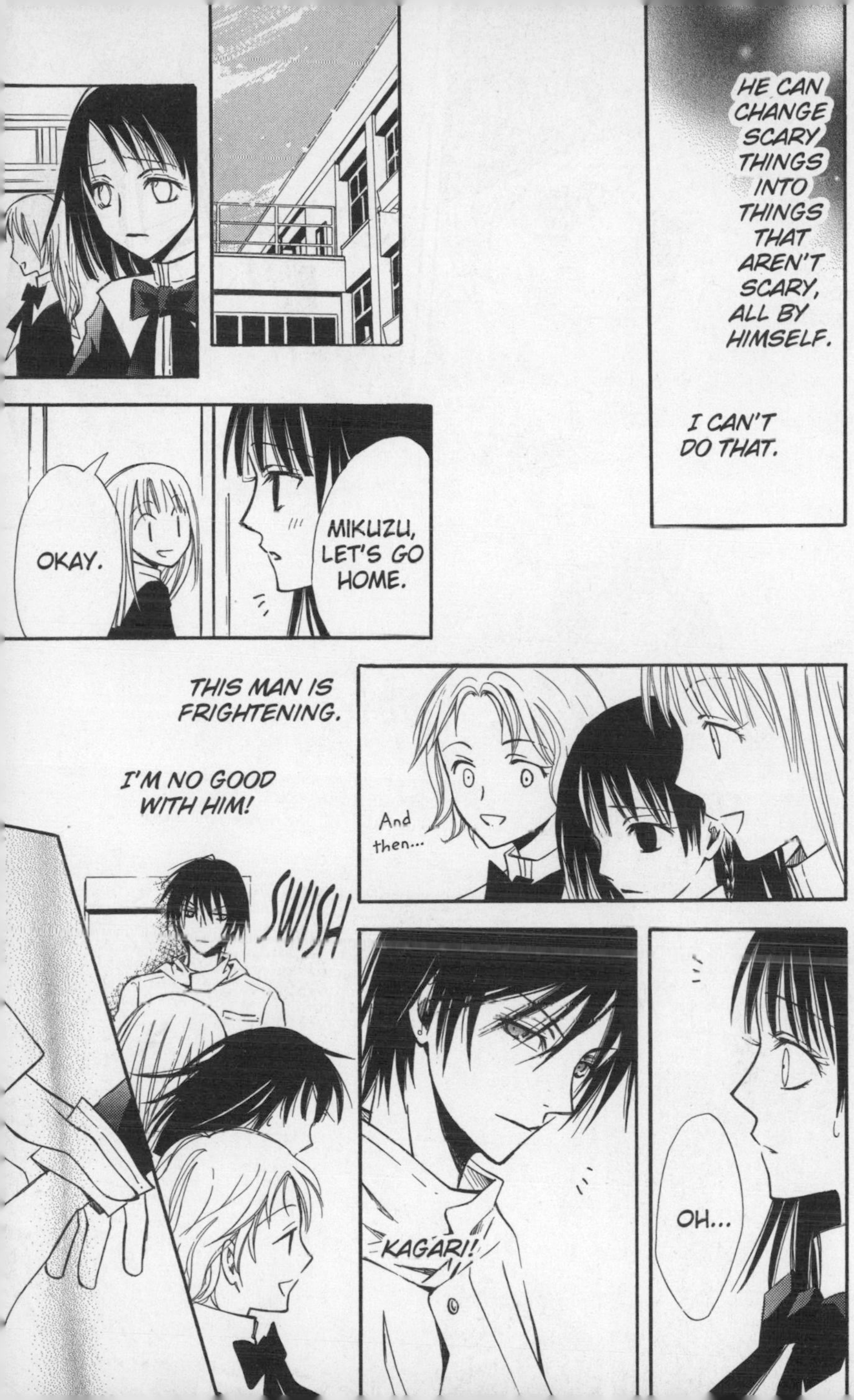

HE CAN CHANGE SCARY THINGS INTO THINGS THAT AREN'T SCARY, ALL BY HIMSELF.
I CAN'T DO THAT.
MIKUZU, LET'S GO HOME.
OKAY.
And then...
THIS MAN IS FRIGHTENING.
I'M NO GOOD WITH HIM!
OH...
KAGARI!
SWISH

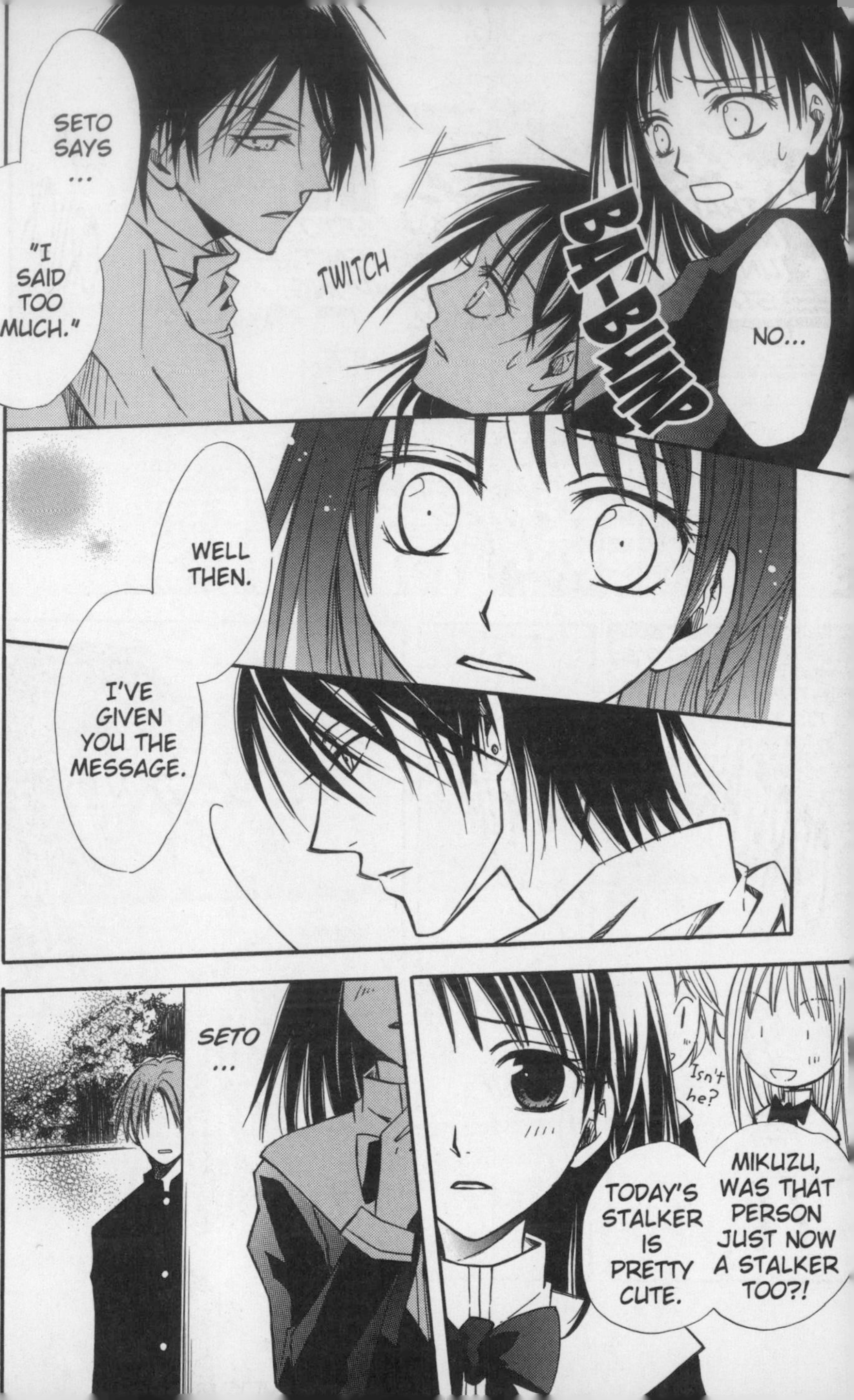
SETO SAYS ...
"I SAID TOO MUCH."
TWITCH
BA-BUMP
NO...
WELL THEN.
I'VE GIVEN YOU THE MESSAGE.
MIKUZU, WAS THAT PERSON JUST NOW A STALKER TOO?!
TODAY'S STALKER IS PRETTY CUTE.
Isn't he?
SETO ...

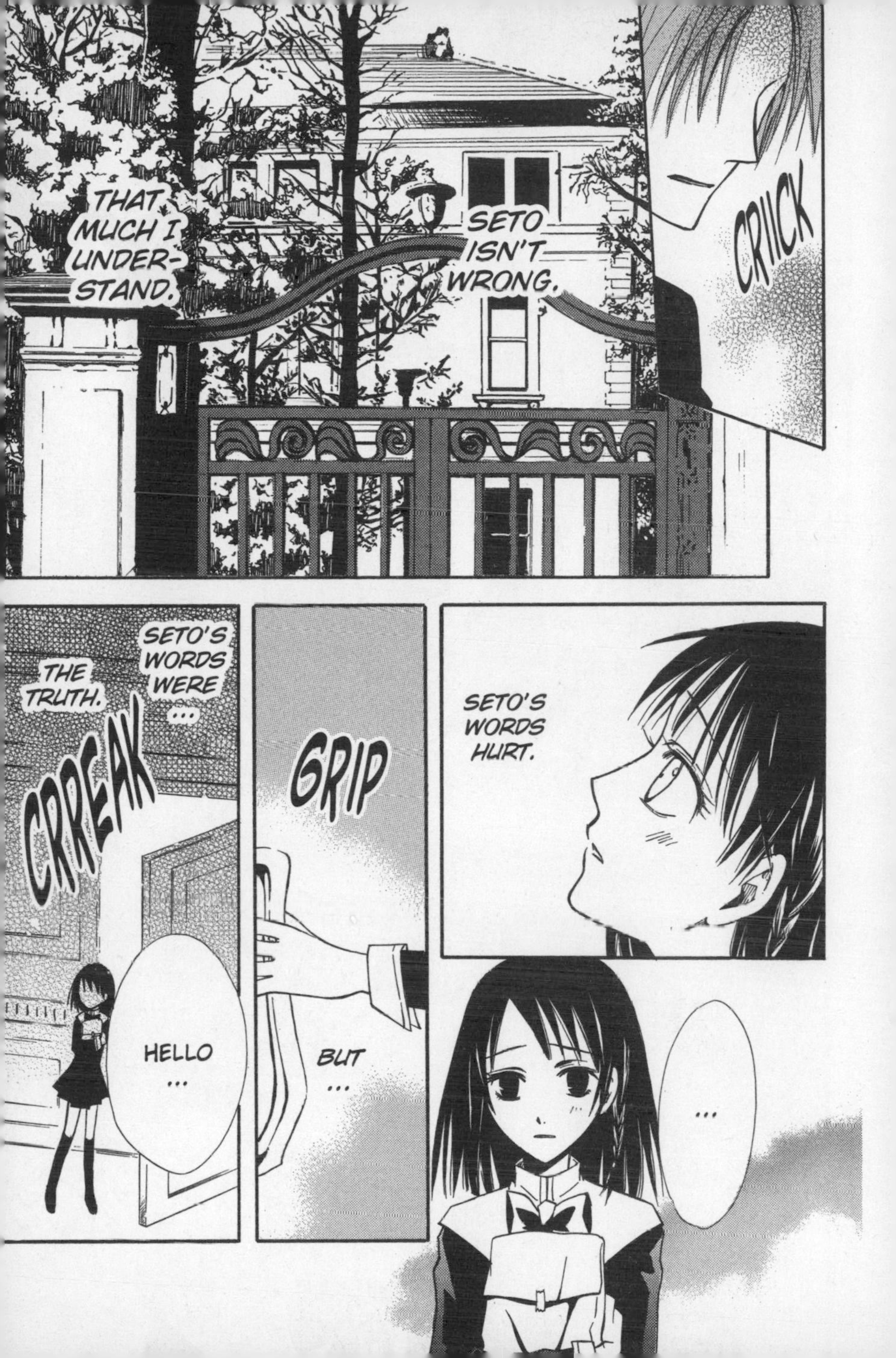
CRIICK
SETO ISN'T WRONG.
THAT MUCH I UNDER-STAND.
SETO'S WORDS HURT.
...
GRIP
BUT ...
SETO'S WORDS WERE ...
THE TRUTH.
CRREAK
HELLO ...

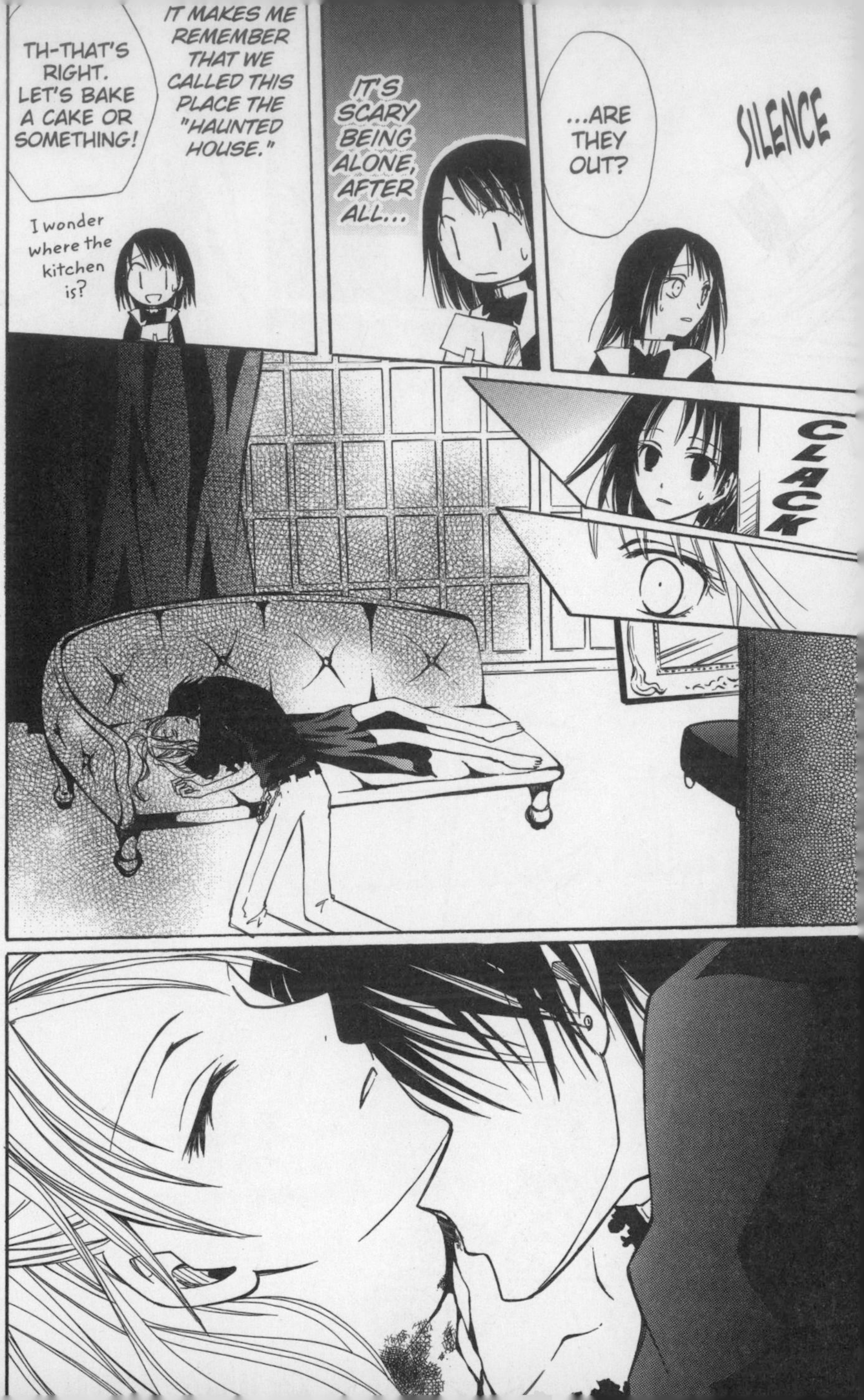
SILENCE
...ARE THEY OUT?
IT'S SCARY BEING ALONE, AFTER ALL...
IT MAKES ME REMEMBER THAT WE CALLED THIS PLACE THE "HAUNTED HOUSE."
TH-THAT'S RIGHT. LET'S BAKE A CAKE OR SOMETHING!
I wonder where the kitchen is?
CLACK

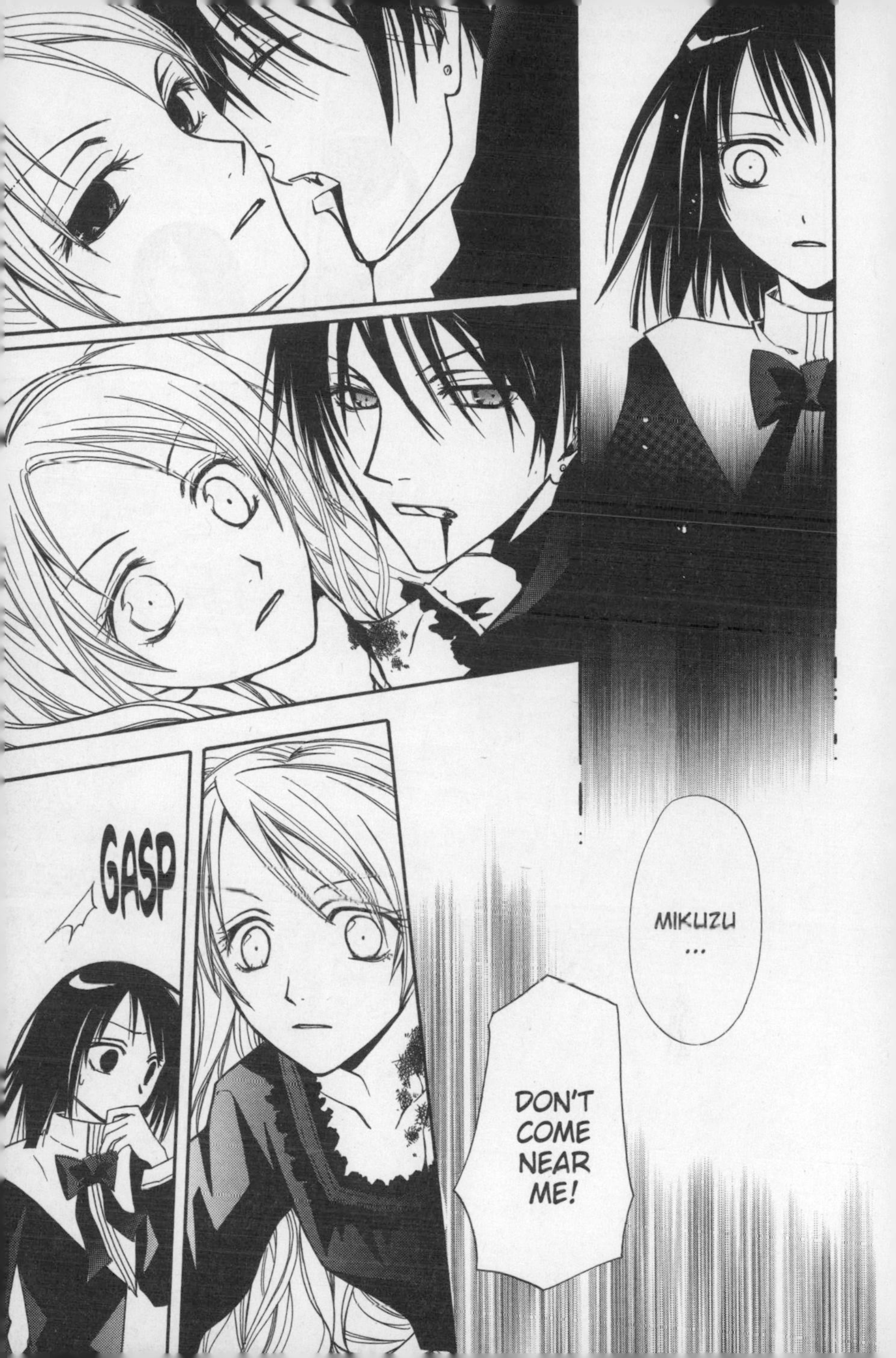
MIKUZU ...
DON'T COME NEAR ME!
GASP

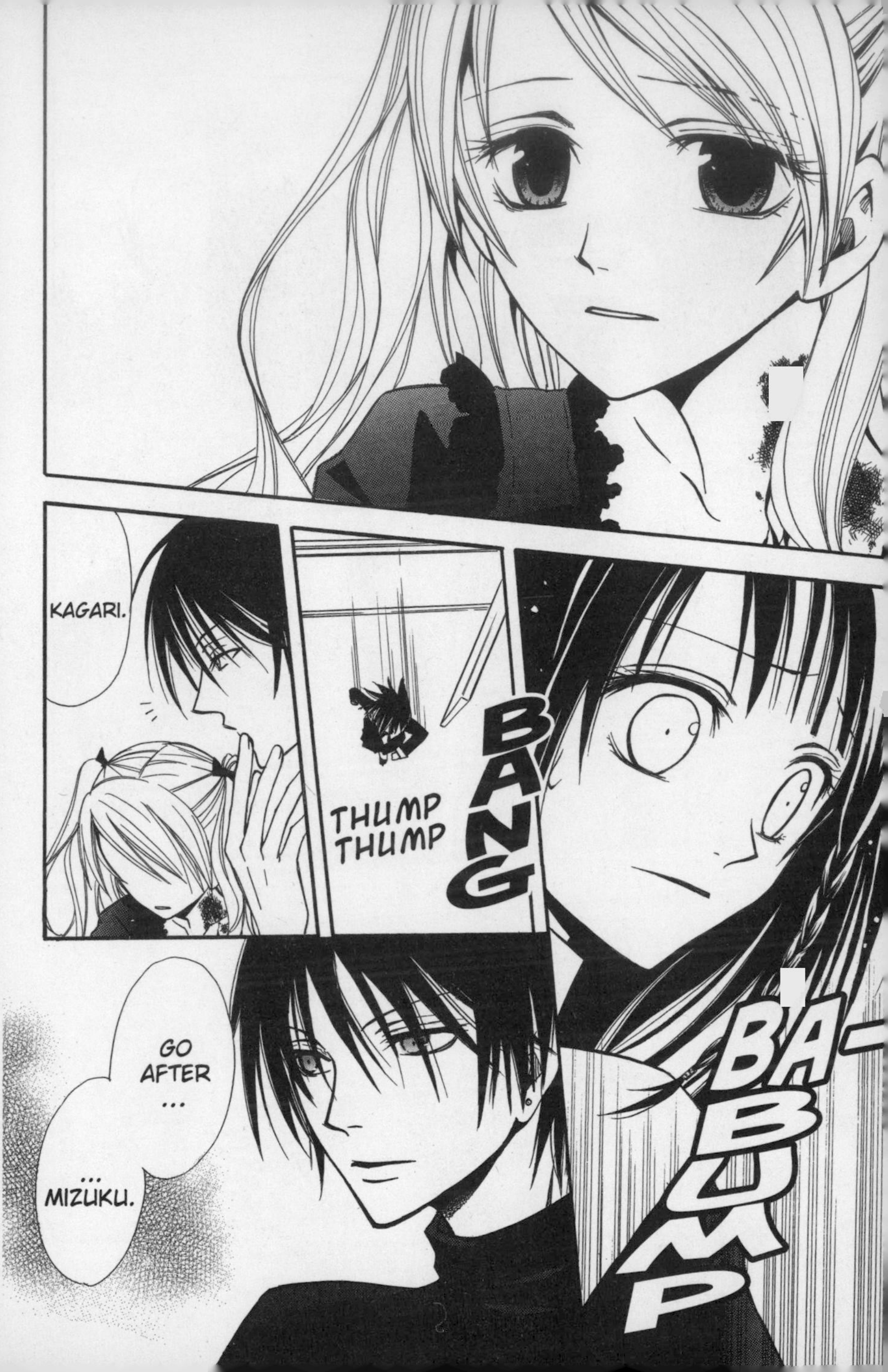
BANG
THUMP THUMP
KAGARI.
BA-BUMP
GO AFTER ...
... MIZUKU.

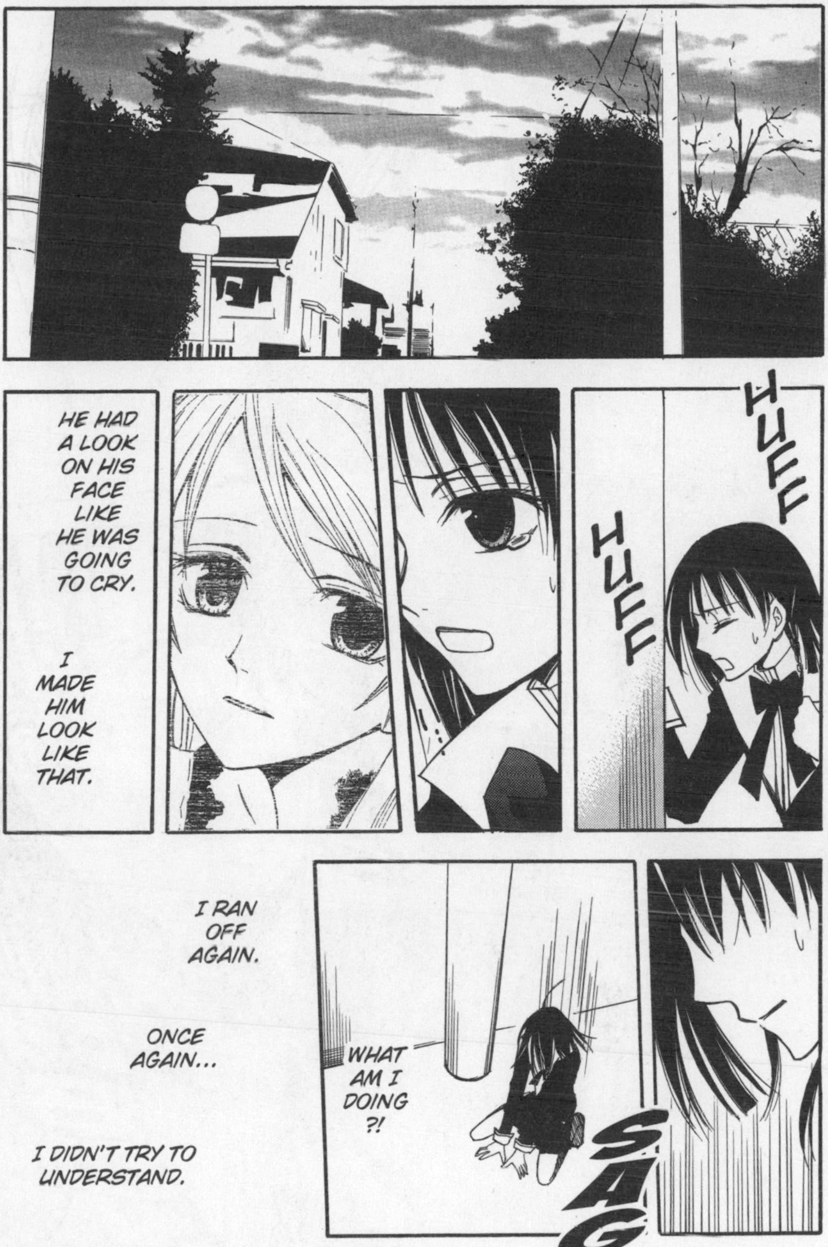
HUFF
HUFF
HE HAD A LOOK ON HIS FACE LIKE HE WAS GOING TO CRY.
I MADE HIM LOOK LIKE THAT.
SAG
WHAT AM I DOING?!
I RAN OFF AGAIN.
ONCE AGAIN...
I DIDN'T TRY TO UNDERSTAND.

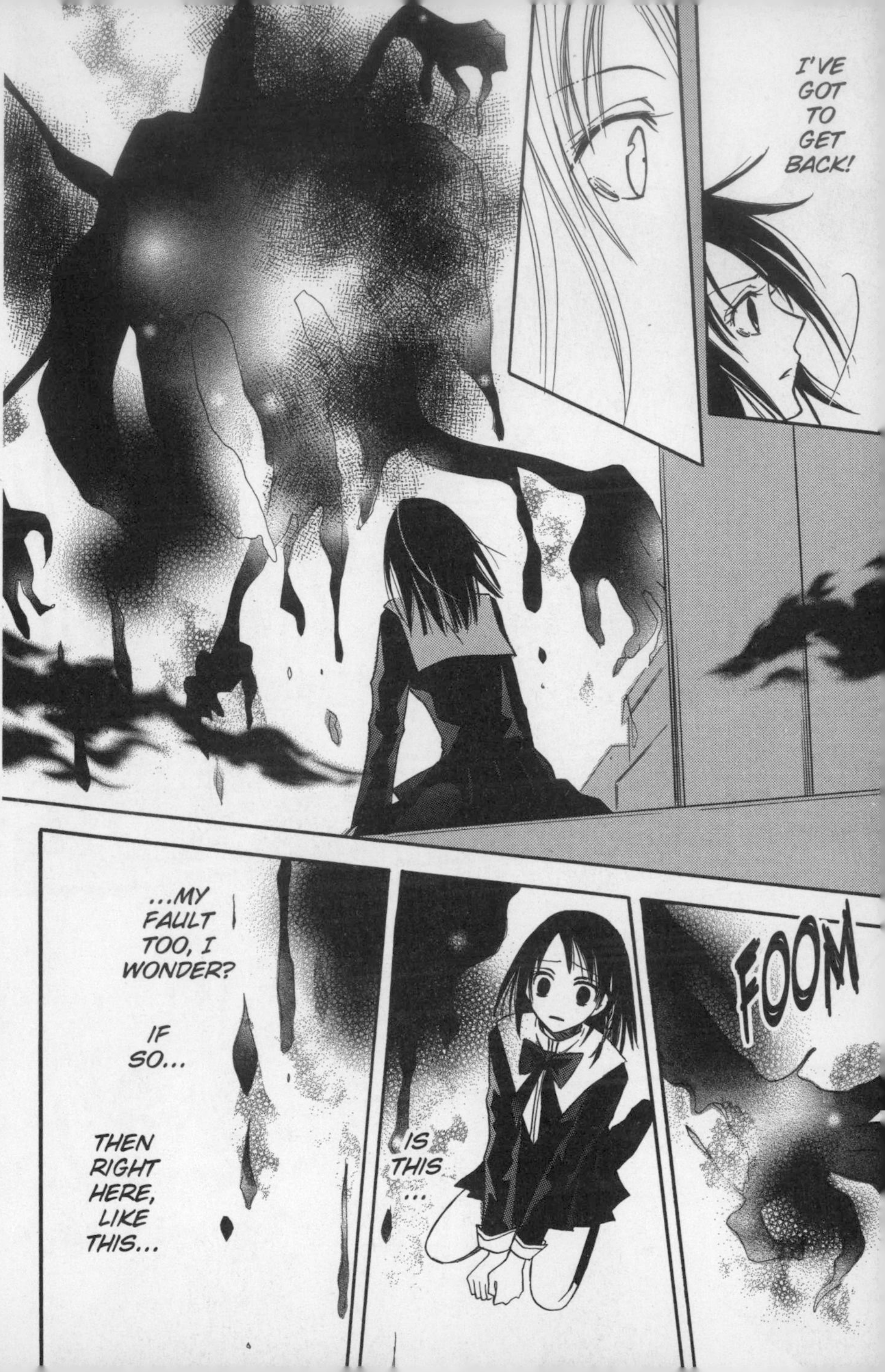
I'VE GOT TO GET BACK!
FOOM
IS THIS ...
...MY FAULT TOO, I WONDER?
IF SO...
THEN RIGHT HERE, LIKE THIS...

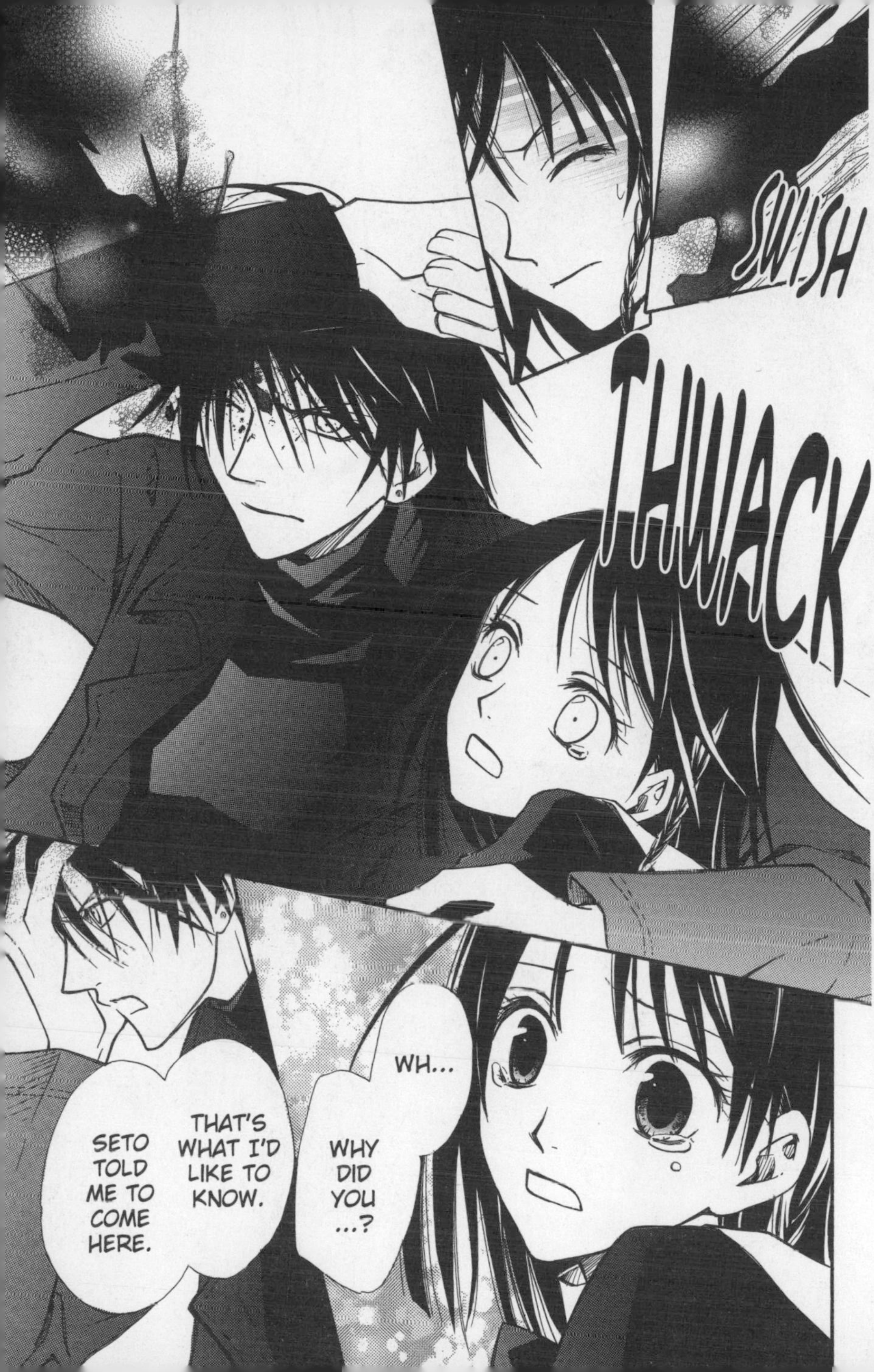
SWISH
THWACK
WH...
WHY DID YOU ...?
THAT'S WHAT I'D LIKE TO KNOW.
SETO TOLD ME TO COME HERE.

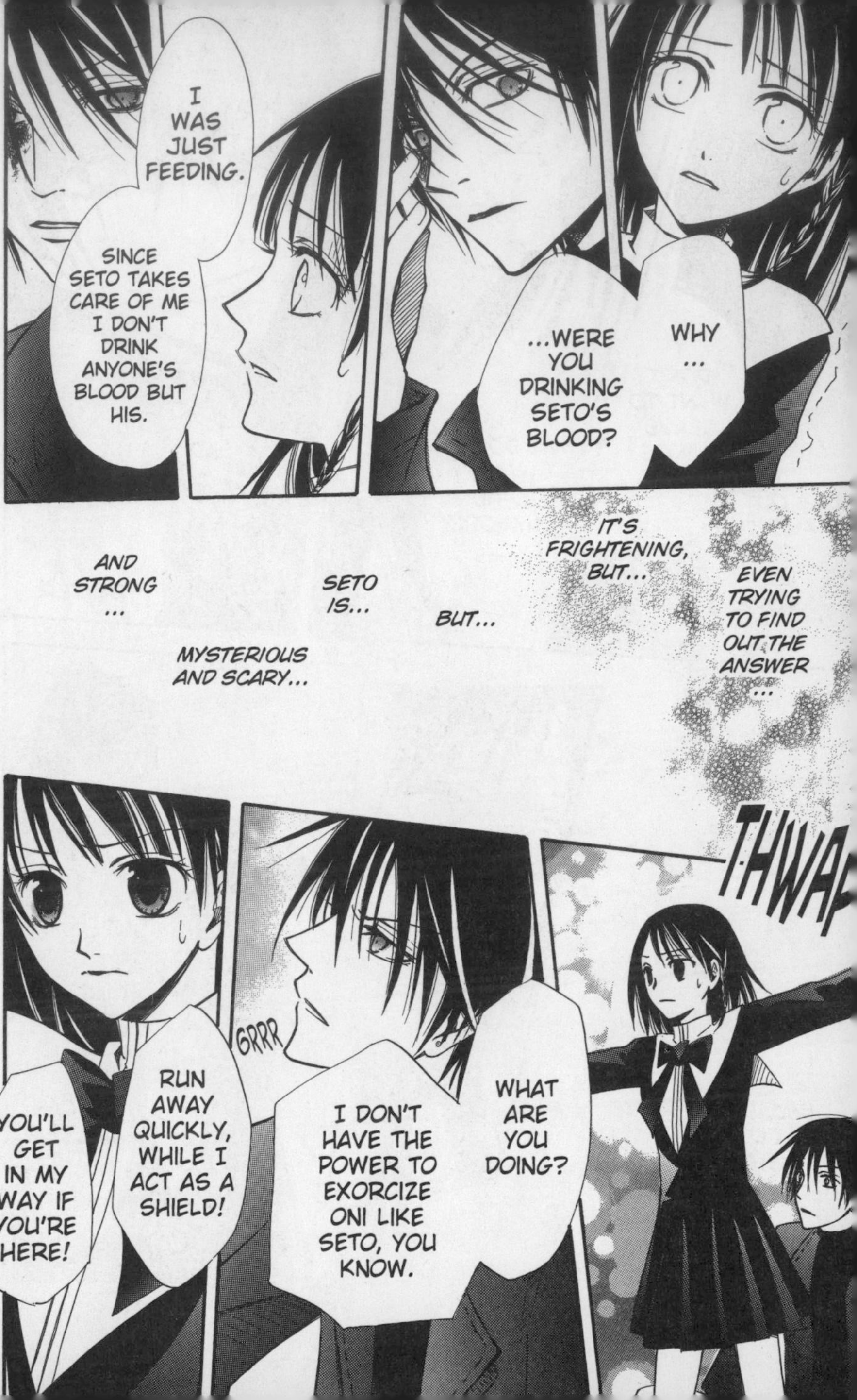
WHY ...
...WERE YOU DRINKING SETO'S BLOOD?
I WAS JUST FEEDING.
SINCE SETO TAKES CARE OF ME I DON'T DRINK ANYONE'S BLOOD BUT HIS.
EVEN TRYING TO FIND OUT THE ANSWER ...
IT'S FRIGHTENING, BUT...
BUT...
SETO IS...
MYSTERIOUS AND SCARY...
AND STRONG ...
THWAP
WHAT ARE YOU DOING?
I DON'T HAVE THE POWER TO EXORCIZE ONI LIKE SETO, YOU KNOW.
GRRR
RUN AWAY QUICKLY, WHILE I ACT AS A SHIELD!
YOU'LL GET IN MY WAY IF YOU'RE HERE!

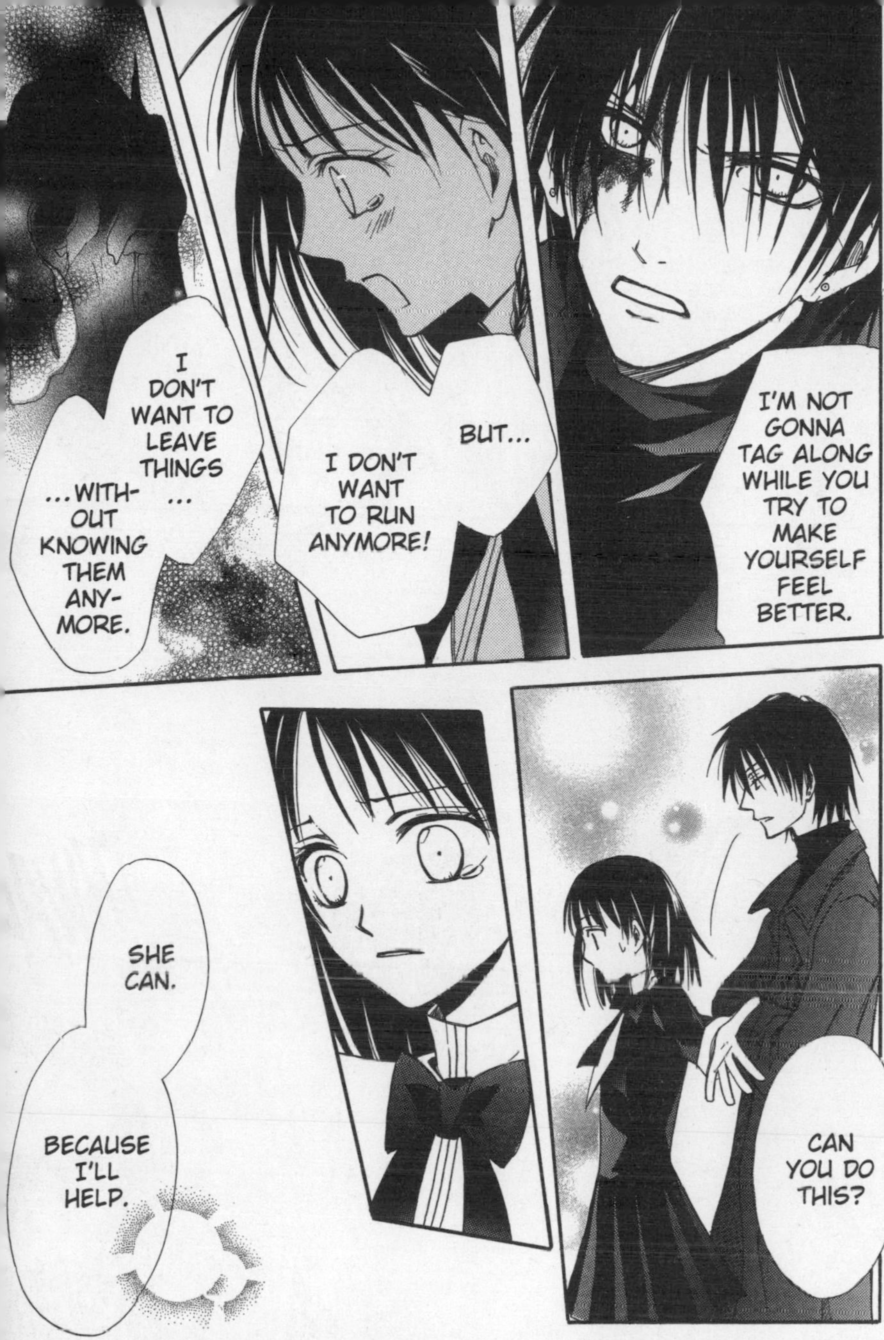
I'M NOT GONNA TAG ALONG WHILE YOU TRY TO MAKE YOURSELF FEEL BETTER.
BUT... I DON'T WANT TO RUN ANYMORE!
I DON'T WANT TO LEAVE THINGS ...
...WITH-OUT KNOWING THEM ANY-MORE.
CAN YOU DO THIS?
SHE CAN.
BECAUSE I'LL HELP.

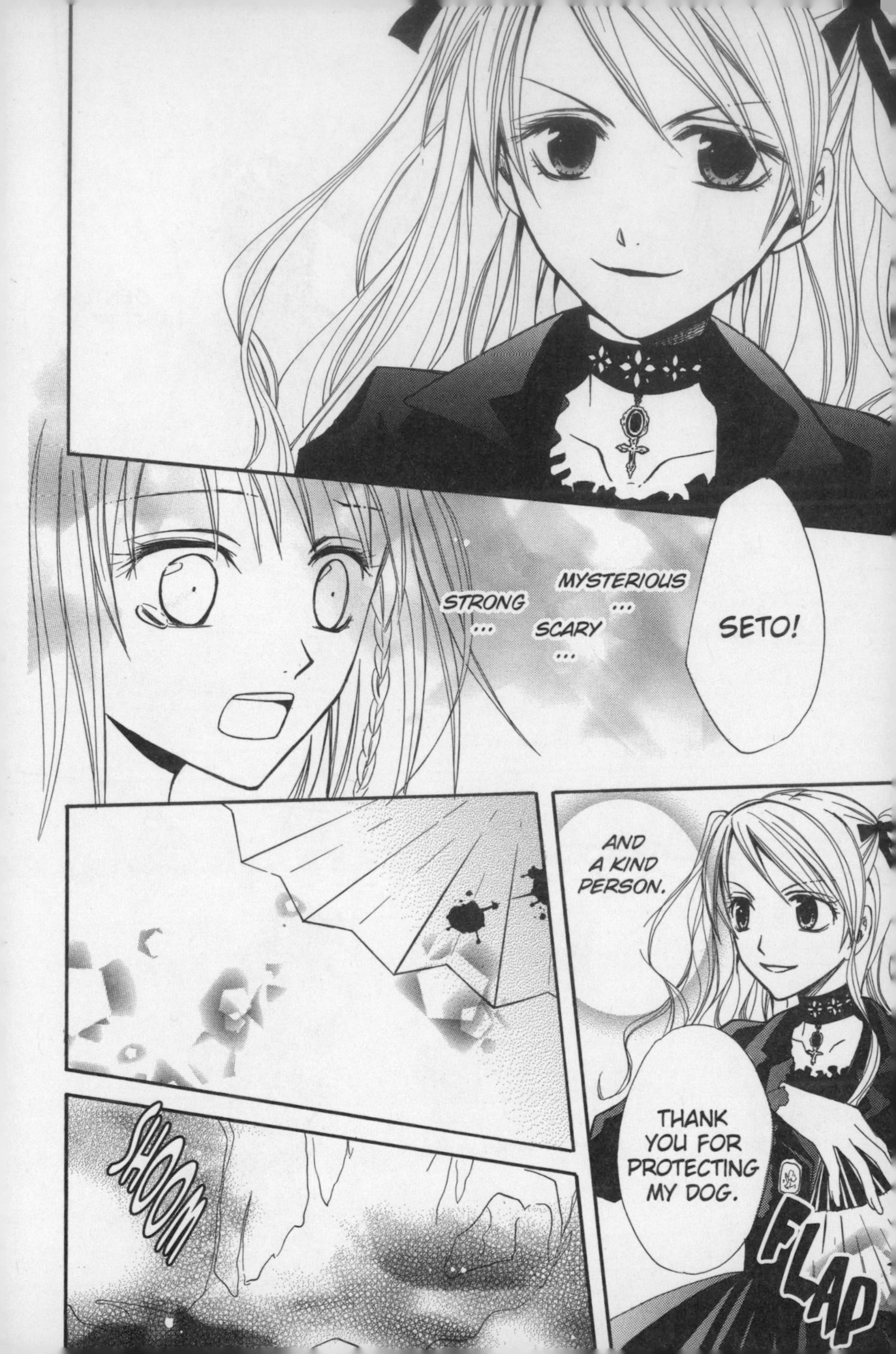
SETO!
MYSTERIOUS...
STRONG...
SCARY...
AND A KIND PERSON.
THANK YOU FOR PROTECTING MY DOG.
FLAP
SHOOM

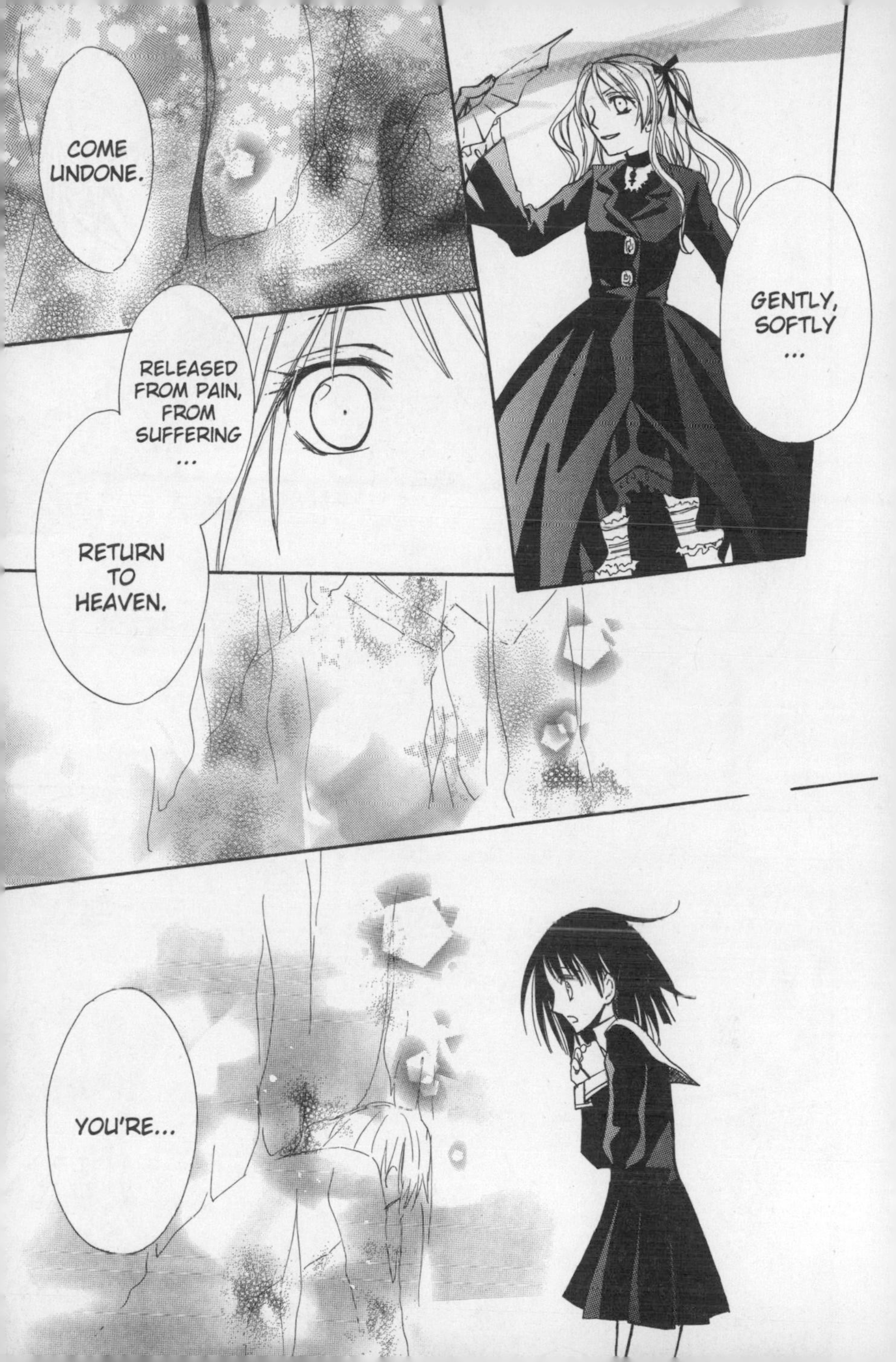

GENTLY, SOFTLY ...
COME UNDONE.
RELEASED FROM PAIN, FROM SUFFERING ...
RETURN TO HEAVEN.
YOU'RE...

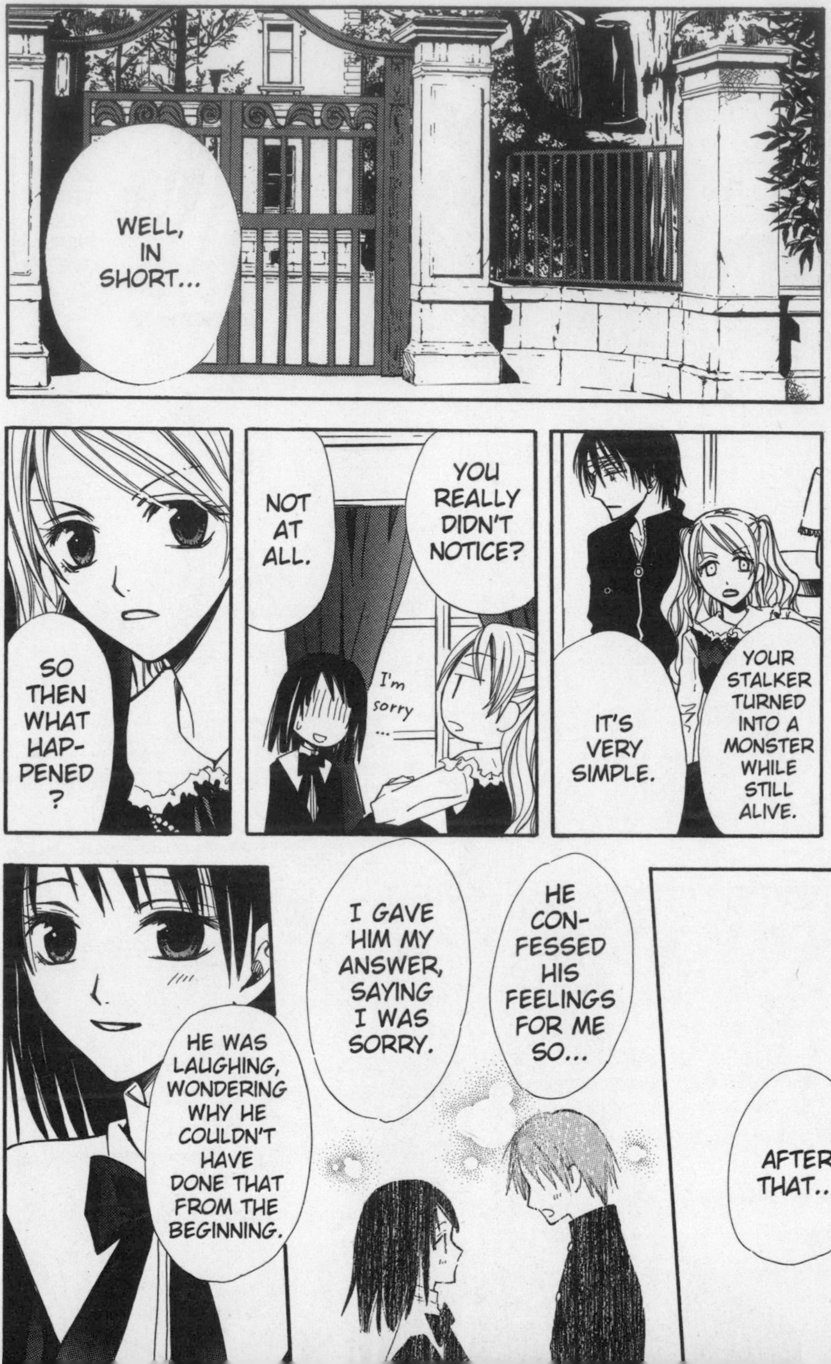
WELL, IN SHORT...
YOUR STALKER TURNED INTO A MONSTER WHILE STILL ALIVE.
IT'S VERY SIMPLE.
YOU REALLY DIDN'T NOTICE?
NOT AT ALL.
I'm sorry...
SO THEN WHAT HAP-PENED?
AFTER THAT...
HE CON-FESSED HIS FEELINGS FOR ME SO...
I GAVE HIM MY ANSWER, SAYING I WAS SORRY.
HE WAS LAUGHING, WONDERING WHY HE COULDN'T HAVE DONE THAT FROM THE BEGINNING.

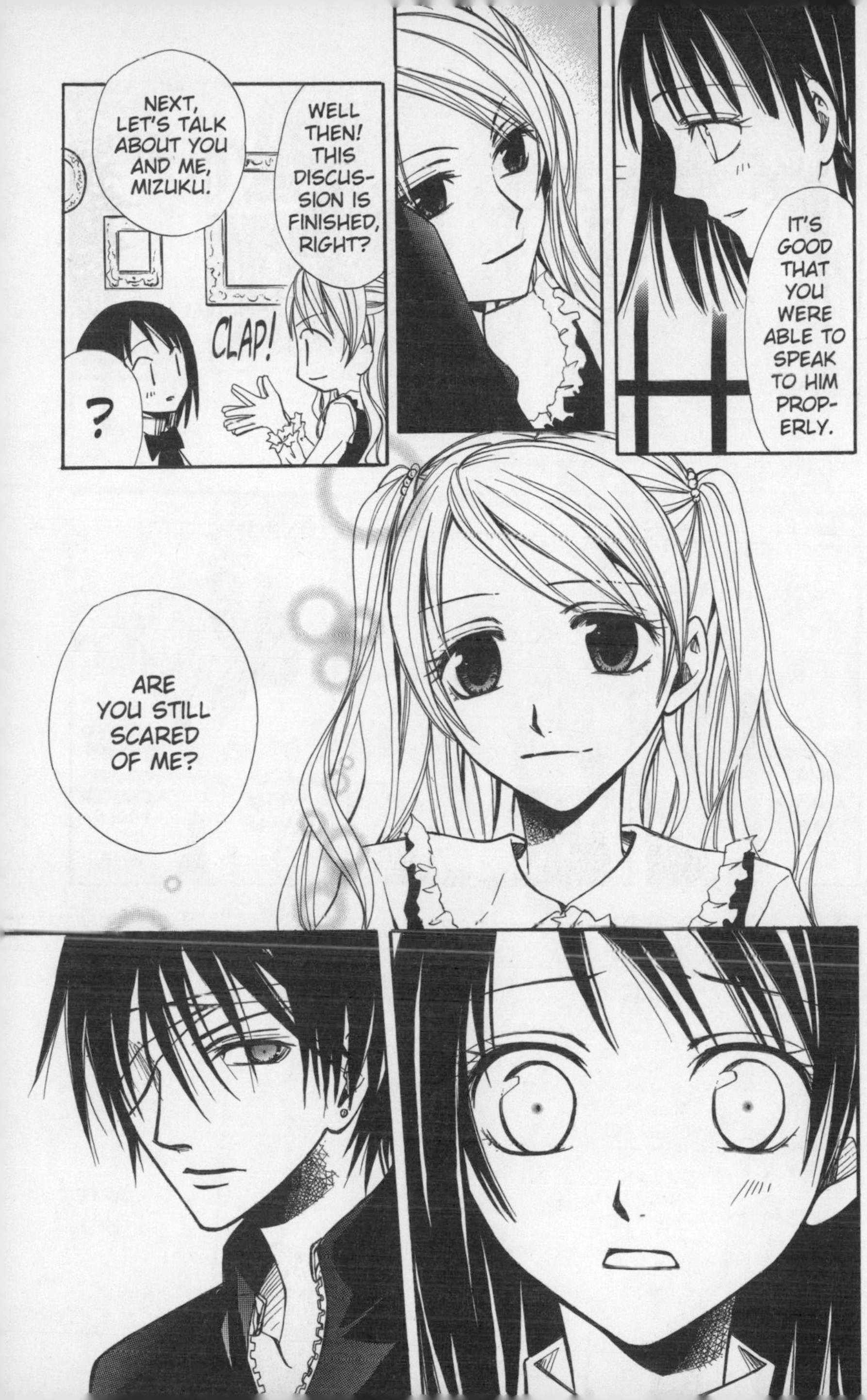
IT'S GOOD THAT YOU WERE ABLE TO SPEAK TO HIM PROPERLY.
WELL THEN! THIS DISCUSSION IS FINISHED, RIGHT?
NEXT, LET'S TALK ABOUT YOU AND ME, MIZUKU.
CLAP!
?
ARE YOU STILL SCARED OF ME?

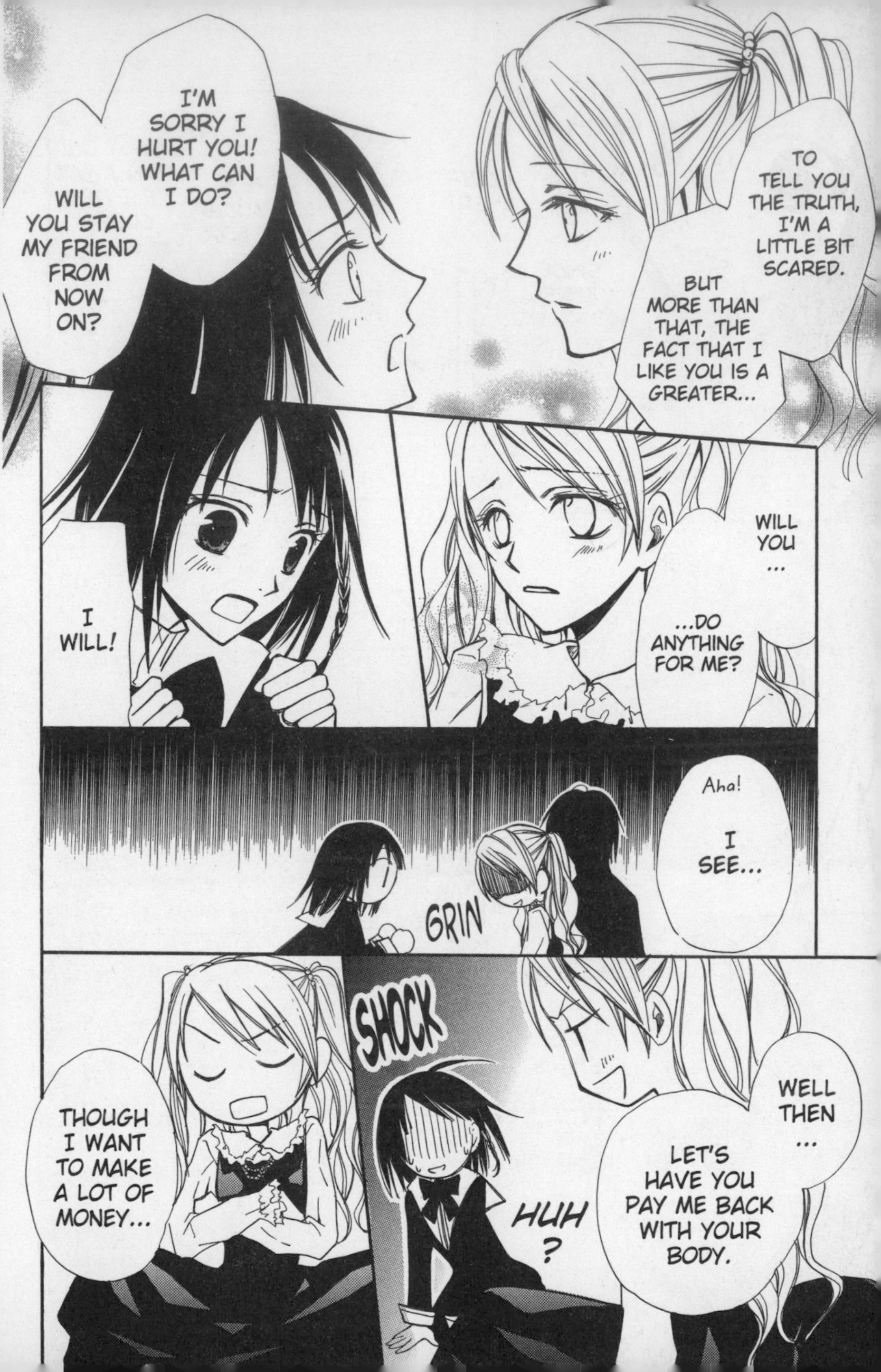
TO TELL YOU THE TRUTH, I'M A LITTLE BIT SCARED.
BUT MORE THAN THAT, THE FACT THAT I LIKE YOU IS A GREATER...
I'M SORRY I HURT YOU! WHAT CAN I DO?
WILL YOU STAY MY FRIEND FROM NOW ON?
WILL YOU ...
...DO ANYTHING FOR ME?
I WILL!
Aha!
I SEE...
GRIN
WELL THEN ...
LET'S HAVE YOU PAY ME BACK WITH YOUR BODY.
SHOCK
HUH?
THOUGH I WANT TO MAKE A LOT OF MONEY...

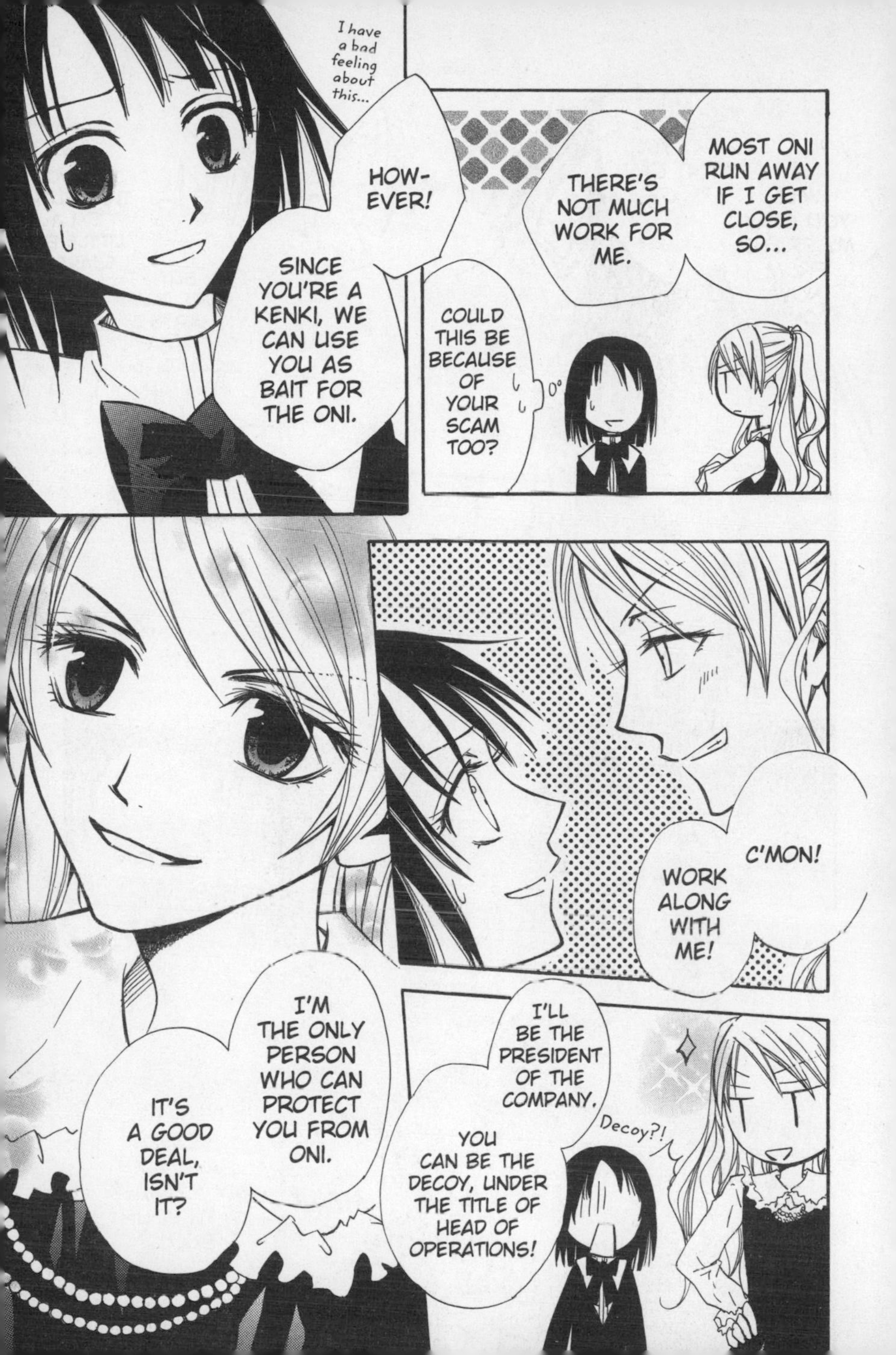
MOST ONI RUN AWAY IF I GET CLOSE, SO...
THERE'S NOT MUCH WORK FOR ME.
COULD THIS BE BECAUSE OF YOUR SCAM TOO?
I have a bad feeling about this...
HOW-EVER!
SINCE YOU'RE A KENKI, WE CAN USE YOU AS BAIT FOR THE ONI.
C'MON!
WORK ALONG WITH ME!
I'LL BE THE PRESIDENT OF THE COMPANY.
YOU CAN BE THE DECOY, UNDER THE TITLE OF HEAD OF OPERATIONS!
Decoy?!
I'M THE ONLY PERSON WHO CAN PROTECT YOU FROM ONI.
IT'S A GOOD DEAL, ISN'T IT?

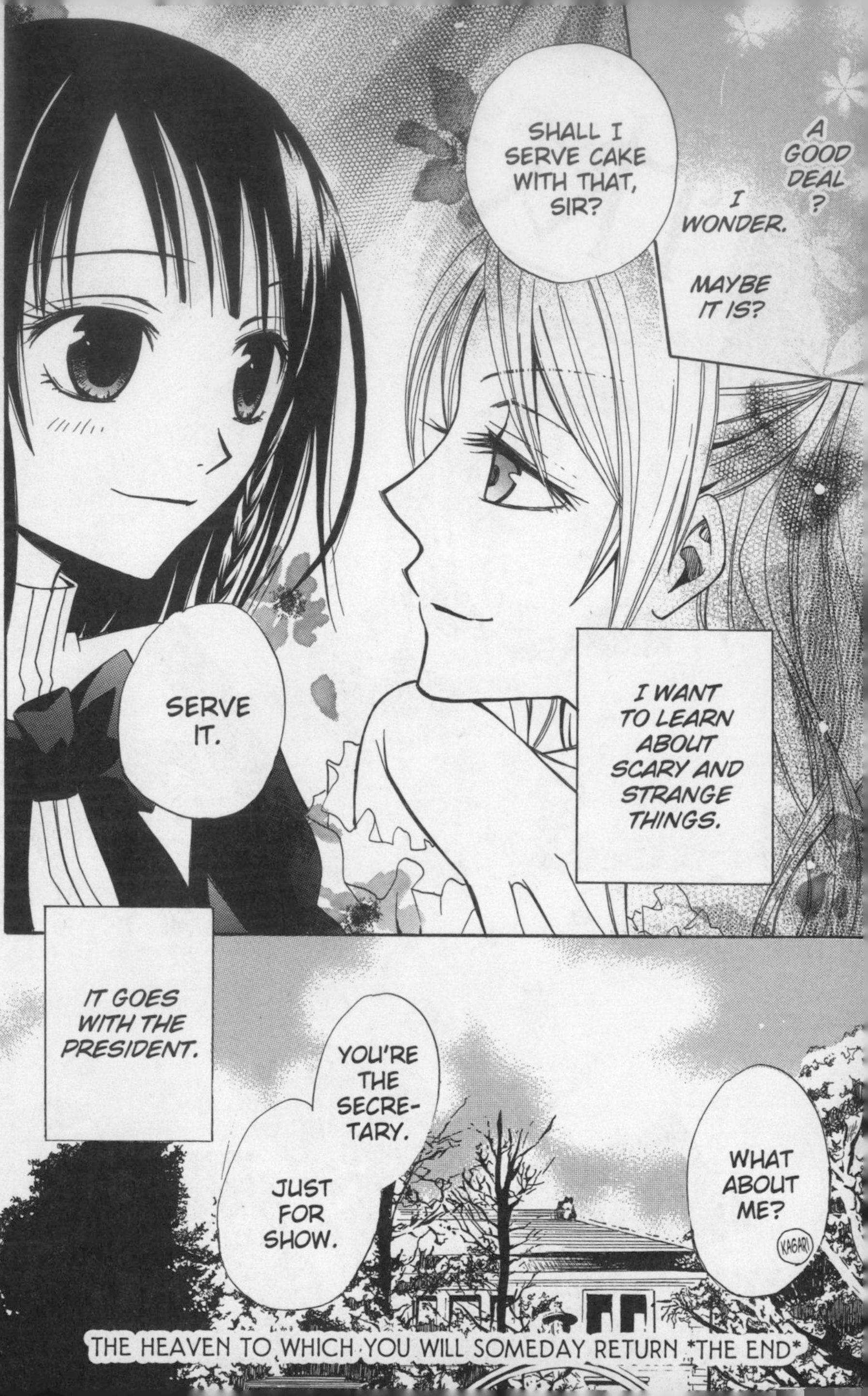
A GOOD DEAL?
I WONDER.
MAYBE IT IS?
SHALL I SERVE CAKE WITH THAT, SIR?
I WANT TO LEARN ABOUT SCARY AND STRANGE THINGS.
SERVE IT.
IT GOES WITH THE PRESIDENT.
WHAT ABOUT ME?
KAGARI
YOU'RE THE SECRETARY.
JUST FOR SHOW.
THE HEAVEN TO WHICH YOU WILL SOMEDAY RETURN *THE END*

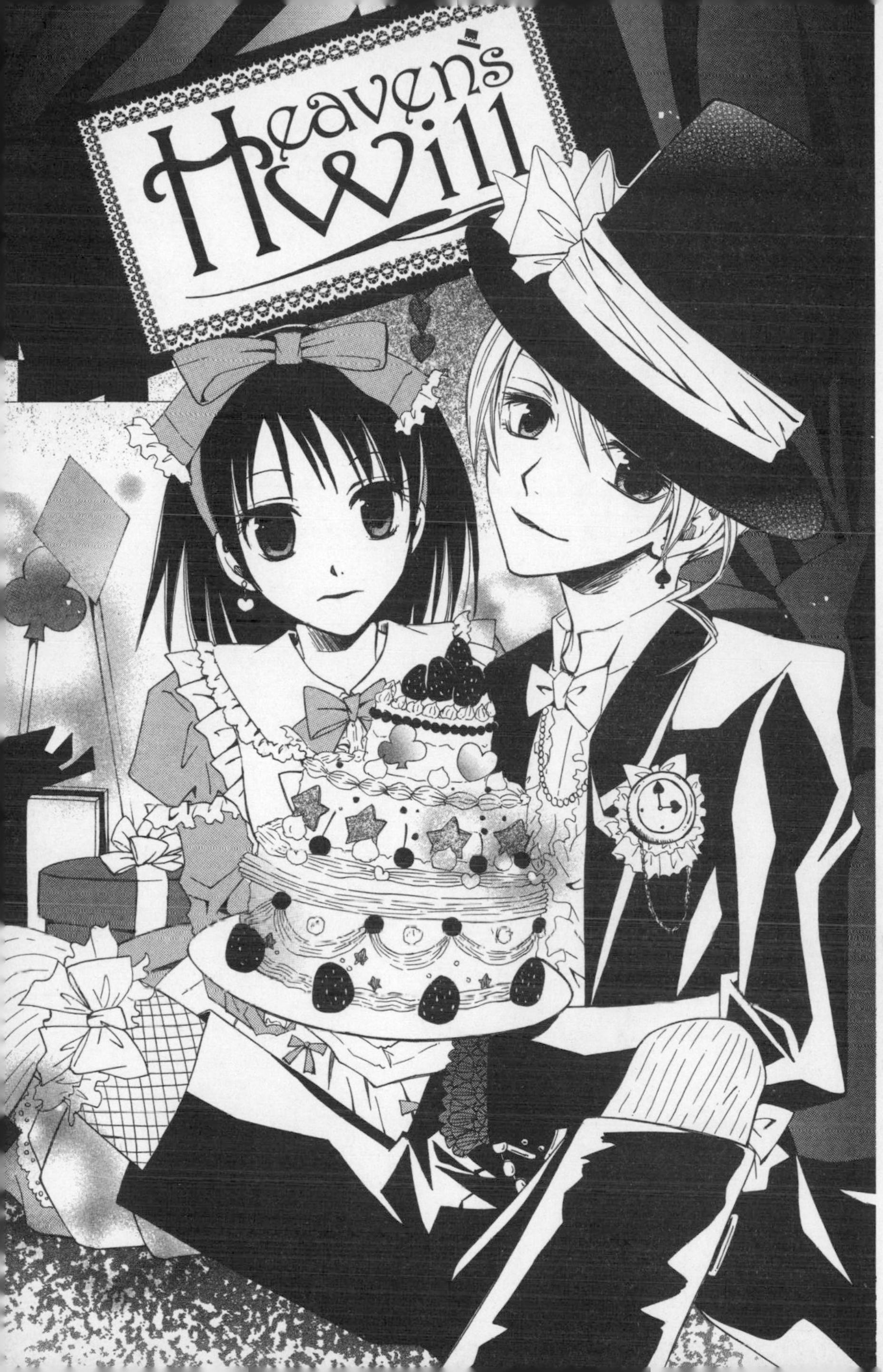
Heaven's Will

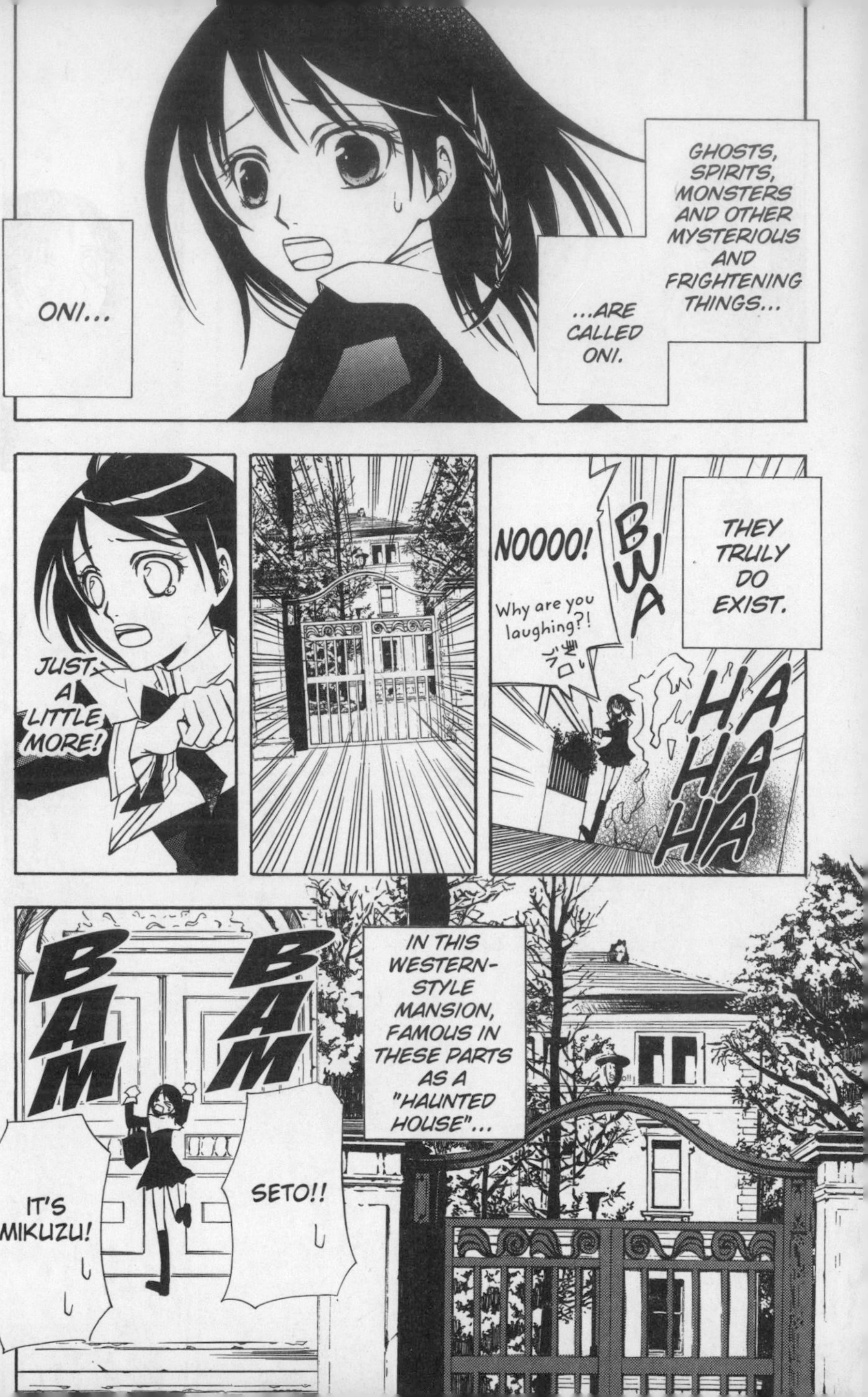
GHOSTS, SPIRITS, MONSTERS AND OTHER MYSTERIOUS AND FRIGHTENING THINGS...
...ARE CALLED ONI.
ONI...
THEY TRULY DO EXIST.
BWA
HA HA HA HA
NOOOO!
Why are you laughing?!
JUST A LITTLE MORE!
IN THIS WESTERN-STYLE MANSION, FAMOUS IN THESE PARTS AS A "HAUNTED HOUSE"...
BAM
BAM
SETO!!
IT'S MIKUZU!

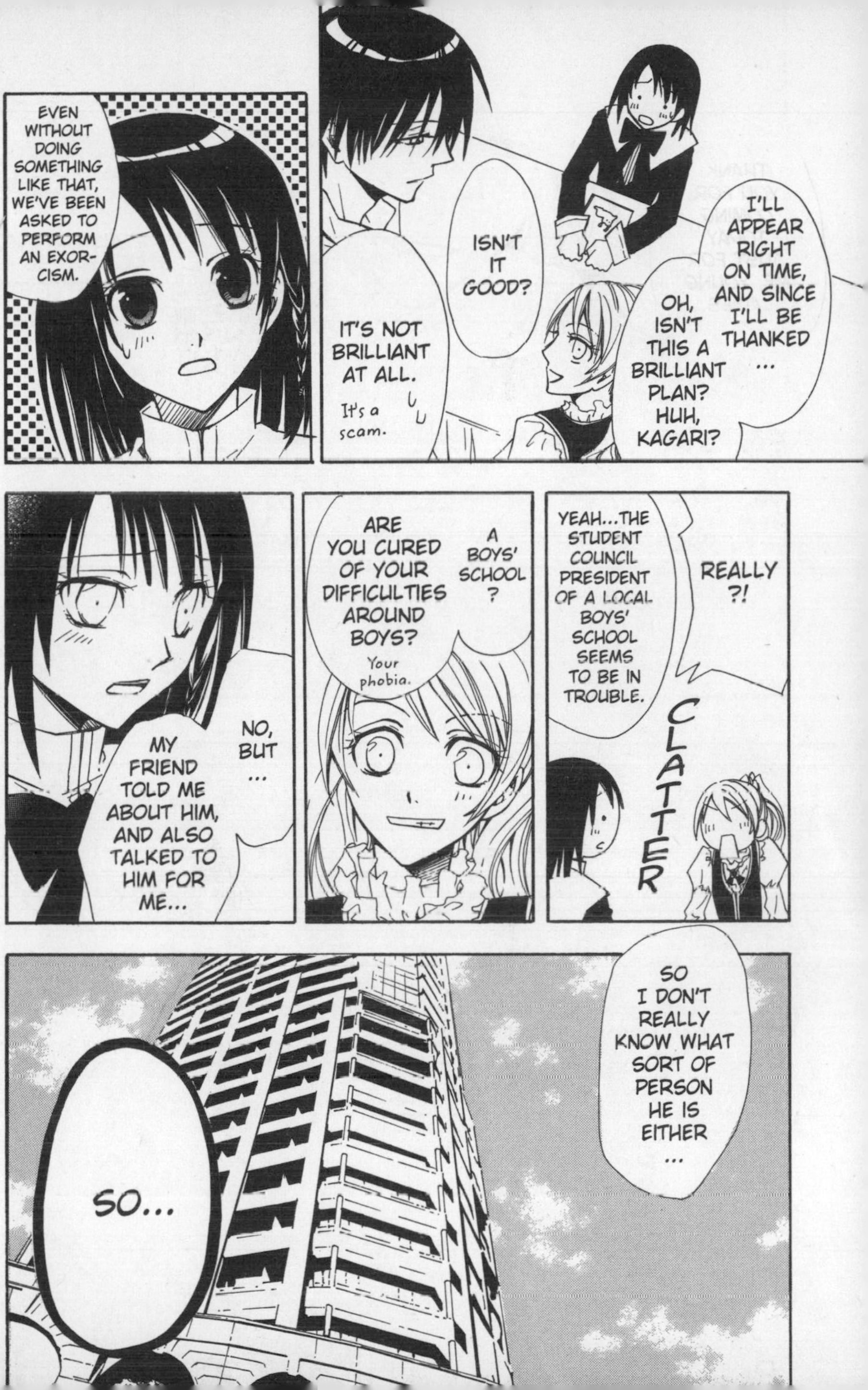

I'LL APPEAR RIGHT ON TIME, AND SINCE I'LL BE THANKED ...
OH, ISN'T THIS A BRILLIANT PLAN? HUH, KAGARI?
ISN'T IT GOOD?
IT'S NOT BRILLIANT AT ALL.
It's a scam.
EVEN WITHOUT DOING SOMETHING LIKE THAT, WE'VE BEEN ASKED TO PERFORM AN EXOR-CISM.
REALLY ?!
YEAH...THE STUDENT COUNCIL PRESIDENT OF A LOCAL BOYS' SCHOOL SEEMS TO BE IN TROUBLE.
CLATTER
A BOYS' SCHOOL ?
ARE YOU CURED OF YOUR DIFFICULTIES AROUND BOYS?
Your phobia.
NO, BUT ...
MY FRIEND TOLD ME ABOUT HIM, AND ALSO TALKED TO HIM FOR ME...
SO I DON'T REALLY KNOW WHAT SORT OF PERSON HE IS EITHER ...
SO...

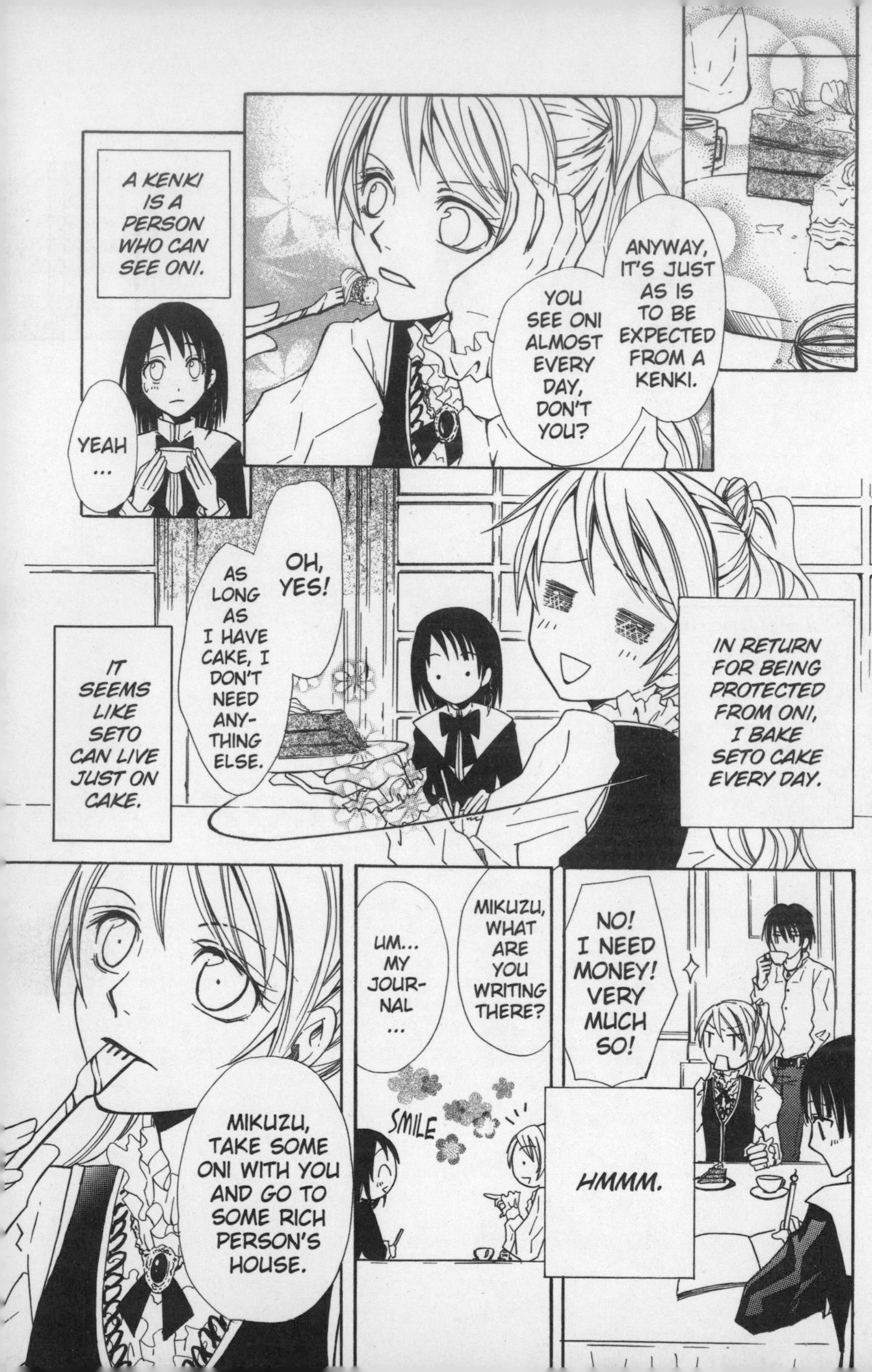
ANYWAY, IT'S JUST AS IS TO BE EXPECTED FROM A KENKI.
YOU SEE ONI ALMOST EVERY DAY, DON'T YOU?
A KENKI IS A PERSON WHO CAN SEE ONI.
YEAH ...
IN RETURN FOR BEING PROTECTED FROM ONI, I BAKE SETO CAKE EVERY DAY.
OH, YES!
AS LONG AS I HAVE CAKE, I DON'T NEED ANY-THING ELSE.
IT SEEMS LIKE SETO CAN LIVE JUST ON CAKE.
NO! I NEED MONEY! VERY MUCH SO!
HMMM.
MIKUZU, WHAT ARE YOU WRITING THERE?
UM... MY JOUR-NAL ...
SMILE
MIKUZU, TAKE SOME ONI WITH YOU AND GO TO SOME RICH PERSON'S HOUSE.

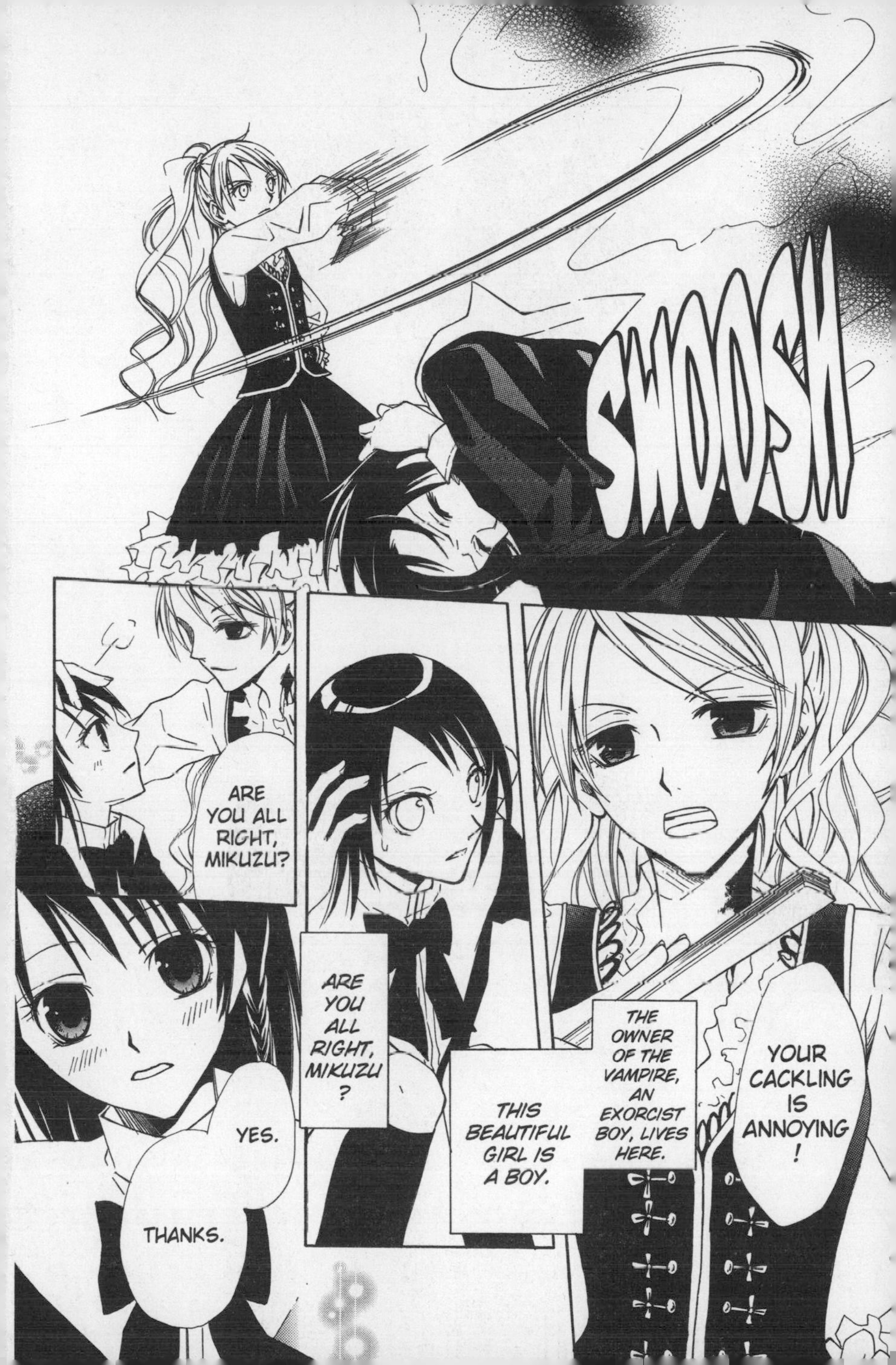
SHOOSH
YOUR CACKLING IS ANNOYING!
THE OWNER OF THE VAMPIRE, AN EXORCIST BOY, LIVES HERE.
THIS BEAUTIFUL GIRL IS A BOY.
ARE YOU ALL RIGHT, MIKUZU?
ARE YOU ALL RIGHT, MIKUZU?
YES.
THANKS.

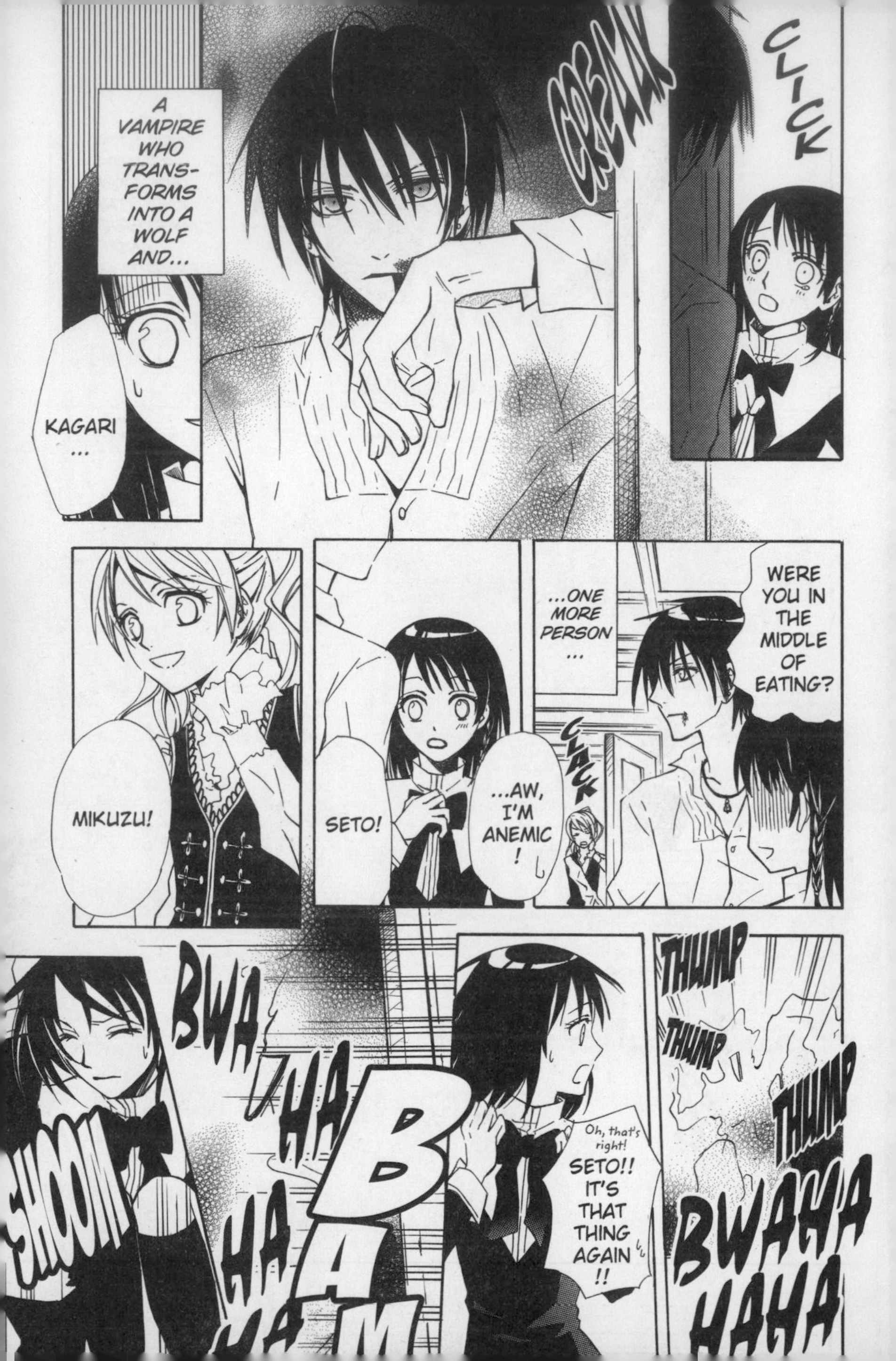
CLICK
CREAKY
A VAMPIRE WHO TRANSFORMS INTO A WOLF AND...
KAGARI ...
WERE YOU IN THE MIDDLE OF EATING?
...ONE MORE PERSON ...
CLACK
...AW, I'M ANEMIC!
SETO!
MIKUZU!
THUMP
THUMP
THUMP
BWAHA HAHA
Oh, that's right!
SETO!! IT'S THAT THING AGAIN!!
BWA HA HA HA
B A
SHOOM

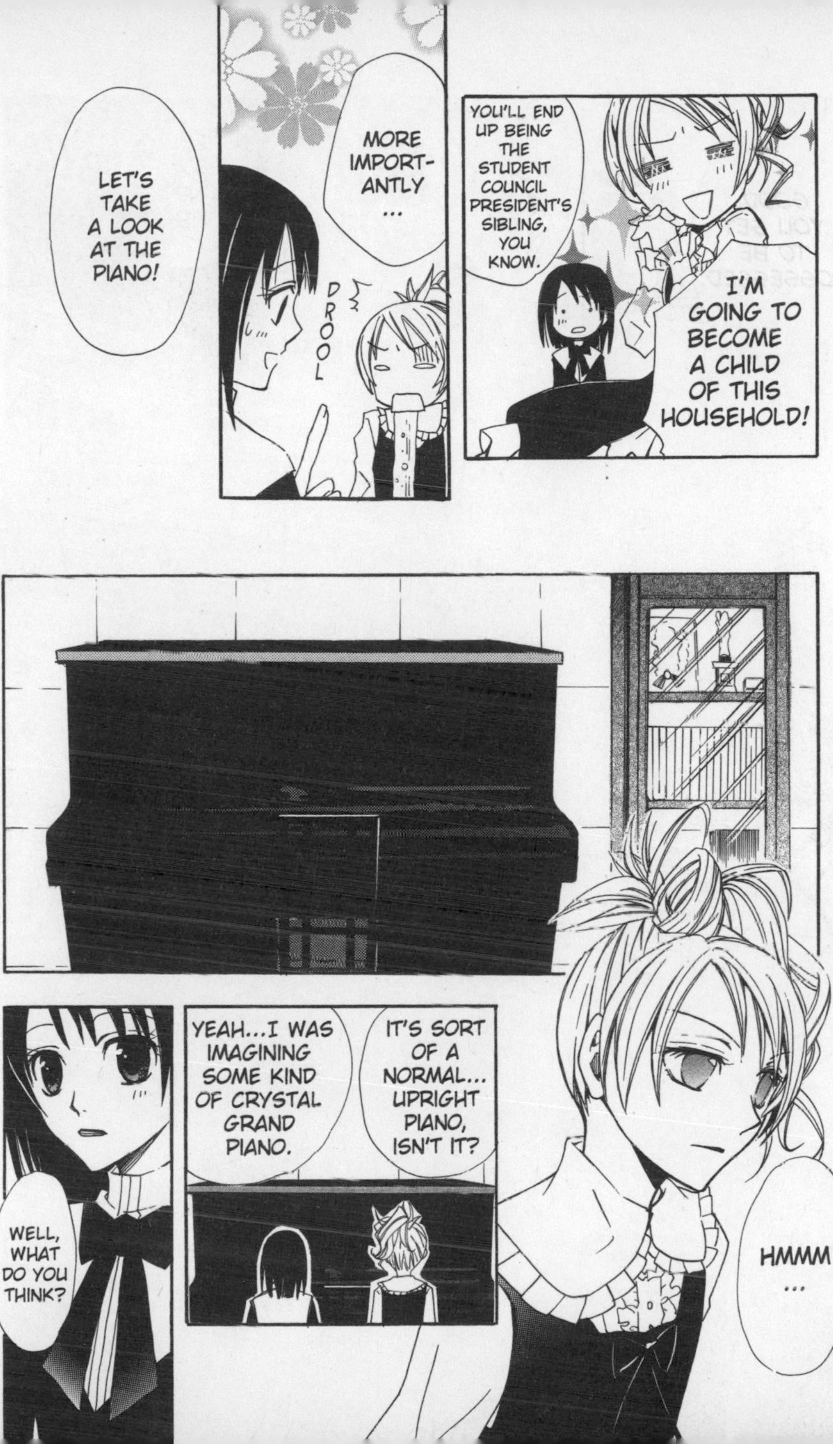
I'M GOING TO BECOME A CHILD OF THIS HOUSEHOLD!
YOU'LL END UP BEING THE STUDENT COUNCIL PRESIDENT'S SIBLING, YOU KNOW.
MORE IMPORT-ANTLY ...
DROOL
LET'S TAKE A LOOK AT THE PIANO!
HMMM ...
IT'S SORT OF A NORMAL... UPRIGHT PIANO, ISN'T IT?
YEAH...I WAS IMAGINING SOME KIND OF CRYSTAL GRAND PIANO.
WELL, WHAT DO YOU THINK?

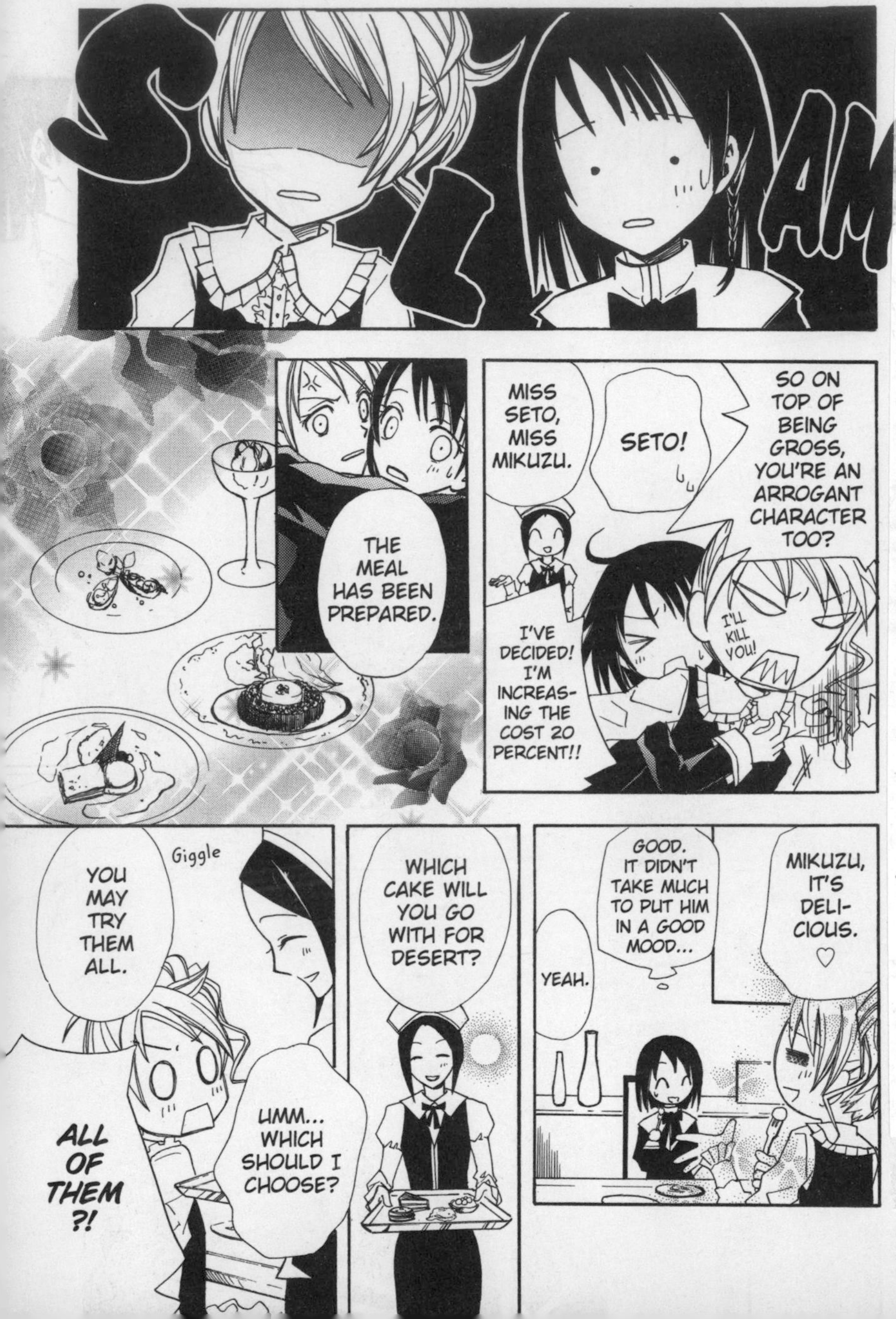
SLAM
SO ON TOP OF BEING GROSS, YOU'RE AN ARROGANT CHARACTER TOO?
SETO!
MISS SETO, MISS MIKUZU.
I'LL KILL YOU!
I'VE DECIDED! I'M INCREAS-ING THE COST 20 PERCENT!!
THE MEAL HAS BEEN PREPARED.
MIKUZU, IT'S DELI-CIOUS. ♡
GOOD. IT DIDN'T TAKE MUCH TO PUT HIM IN A GOOD MOOD...
YEAH.
WHICH CAKE WILL YOU GO WITH FOR DESERT?
UMM... WHICH SHOULD I CHOOSE?
Giggle
YOU MAY TRY THEM ALL.
ALL OF THEM ?!

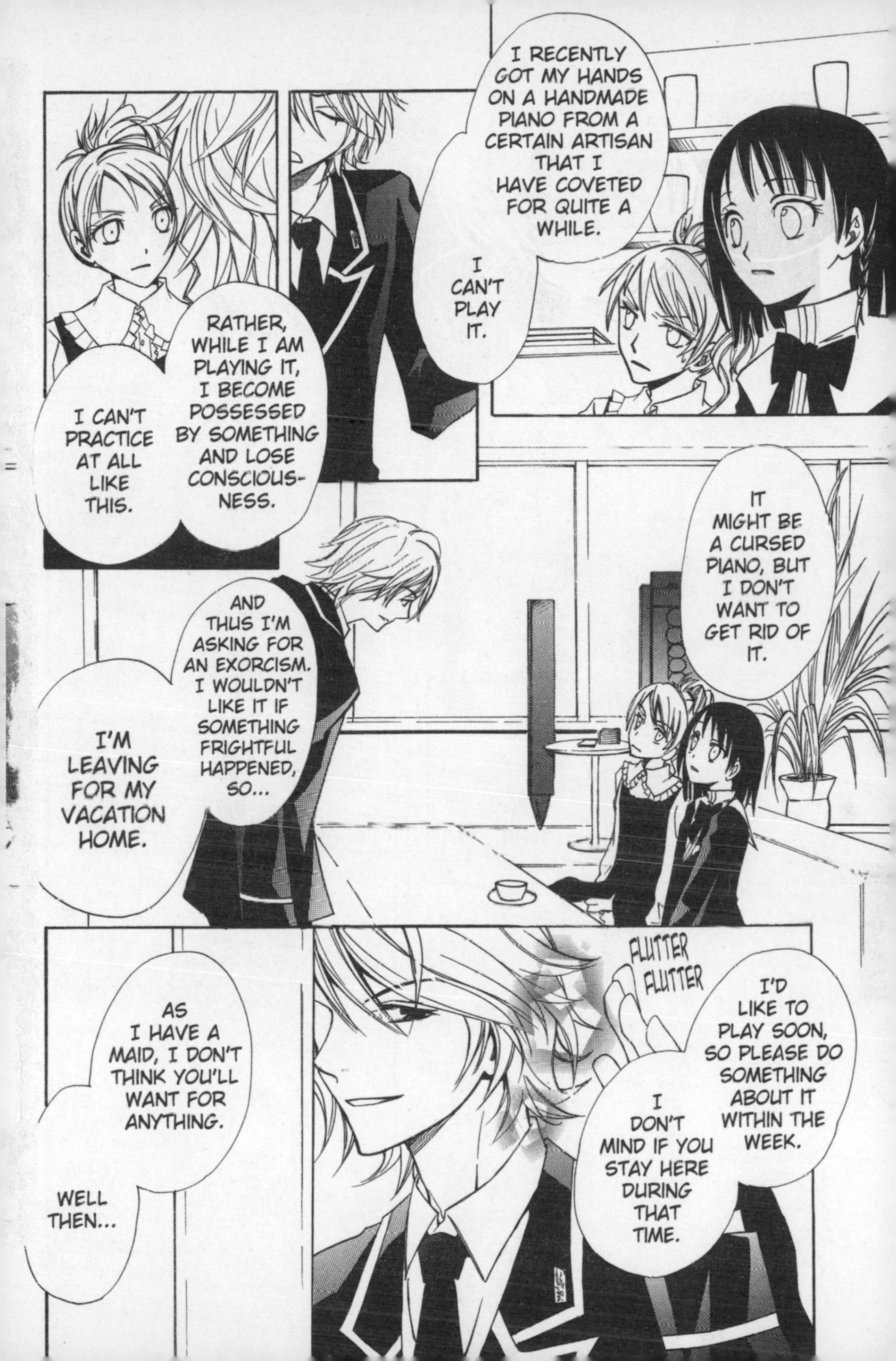
I RECENTLY GOT MY HANDS ON A HANDMADE PIANO FROM A CERTAIN ARTISAN THAT I HAVE COVETED FOR QUITE A WHILE.
I CAN'T PLAY IT.
RATHER, WHILE I AM PLAYING IT, I BECOME POSSESSED BY SOMETHING AND LOSE CONSCIOUS-NESS.
I CAN'T PRACTICE AT ALL LIKE THIS.
IT MIGHT BE A CURSED PIANO, BUT I DON'T WANT TO GET RID OF IT.
AND THUS I'M ASKING FOR AN EXORCISM. I WOULDN'T LIKE IT IF SOMETHING FRIGHTFUL HAPPENED, SO...
I'M LEAVING FOR MY VACATION HOME.
FLUTTER FLUTTER
I'D LIKE TO PLAY SOON, SO PLEASE DO SOMETHING ABOUT IT WITHIN THE WEEK.
I DON'T MIND IF YOU STAY HERE DURING THAT TIME.
AS I HAVE A MAID, I DON'T THINK YOU'LL WANT FOR ANYTHING.
WELL THEN...

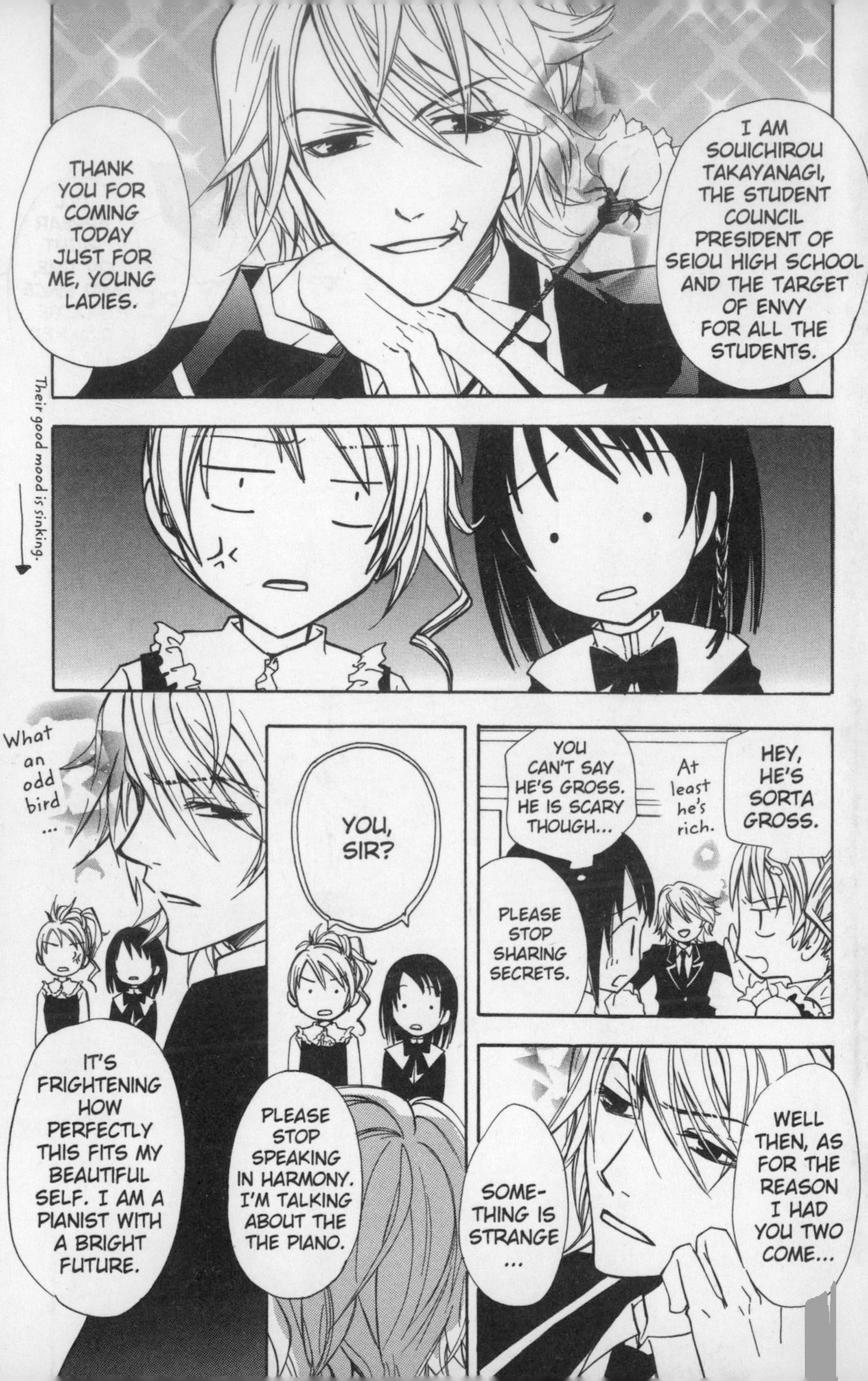
I AM SOUICHIROU TAKAYANAGI, THE STUDENT COUNCIL PRESIDENT OF SEIOU HIGH SCHOOL AND THE TARGET OF ENVY FOR ALL THE STUDENTS.
THANK YOU FOR COMING TODAY JUST FOR ME, YOUNG LADIES.
Their good mood is sinking.
HEY, HE'S SORTA GROSS.
At least he's rich.
YOU CAN'T SAY HE'S GROSS. HE IS SCARY THOUGH...
PLEASE STOP SHARING SECRETS.
WELL THEN, AS FOR THE REASON I HAD YOU TWO COME...
SOME-THING IS STRANGE ...
YOU, SIR?
PLEASE STOP SPEAKING IN HARMONY. I'M TALKING ABOUT THE THE PIANO.
What an odd bird ...
IT'S FRIGHTENING HOW PERFECTLY THIS FITS MY BEAUTIFUL SELF. I AM A PIANIST WITH A BRIGHT FUTURE.

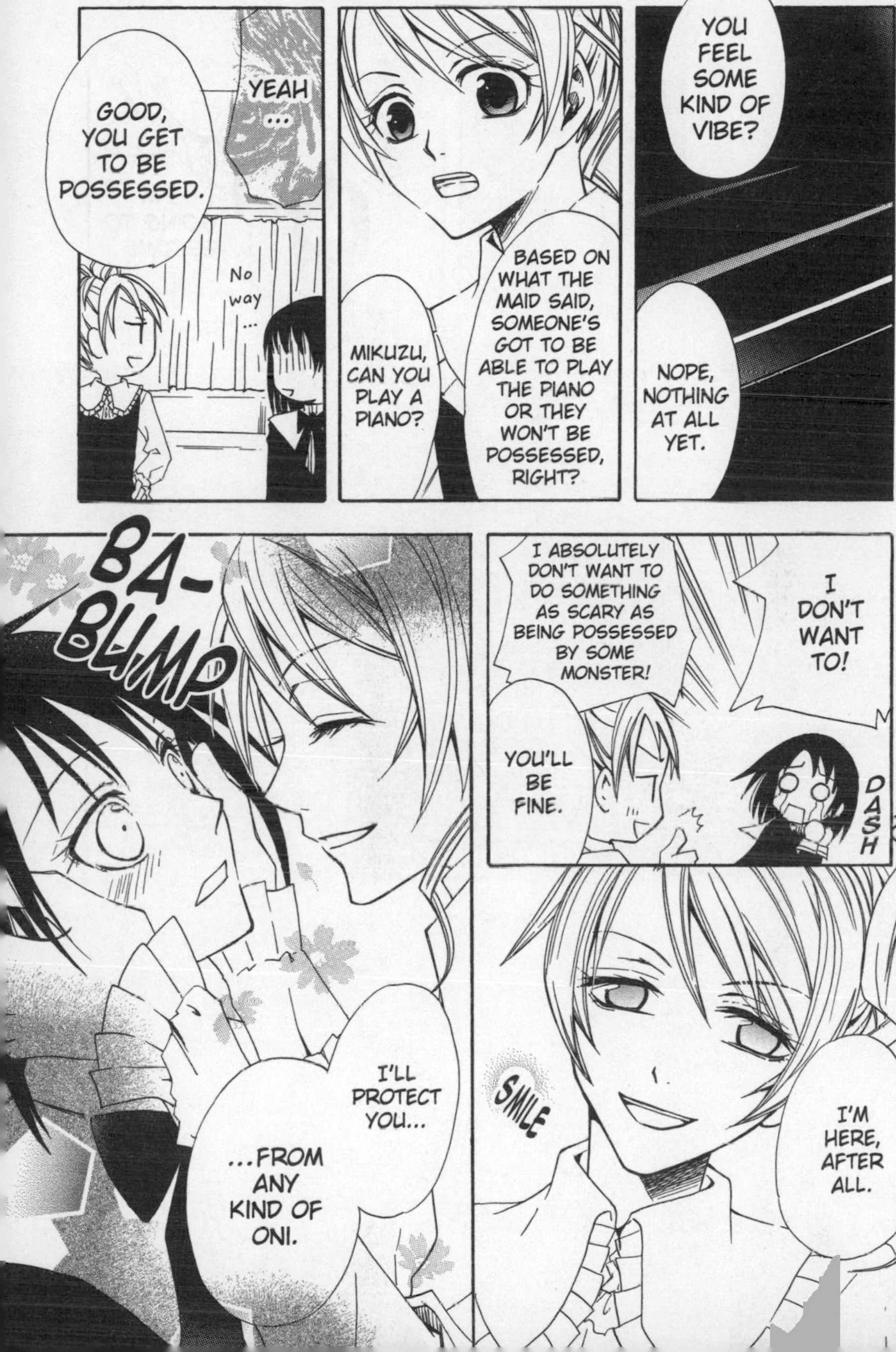
YOU FEEL SOME KIND OF VIBE?
NOPE, NOTHING AT ALL YET.
BASED ON WHAT THE MAID SAID, SOMEONE'S GOT TO BE ABLE TO PLAY THE PIANO OR THEY WON'T BE POSSESSED, RIGHT?
MIKUZU, CAN YOU PLAY A PIANO?
YEAH ...
GOOD, YOU GET TO BE POSSESSED.
No way ...
I DON'T WANT TO!
I ABSOLUTELY DON'T WANT TO DO SOMETHING AS SCARY AS BEING POSSESSED BY SOME MONSTER!
DASH
YOU'LL BE FINE.
I'M HERE, AFTER ALL.
SMILE
BA-BUMP
I'LL PROTECT YOU...
...FROM ANY KIND OF ONI.

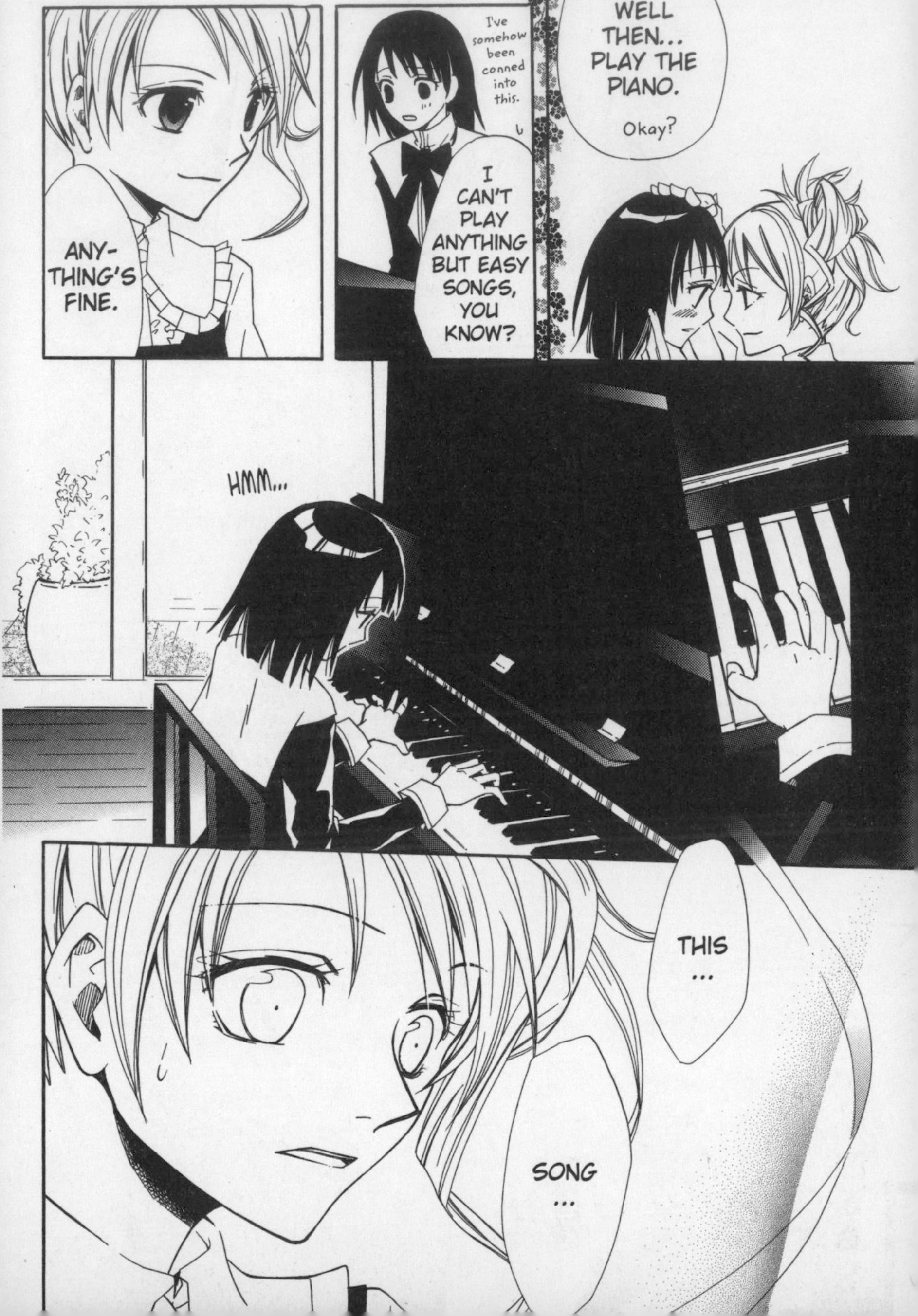
WELL THEN... PLAY THE PIANO.
Okay?
I've somehow been conned into this.
I CAN'T PLAY ANYTHING BUT EASY SONGS, YOU KNOW?
ANY-THING'S FINE.
HMM...
THIS ...
SONG ...

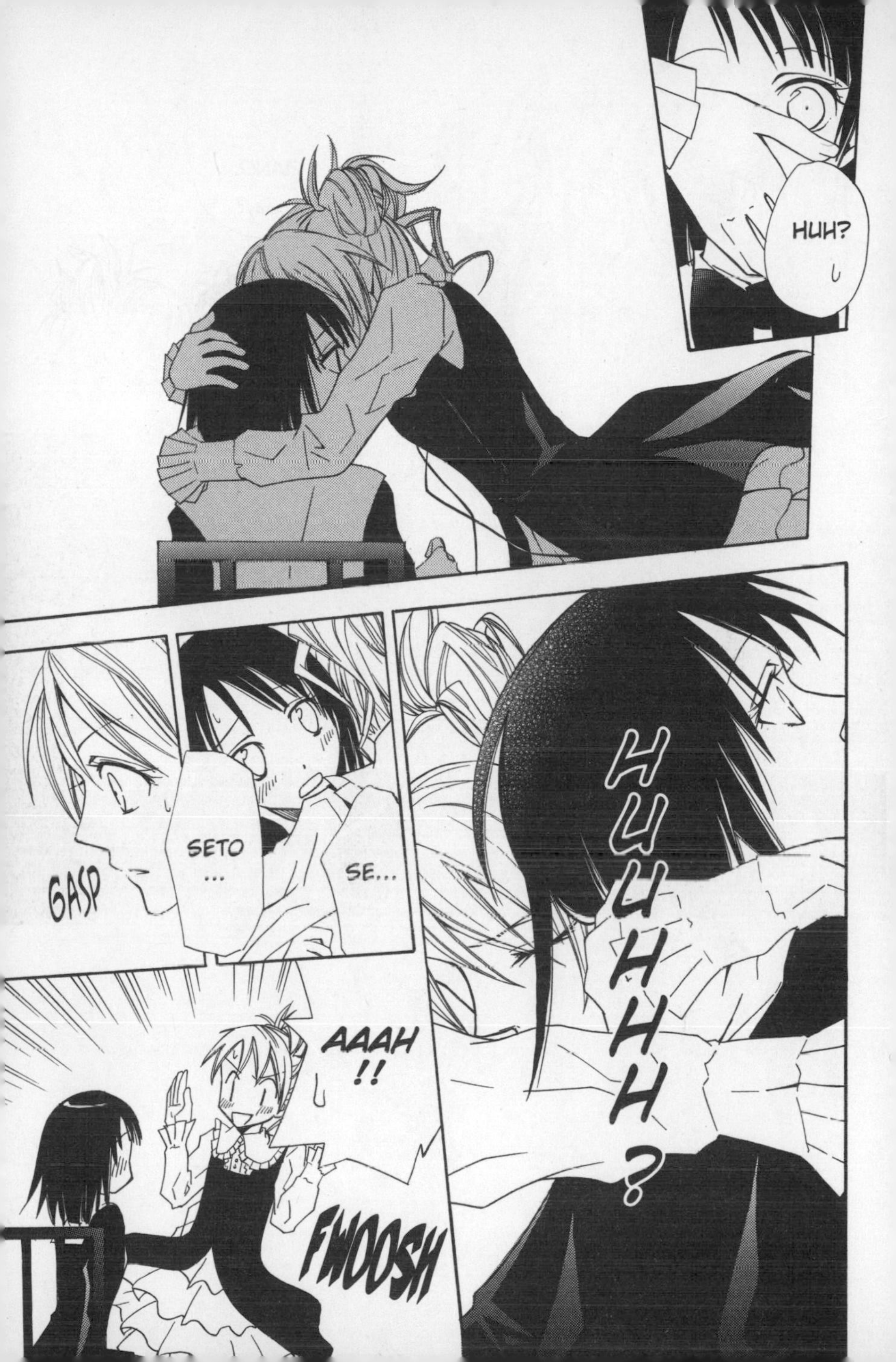
HUH?
HUUUHHH?
SE...
SETO ...
GASP
AAAH !!
FWOOSH

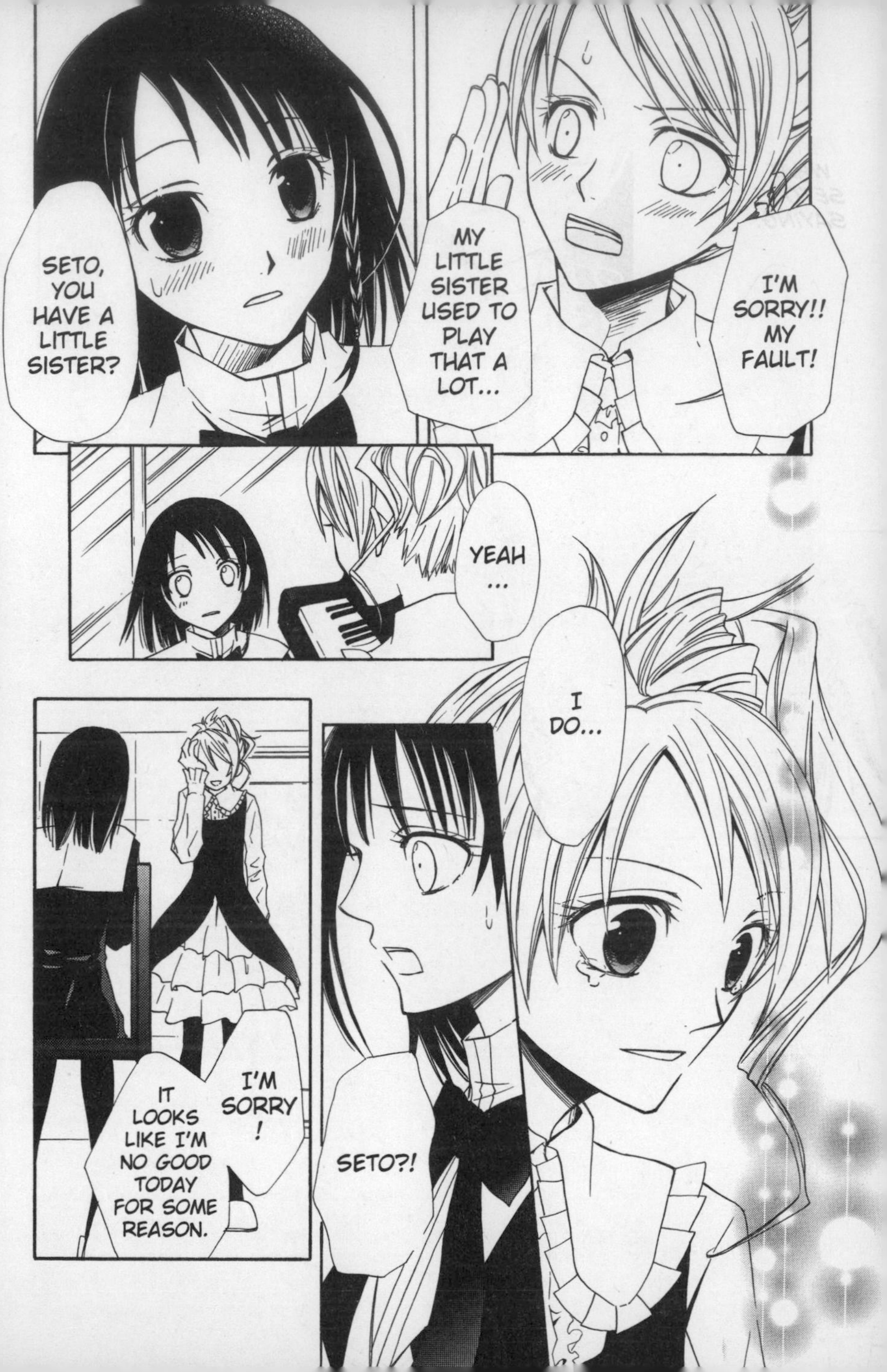
I'M SORRY!! MY FAULT!
MY LITTLE SISTER USED TO PLAY THAT A LOT...
SETO, YOU HAVE A LITTLE SISTER?
YEAH ...
I DO...
SETO?!
I'M SORRY !
IT LOOKS LIKE I'M NO GOOD TODAY FOR SOME REASON.

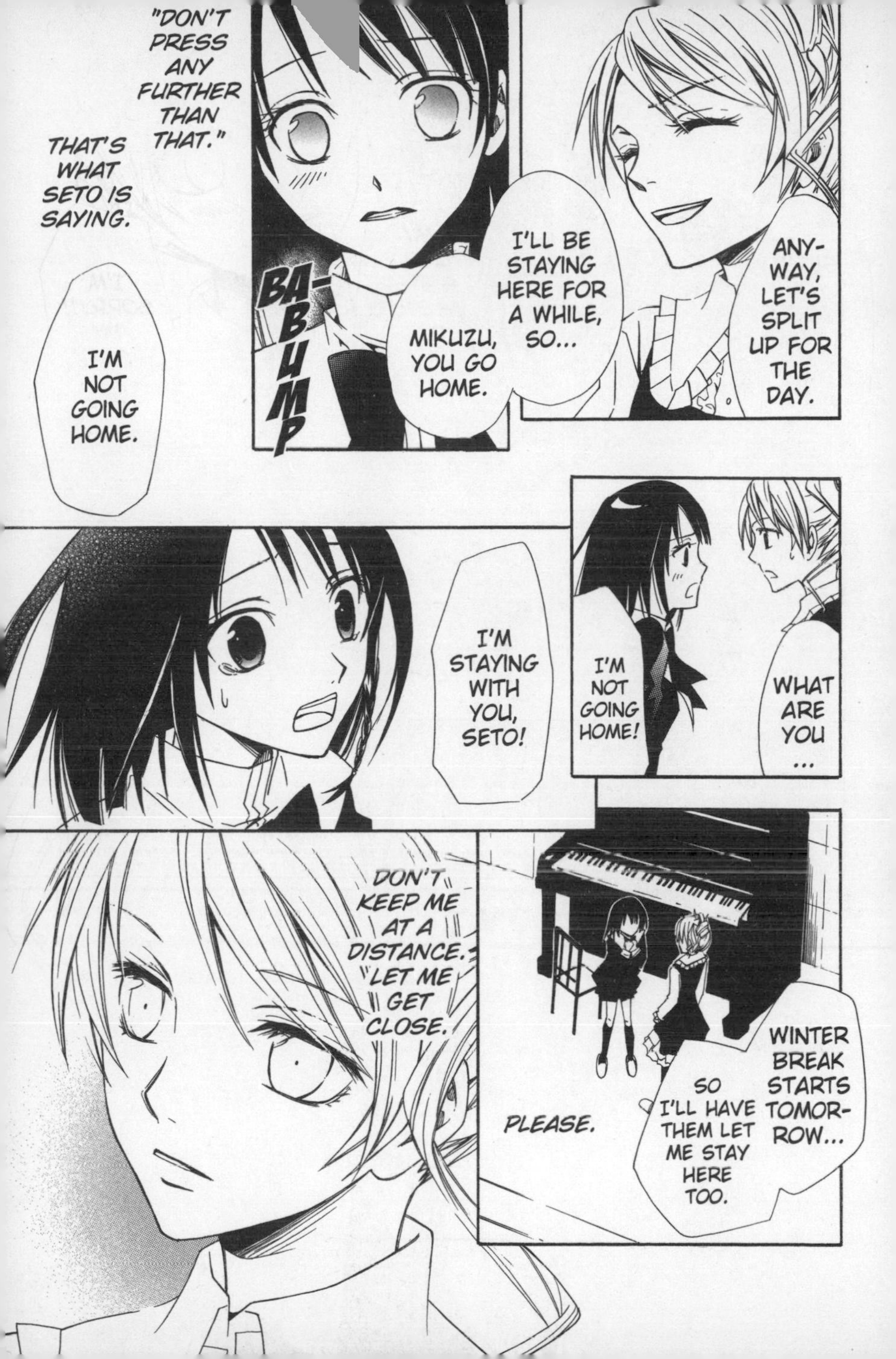
ANY-WAY, LET'S SPLIT UP FOR THE DAY.
I'LL BE STAYING HERE FOR A WHILE, SO...
MIKUZU, YOU GO HOME.
BA-BUMP
"DON'T PRESS ANY FURTHER THAN THAT."
THAT'S WHAT SETO IS SAYING.
I'M NOT GOING HOME.
WHAT ARE YOU ...
I'M NOT GOING HOME!
I'M STAYING WITH YOU, SETO!
WINTER BREAK STARTS TOMORROW...
SO I'LL HAVE THEM LET ME STAY HERE TOO.
PLEASE.
DON'T KEEP ME AT A DISTANCE. LET ME GET CLOSE.

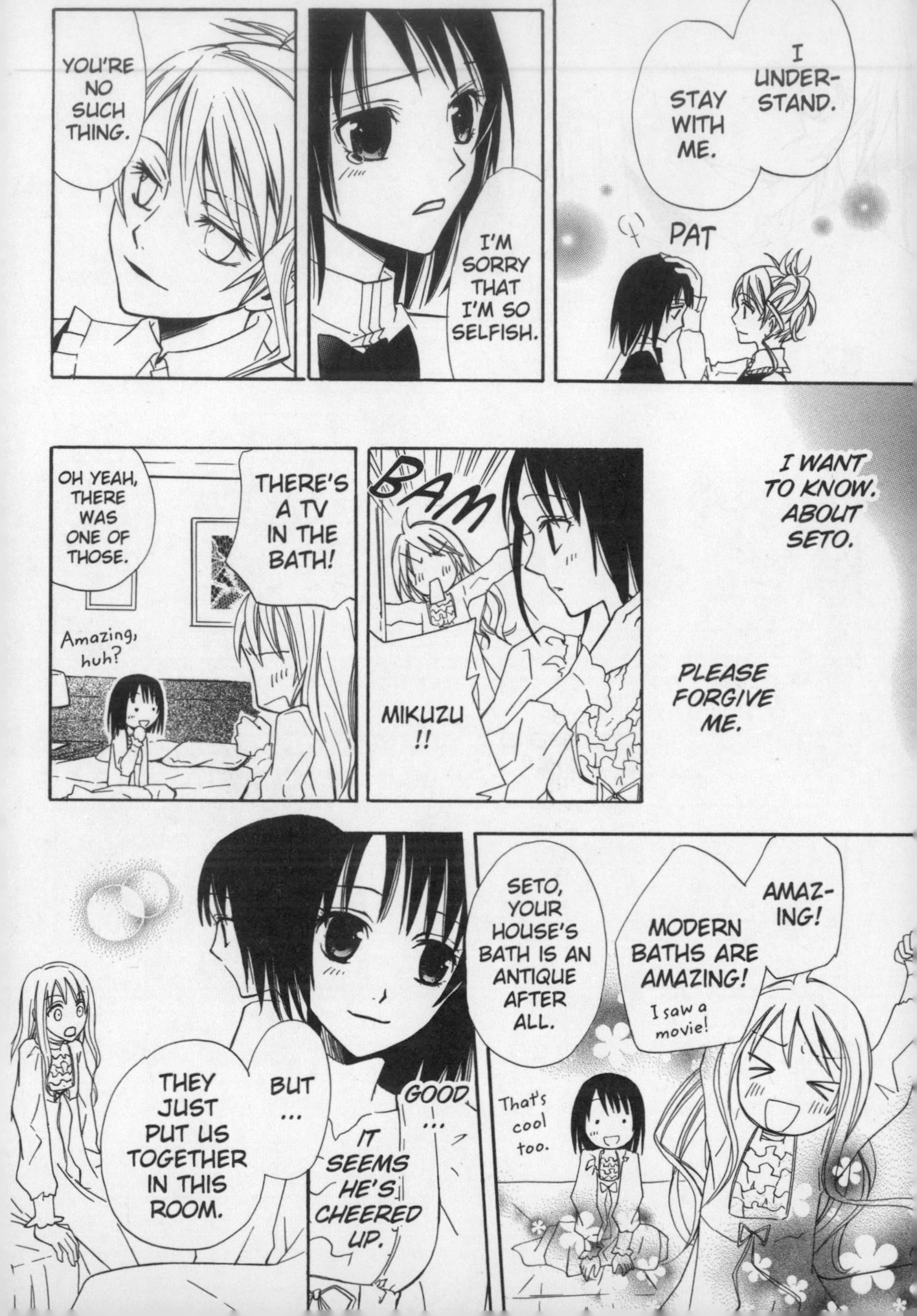
I UNDERSTAND.
STAY WITH ME.
PAT
I'M SORRY THAT I'M SO SELFISH.
YOU'RE NO SUCH THING.
I WANT TO KNOW. ABOUT SETO.
PLEASE FORGIVE ME.
BAM
MIKUZU !!
THERE'S A TV IN THE BATH!
OH YEAH, THERE WAS ONE OF THOSE.
Amazing, huh?
AMAZ-ING!
MODERN BATHS ARE AMAZING!
I saw a movie!
SETO, YOUR HOUSE'S BATH IS AN ANTIQUE AFTER ALL.
That's cool too.
GOOD...
IT SEEMS HE'S CHEERED UP.
BUT...
THEY JUST PUT US TOGETHER IN THIS ROOM.

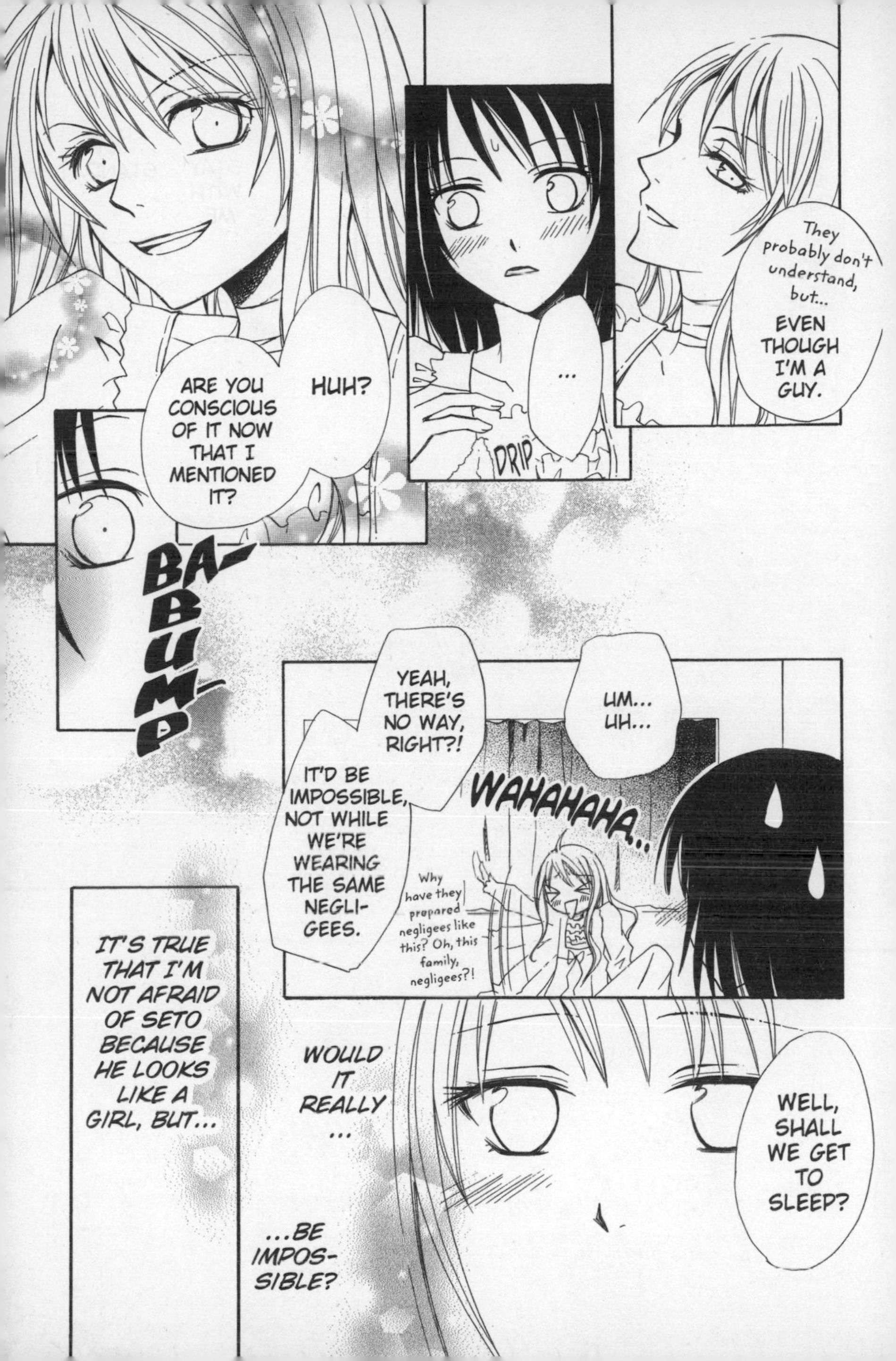
They probably don't understand, but...
EVEN THOUGH I'M A GUY.
...
DRIP
HUH?
ARE YOU CONSCIOUS OF IT NOW THAT I MENTIONED IT?
BA-BUMP
UM... UH...
YEAH, THERE'S NO WAY, RIGHT?!
IT'D BE IMPOSSIBLE, NOT WHILE WE'RE WEARING THE SAME NEGLI-GEES.
WAHAHAHA...
Why have they prepared negligees like this? Oh, this family, negligees?!
WELL, SHALL WE GET TO SLEEP?
WOULD IT REALLY ...
...BE IMPOS-SIBLE?
IT'S TRUE THAT I'M NOT AFRAID OF SETO BECAUSE HE LOOKS LIKE A GIRL, BUT...

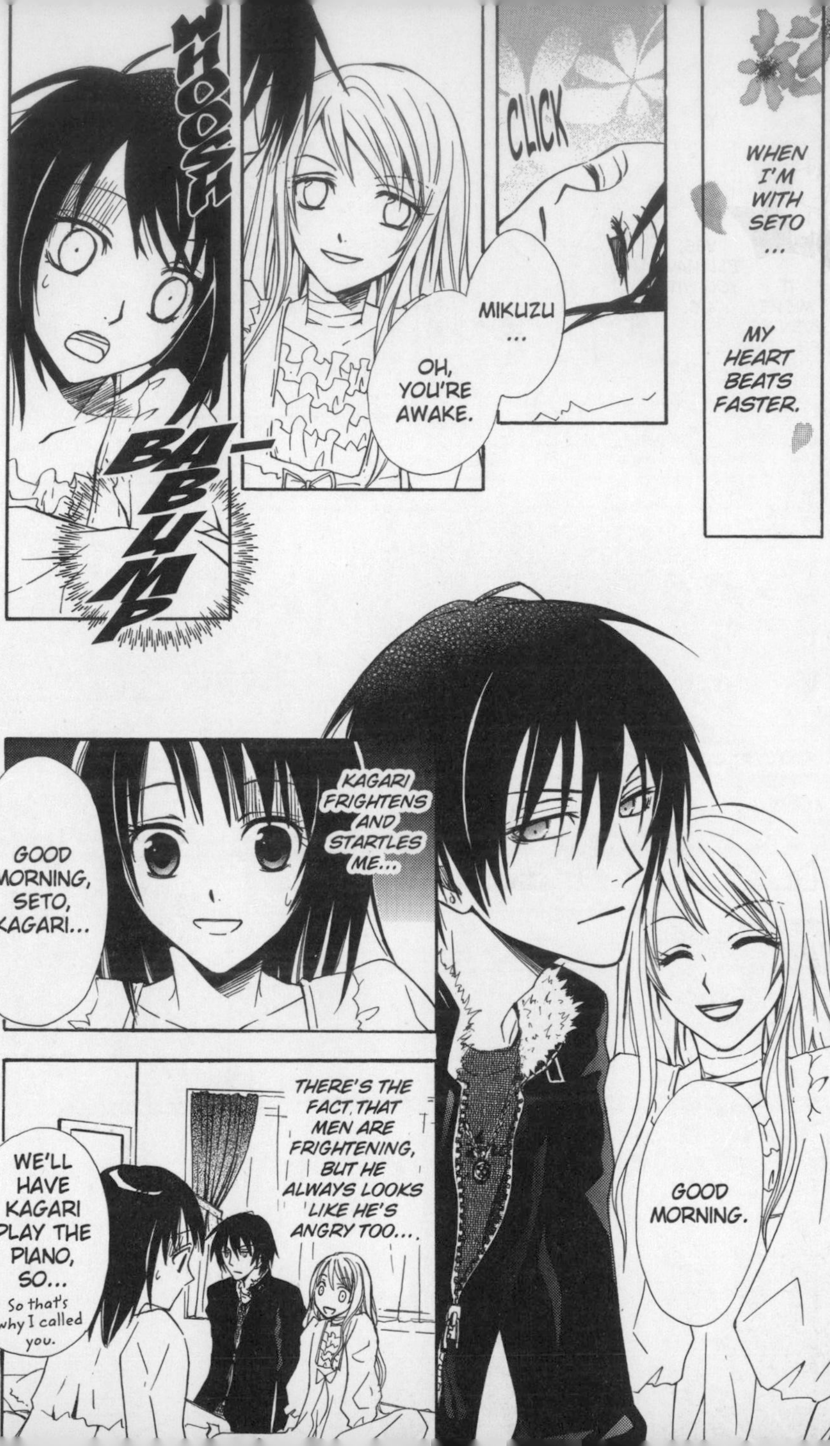
WHEN I'M WITH SETO...
MY HEART BEATS FASTER.
CLICK
MIKUZU...
OH, YOU'RE AWAKE.
WHOOSH
BA-BABUMP
GOOD MORNING.
KAGARI FRIGHTENS AND STARTLES ME...
GOOD MORNING, SETO, KAGARI...
THERE'S THE FACT THAT MEN ARE FRIGHTENING, BUT HE ALWAYS LOOKS LIKE HE'S ANGRY TOO...
WE'LL HAVE KAGARI PLAY THE PIANO, SO...
So that's why I called you.

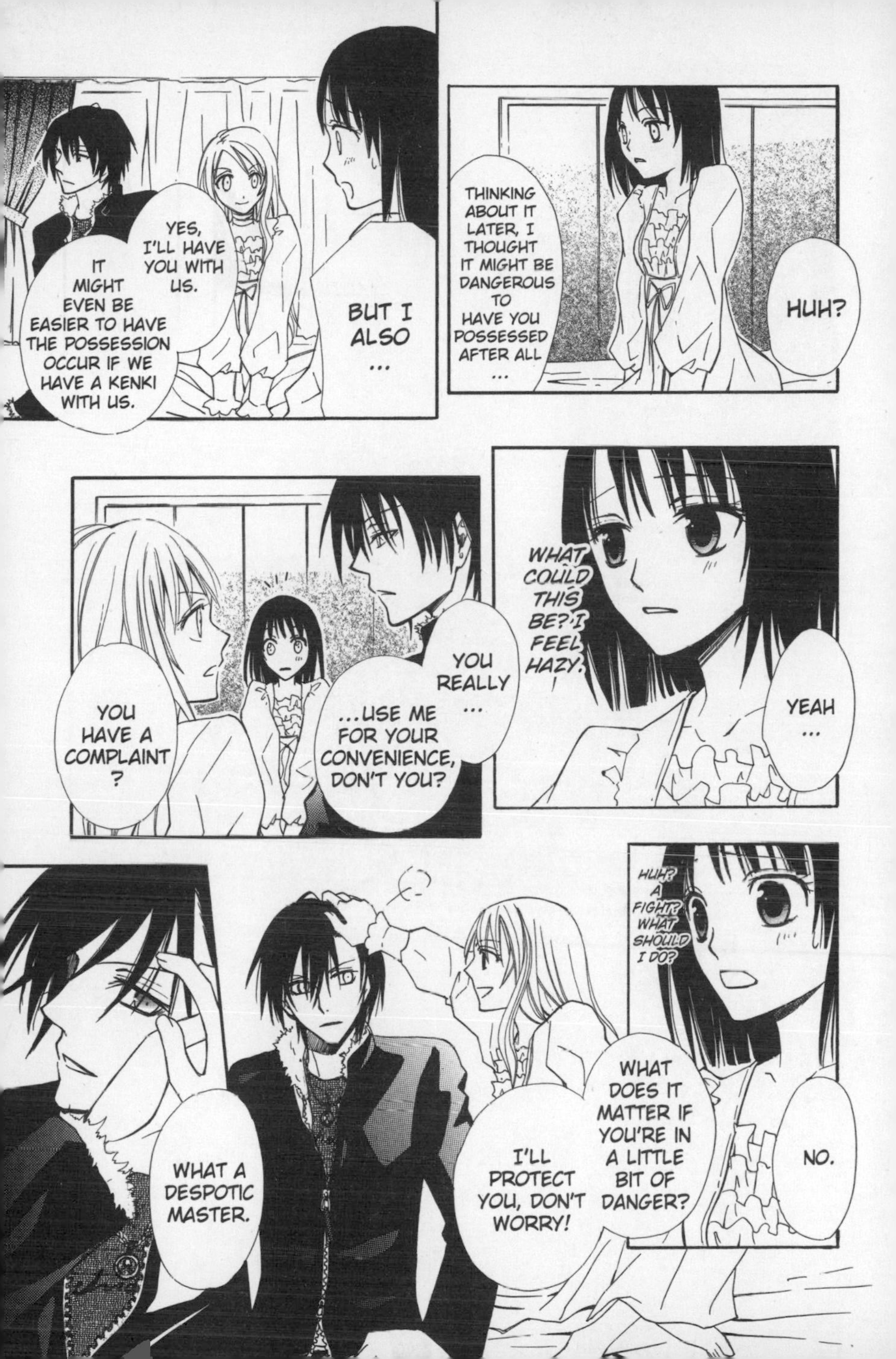
THINKING ABOUT IT LATER, I THOUGHT IT MIGHT BE DANGEROUS TO HAVE YOU POSSESSED AFTER ALL ...
HUH?
BUT I ALSO ...
YES, I'LL HAVE YOU WITH US.
IT MIGHT EVEN BE EASIER TO HAVE THE POSSESSION OCCUR IF WE HAVE A KENKI WITH US.
WHAT COULD THIS BE? I FEEL HAZY.
YEAH ...
YOU REALLY ...
...USE ME FOR YOUR CONVENIENCE, DON'T YOU?
YOU HAVE A COMPLAINT?
HUH? A FIGHT? WHAT SHOULD I DO?
NO.
WHAT DOES IT MATTER IF YOU'RE IN A LITTLE BIT OF DANGER?
I'LL PROTECT YOU, DON'T WORRY!
WHAT A DESPOTIC MASTER.

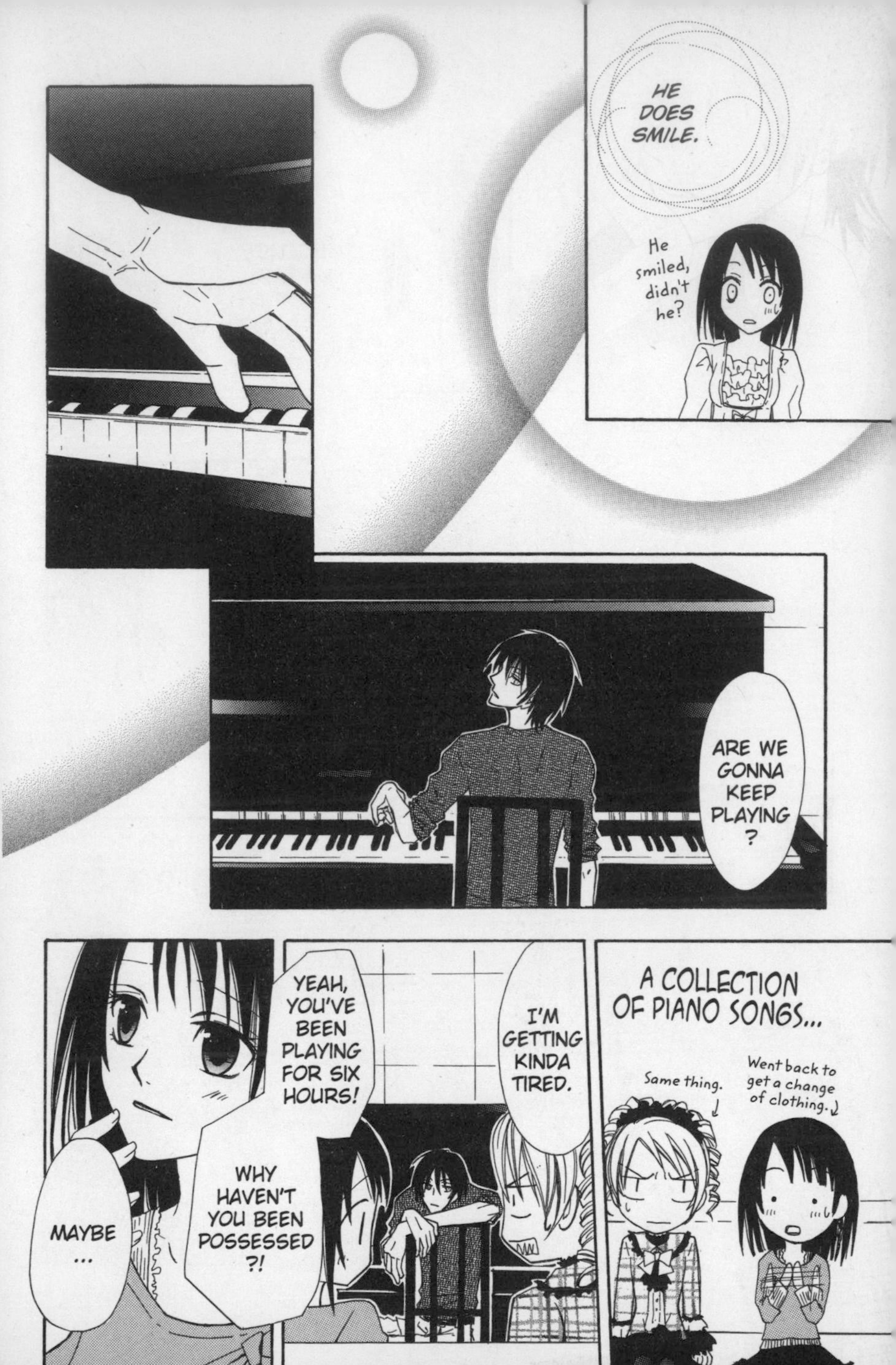
HE DOES SMILE.
He smiled, didn't he?
ARE WE GONNA KEEP PLAYING?
A COLLECTION OF PIANO SONGS...
Went back to get a change of clothing.
Same thing.
I'M GETTING KINDA TIRED.
YEAH, YOU'VE BEEN PLAYING FOR SIX HOURS!
WHY HAVEN'T YOU BEEN POSSESSED?!
MAYBE...

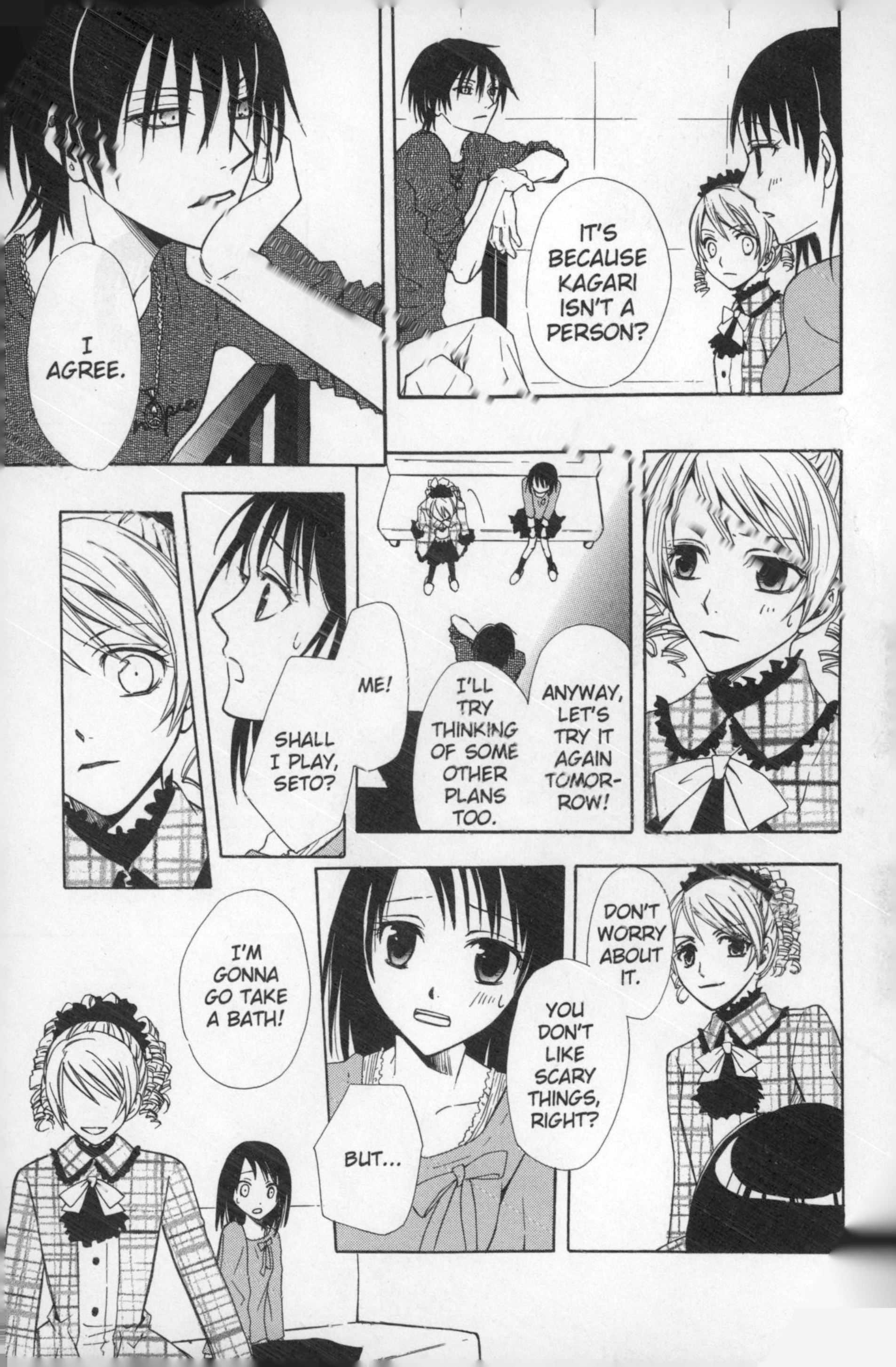
IT'S BECAUSE KAGARI ISN'T A PERSON?
I AGREE.
ANYWAY, LET'S TRY IT AGAIN TOMORROW!
I'LL TRY THINKING OF SOME OTHER PLANS TOO.
ME!
SHALL I PLAY, SETO?
DON'T WORRY ABOUT IT.
YOU DON'T LIKE SCARY THINGS, RIGHT?
BUT...
I'M GONNA GO TAKE A BATH!

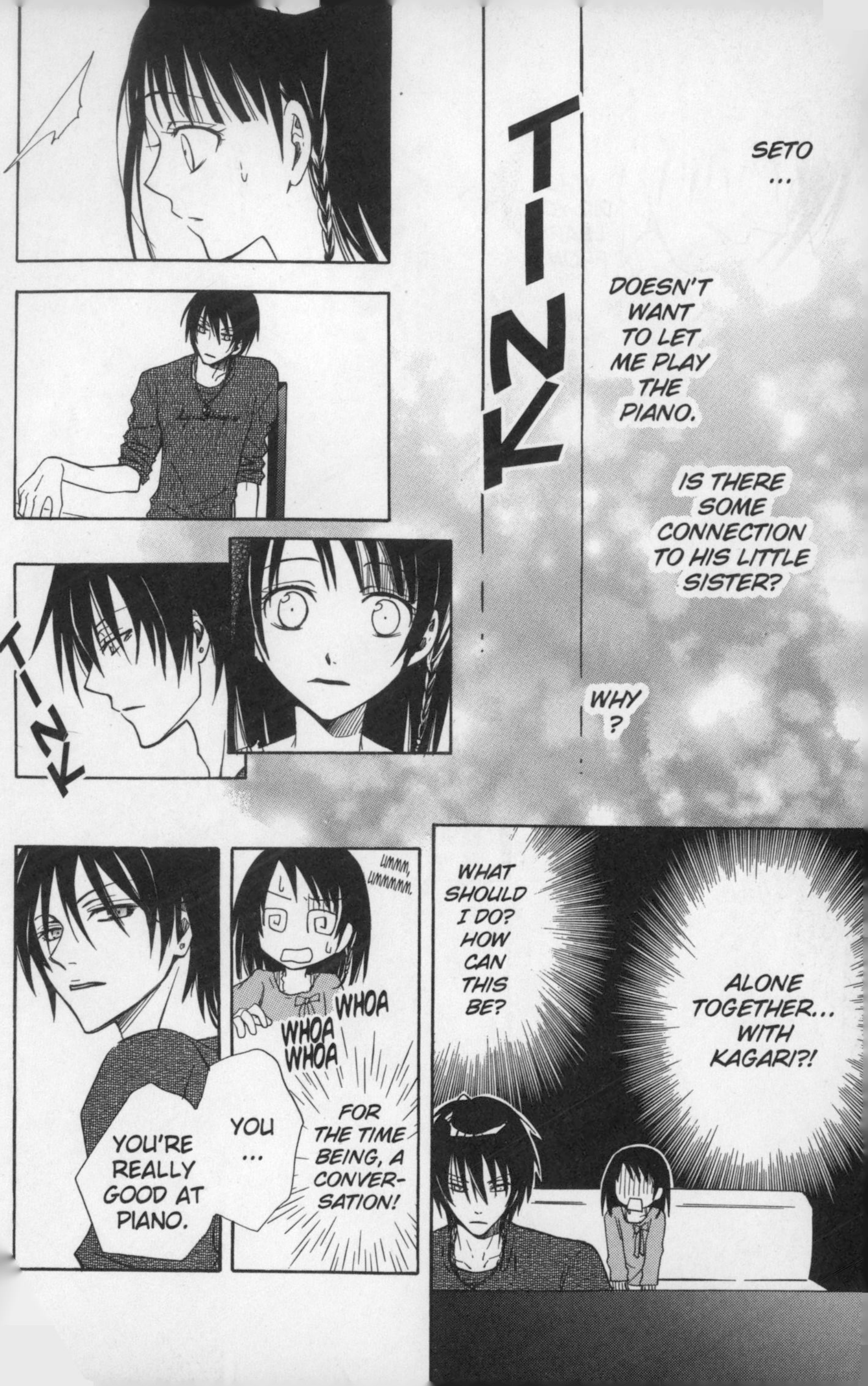
SETO ...
DOESN'T WANT TO LET ME PLAY THE PIANO.
IS THERE SOME CONNECTION TO HIS LITTLE SISTER?
WHY?
TINK
TINK
ALONE TOGETHER... WITH KAGARI?!
WHAT SHOULD I DO? HOW CAN THIS BE?
UMMM, UMMMMM.
WHOA WHOA WHOA
FOR THE TIME BEING, A CONVERSATION!
YOU ...
YOU'RE REALLY GOOD AT PIANO.

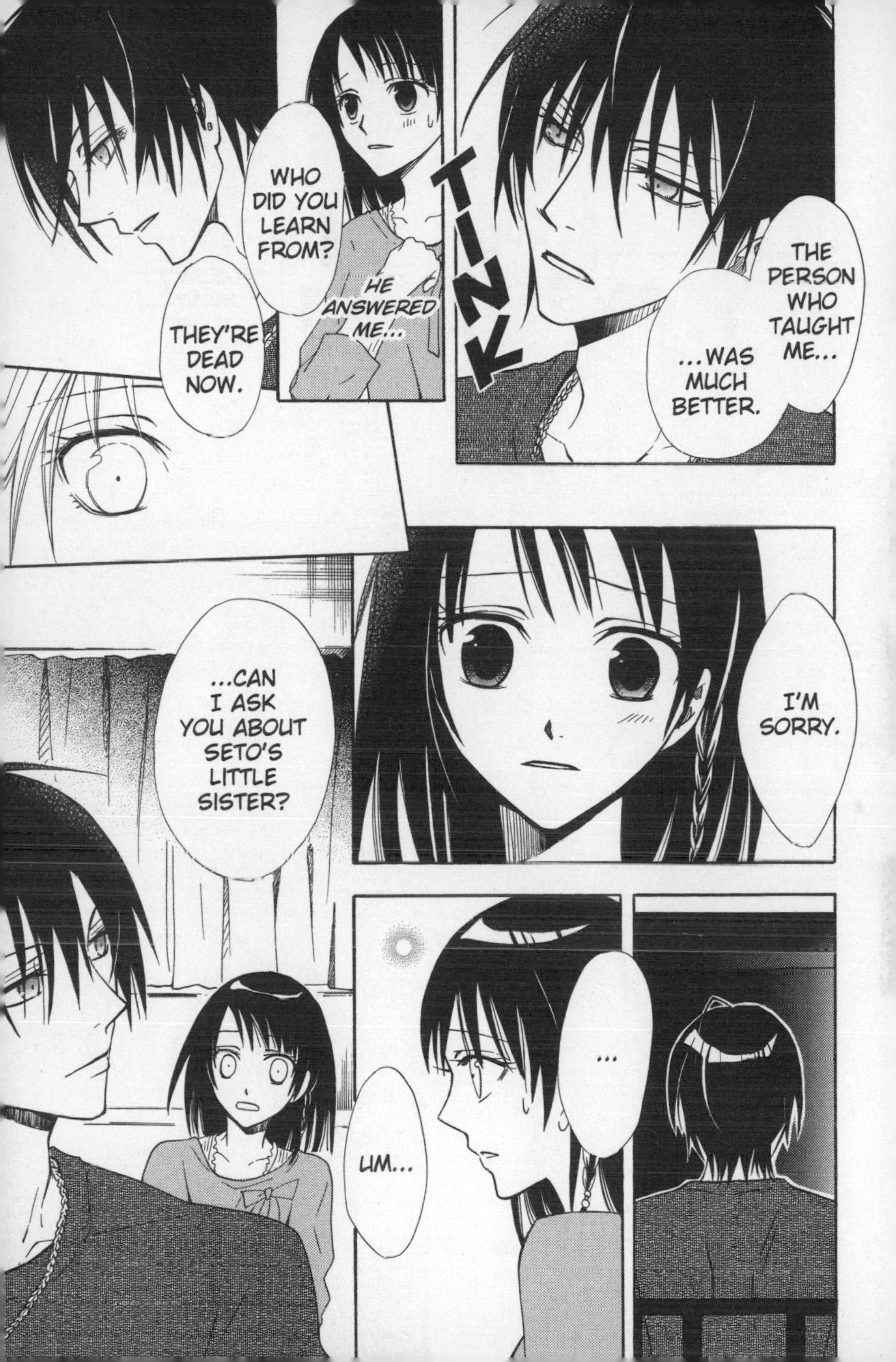
TINK
THE PERSON WHO TAUGHT ME...
...WAS MUCH BETTER.
WHO DID YOU LEARN FROM?
HE ANSWERED ME...
THEY'RE DEAD NOW.
I'M SORRY.
...CAN I ASK YOU ABOUT SETO'S LITTLE SISTER?
...
UM...

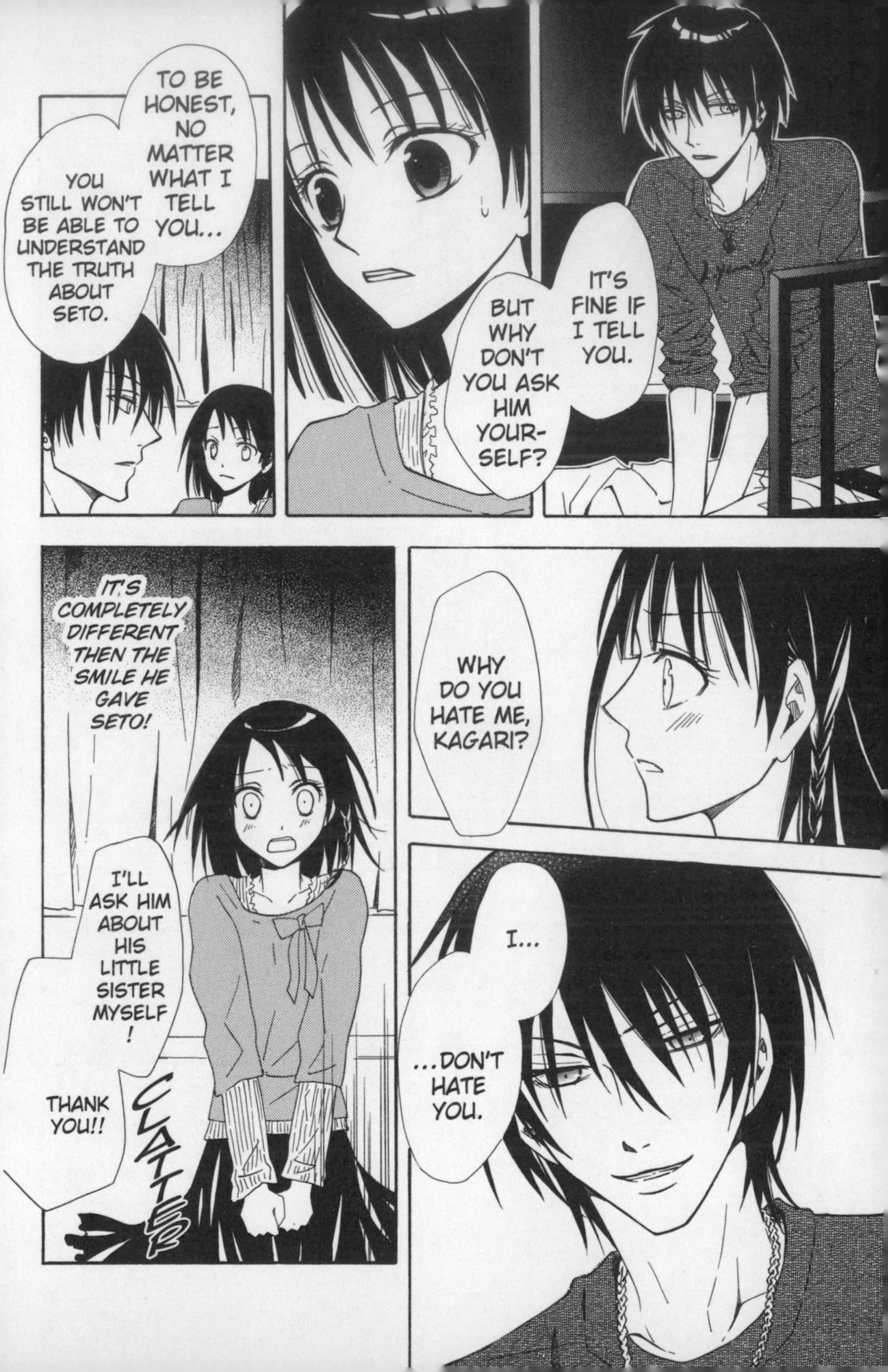
IT'S FINE IF I TELL YOU.
BUT WHY DON'T YOU ASK HIM YOURSELF?
TO BE HONEST, NO MATTER WHAT I TELL YOU...
YOU STILL WON'T BE ABLE TO UNDERSTAND THE TRUTH ABOUT SETO.
WHY DO YOU HATE ME, KAGARI?
I...
...DON'T HATE YOU.
IT'S COMPLETELY DIFFERENT THEN THE SMILE HE GAVE SETO!
I'LL ASK HIM ABOUT HIS LITTLE SISTER MYSELF!
THANK YOU!!
CLATTER

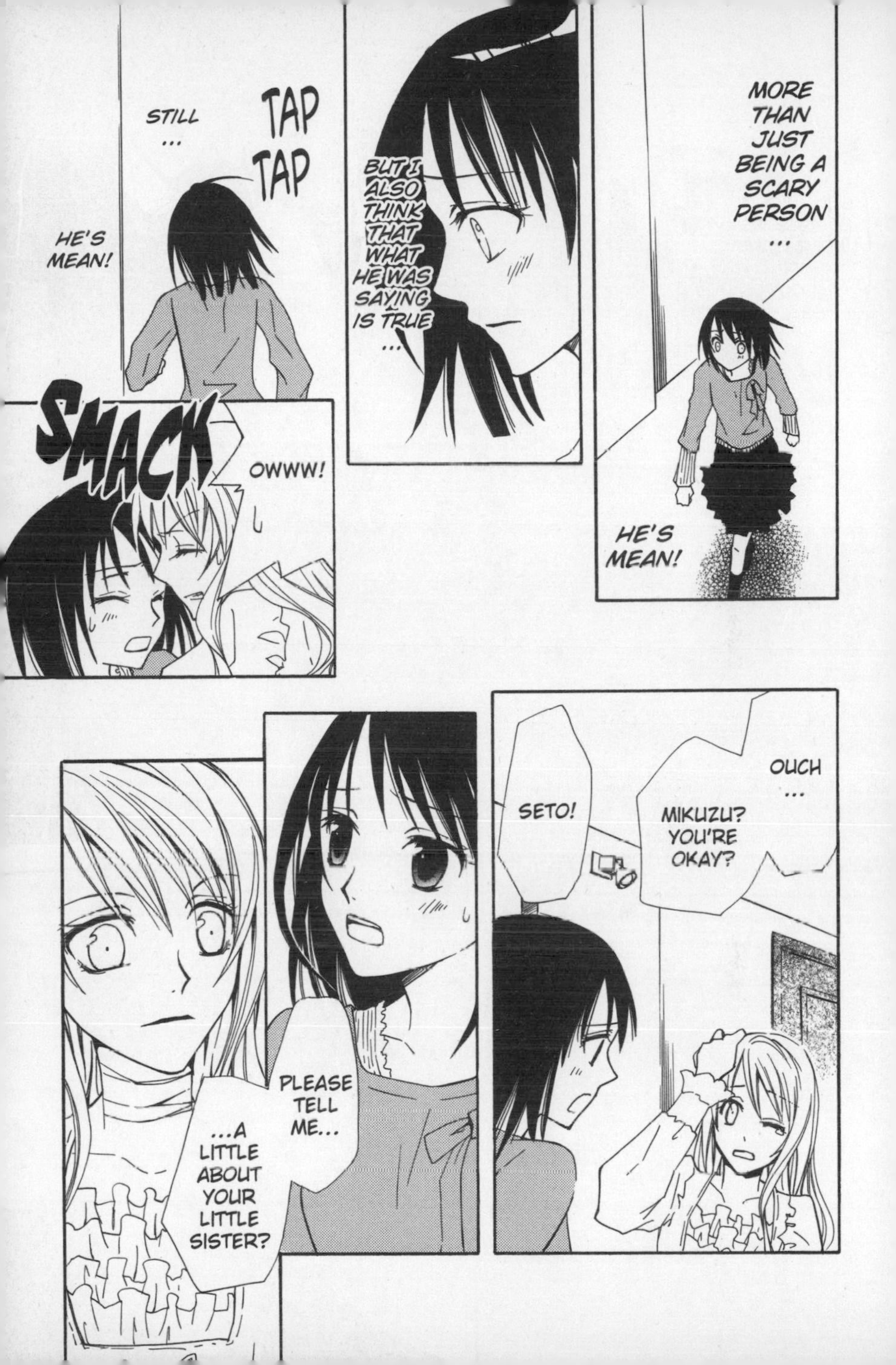
MORE THAN JUST BEING A SCARY PERSON ...
HE'S MEAN!
BUT I ALSO THINK THAT WHAT HE WAS SAYING IS TRUE ...
TAP TAP
STILL ...
HE'S MEAN!
SMACK
OWWW!
OUCH ...
MIKUZU? YOU'RE OKAY?
SETO!
PLEASE TELL ME...
...A LITTLE ABOUT YOUR LITTLE SISTER?

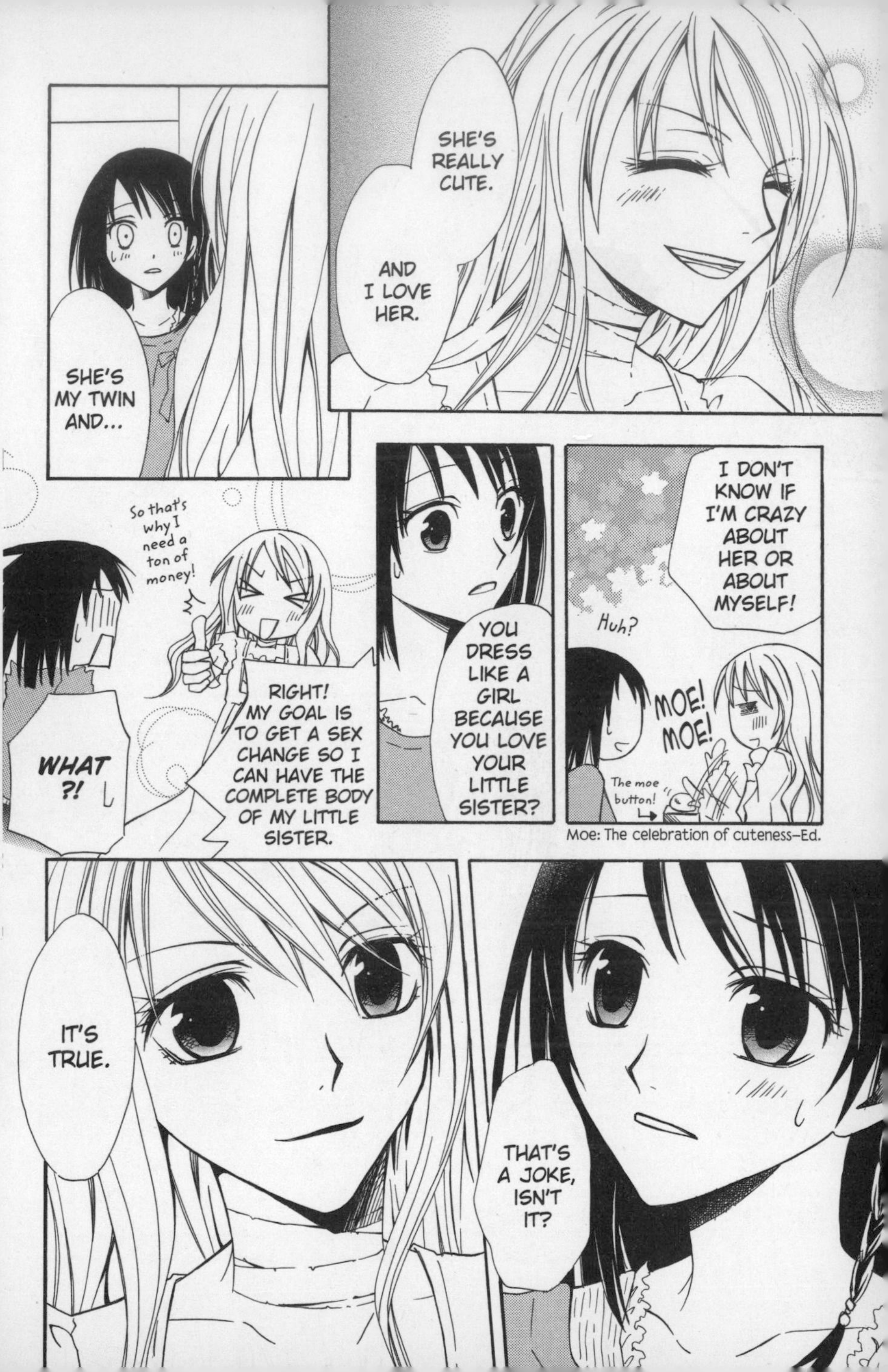
SHE'S REALLY CUTE.
AND I LOVE HER.
SHE'S MY TWIN AND...
I DON'T KNOW IF I'M CRAZY ABOUT HER OR ABOUT MYSELF!
Huh?
MOE! MOE!
The moe button!
Moe: The celebration of cuteness–Ed.
YOU DRESS LIKE A GIRL BECAUSE YOU LOVE YOUR LITTLE SISTER?
RIGHT! MY GOAL IS TO GET A SEX CHANGE SO I CAN HAVE THE COMPLETE BODY OF MY LITTLE SISTER.
So that's why I need a ton of money!
WHAT?!
THAT'S A JOKE, ISN'T IT?
IT'S TRUE.

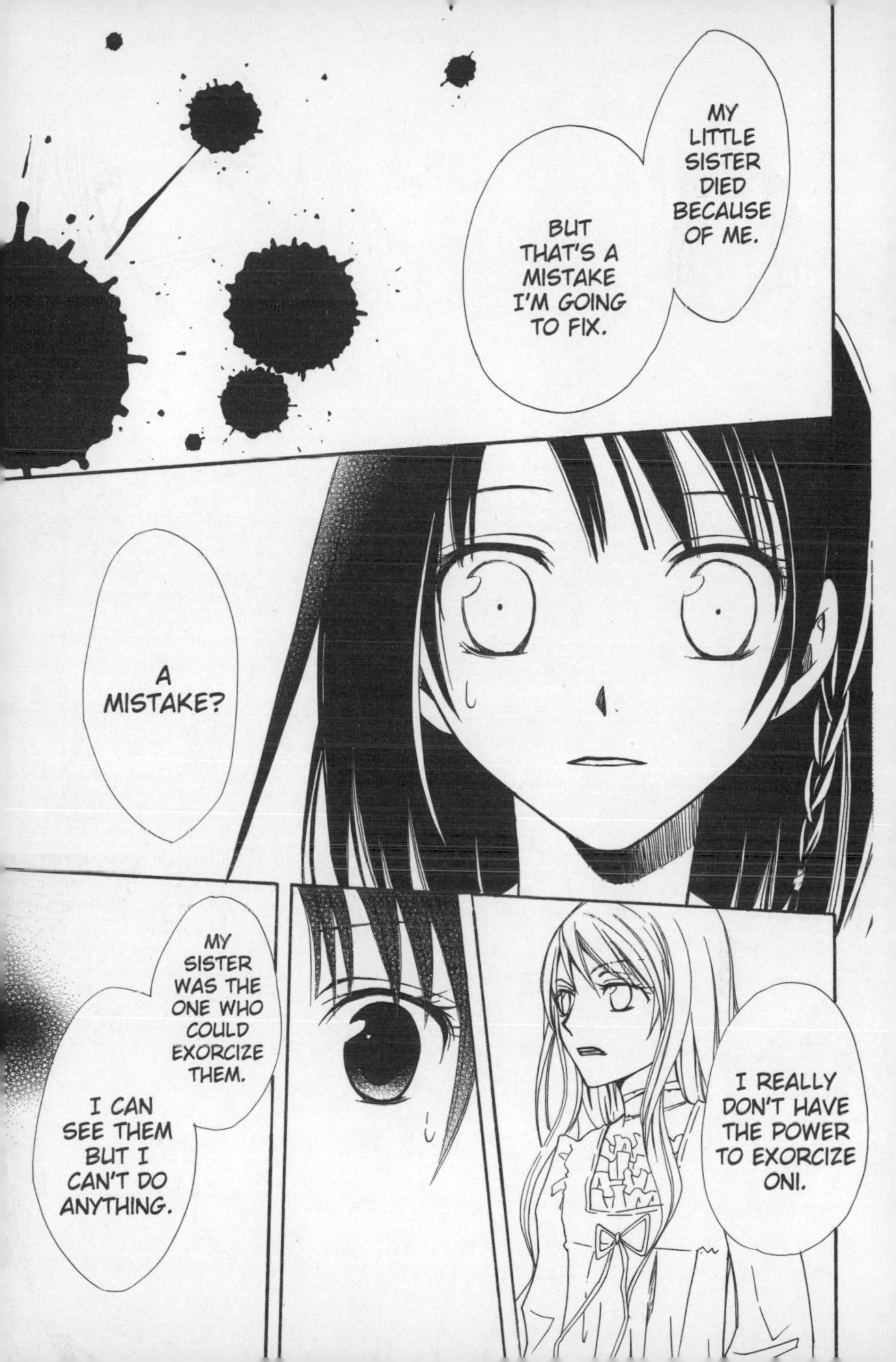
MY LITTLE SISTER DIED BECAUSE OF ME.
BUT THAT'S A MISTAKE I'M GOING TO FIX.
A MISTAKE?
I REALLY DON'T HAVE THE POWER TO EXORCIZE ONI.
MY SISTER WAS THE ONE WHO COULD EXORCIZE THEM.
I CAN SEE THEM BUT I CAN'T DO ANYTHING.

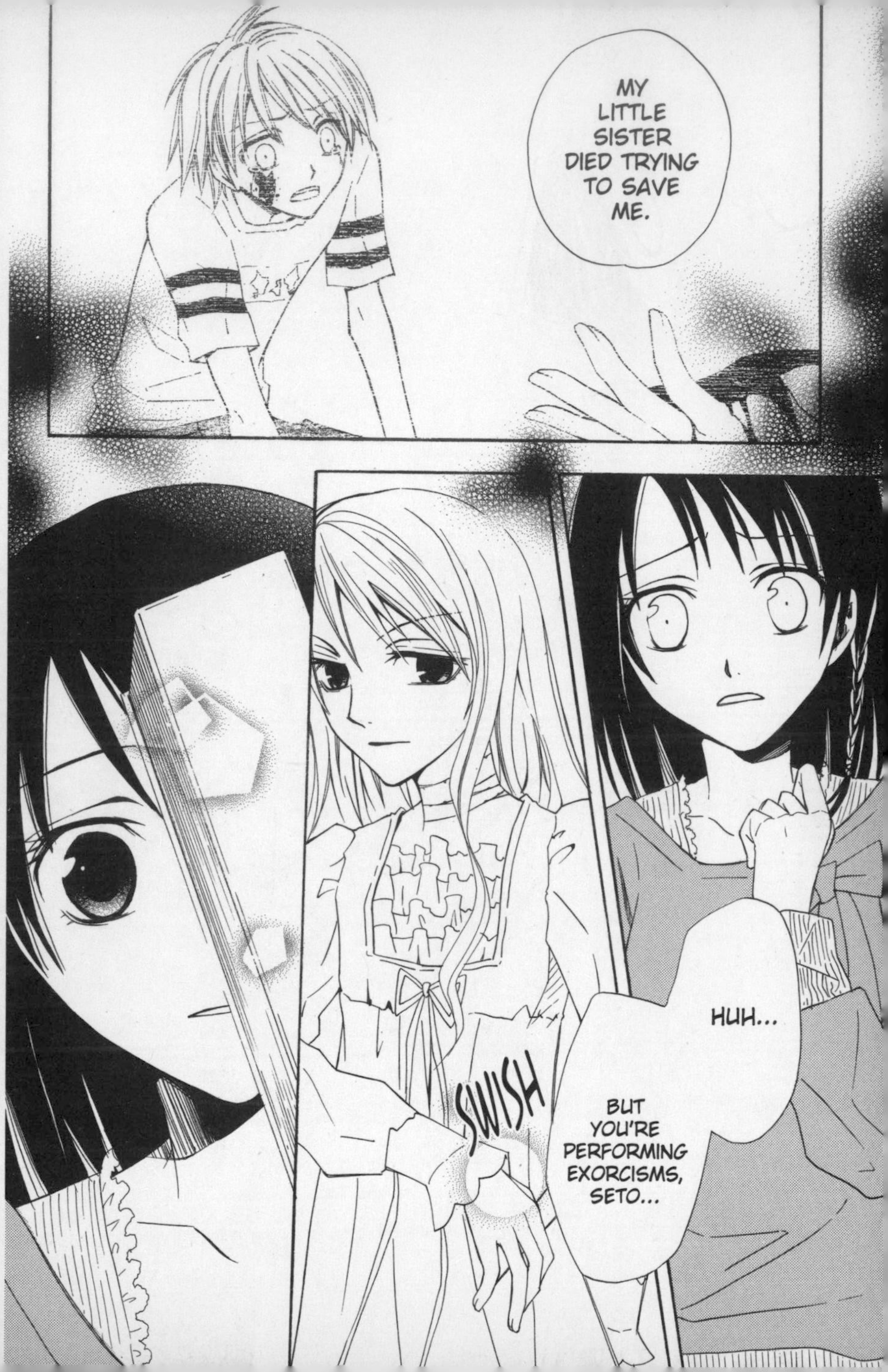
MY LITTLE SISTER DIED TRYING TO SAVE ME.
HUH...
BUT YOU'RE PERFORMING EXORCISMS, SETO...
SWISH

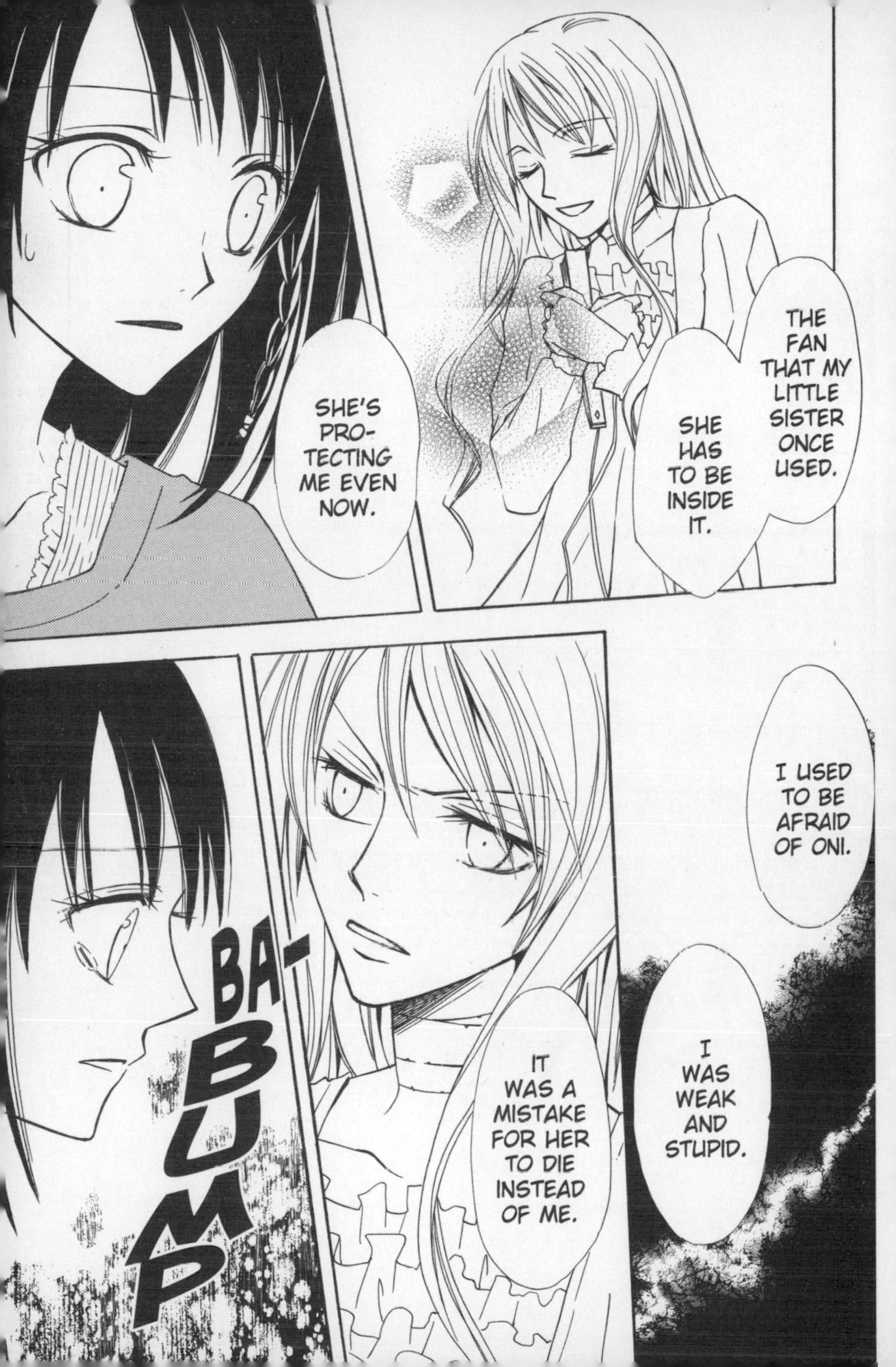
THE FAN THAT MY LITTLE SISTER ONCE USED.
SHE HAS TO BE INSIDE IT.
SHE'S PRO-TECTING ME EVEN NOW.
I USED TO BE AFRAID OF ONI.
I WAS WEAK AND STUPID.
IT WAS A MISTAKE FOR HER TO DIE INSTEAD OF ME.
BA-BUMP

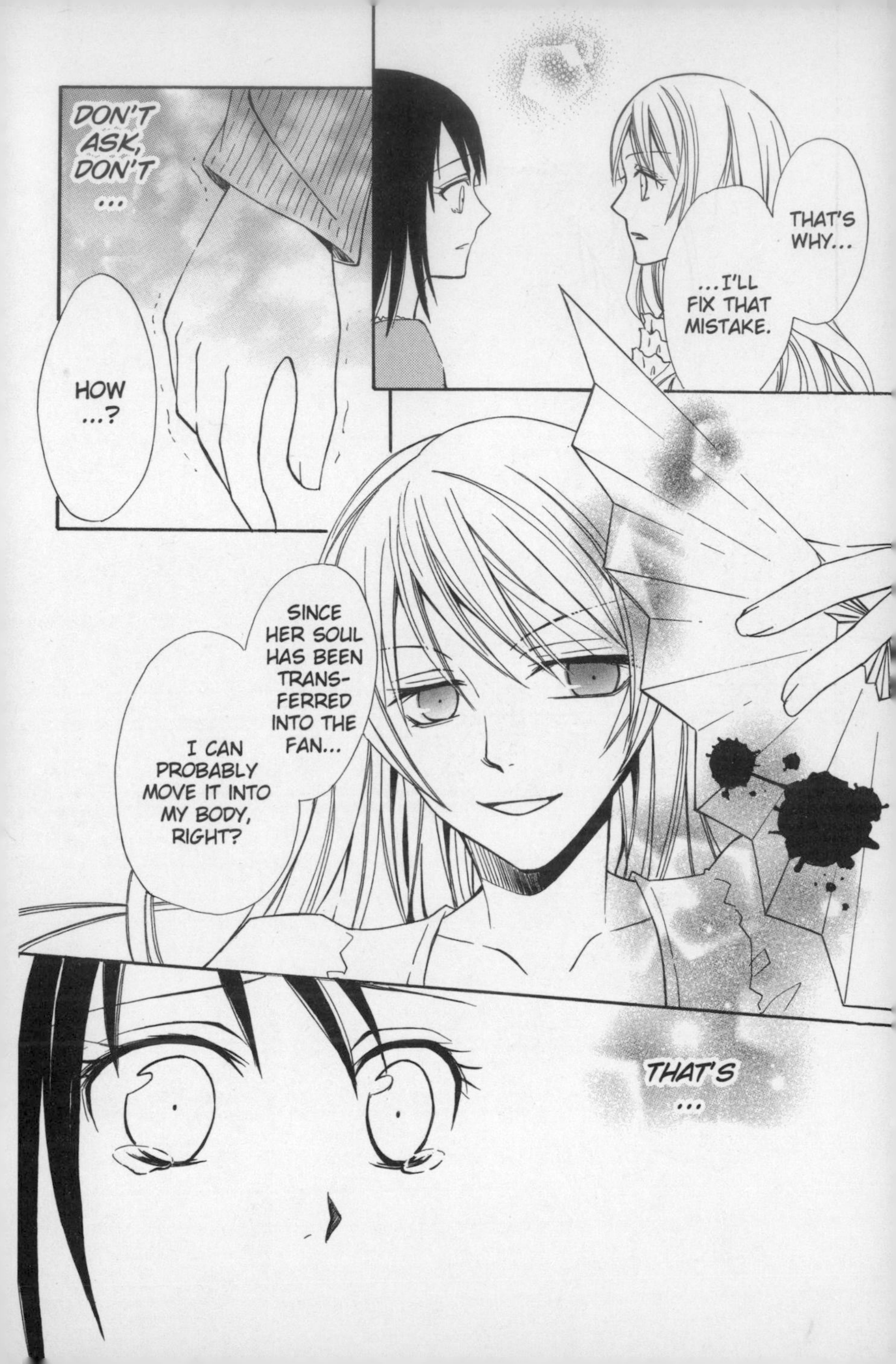
THAT'S WHY...
...I'LL FIX THAT MISTAKE.
DON'T ASK, DON'T ...
HOW ...?
SINCE HER SOUL HAS BEEN TRANS- FERRED INTO THE FAN...
I CAN PROBABLY MOVE IT INTO MY BODY, RIGHT?
THAT'S ...

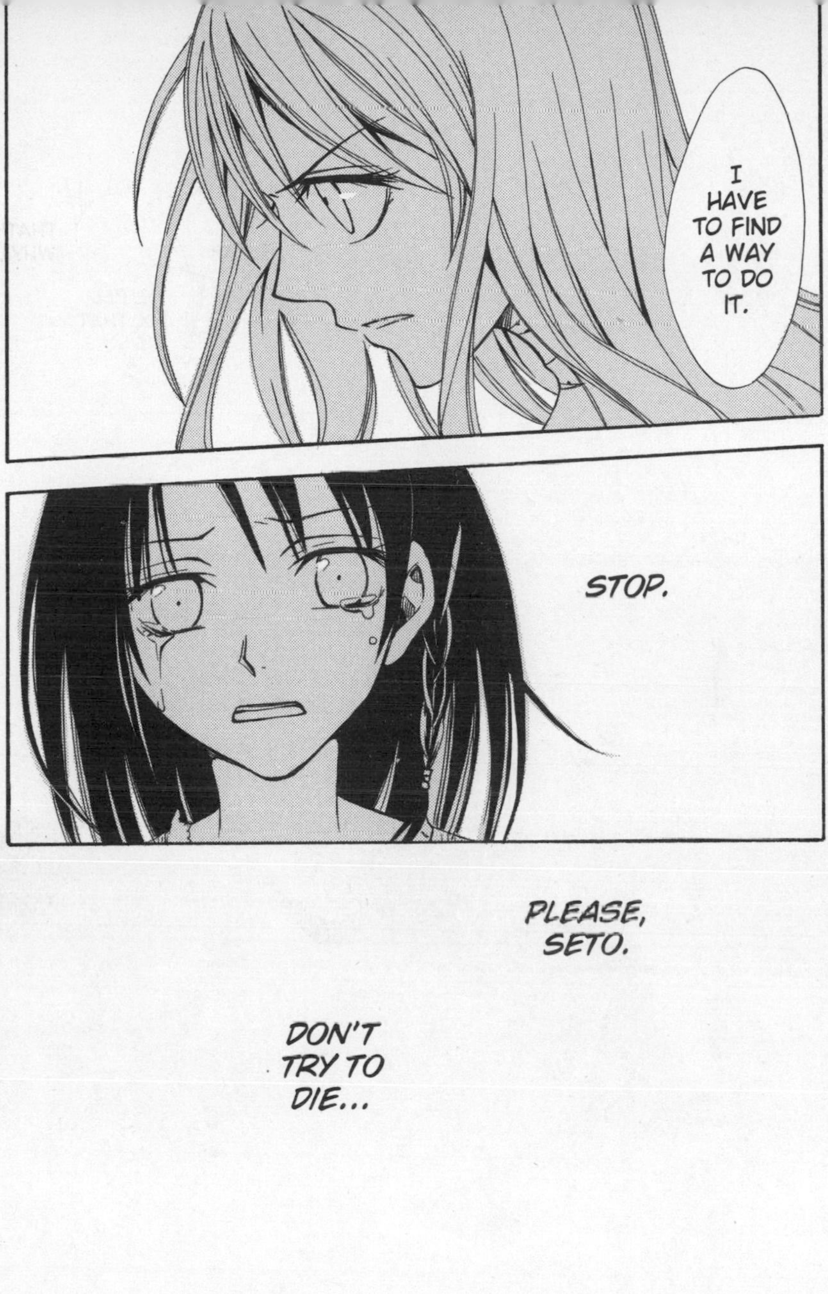
I HAVE TO FIND A WAY TO DO IT.
STOP.
PLEASE, SETO.
DON'T TRY TO DIE...

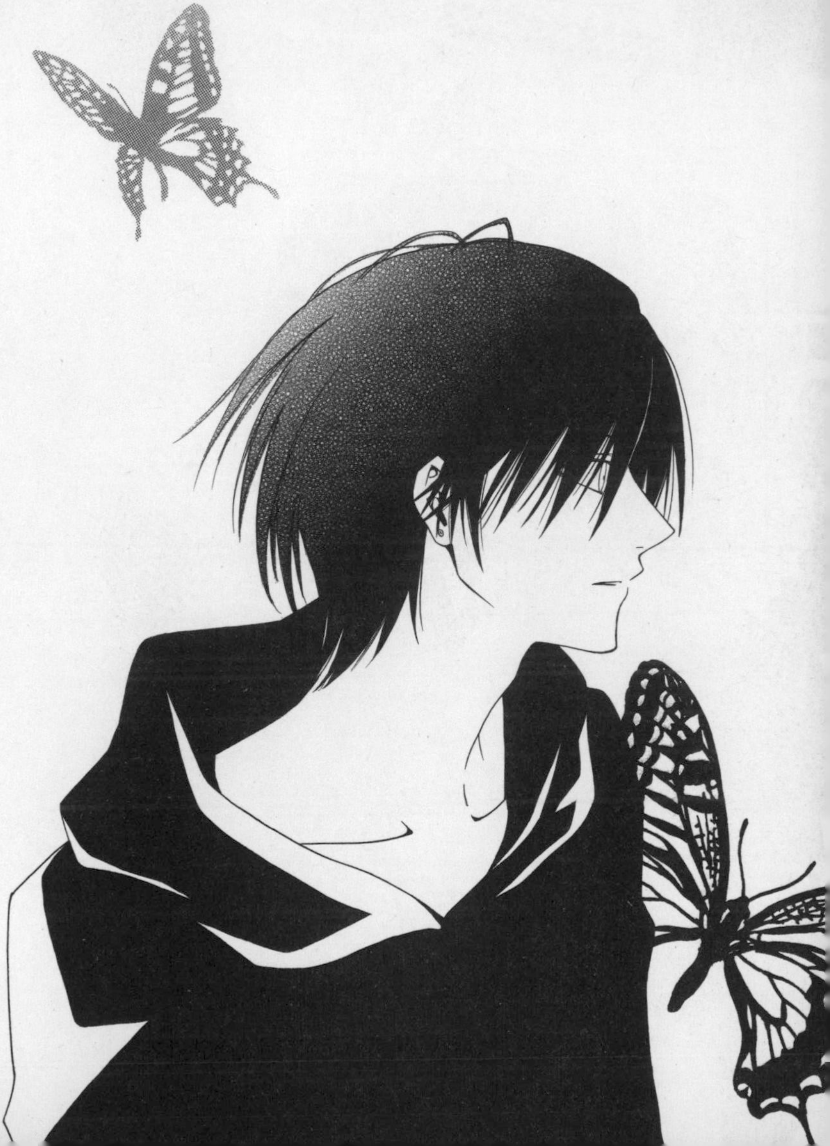

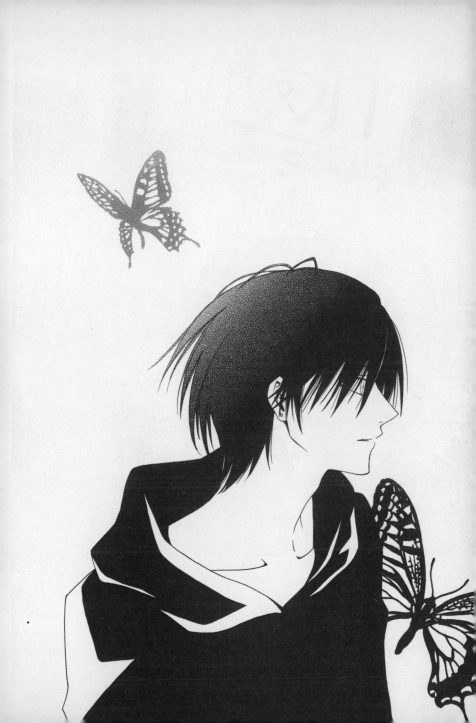

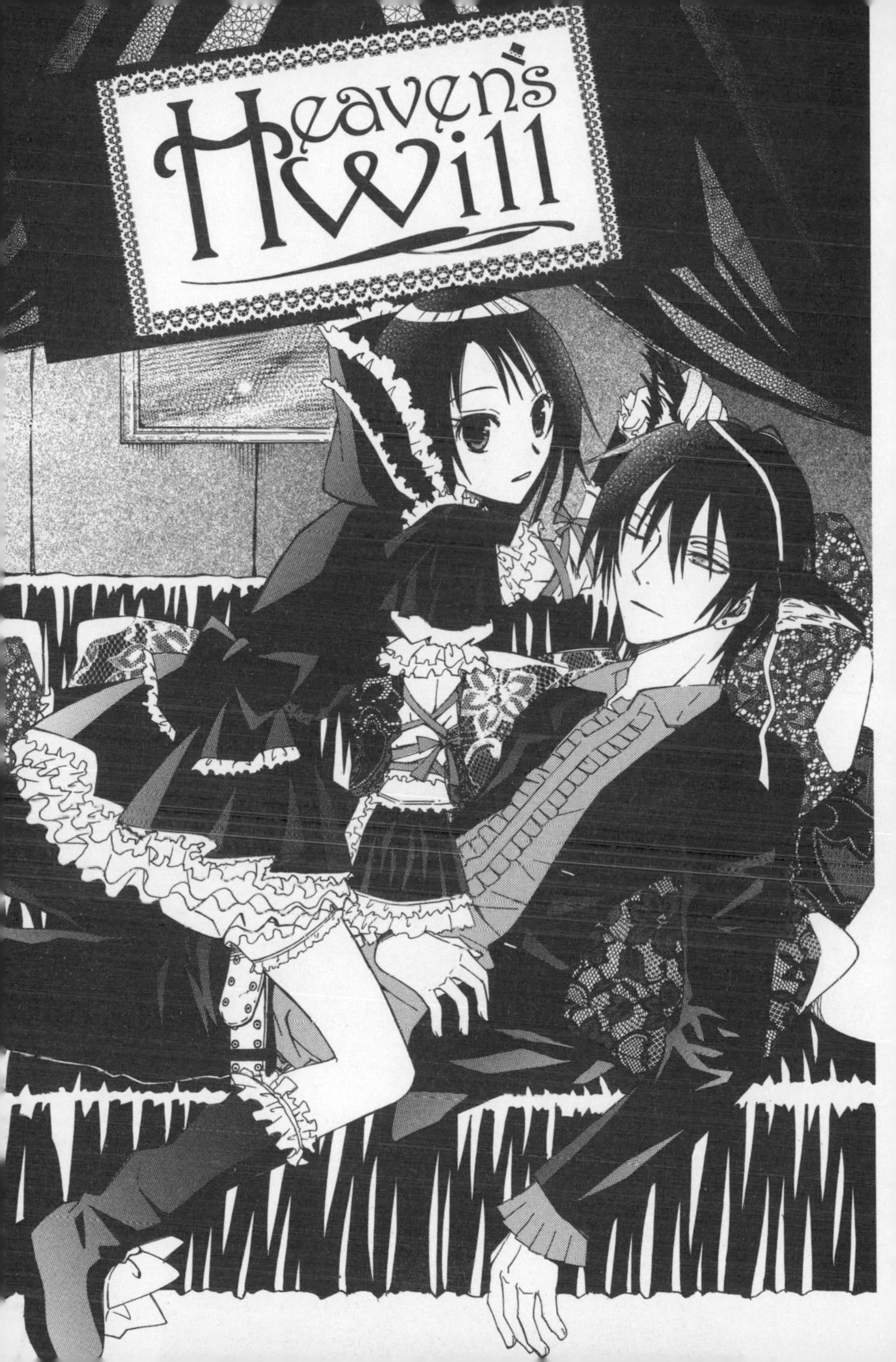
Heaven's Will

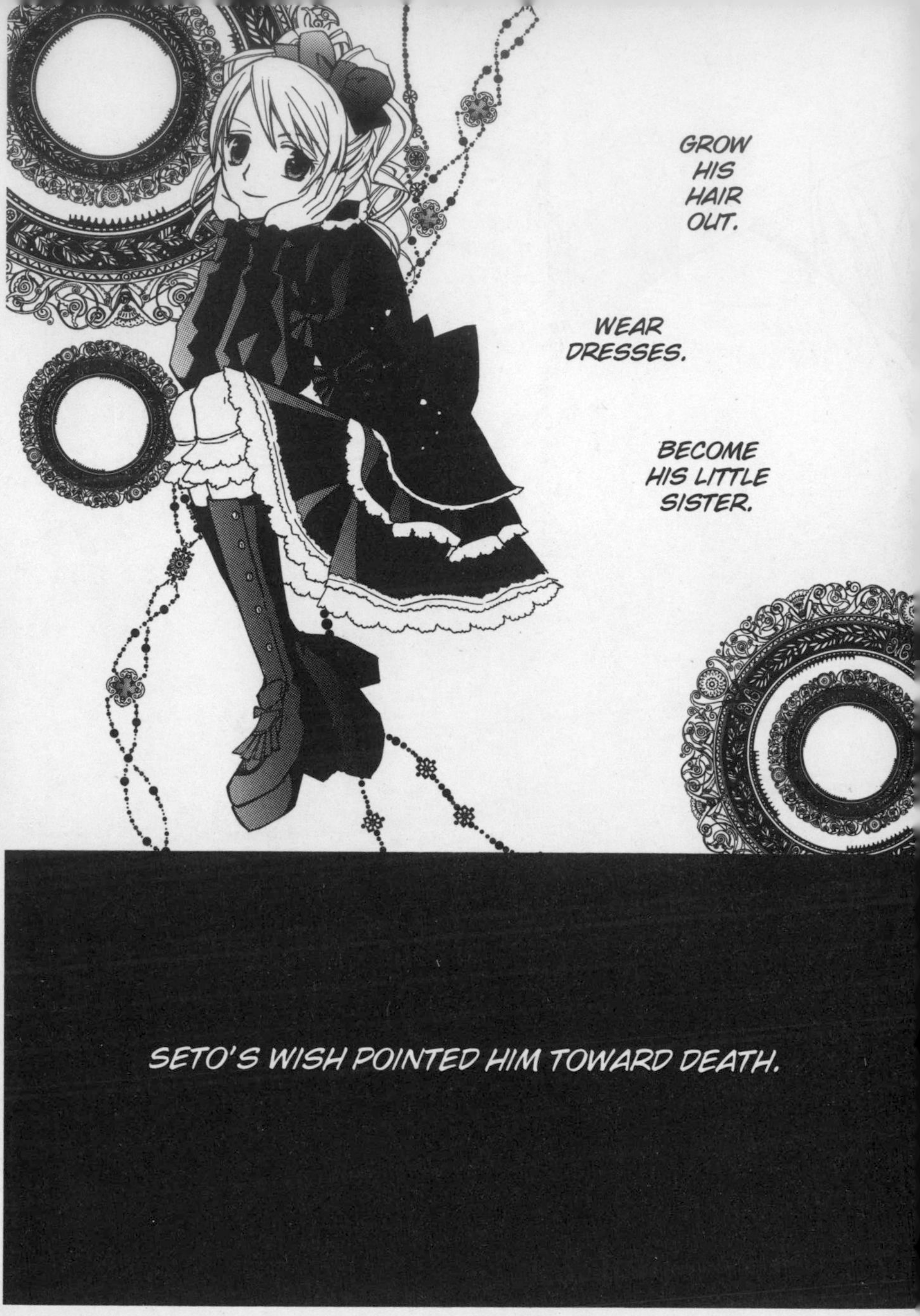
GROW HIS HAIR OUT.
WEAR DRESSES.
BECOME HIS LITTLE SISTER.
SETO'S WISH POINTED HIM TOWARD DEATH.

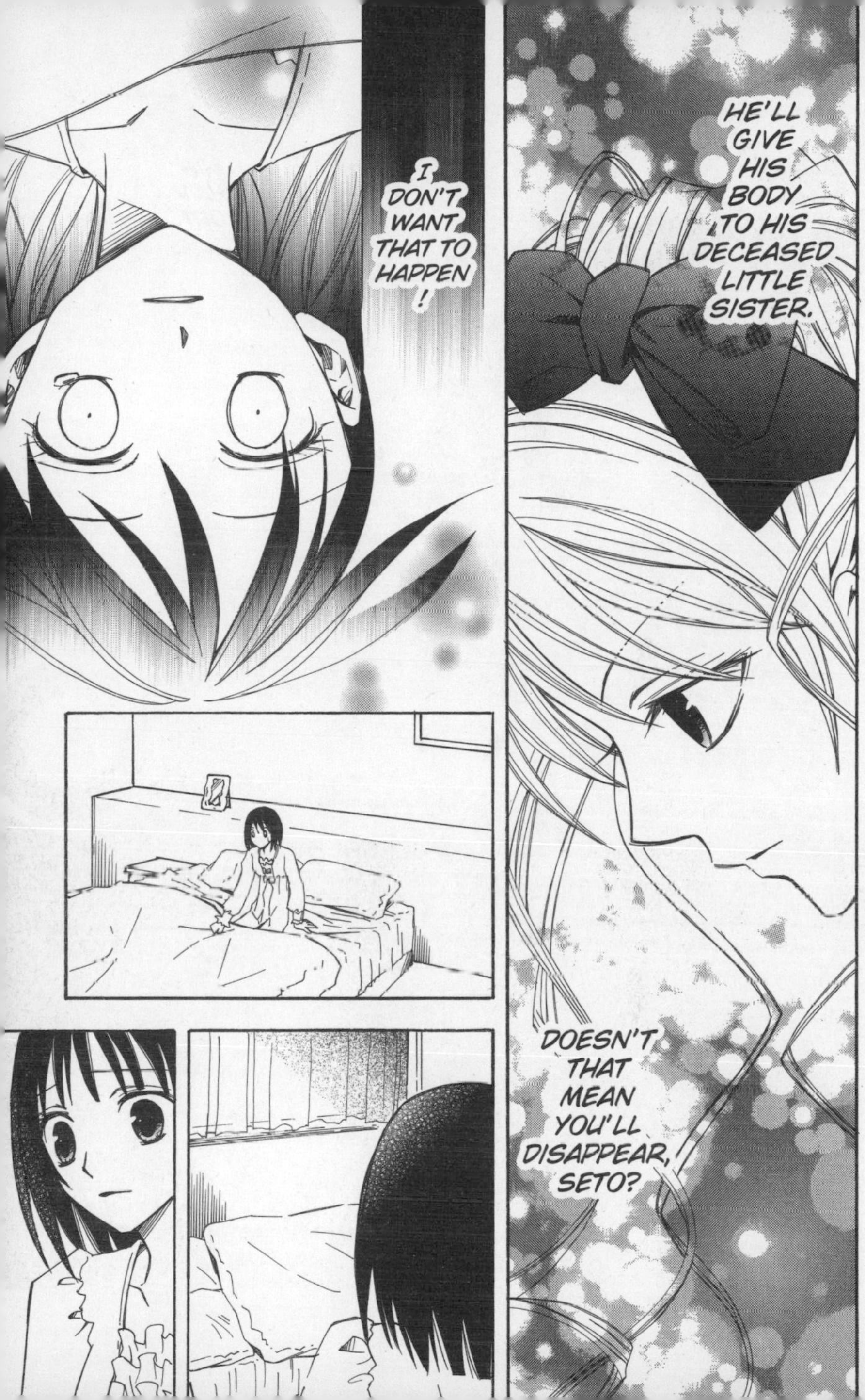
HE'LL GIVE HIS BODY TO HIS DECEASED LITTLE SISTER.
DOESN'T THAT MEAN YOU'LL DISAPPEAR, SETO?
I DON'T WANT THAT TO HAPPEN!

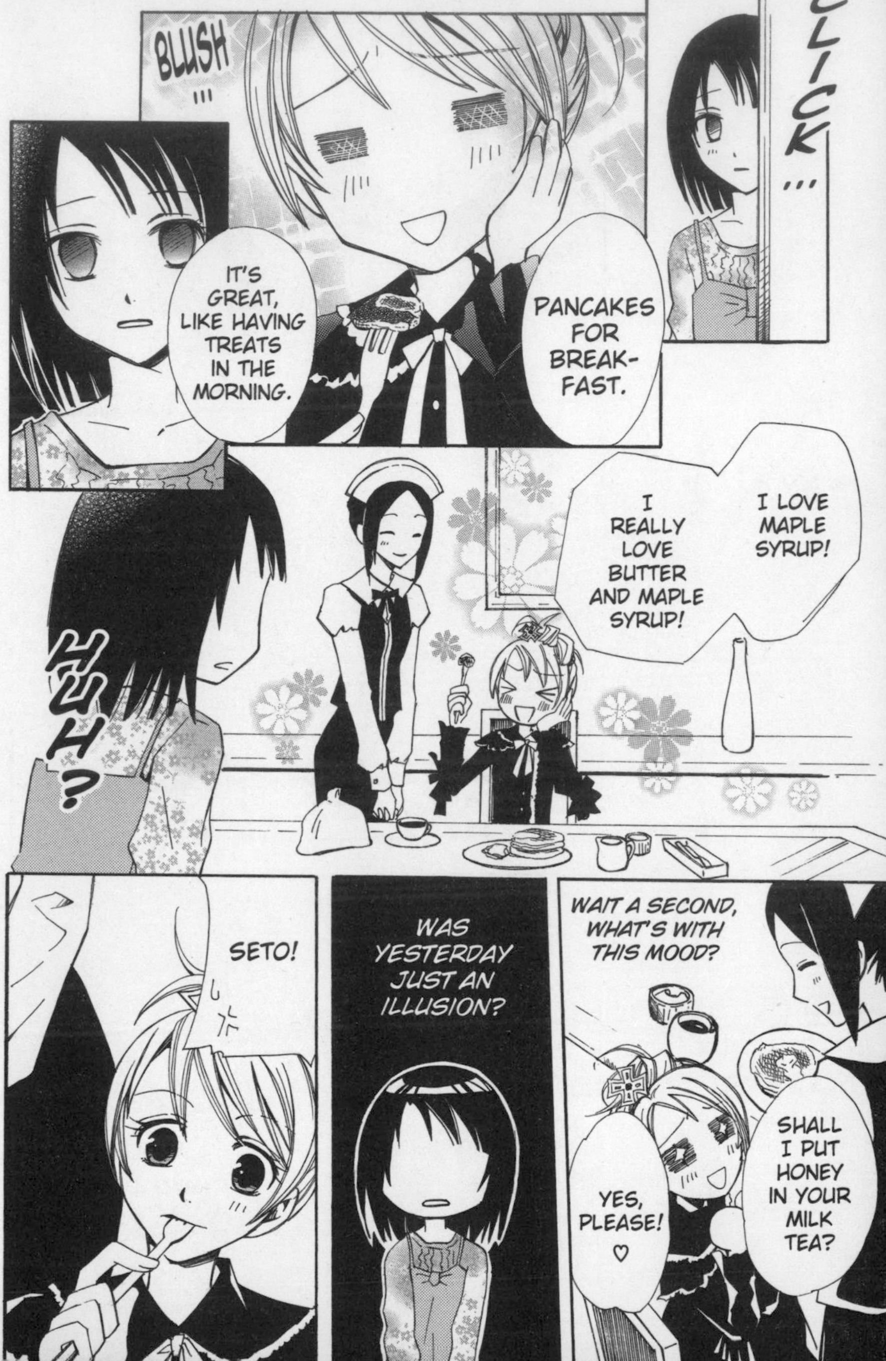
CLICK...
BLUSH
PANCAKES FOR BREAKFAST.
IT'S GREAT, LIKE HAVING TREATS IN THE MORNING.
I LOVE MAPLE SYRUP!
I REALLY LOVE BUTTER AND MAPLE SYRUP!
HUH?
WAIT A SECOND, WHAT'S WITH THIS MOOD?
SHALL I PUT HONEY IN YOUR MILK TEA?
YES, PLEASE! ♡
WAS YESTERDAY JUST AN ILLUSION?
SETO!

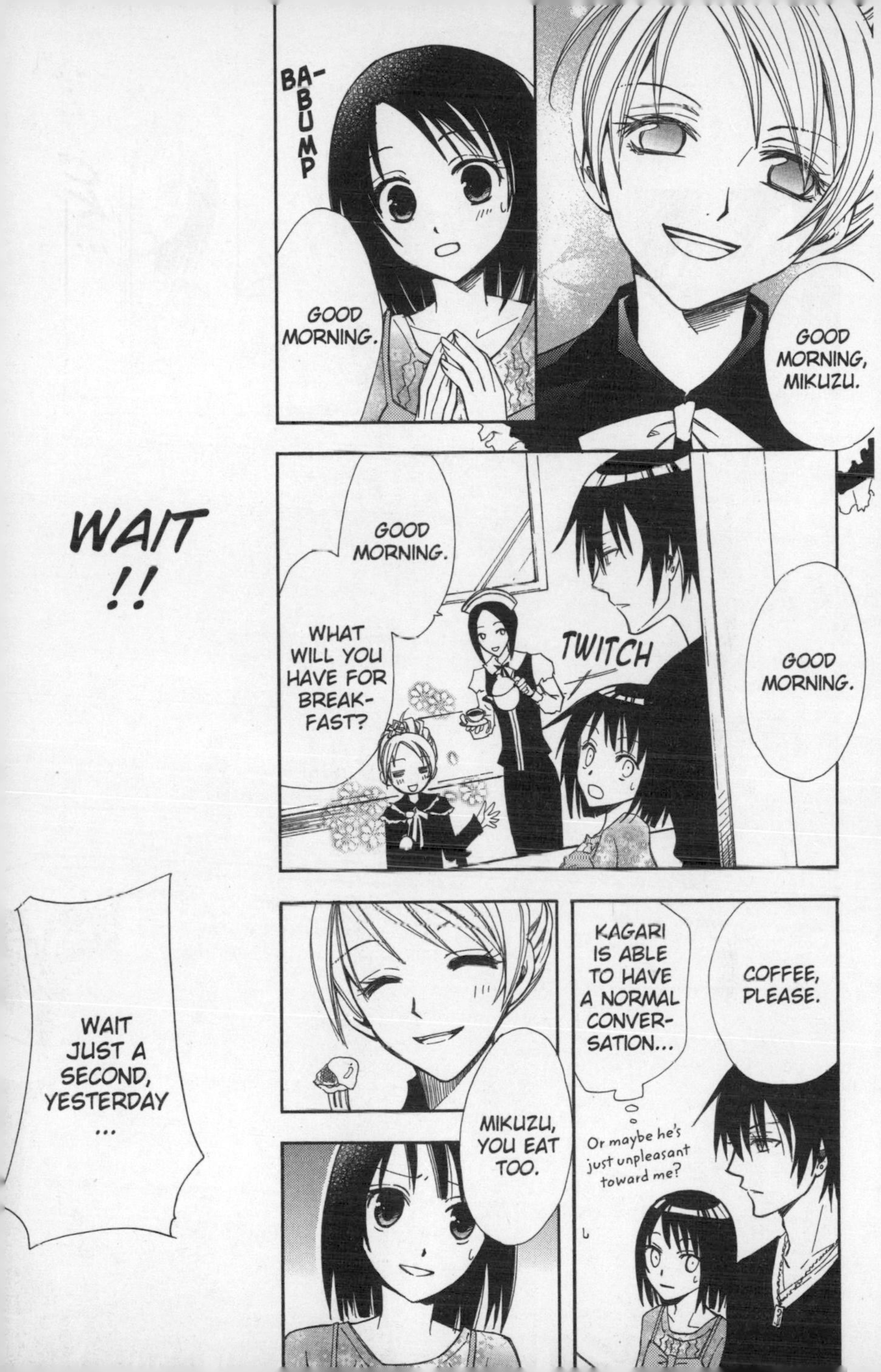
GOOD MORNING, MIKUZU.
BA-BUMP
GOOD MORNING.
GOOD MORNING.
TWITCH
GOOD MORNING.
WHAT WILL YOU HAVE FOR BREAKFAST?
WAIT !!
COFFEE, PLEASE.
KAGARI IS ABLE TO HAVE A NORMAL CONVERSATION...
Or maybe he's just unpleasant toward me?
MIKUZU, YOU EAT TOO.
WAIT JUST A SECOND, YESTERDAY ...

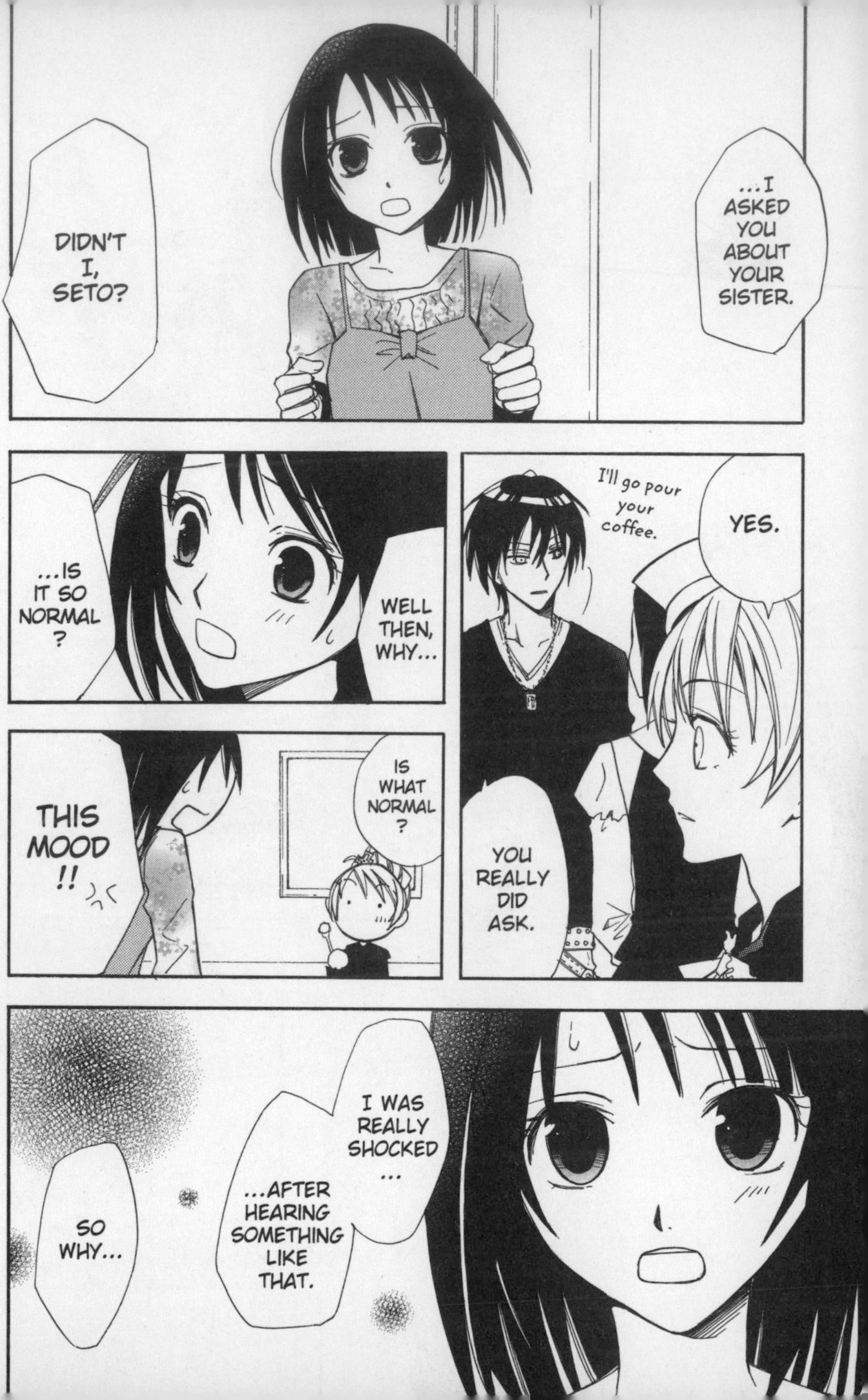
...I ASKED YOU ABOUT YOUR SISTER.
DIDN'T I, SETO?
YES.
I'll go pour your coffee.
YOU REALLY DID ASK.
WELL THEN, WHY...
...IS IT SO NORMAL?
IS WHAT NORMAL?
THIS MOOD!!
I WAS REALLY SHOCKED...
...AFTER HEARING SOMETHING LIKE THAT.
SO WHY...

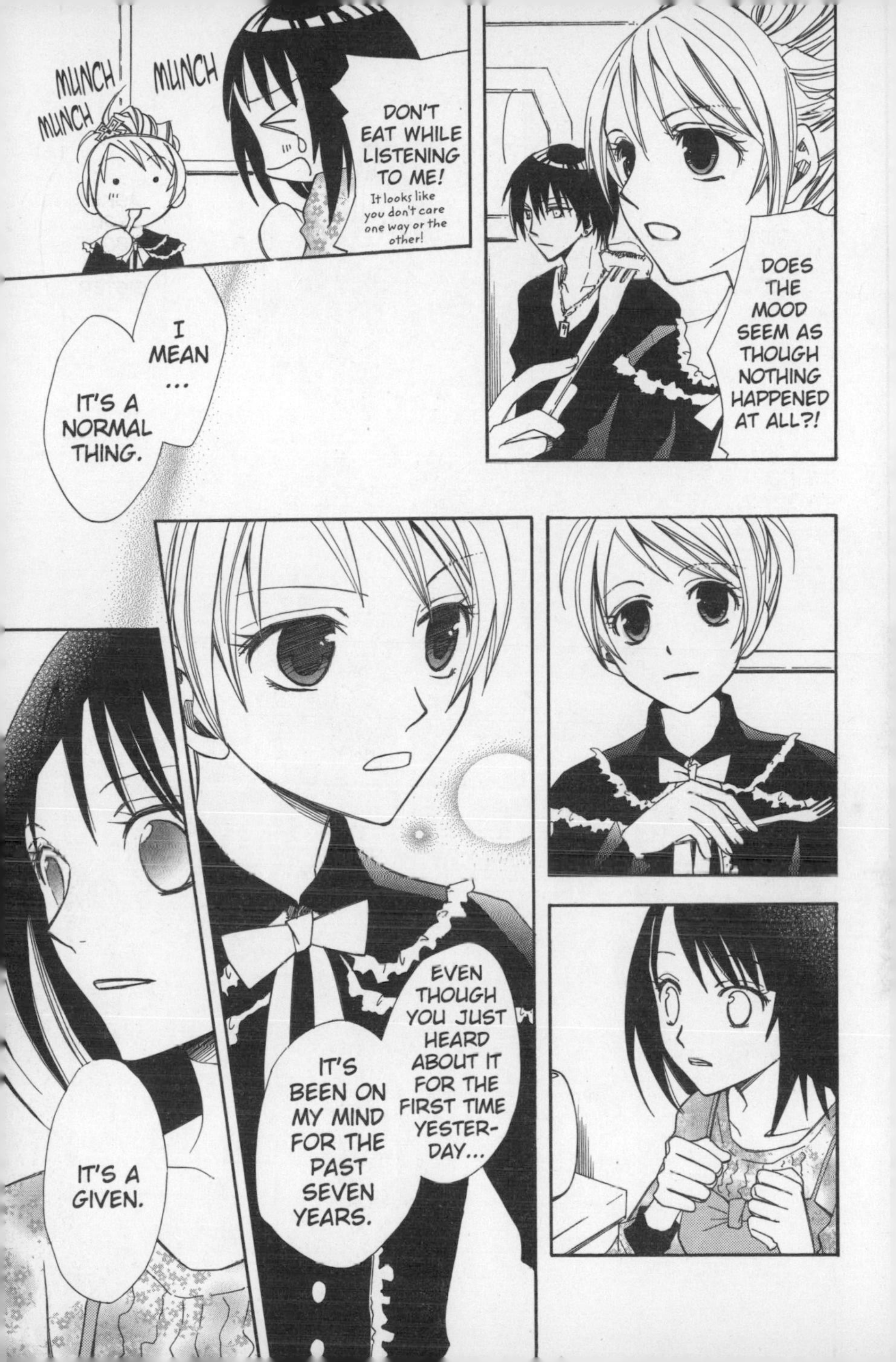
DOES THE MOOD SEEM AS THOUGH NOTHING HAPPENED AT ALL?!
DON'T EAT WHILE LISTENING TO ME!
It looks like you don't care one way or the other!
MUNCH
MUNCH
MUNCH
I MEAN ...
IT'S A NORMAL THING.
EVEN THOUGH YOU JUST HEARD ABOUT IT FOR THE FIRST TIME YESTER-DAY...
IT'S BEEN ON MY MIND FOR THE PAST SEVEN YEARS.
IT'S A GIVEN.

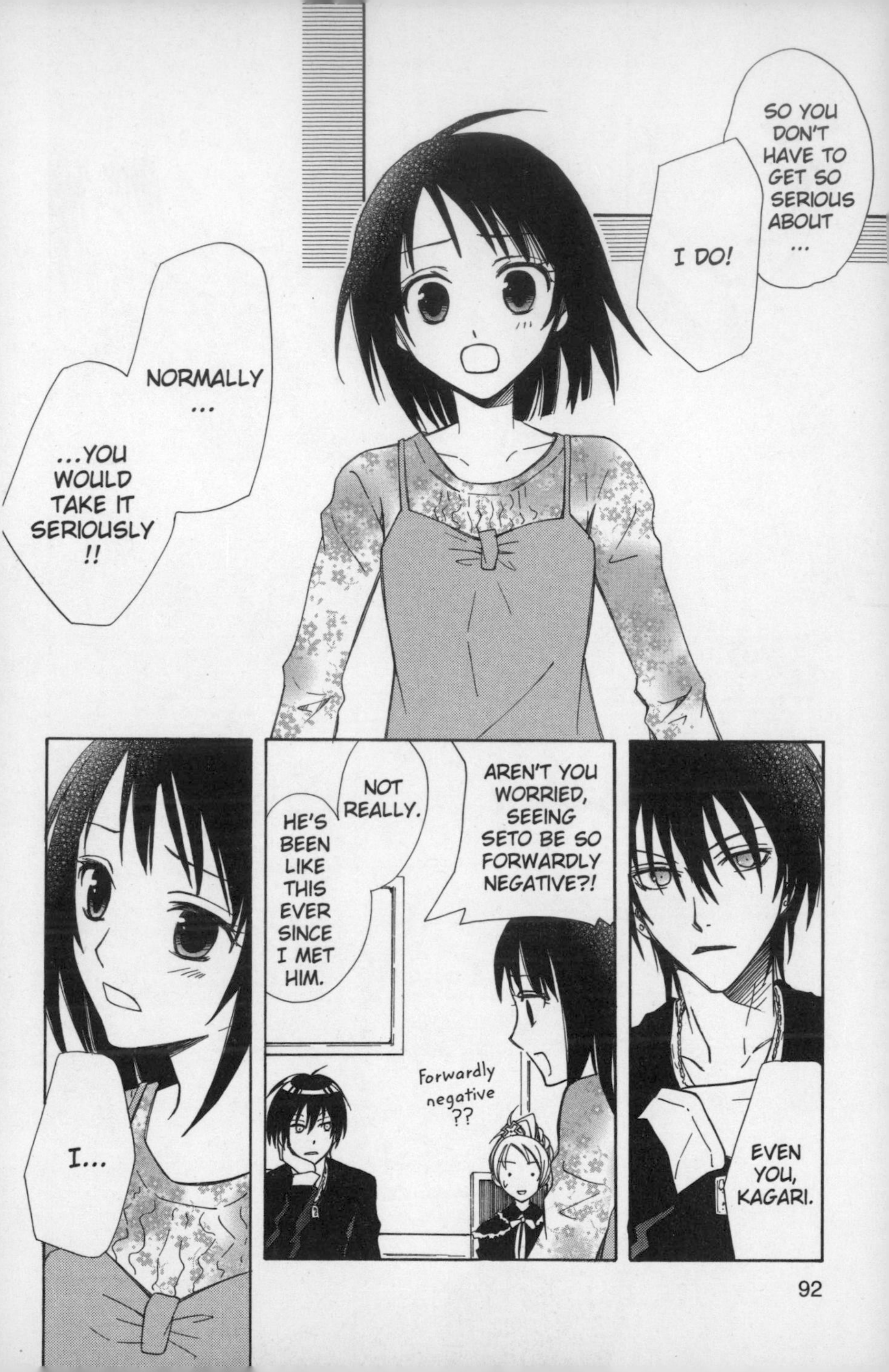
SO YOU DON'T HAVE TO GET SO SERIOUS ABOUT ...
I DO!
NORMALLY ...
...YOU WOULD TAKE IT SERIOUSLY !!
EVEN YOU, KAGARI.
AREN'T YOU WORRIED, SEEING SETO BE SO FORWARDLY NEGATIVE?!
NOT REALLY.
HE'S BEEN LIKE THIS EVER SINCE I MET HIM.
Forwardly negative ??
I...

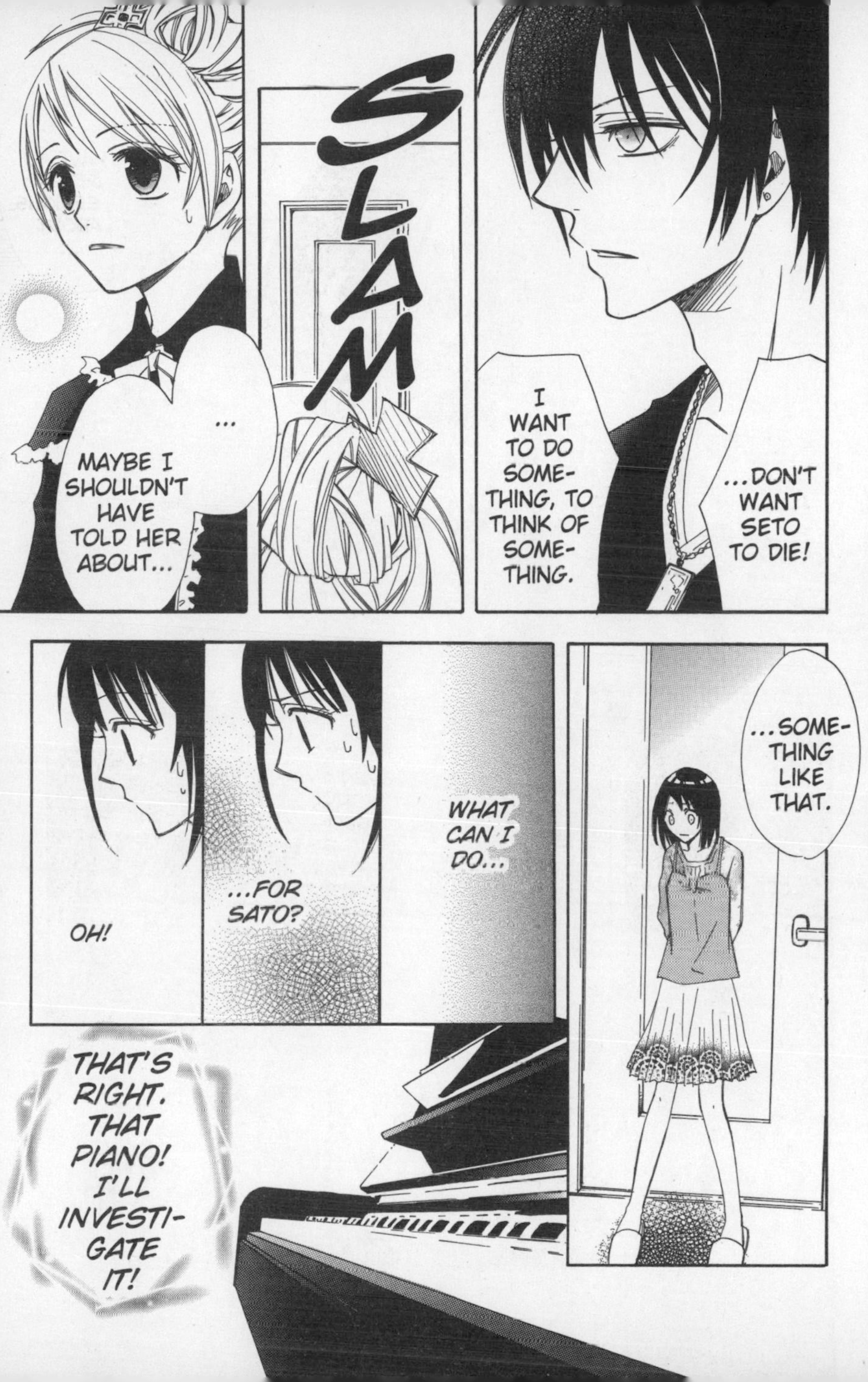
...DON'T WANT SETO TO DIE!
I WANT TO DO SOME-THING, TO THINK OF SOME-THING.
SLAM
...
MAYBE I SHOULDN'T HAVE TOLD HER ABOUT...
...SOME-THING LIKE THAT.
WHAT CAN I DO...
...FOR SATO?
OH!
THAT'S RIGHT. THAT PIANO! I'LL INVESTI-GATE IT!

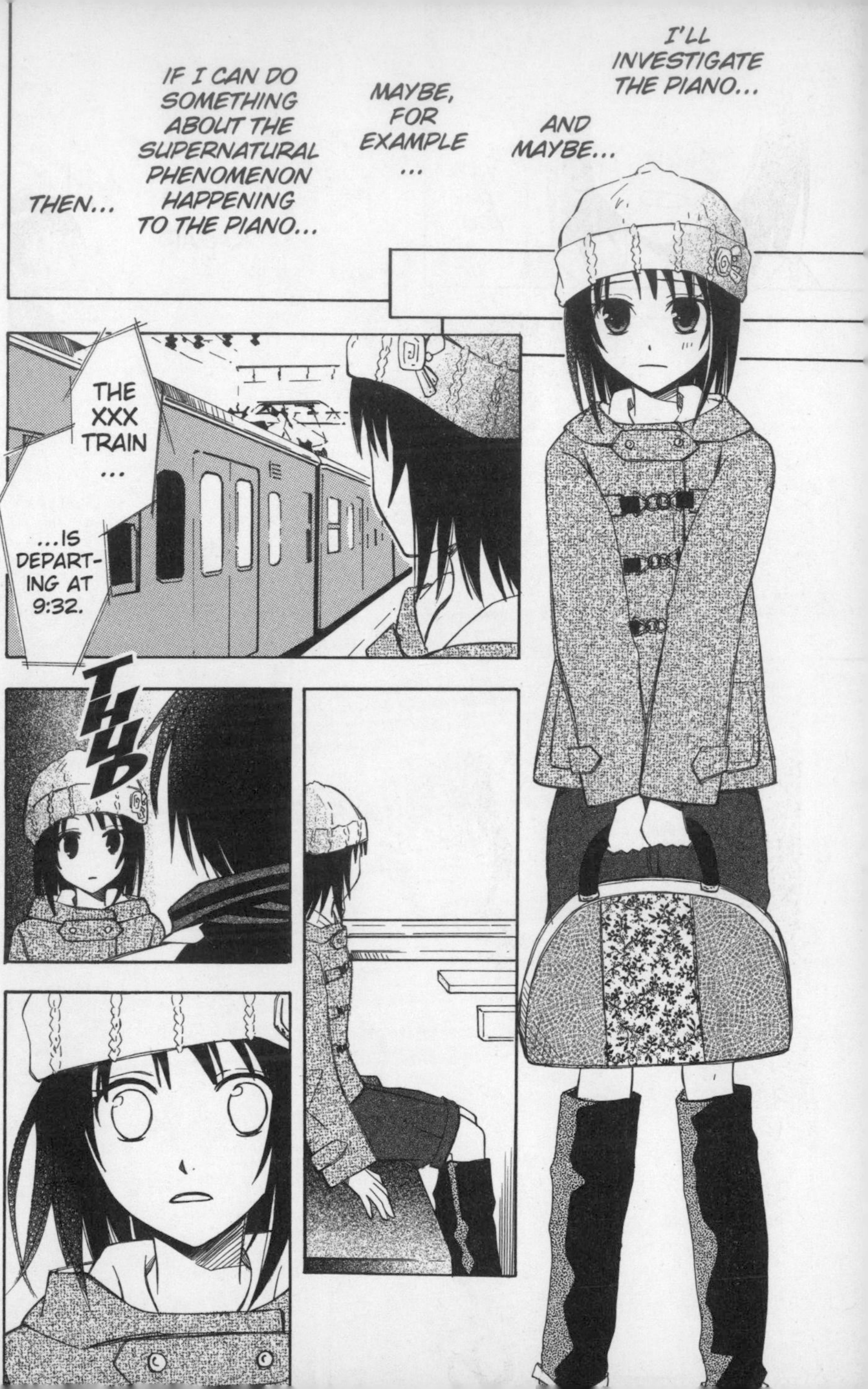
I'LL INVESTIGATE THE PIANO...
AND MAYBE...
MAYBE, FOR EXAMPLE ...
IF I CAN DO SOMETHING ABOUT THE SUPERNATURAL PHENOMENON HAPPENING TO THE PIANO...
THEN...
THE XXX TRAIN ...
...IS DEPARTING AT 9:32.
THUD

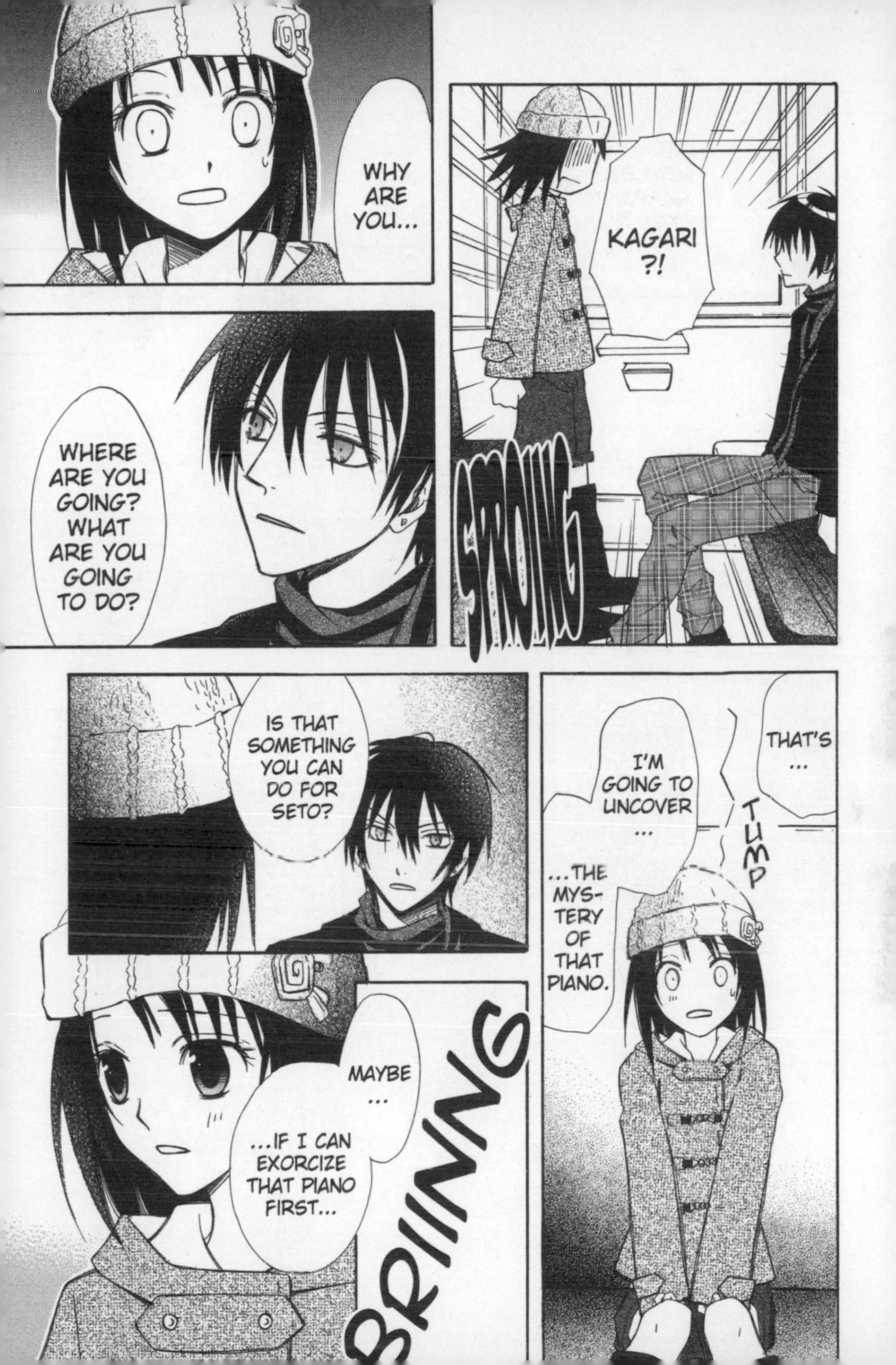
KAGARI ?!
SPROING
WHY ARE YOU...
WHERE ARE YOU GOING? WHAT ARE YOU GOING TO DO?
THAT'S ...
I'M GOING TO UNCOVER ...
TUMP
...THE MYSTERY OF THAT PIANO.
IS THAT SOMETHING YOU CAN DO FOR SETO?
MAYBE ...
...IF I CAN EXORCIZE THAT PIANO FIRST...
BRIING

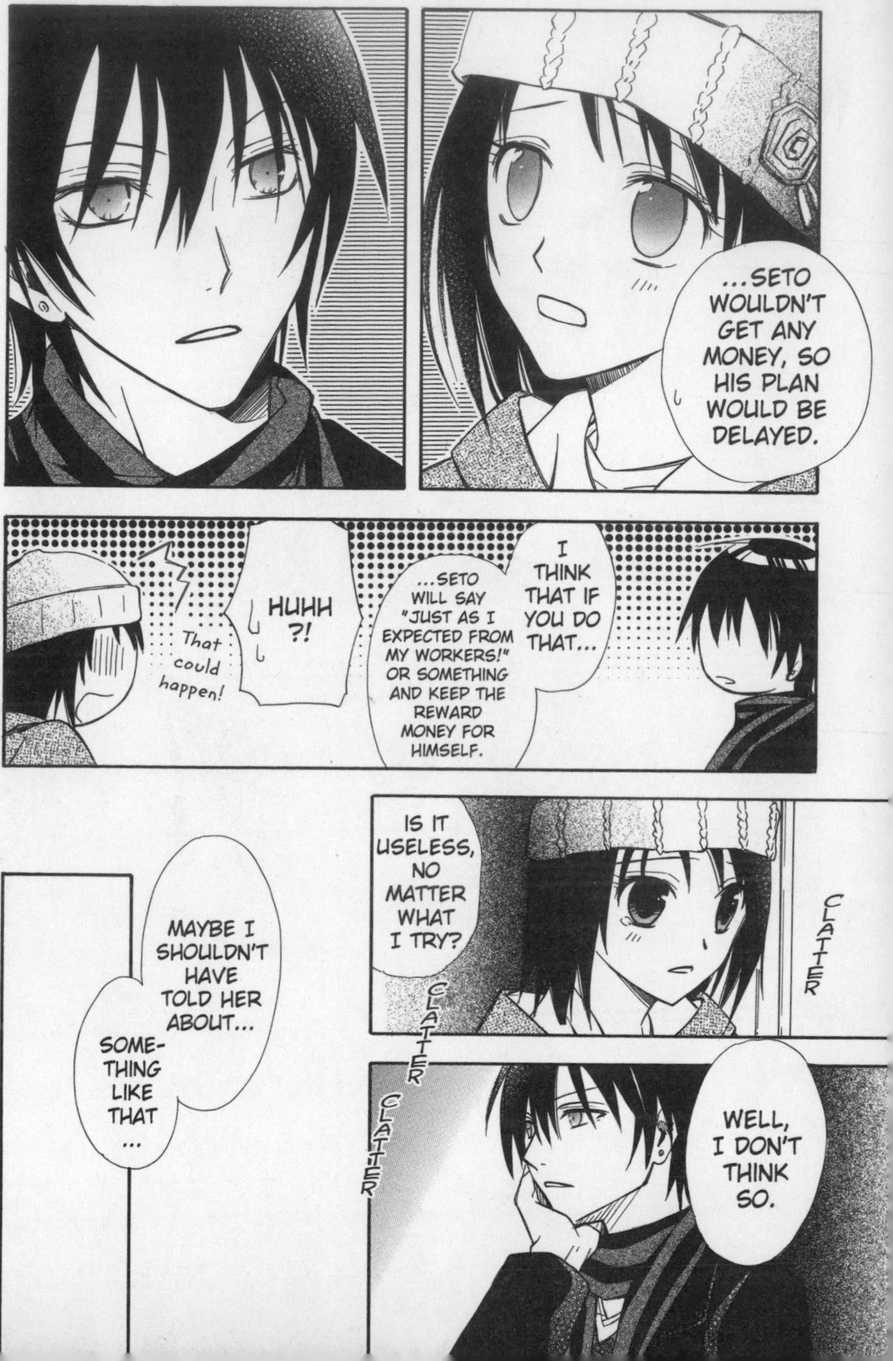
...SETO WOULDN'T GET ANY MONEY, SO HIS PLAN WOULD BE DELAYED.
I THINK THAT IF YOU DO THAT...
...SETO WILL SAY "JUST AS I EXPECTED FROM MY WORKERS!" OR SOMETHING AND KEEP THE REWARD MONEY FOR HIMSELF.
HUHH ?!
That could happen!
CLATTER
IS IT USELESS, NO MATTER WHAT I TRY?
CLATTER
WELL, I DON'T THINK SO.
CLATTER
MAYBE I SHOULDN'T HAVE TOLD HER ABOUT...
SOME-THING LIKE THAT ...

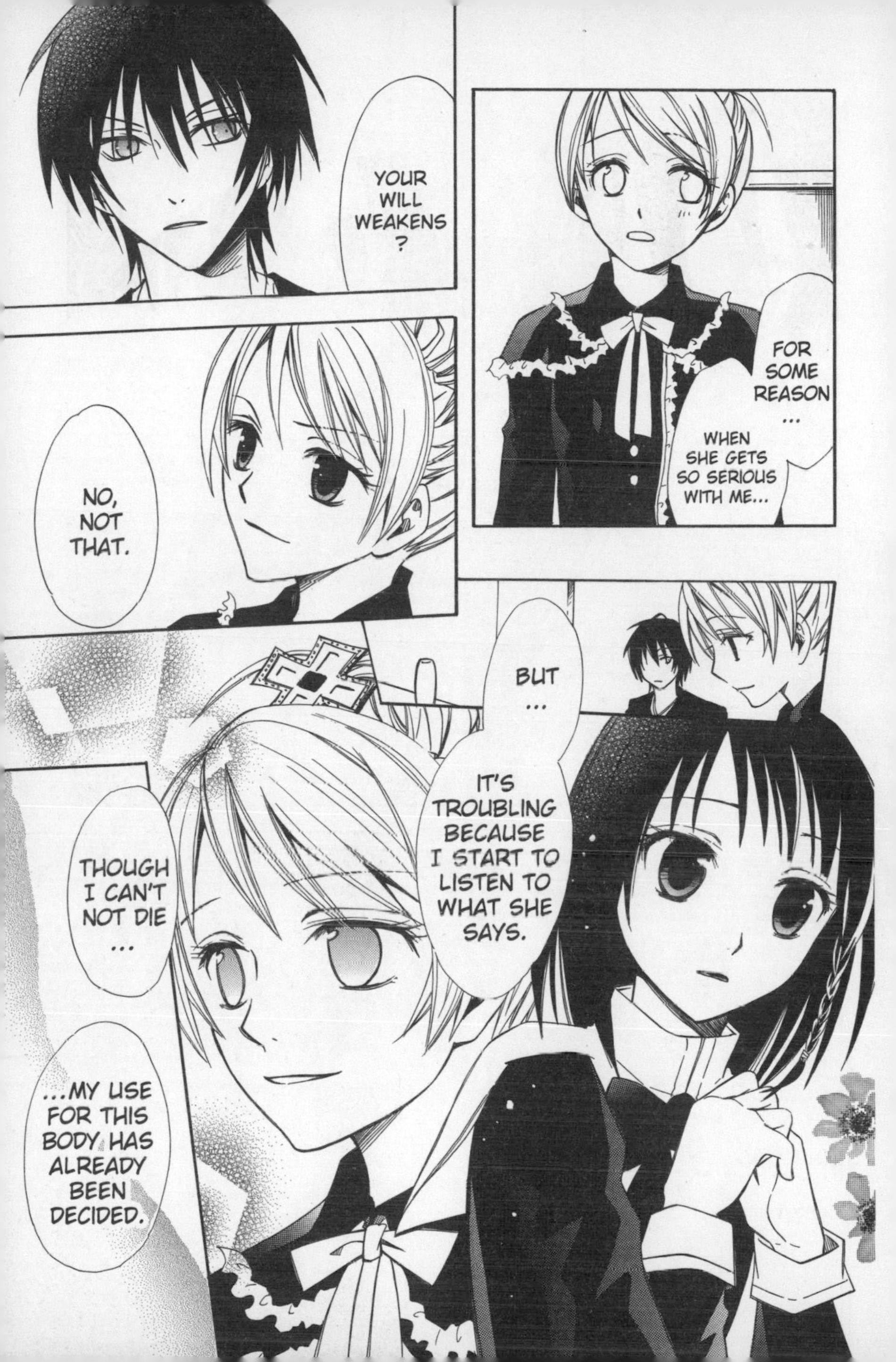
FOR SOME REASON ...
WHEN SHE GETS SO SERIOUS WITH ME...
YOUR WILL WEAKENS?
NO, NOT THAT.
BUT ...
IT'S TROUBLING BECAUSE I START TO LISTEN TO WHAT SHE SAYS.
THOUGH I CAN'T NOT DIE ...
...MY USE FOR THIS BODY HAS ALREADY BEEN DECIDED.

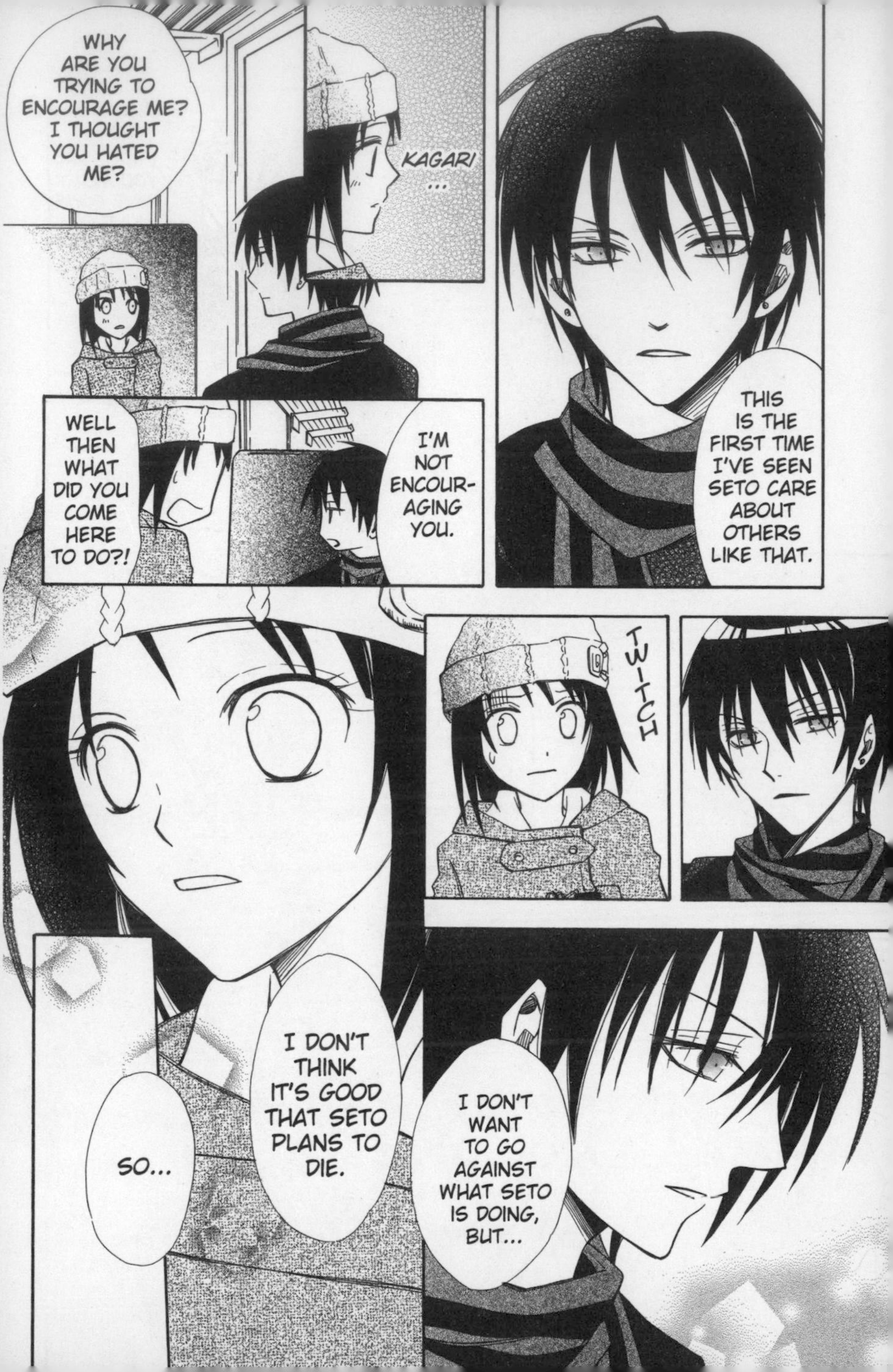

THIS IS THE FIRST TIME I'VE SEEN SETO CARE ABOUT OTHERS LIKE THAT.
KAGARI ...
WHY ARE YOU TRYING TO ENCOURAGE ME? I THOUGHT YOU HATED ME?
I'M NOT ENCOURAGING YOU.
WELL THEN WHAT DID YOU COME HERE TO DO?!
TWITCH
I DON'T WANT TO GO AGAINST WHAT SETO IS DOING, BUT...
I DON'T THINK IT'S GOOD THAT SETO PLANS TO DIE.
SO...

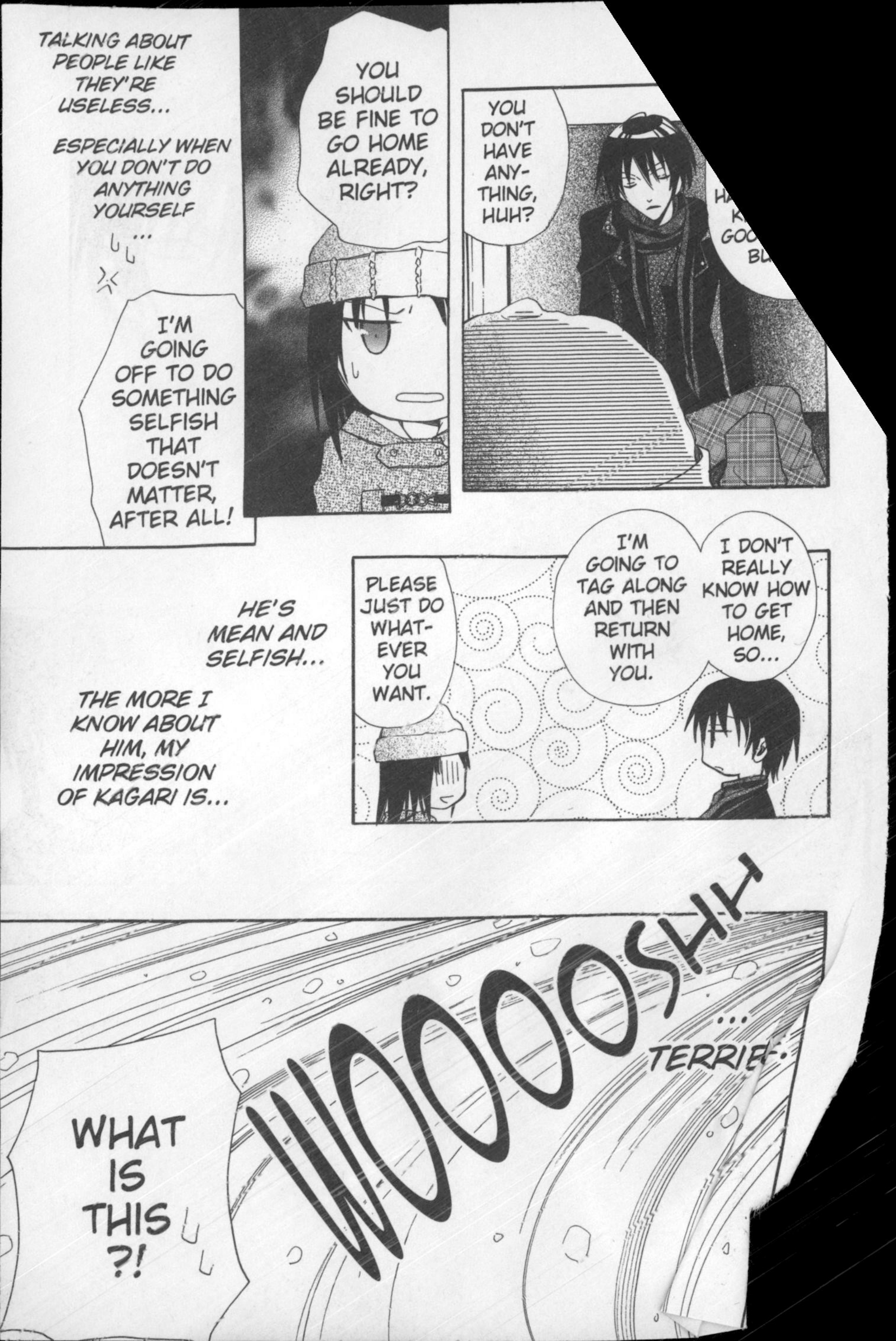
YOU DON'T HAVE ANY-THING, HUH?
YOU SHOULD BE FINE TO GO HOME ALREADY, RIGHT?
TALKING ABOUT PEOPLE LIKE THEY'RE USELESS...
ESPECIALLY WHEN YOU DON'T DO ANYTHING YOURSELF...
I'M GOING OFF TO DO SOMETHING SELFISH THAT DOESN'T MATTER, AFTER ALL!
I DON'T REALLY KNOW HOW TO GET HOME, SO...
I'M GOING TO TAG ALONG AND THEN RETURN WITH YOU.
PLEASE JUST DO WHAT-EVER YOU WANT.
HE'S MEAN AND SELFISH...
THE MORE I KNOW ABOUT HIM, MY IMPRESSION OF KAGARI IS...
... TERRIF
WOOOOSHH
WHAT IS THIS?!

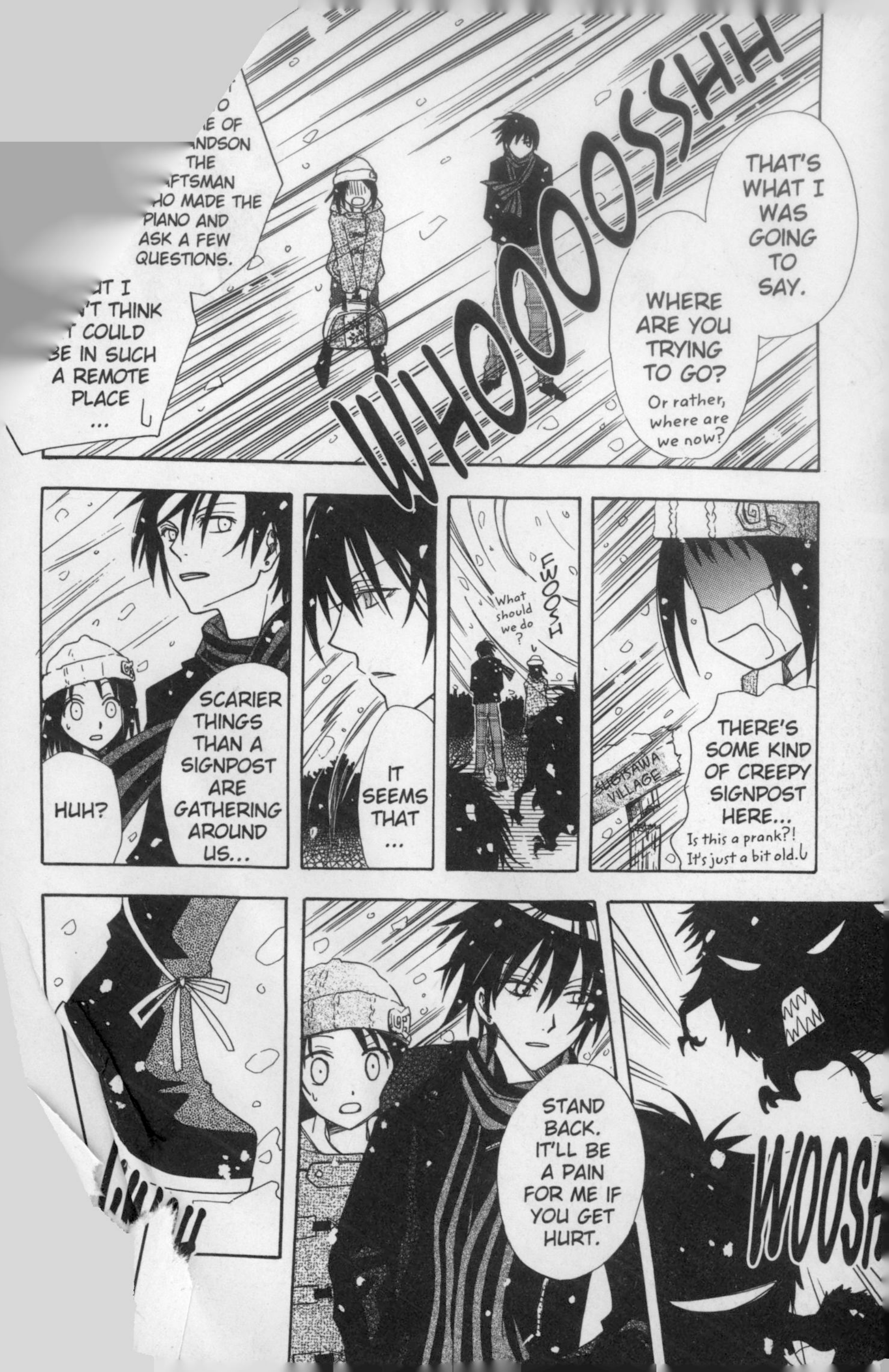

THAT'S WHAT I WAS GOING TO SAY.
WHERE ARE YOU TRYING TO GO?
Or rather, where are we now?
WHOOOOSSHH
...TO ...E OF ...ANDSON THE ...AFTSMAN ...HO MADE THE PIANO AND ASK A FEW QUESTIONS.
...T I ...N'T THINK ...T COULD BE IN SUCH A REMOTE PLACE...
THERE'S SOME KIND OF CREEPY SIGNPOST HERE...
Is this a prank?! It's just a bit old.
SHOISAWA VILLAGE
FWOOSH
What should we do?
IT SEEMS THAT...
SCARIER THINGS THAN A SIGNPOST ARE GATHERING AROUND US...
HUH?
WOOSH
STAND BACK. IT'LL BE A PAIN FOR ME IF YOU GET HURT.

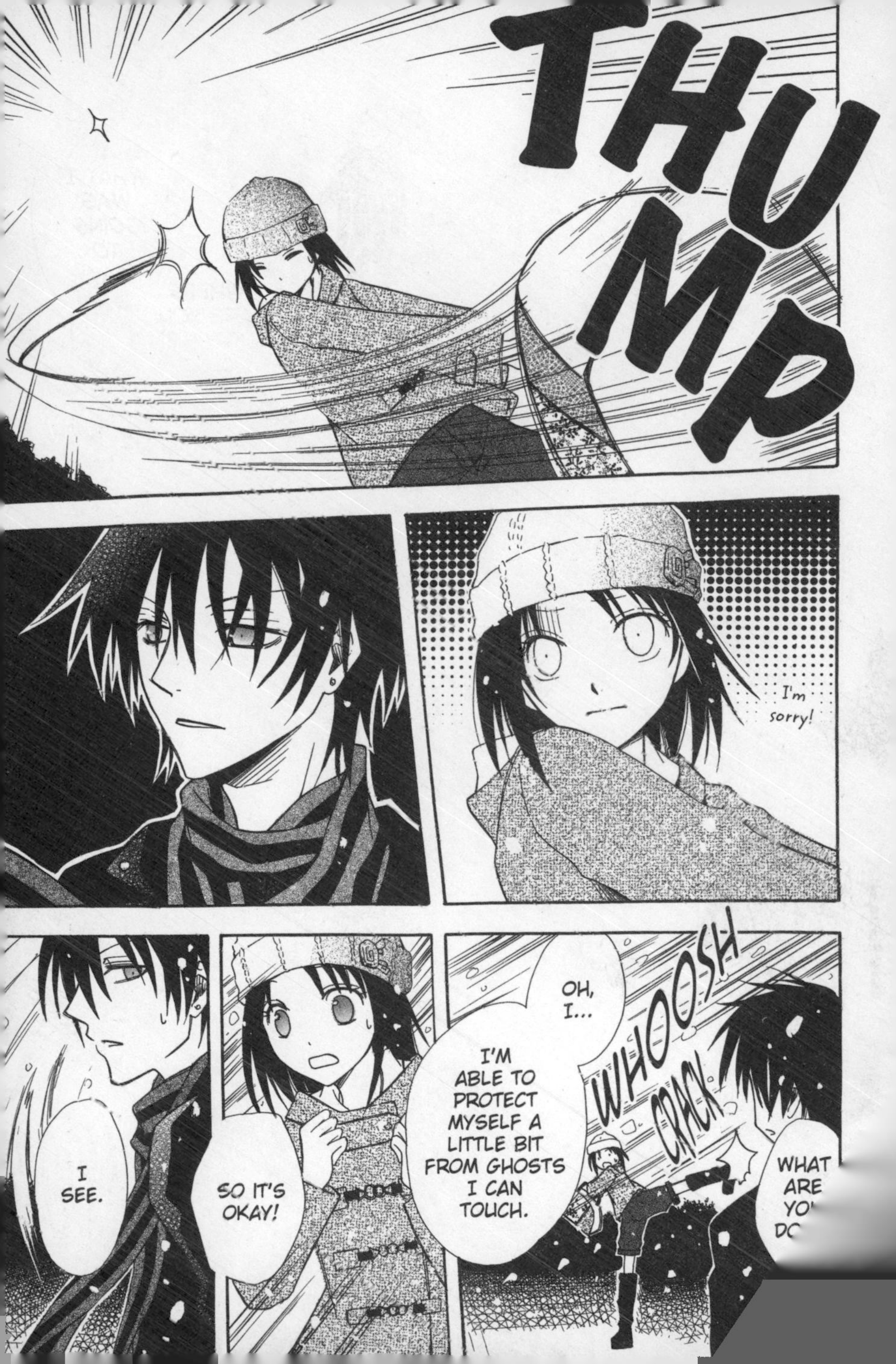
THUMP
I'm sorry!
WHOOSH
CRACK
WHAT ARE YO DO
OH, I...
I'M ABLE TO PROTECT MYSELF A LITTLE BIT FROM GHOSTS I CAN TOUCH.
SO IT'S OKAY!
I SEE.

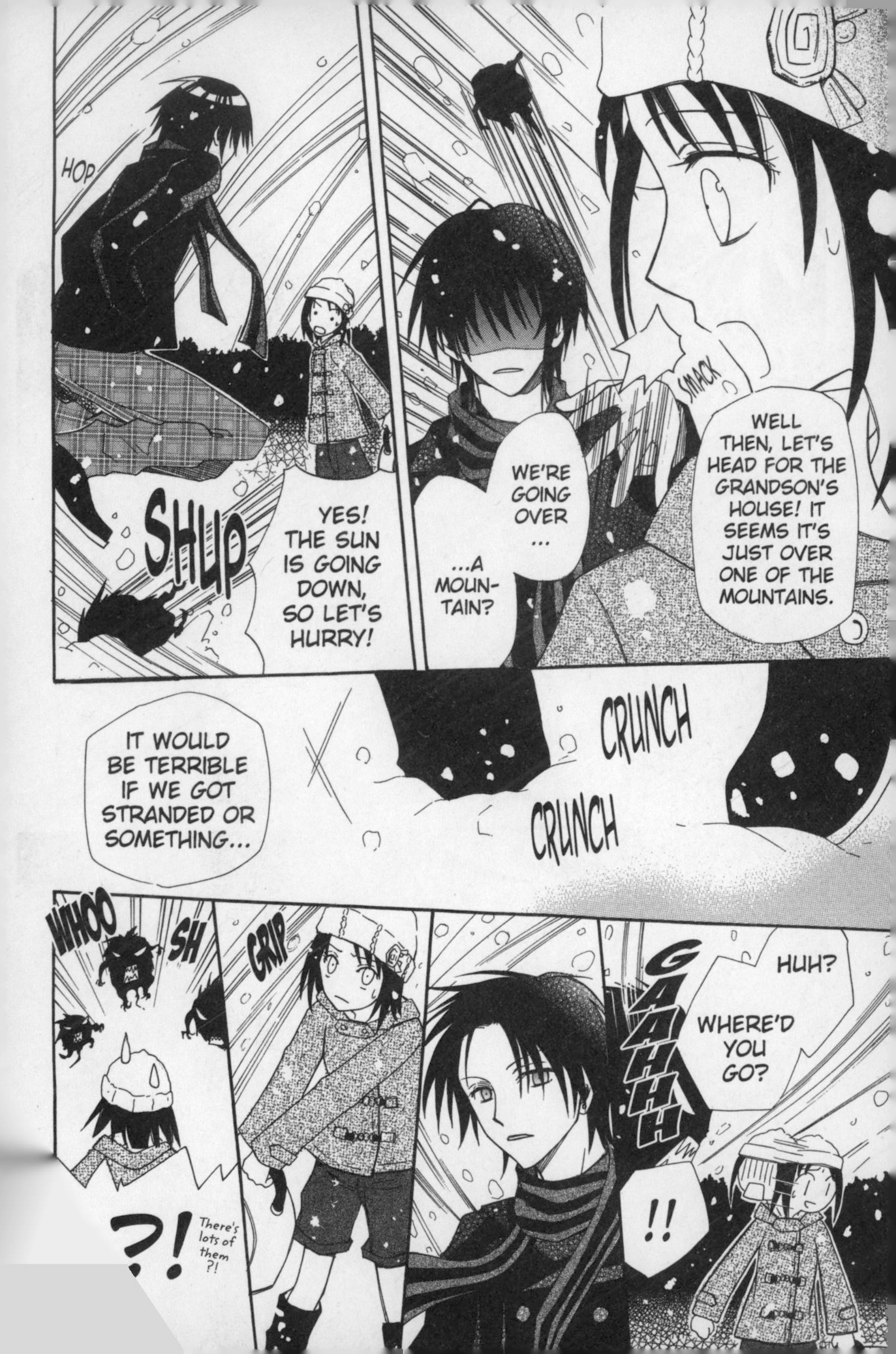
SMACK
WELL THEN, LET'S HEAD FOR THE GRANDSON'S HOUSE! IT SEEMS IT'S JUST OVER ONE OF THE MOUNTAINS.
WE'RE GOING OVER ...
...A MOUNTAIN?
HOP
YES! THE SUN IS GOING DOWN, SO LET'S HURRY!
SHLIP
CRUNCH
CRUNCH
IT WOULD BE TERRIBLE IF WE GOT STRANDED OR SOMETHING...
HUH?
WHERE'D YOU GO?
GAAHHH
!!
GRIP
WHOOSH
?!
There's lots of them ?!

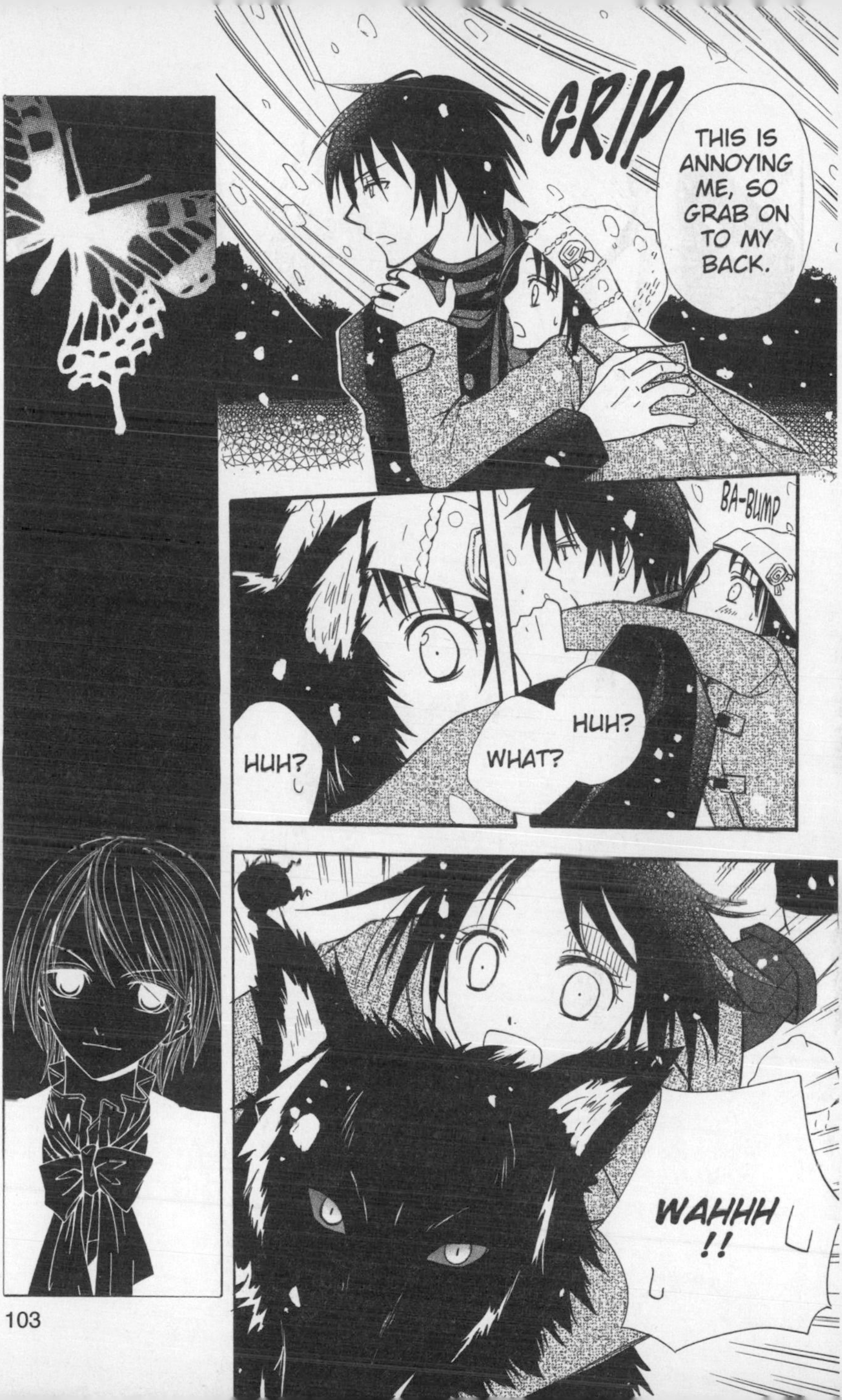

GRIP
THIS IS ANNOYING ME, SO GRAB ON TO MY BACK.
BA-BUMP
HUH?
WHAT?
HUH?
WAHHH !!

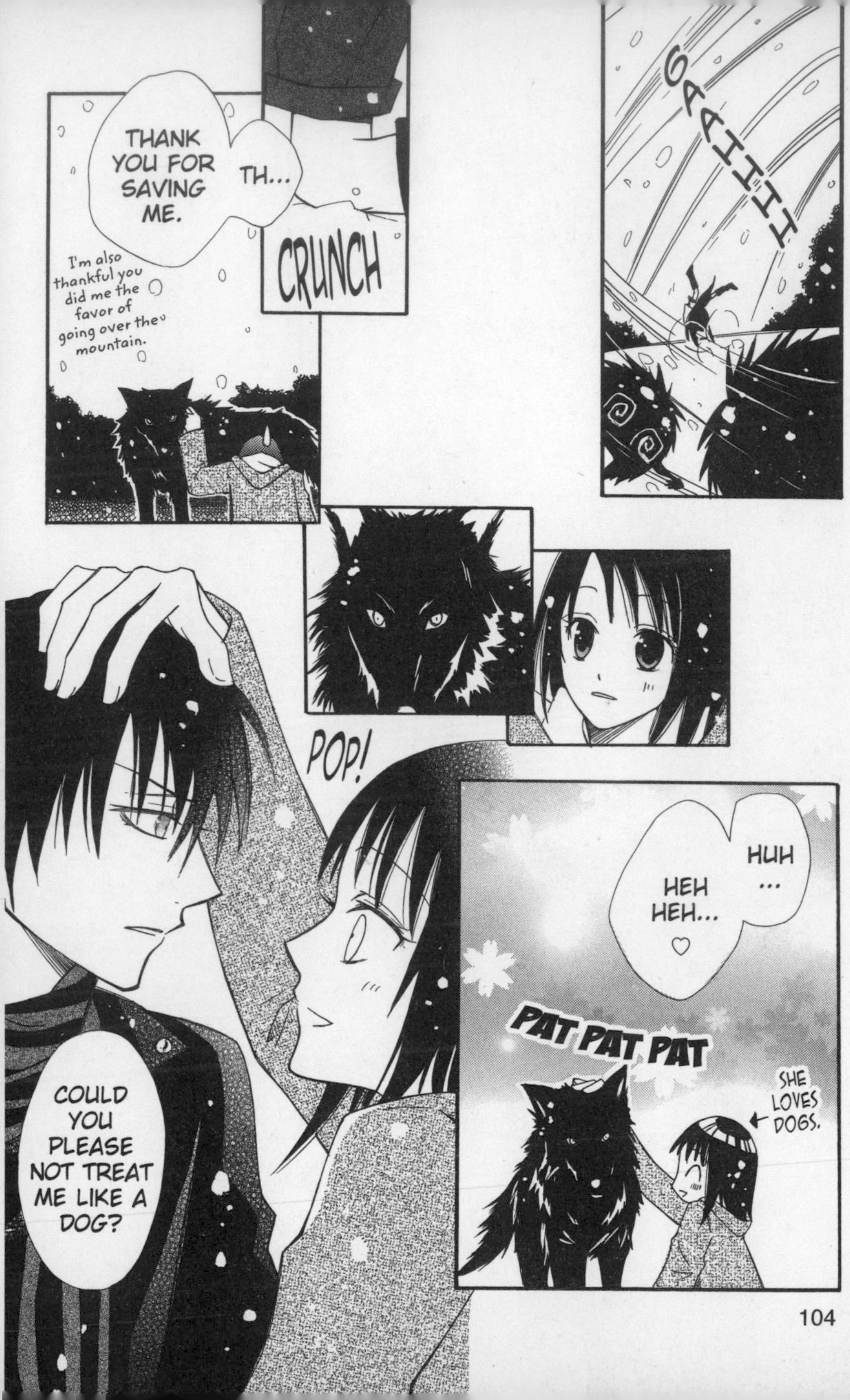
SAAIIIII
CRUNCH
TH...
THANK YOU FOR SAVING ME.
I'm also thankful you did me the favor of going over the mountain.
HUH... HEH HEH... ♡
PAT PAT PAT
SHE LOVES DOGS.
POP!
COULD YOU PLEASE NOT TREAT ME LIKE A DOG?

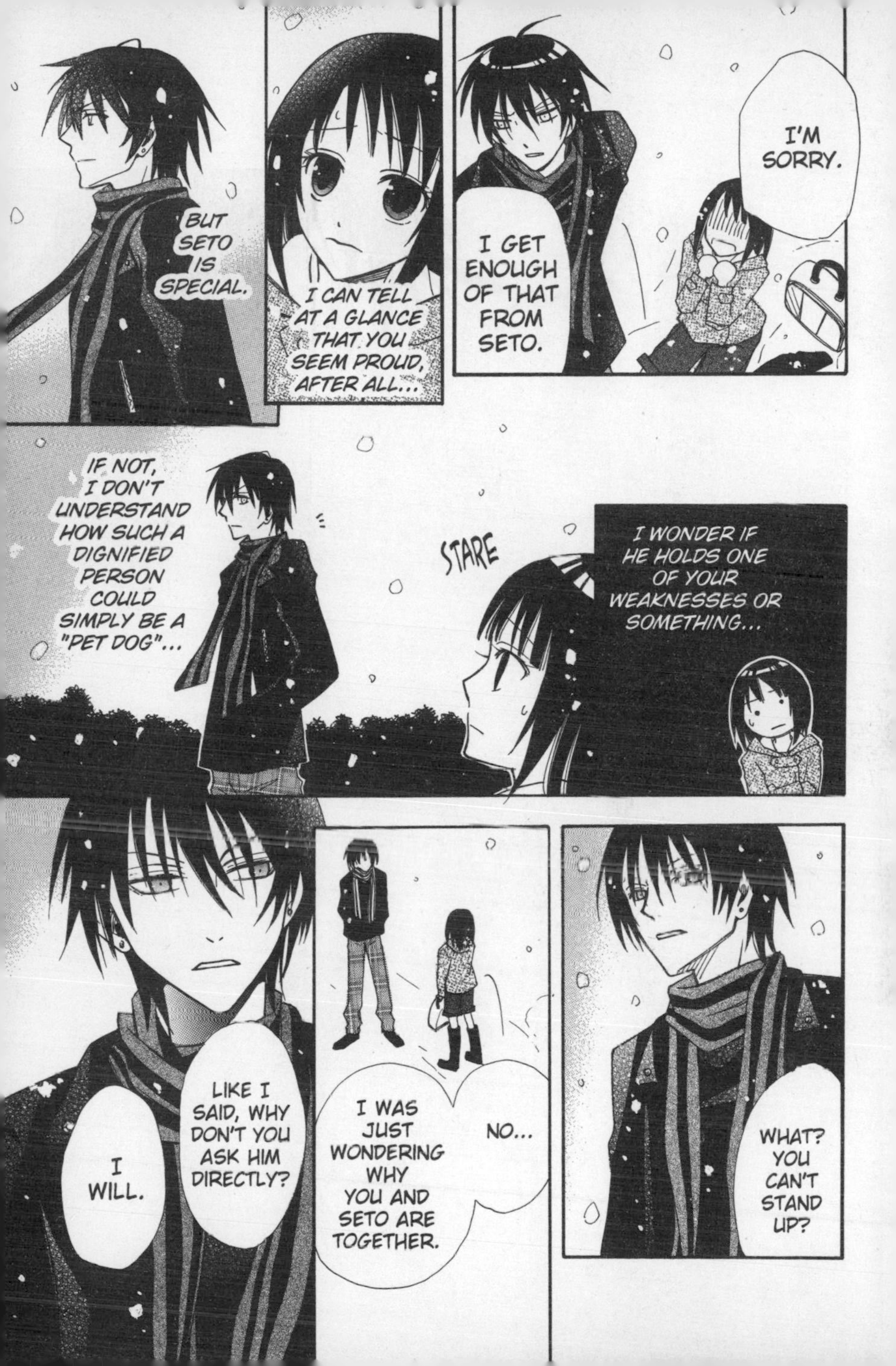
I'M SORRY.
I GET ENOUGH OF THAT FROM SETO.
I CAN TELL AT A GLANCE THAT YOU SEEM PROUD, AFTER ALL...
BUT SETO IS SPECIAL.
IF NOT, I DON'T UNDERSTAND HOW SUCH A DIGNIFIED PERSON COULD SIMPLY BE A "PET DOG"...
STARE
I WONDER IF HE HOLDS ONE OF YOUR WEAKNESSES OR SOMETHING...
WHAT? YOU CAN'T STAND UP?
NO...
I WAS JUST WONDERING WHY YOU AND SETO ARE TOGETHER.
LIKE I SAID, WHY DON'T YOU ASK HIM DIRECTLY?
I WILL.

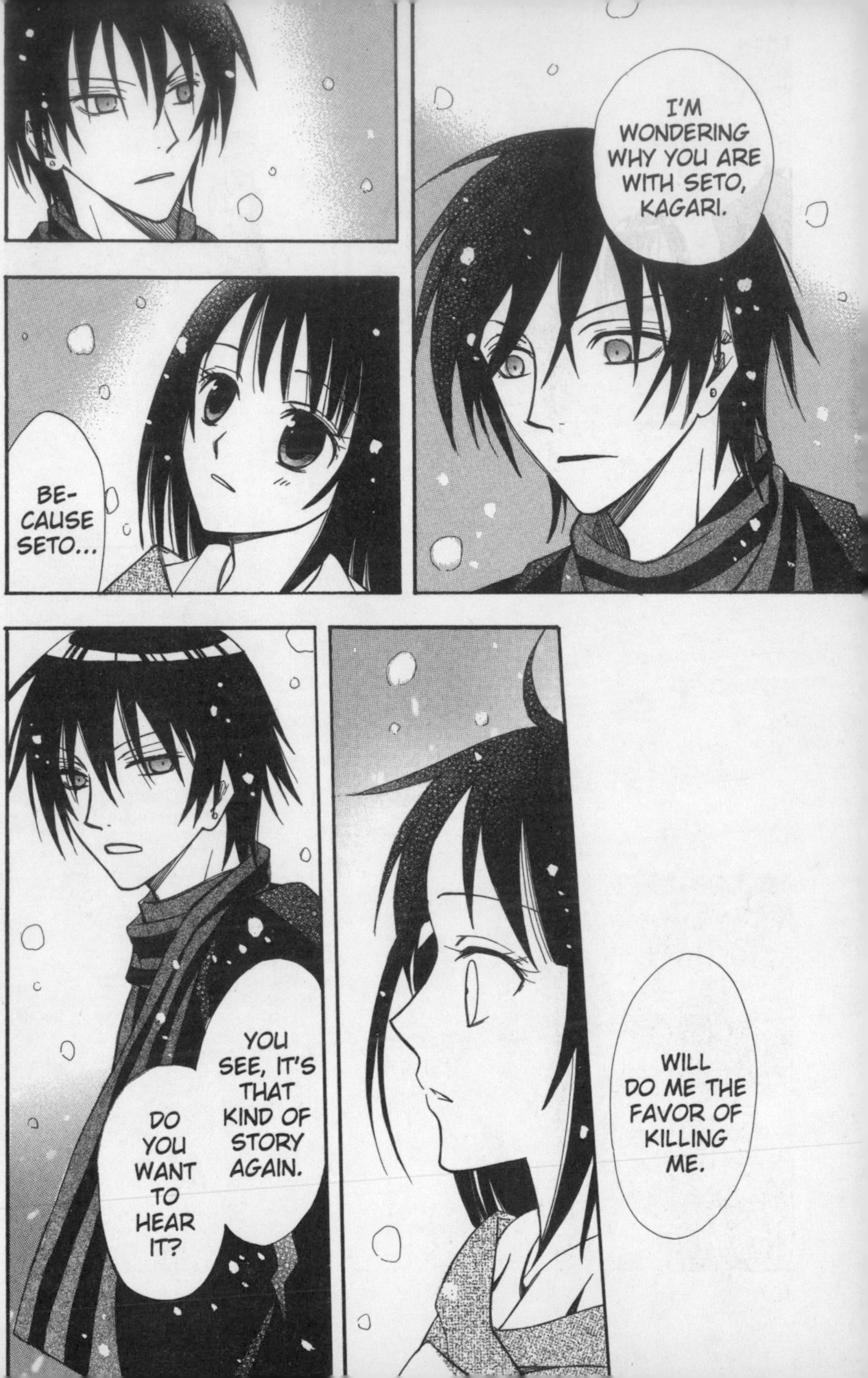
I'M WONDERING WHY YOU ARE WITH SETO, KAGARI.
BE-CAUSE SETO...
WILL DO ME THE FAVOR OF KILLING ME.
YOU SEE, IT'S THAT KIND OF STORY AGAIN.
DO YOU WANT TO HEAR IT?

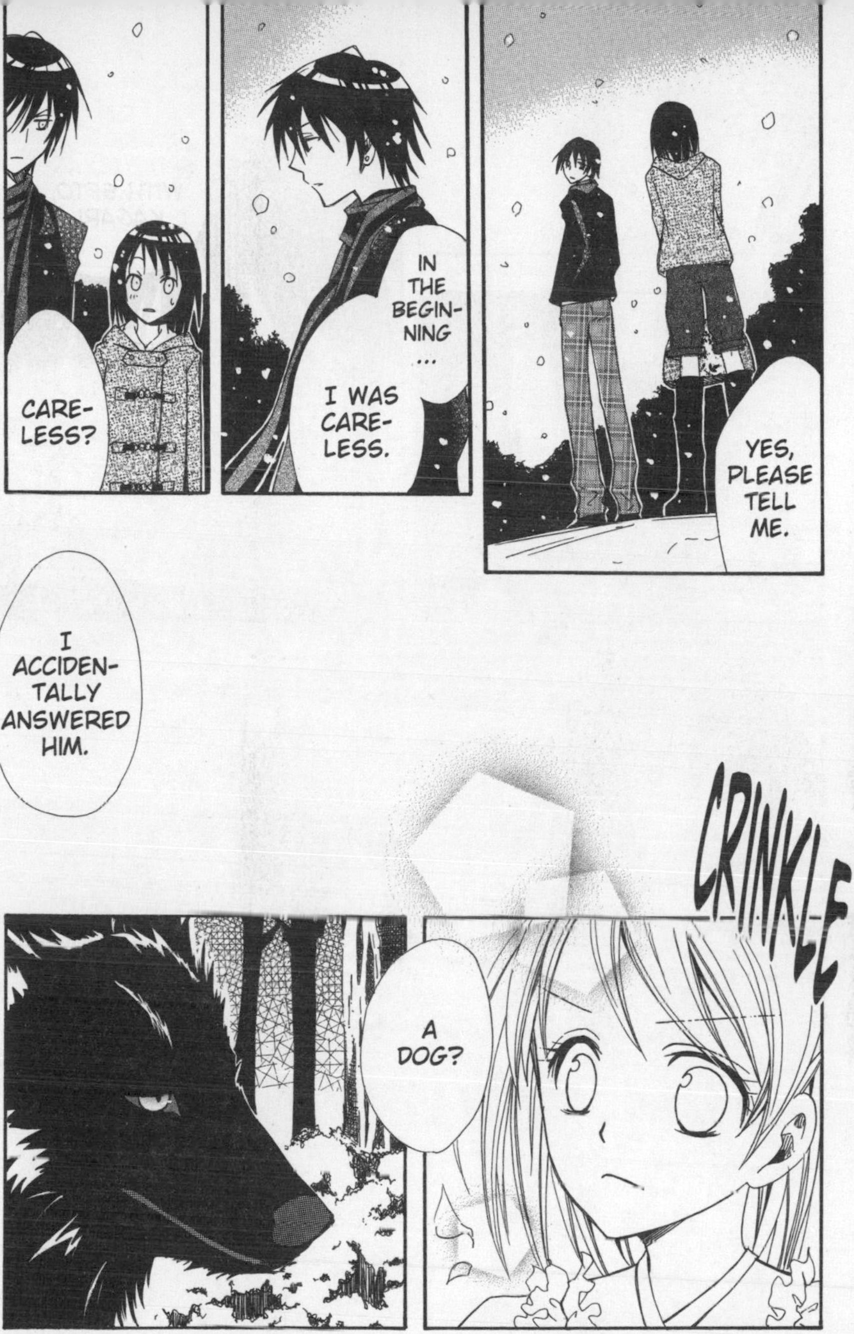
YES, PLEASE TELL ME.
IN THE BEGINNING...
I WAS CARELESS.
CARELESS?
I ACCIDENTALLY ANSWERED HIM.
CRINKLE
A DOG?

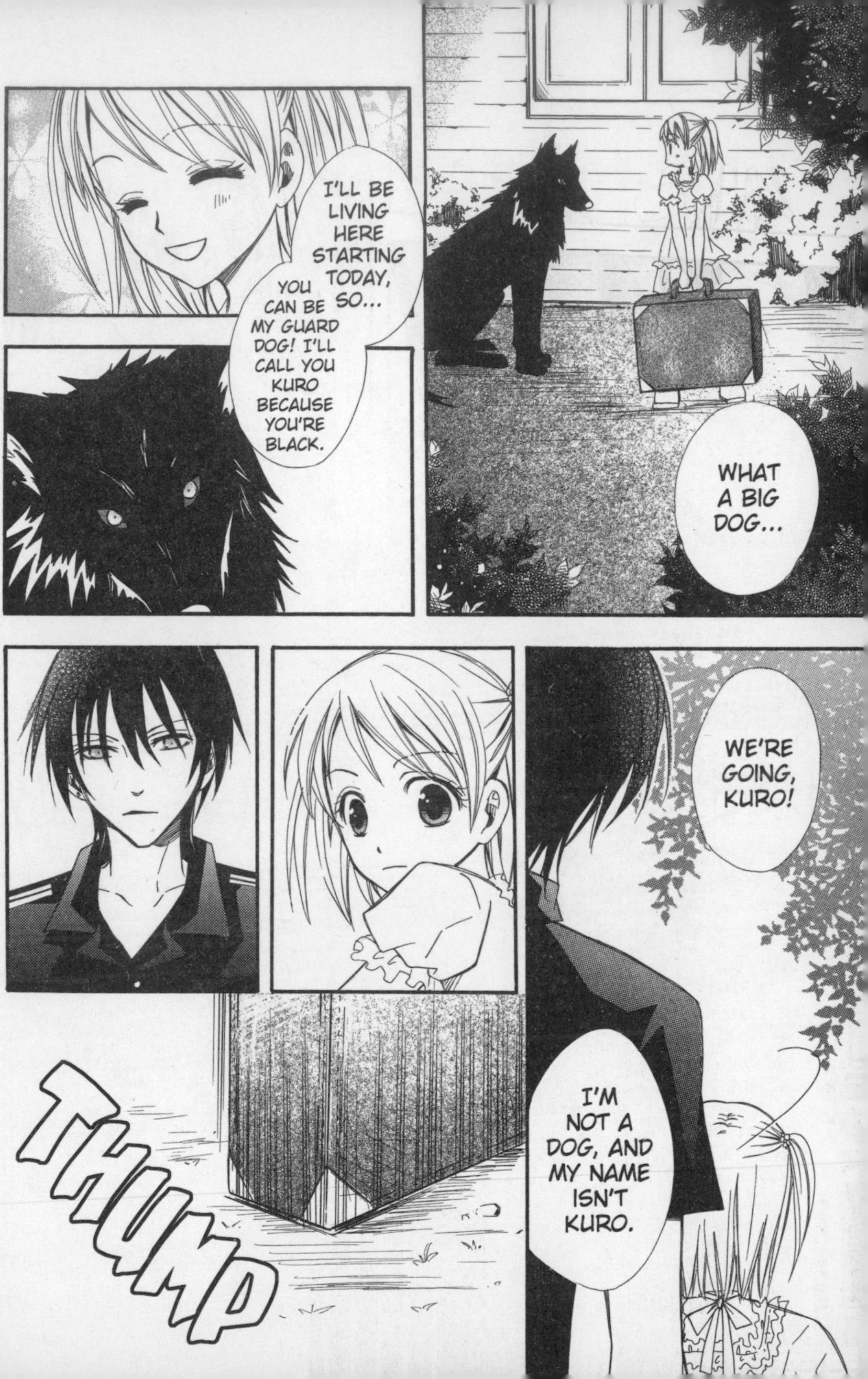
WHAT A BIG DOG...
I'LL BE LIVING HERE STARTING TODAY, SO...
YOU CAN BE MY GUARD DOG! I'LL CALL YOU KURO BECAUSE YOU'RE BLACK.
WE'RE GOING, KURO!
I'M NOT A DOG, AND MY NAME ISN'T KURO.
THUMP

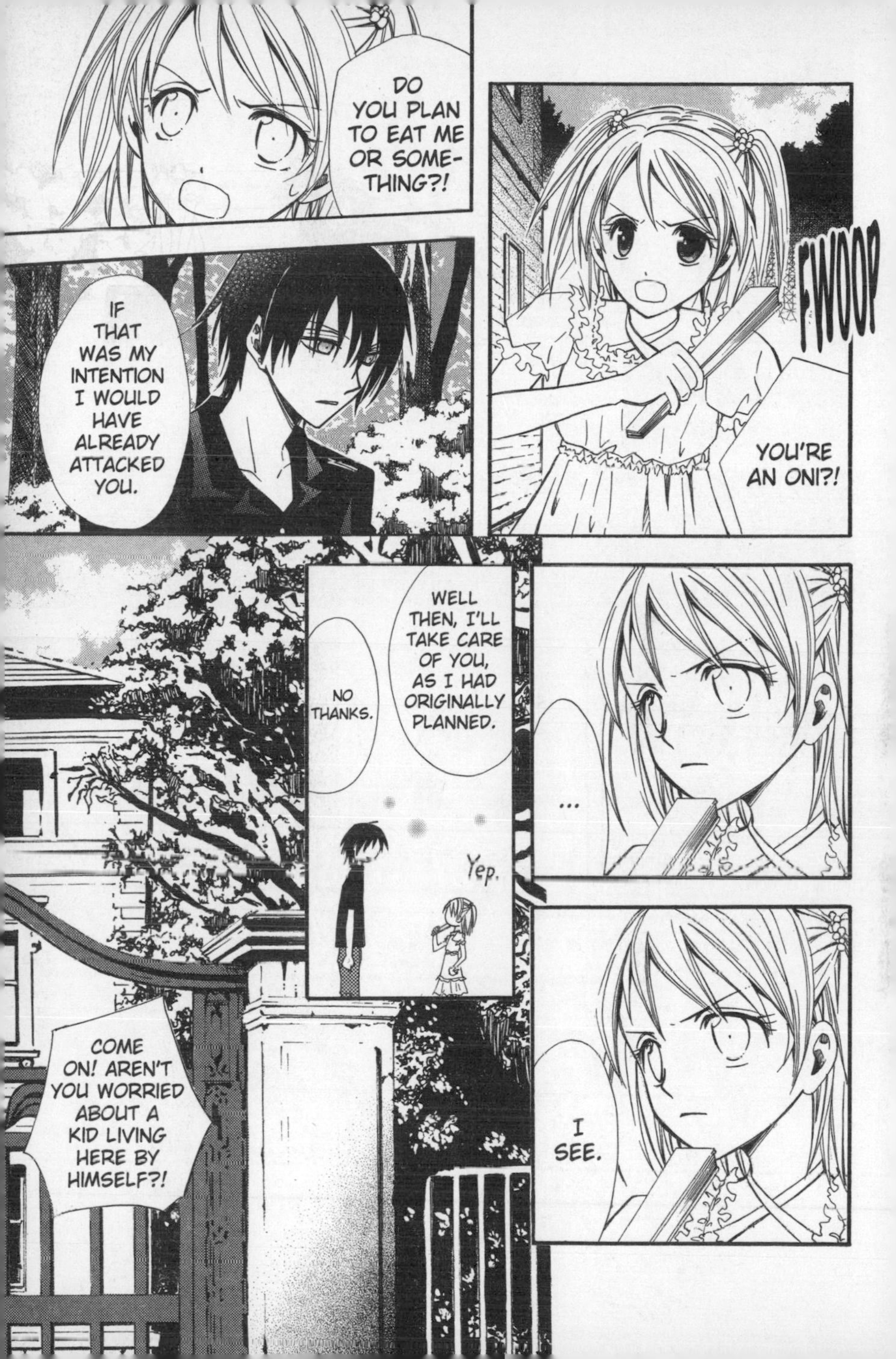
FWOOP
YOU'RE AN ONI?!
DO YOU PLAN TO EAT ME OR SOME-THING?!
IF THAT WAS MY INTENTION I WOULD HAVE ALREADY ATTACKED YOU.
...
I SEE.
WELL THEN, I'LL TAKE CARE OF YOU, AS I HAD ORIGINALLY PLANNED.
NO THANKS.
Yep.
COME ON! AREN'T YOU WORRIED ABOUT A KID LIVING HERE BY HIMSELF?!

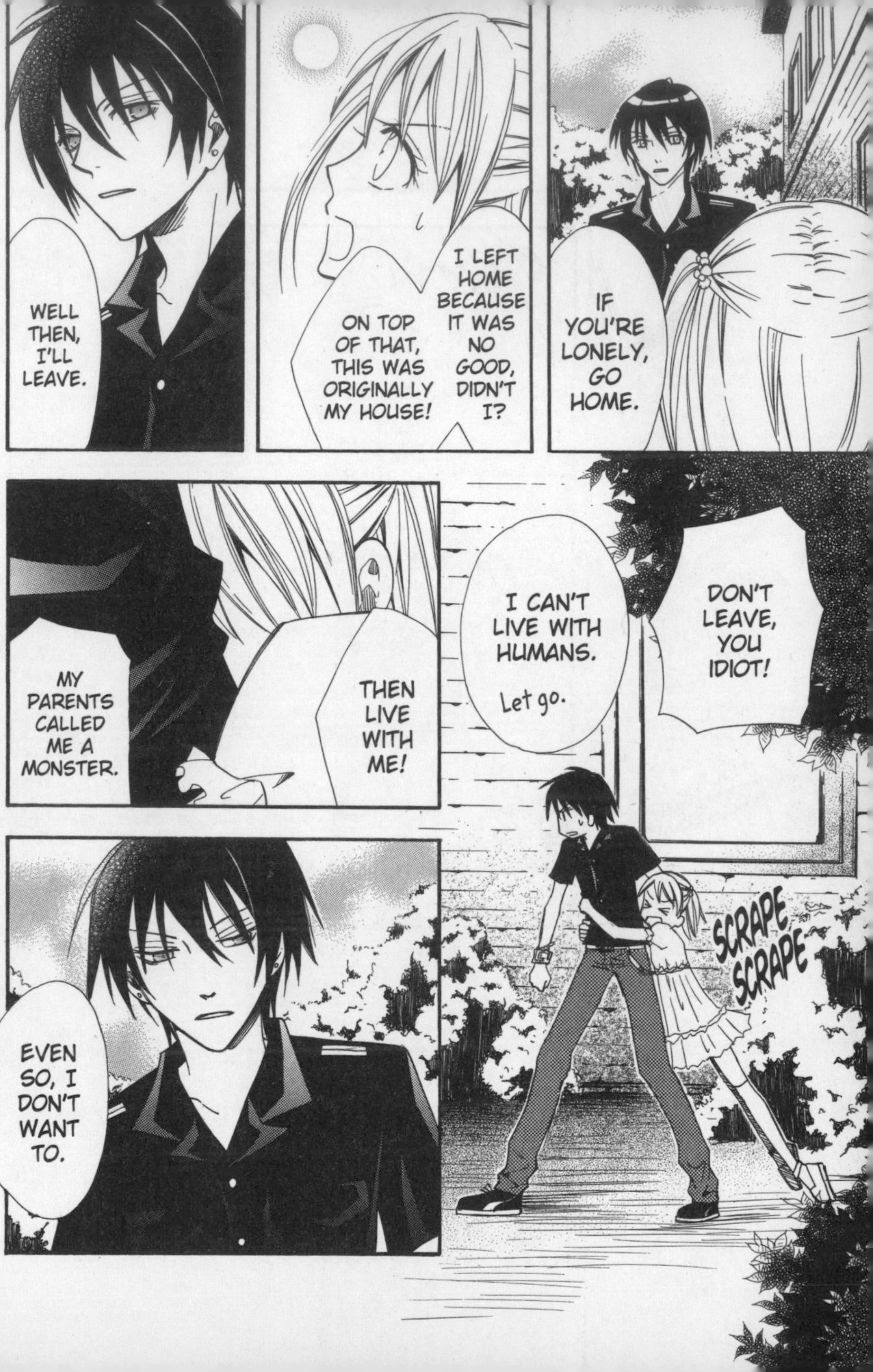
IF YOU'RE LONELY, GO HOME.
I LEFT HOME BECAUSE IT WAS NO GOOD, DIDN'T I?
ON TOP OF THAT, THIS WAS ORIGINALLY MY HOUSE!
WELL THEN, I'LL LEAVE.
DON'T LEAVE, YOU IDIOT!
I CAN'T LIVE WITH HUMANS.
Let go.
SCRAPE SCRAPE
THEN LIVE WITH ME!
MY PARENTS CALLED ME A MONSTER.
EVEN SO, I DON'T WANT TO.

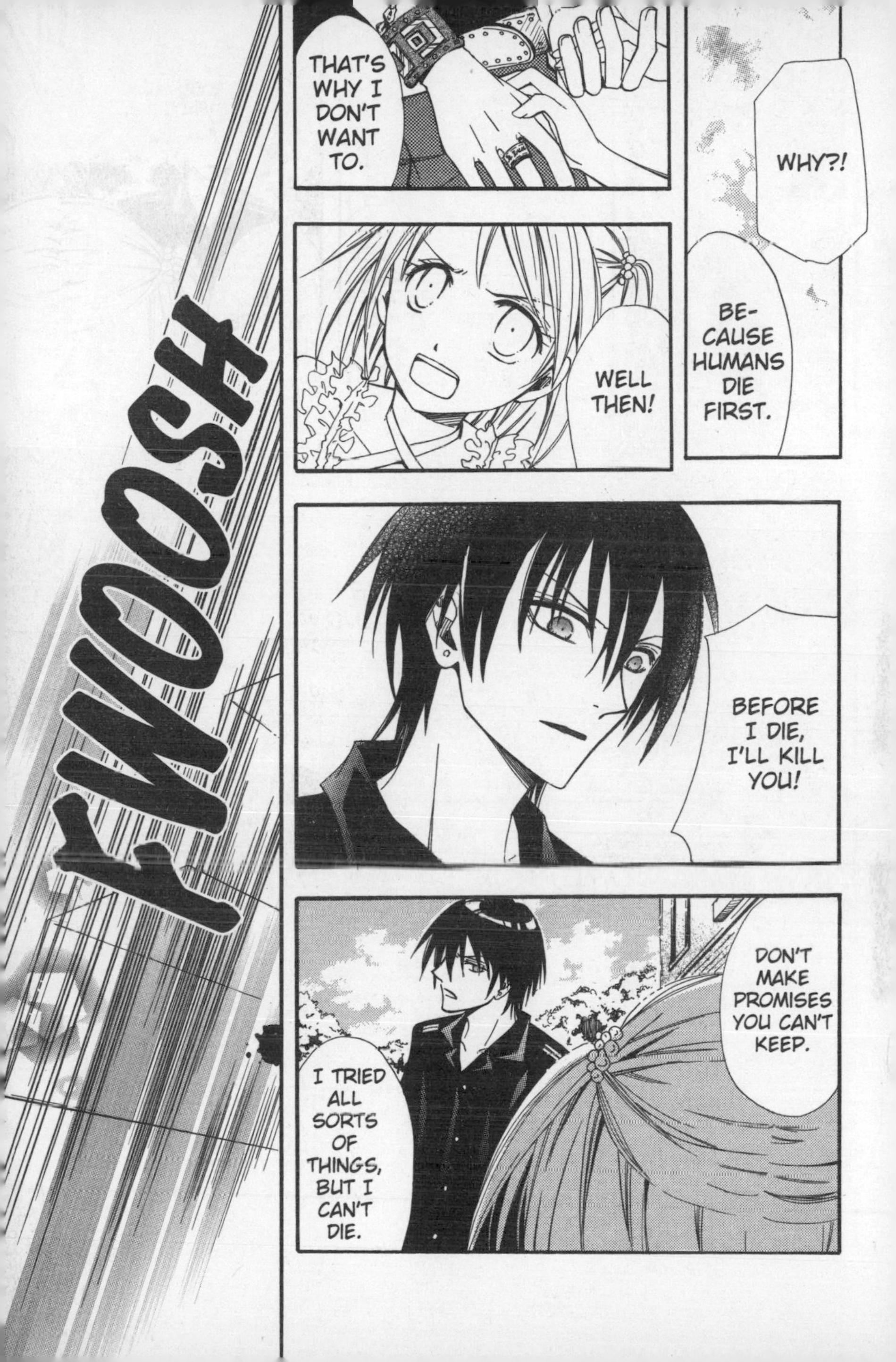
WHY?!
BE-CAUSE HUMANS DIE FIRST.
THAT'S WHY I DON'T WANT TO.
WELL THEN!
BEFORE I DIE, I'LL KILL YOU!
DON'T MAKE PROMISES YOU CAN'T KEEP.
I TRIED ALL SORTS OF THINGS, BUT I CAN'T DIE.
FWOOSH

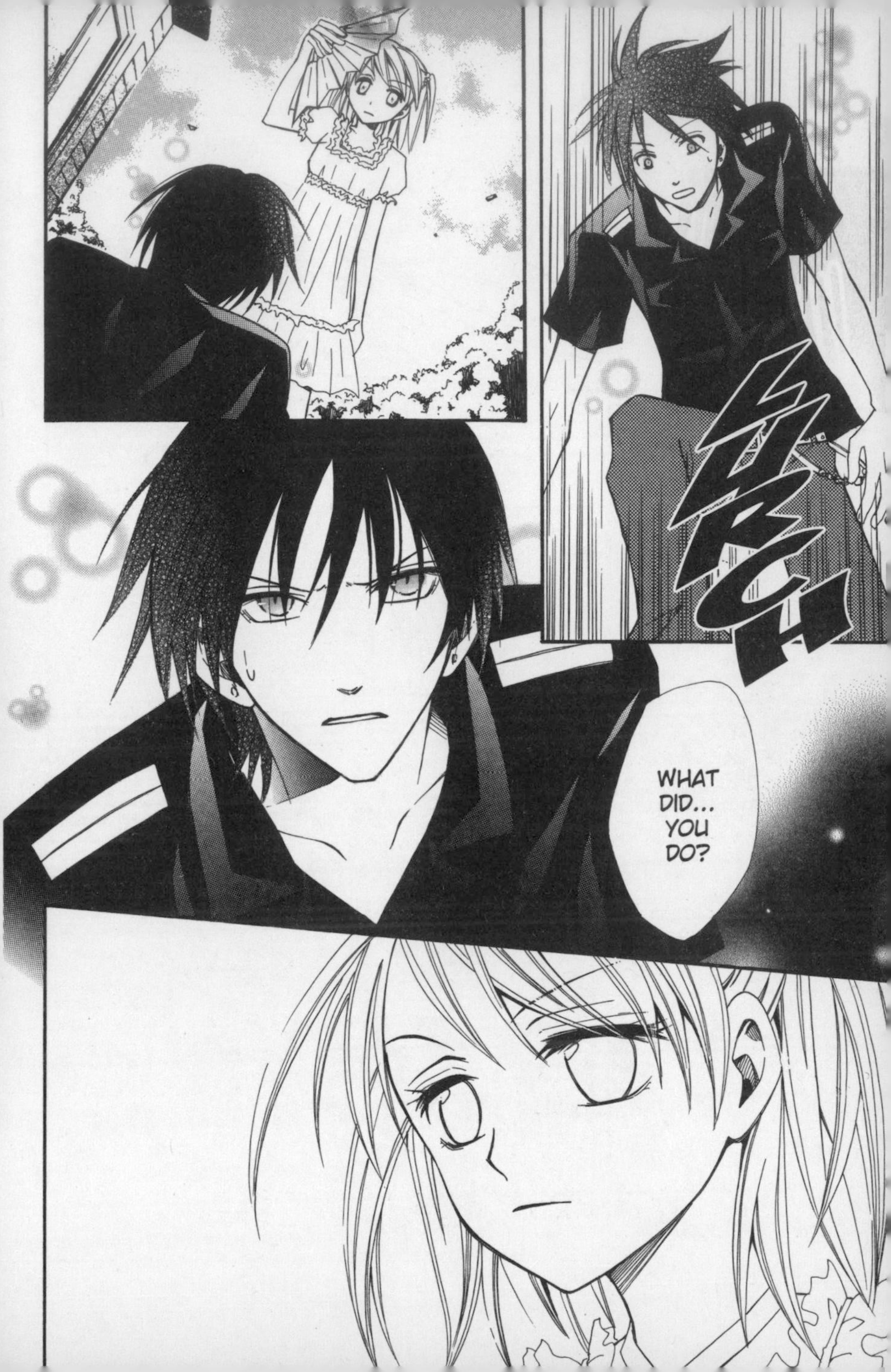
LURCH
WHAT DID... YOU DO?

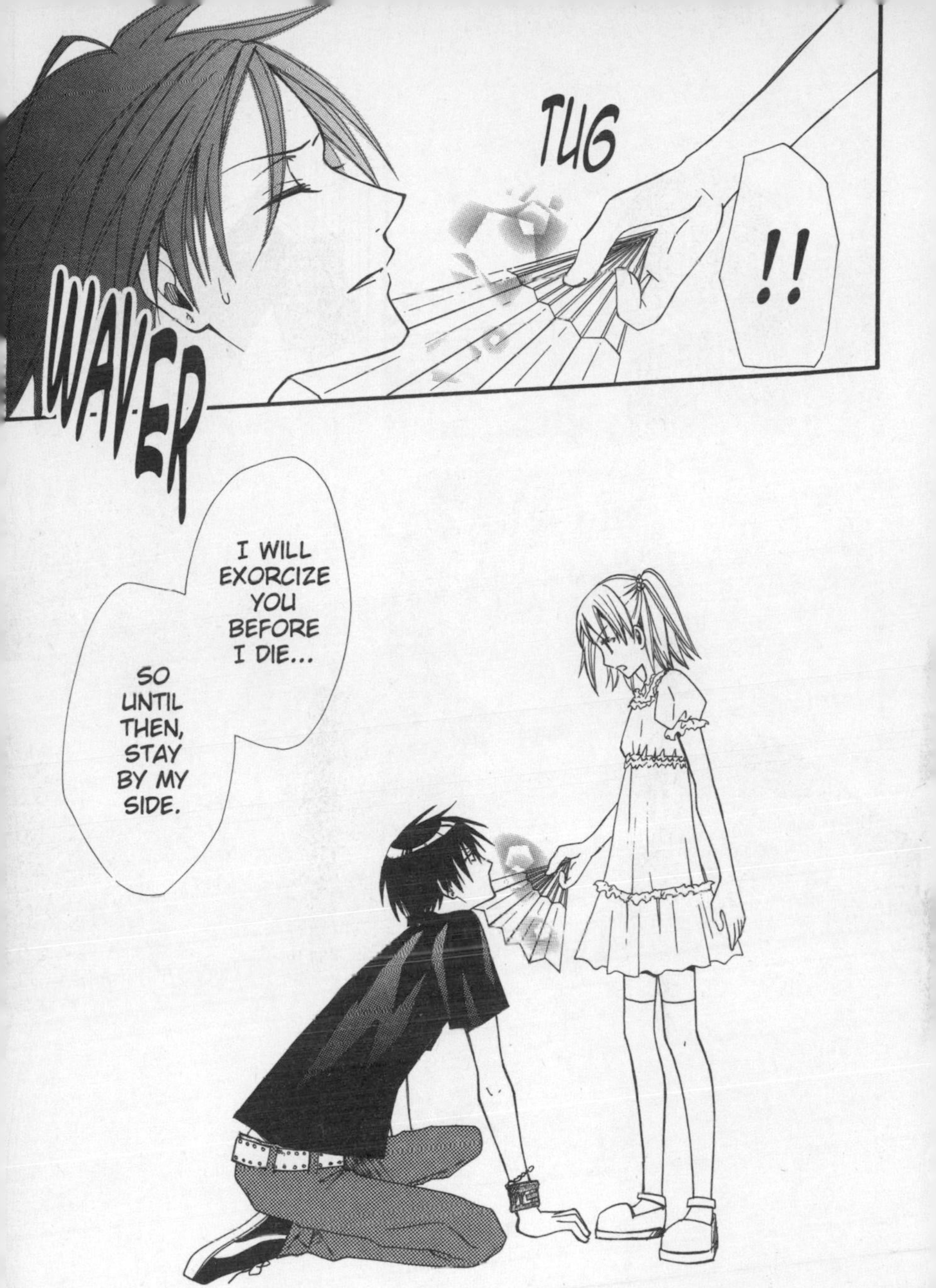
!!
TUG
WAVER
I WILL EXORCIZE YOU BEFORE I DIE...
SO UNTIL THEN, STAY BY MY SIDE.

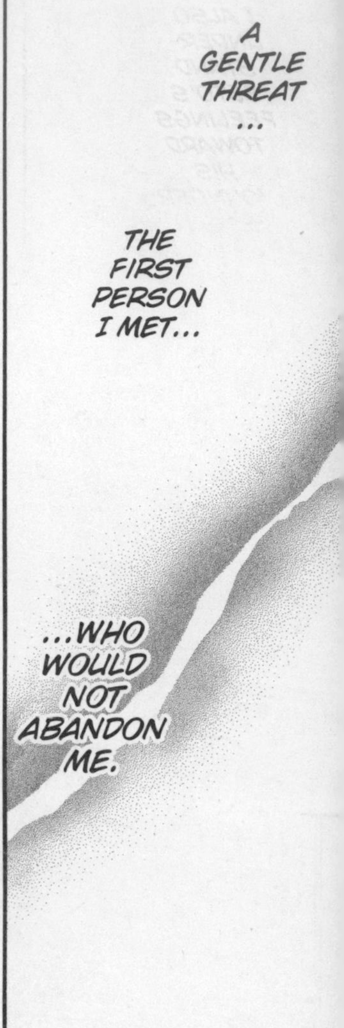
A GENTLE THREAT...
THE FIRST PERSON I MET...
...WHO WOULD NOT ABANDON ME.

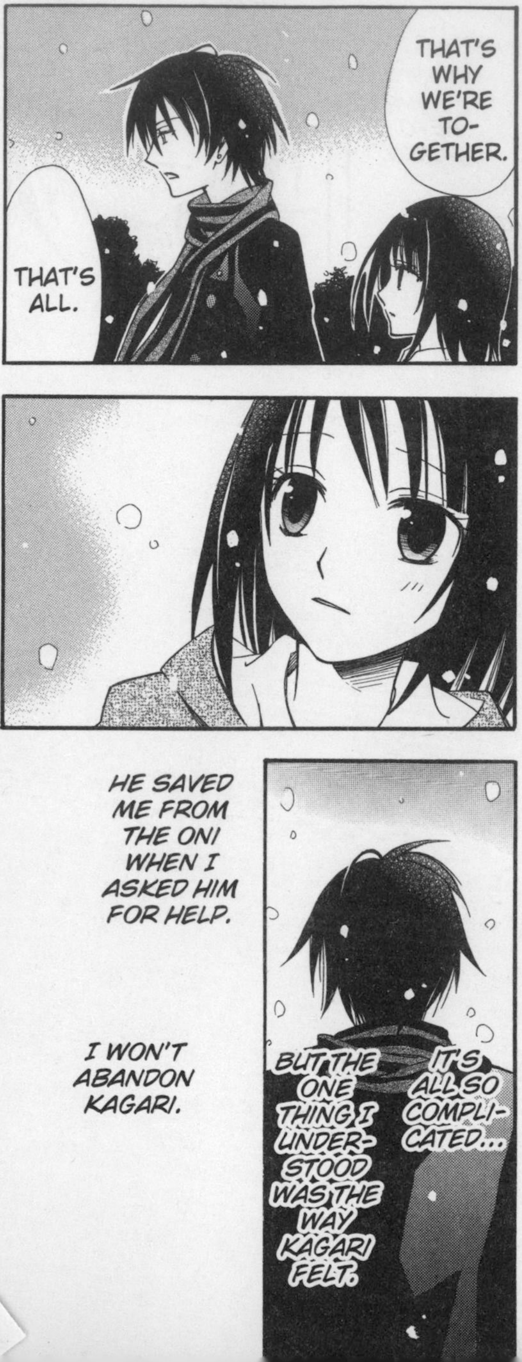
THAT'S WHY WE'RE TO-GETHER.
THAT'S ALL.
IT'S ALL SO COMPLI-CATED...
BUT THE ONE THING I UNDER-STOOD WAS THE WAY KAGARI FELT.
HE SAVED ME FROM THE ONI WHEN I ASKED HIM FOR HELP.
I WON'T ABANDON KAGARI.

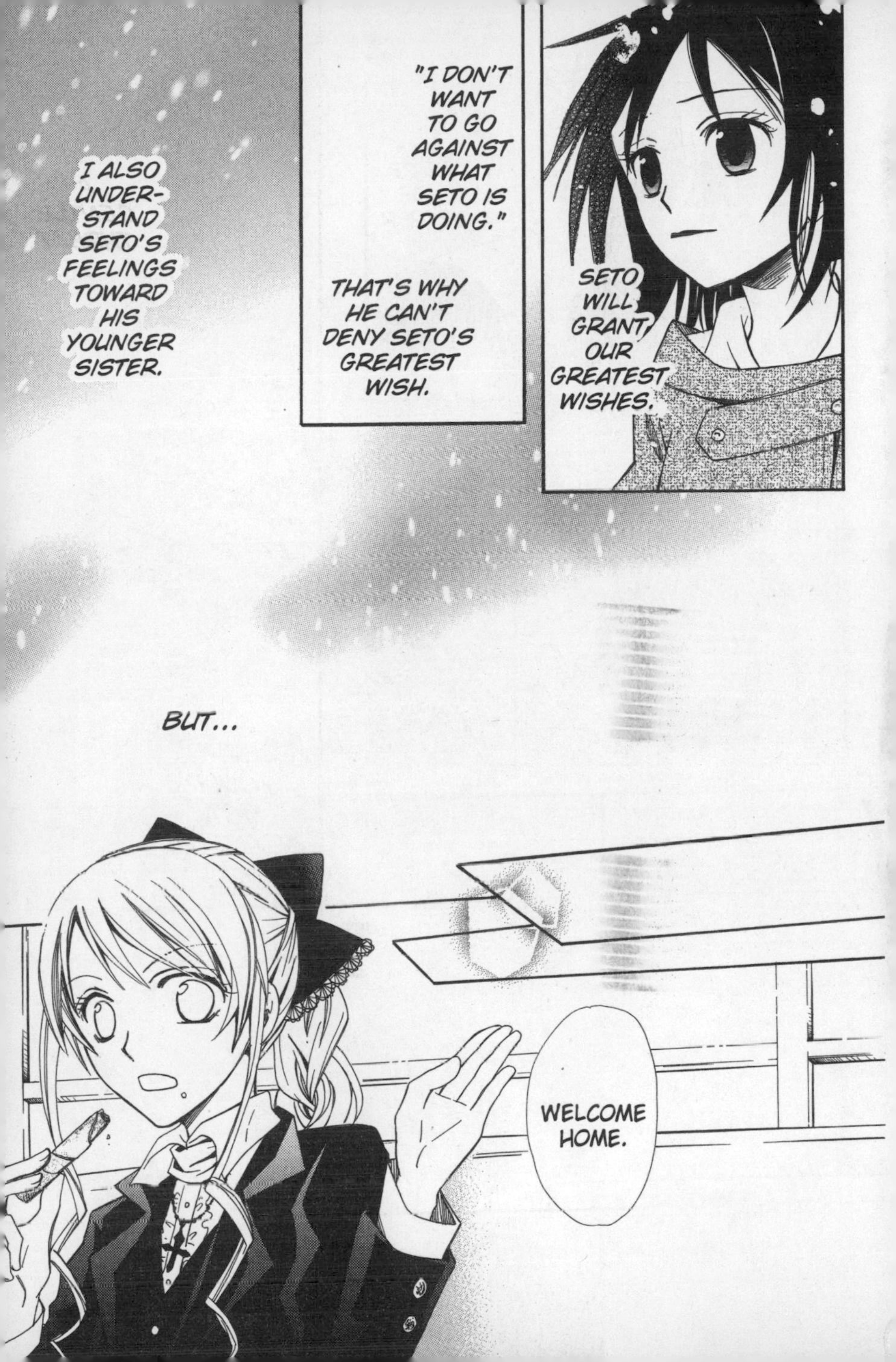
SETO WILL GRANT OUR GREATEST WISHES.
"I DON'T WANT TO GO AGAINST WHAT SETO IS DOING."
THAT'S WHY HE CAN'T DENY SETO'S GREATEST WISH.
I ALSO UNDER-STAND SETO'S FEELINGS TOWARD HIS YOUNGER SISTER.
BUT...
WELCOME HOME.

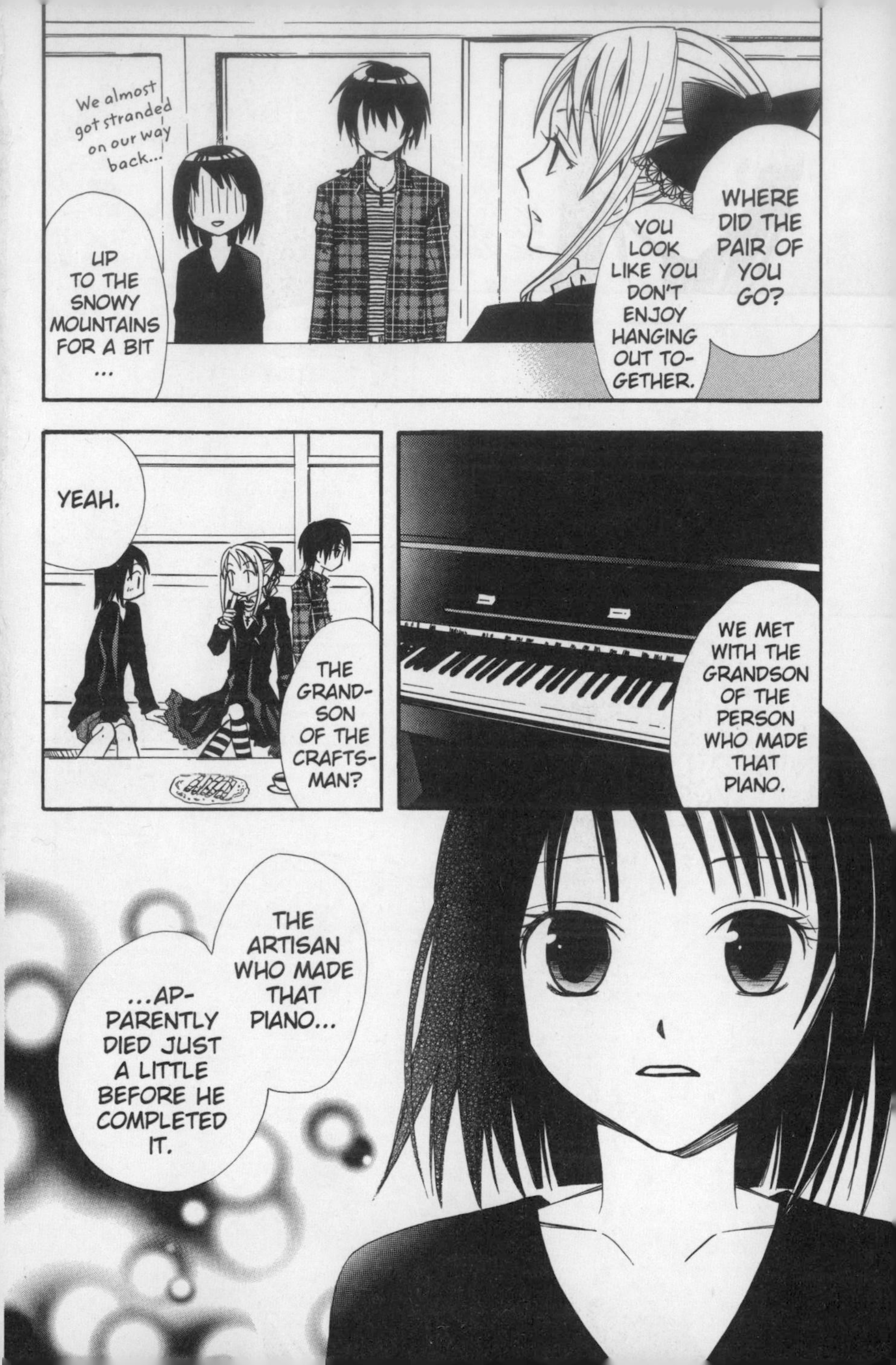
WHERE DID THE PAIR OF YOU GO?
YOU LOOK LIKE YOU DON'T ENJOY HANGING OUT TOGETHER.
UP TO THE SNOWY MOUNTAINS FOR A BIT ...
We almost got stranded on our way back...
WE MET WITH THE GRANDSON OF THE PERSON WHO MADE THAT PIANO.
THE GRANDSON OF THE CRAFTSMAN?
YEAH.
THE ARTISAN WHO MADE THAT PIANO...
...APPARENTLY DIED JUST A LITTLE BEFORE HE COMPLETED IT.

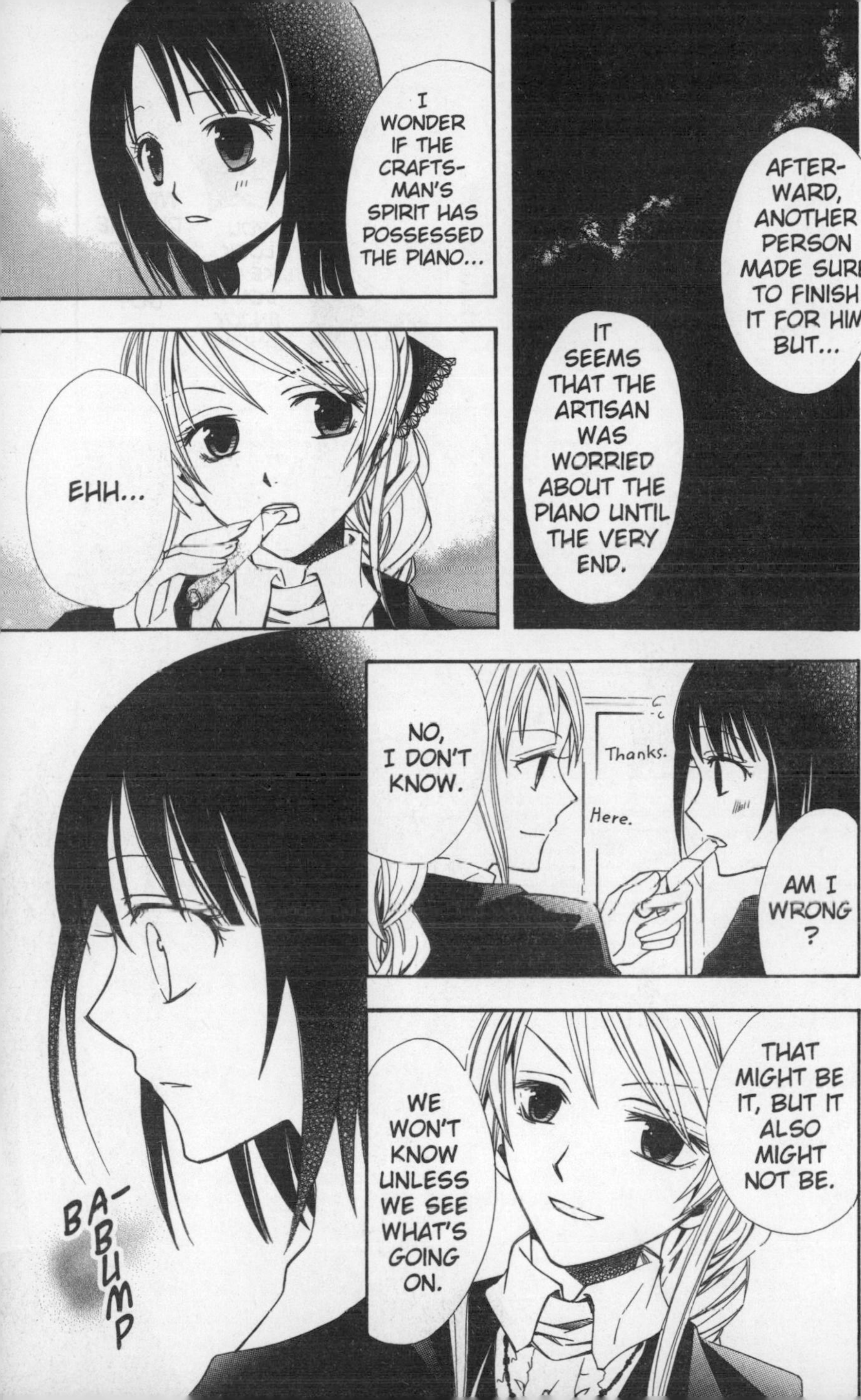
AFTER-WARD, ANOTHER PERSON MADE SURE TO FINISH IT FOR HIM BUT...
IT SEEMS THAT THE ARTISAN WAS WORRIED ABOUT THE PIANO UNTIL THE VERY END.
I WONDER IF THE CRAFTS-MAN'S SPIRIT HAS POSSESSED THE PIANO...
EHH...
AM I WRONG?
Thanks.
Here.
NO, I DON'T KNOW.
THAT MIGHT BE IT, BUT IT ALSO MIGHT NOT BE.
WE WON'T KNOW UNLESS WE SEE WHAT'S GOING ON.
BA-BUMP

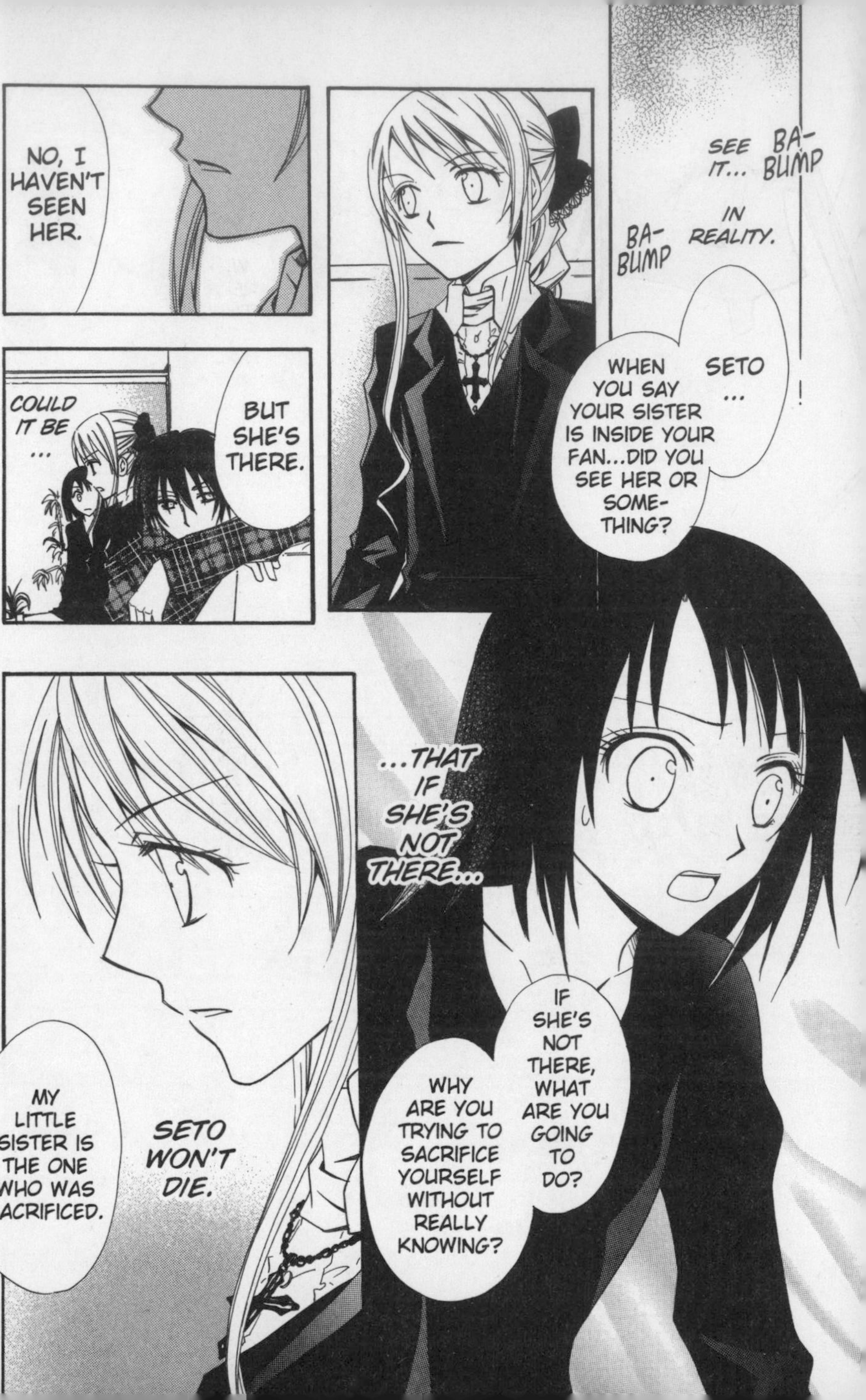
SEE IT... IN REALITY.
BA-BUMP
BA-BUMP
SETO...!
WHEN YOU SAY YOUR SISTER IS INSIDE YOUR FAN...DID YOU SEE HER OR SOME-THING?
NO, I HAVEN'T SEEN HER.
BUT SHE'S THERE.
COULD IT BE...
...THAT IF SHE'S NOT THERE...
IF SHE'S NOT THERE, WHAT ARE YOU GOING TO DO?
WHY ARE YOU TRYING TO SACRIFICE YOURSELF WITHOUT REALLY KNOWING?
SETO WON'T DIE.
MY LITTLE SISTER IS THE ONE WHO WAS SACRIFICED.

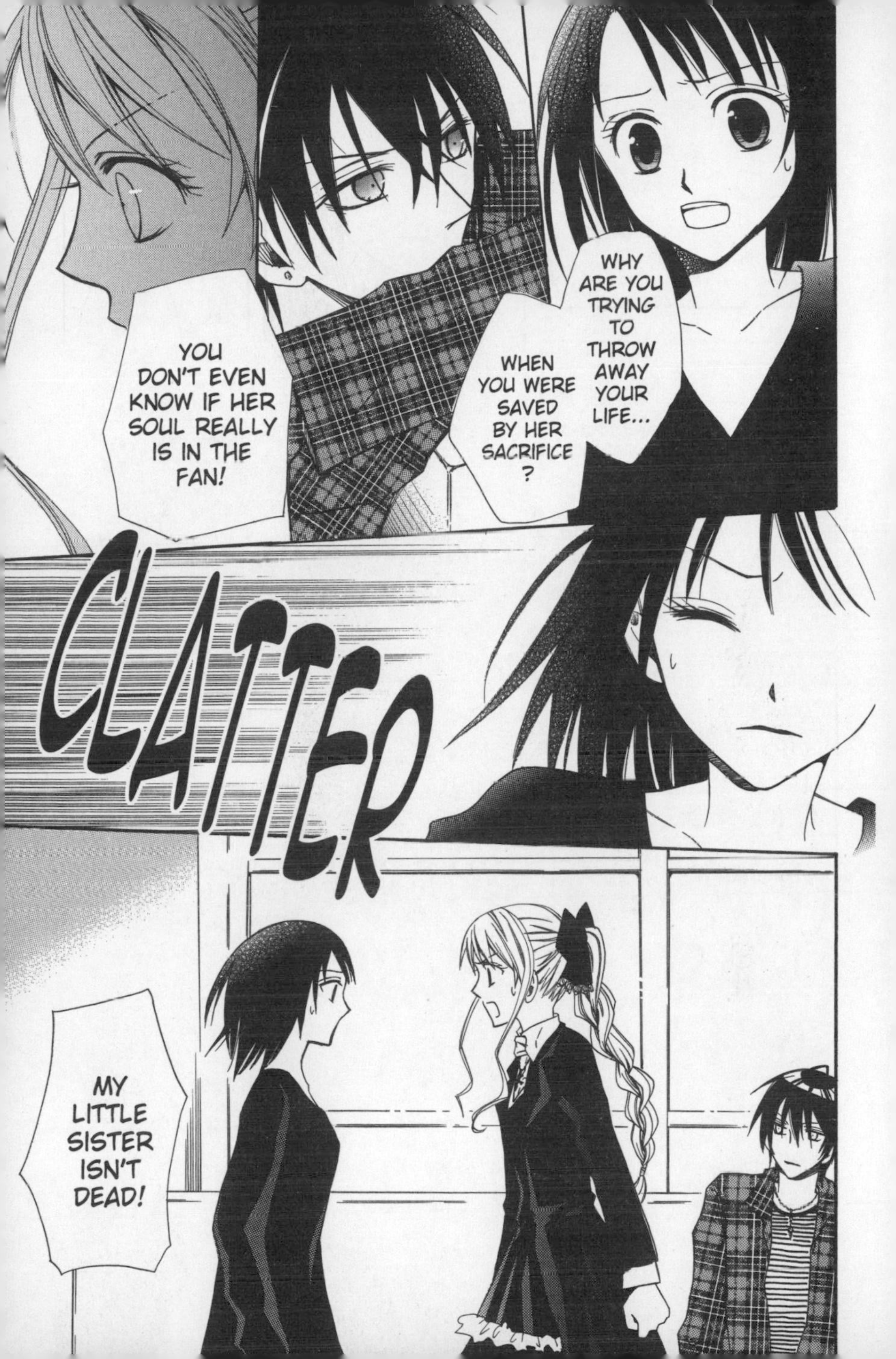
WHY ARE YOU TRYING TO THROW AWAY YOUR LIFE...
WHEN YOU WERE SAVED BY HER SACRIFICE?
YOU DON'T EVEN KNOW IF HER SOUL REALLY IS IN THE FAN!
CLATTER
MY LITTLE SISTER ISN'T DEAD!

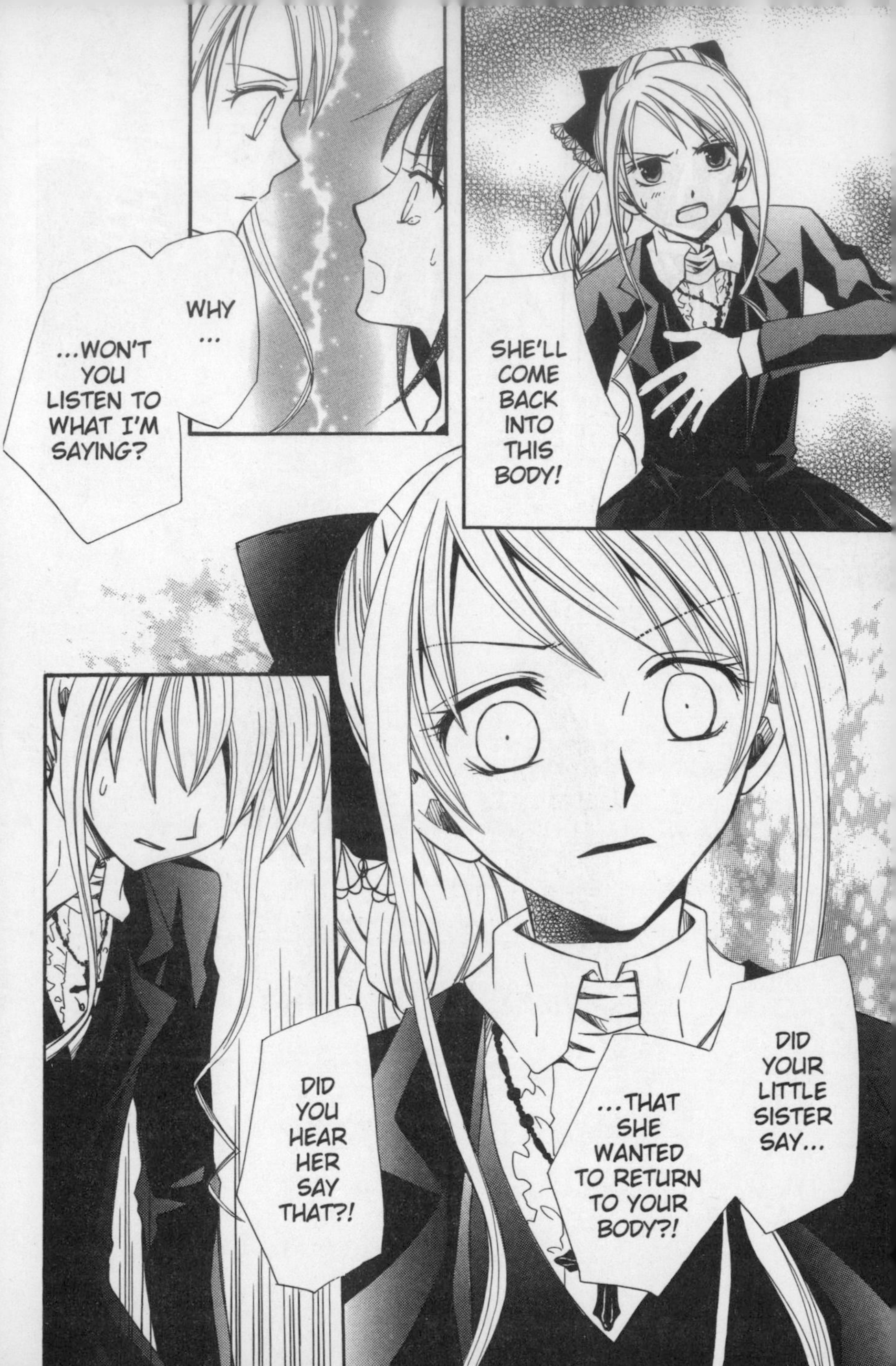
SHE'LL COME BACK INTO THIS BODY!
WHY ...
...WON'T YOU LISTEN TO WHAT I'M SAYING?
DID YOUR LITTLE SISTER SAY...
...THAT SHE WANTED TO RETURN TO YOUR BODY?!
DID YOU HEAR HER SAY THAT?!

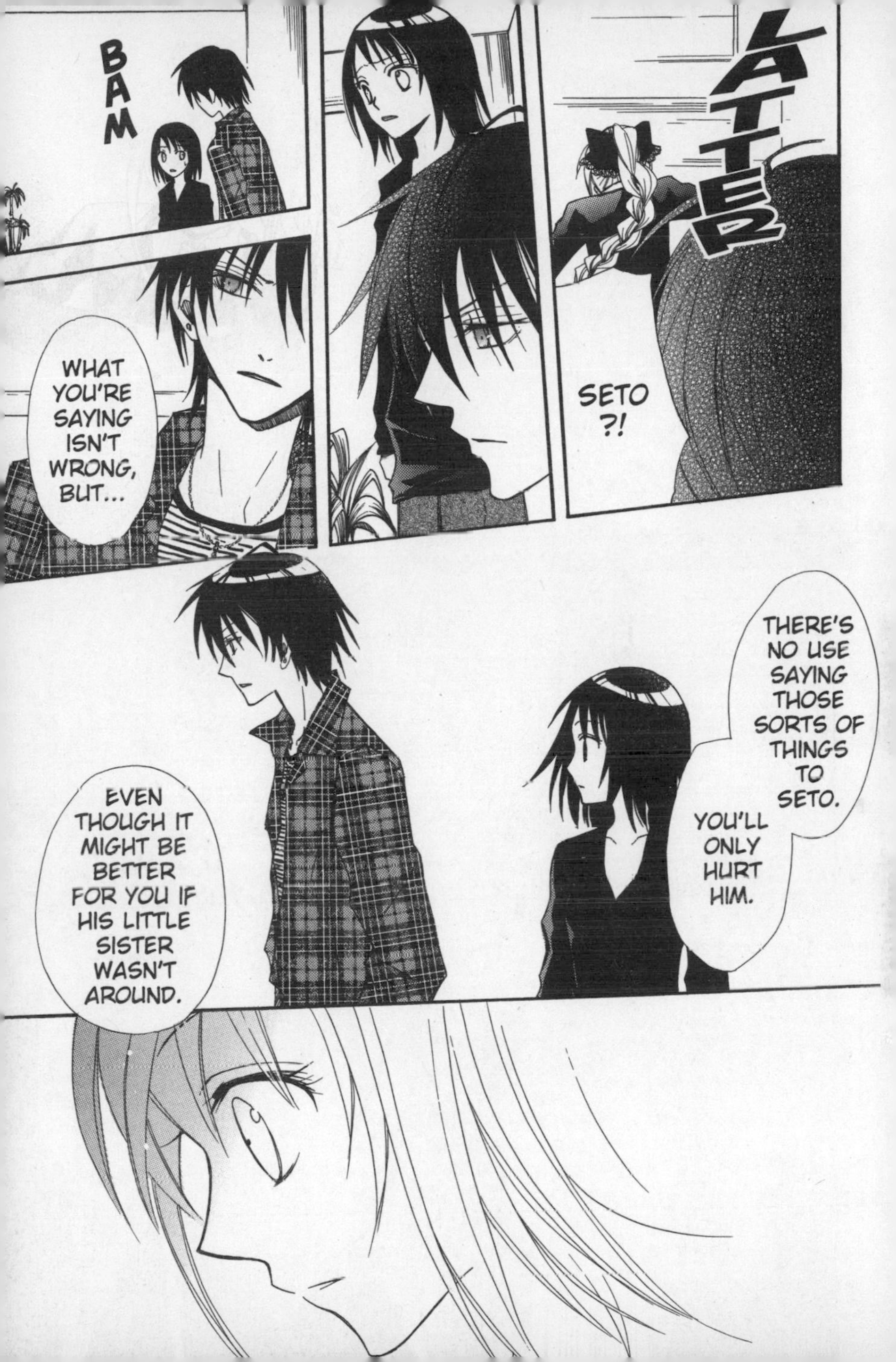
LATER
SETO ?!
BAM
WHAT YOU'RE SAYING ISN'T WRONG, BUT...
THERE'S NO USE SAYING THOSE SORTS OF THINGS TO SETO.
YOU'LL ONLY HURT HIM.
EVEN THOUGH IT MIGHT BE BETTER FOR YOU IF HIS LITTLE SISTER WASN'T AROUND.

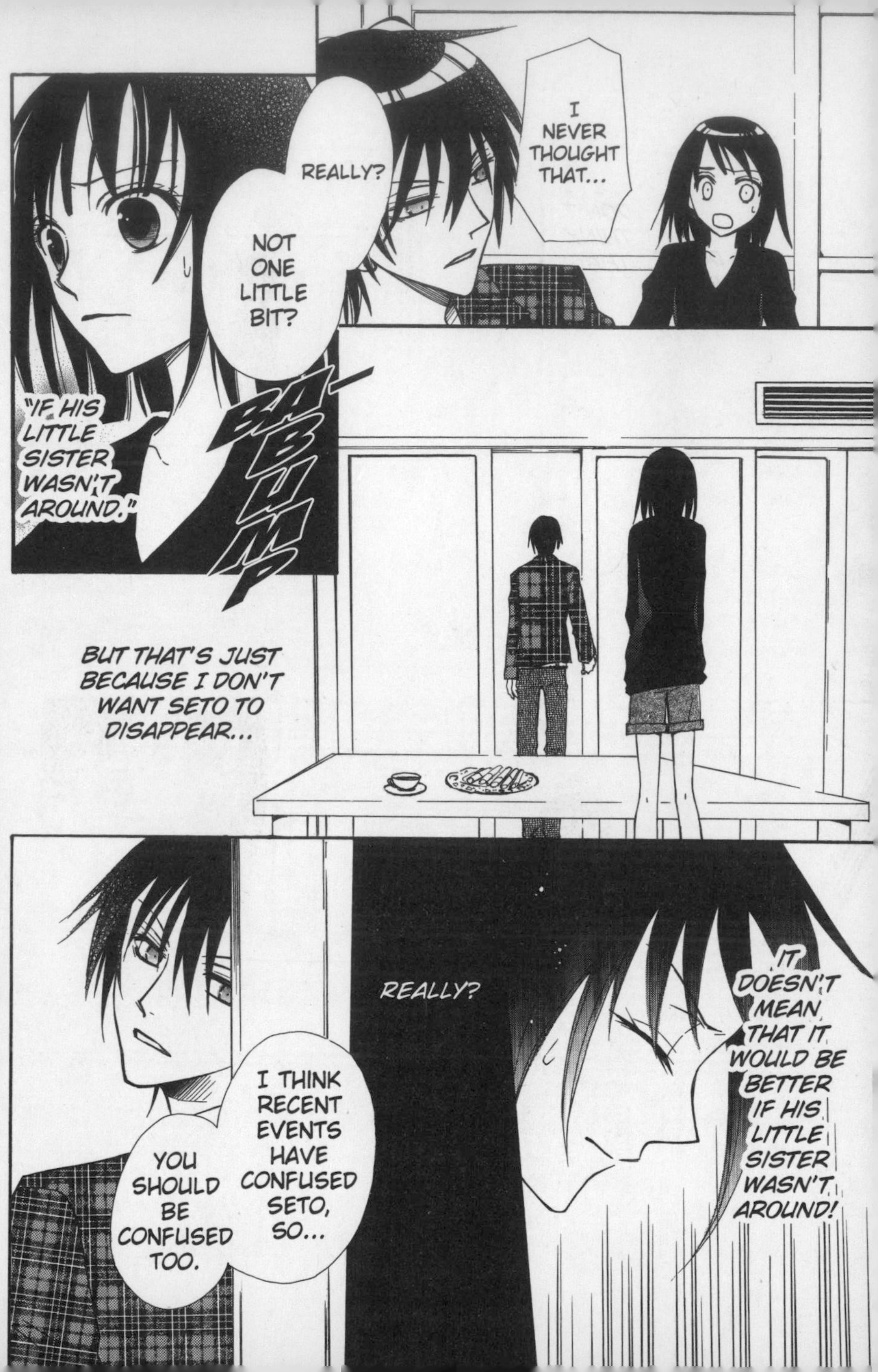

I NEVER THOUGHT THAT...
REALLY?
NOT ONE LITTLE BIT?
"IF HIS LITTLE SISTER WASN'T AROUND."
BA-BUMP
BUT THAT'S JUST BECAUSE I DON'T WANT SETO TO DISAPPEAR...
IT DOESN'T MEAN THAT IT WOULD BE BETTER IF HIS LITTLE SISTER WASN'T AROUND!
REALLY?
I THINK RECENT EVENTS HAVE CONFUSED SETO, SO...
YOU SHOULD BE CONFUSED TOO.

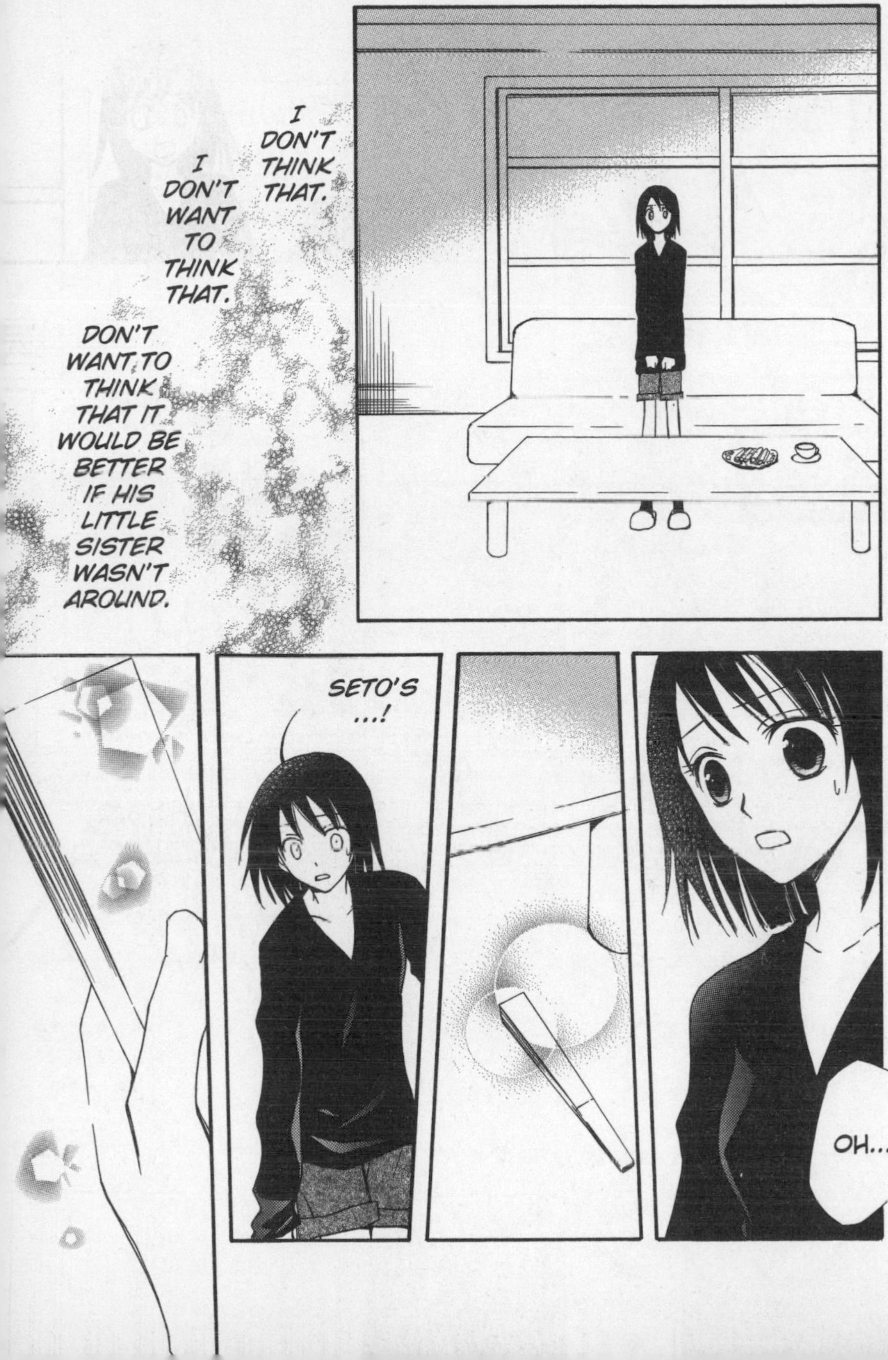
I DON'T THINK THAT.
I DON'T WANT TO THINK THAT.
DON'T WANT TO THINK THAT IT WOULD BE BETTER IF HIS LITTLE SISTER WASN'T AROUND.
OH...
SETO'S ...!

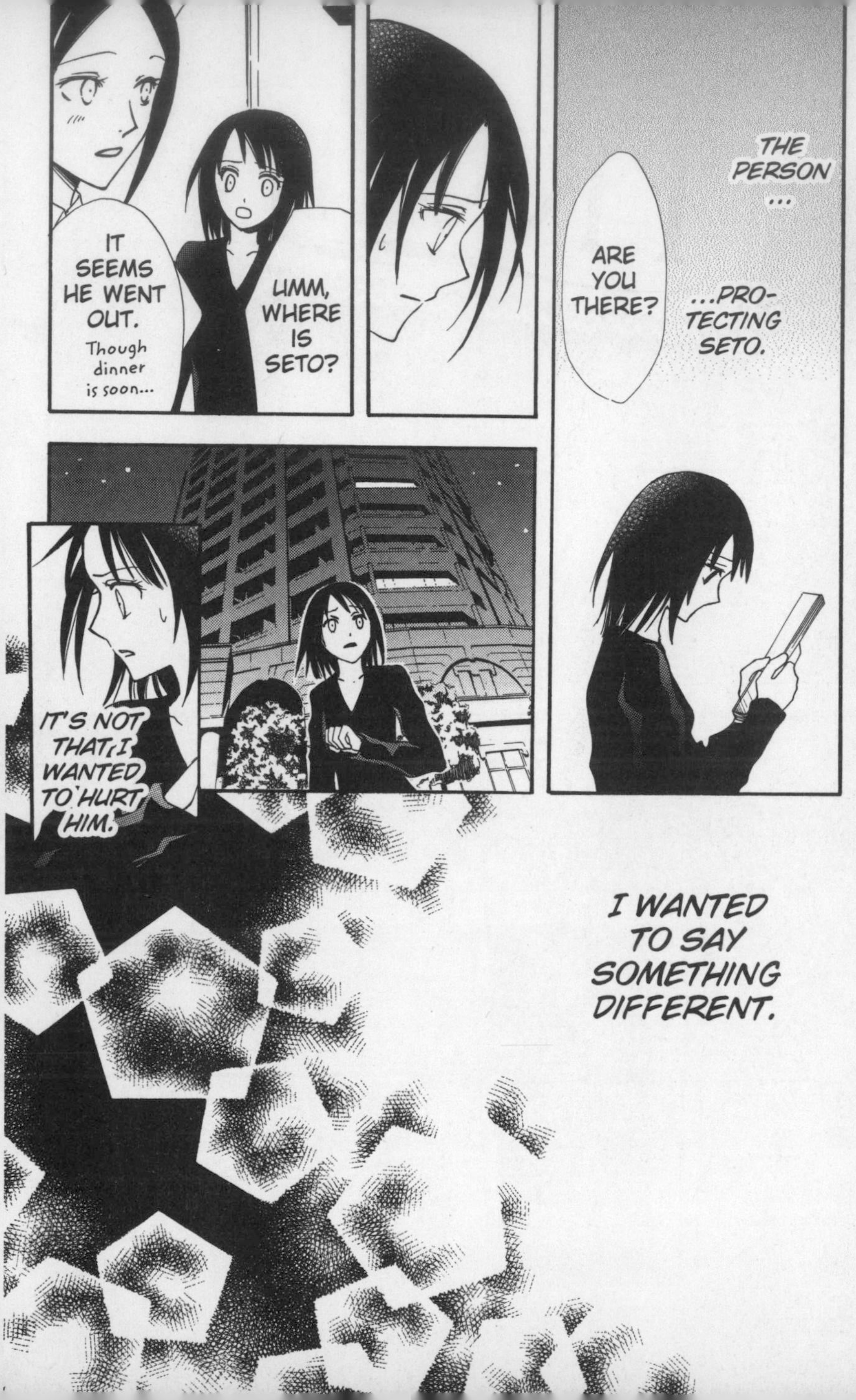
THE PERSON...
ARE YOU THERE?
...PROTECTING SETO.
UMM, WHERE IS SETO?
IT SEEMS HE WENT OUT.
Though dinner is soon...
IT'S NOT THAT I WANTED TO HURT HIM.
I WANTED TO SAY SOMETHING DIFFERENT.

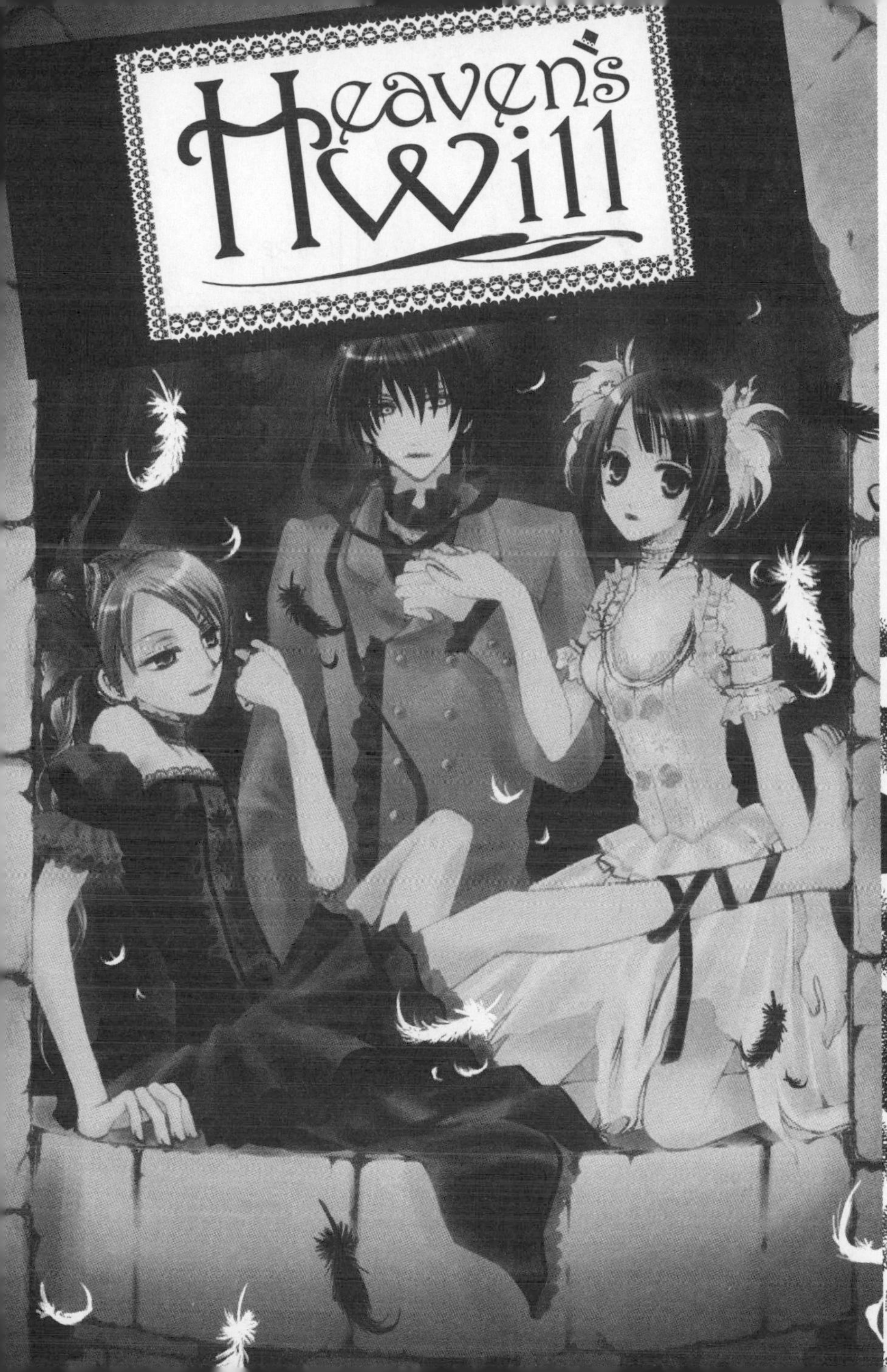
Heaven's
Will

HELLO. THIS IS SATORU TAKAMIYA.
THIS IS MY FIRST COMIC IN A WHILE.

WHILE I WAS GONE I DID A VARIETY OF THINGS,
LIKE MOVING FROM *CHAO* MAGAZINE TO *CHU CHU*.

I WROTE *HEAVEN'S WILL* WHILE IN A STATE OF
CONFUSION. I WAS WORRIED ABOUT THE ART BEING
MAINLY BLACK AND WHITE...THAT WOULD MAKE IT
PLAIN! AND IF I PUT DOWN TONES, WOULD THAT MAKE
THE ART TOO BUSY? ALSO, I DIDN'T WANT MY SCRIPT
TO REFLECT HOW CONFUSED I WAS AROUND APRIL (IT'S
JUNE NOW). CONSEQUENTLY I DID A LOT OF RE-DRAWING.
BUT WHEN JUNE ROLLED AROUND, I REALIZED THAT I
WASN'T ONE HUNDRED PERCENT HAPPY WITH MY SCRIPT
EITHER. SO I THOUGHT, "NEVER MIND! IT'LL JUST BE AN UGLY
LOOKING RECORD OF MY ARTISTIC GROWTH." HYAAA! I DECIDED
TO SEND IT TO MY EDITOR ANYWAY.

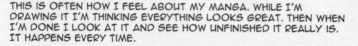

THIS IS OFTEN HOW I FEEL ABOUT MY MANGA. WHILE I'M
DRAWING IT I'M THINKING EVERYTHING LOOKS GREAT. THEN WHEN
I'M DONE I LOOK AT IT AND SEE HOW UNFINISHED IT REALLY IS.
IT HAPPENS EVERY TIME.

FOR SOME REASON THESE ARTISTIC DOUBTS CREEP INTO MY
HEAD WHEN I'M ASKED TO WRITE THESE EPILOGUE-LIKE THINGS.
I ALWAYS WONDER IF I SHOULD SHARE THEM WITH MY READERS
OR NOT. BUT, AS YOU CAN SEE, I CAN'T HELP IT!

SO, FINALLY, I'LL BRING THIS TO AN END.
A SINCERE THANK YOU TO EVERYONE WHO READS THIS MANGA.
UNFORTUNATELY IT ENDED WITHOUT ME BEING ABLE TO EVEN DO
HALF OF WHAT I HAD PLANNED. SETO AND MIKUZU NEVER FELL IN LOVE,
SO IT'S A BRILLIANTLY INCOMPLETE STORY. BUT STILL...I'M GLAD I HAD
A CHANCE TO WRITE IT.

WHEN I WROTE THE SHORT STORY "THE HEAVEN TO
WHICH YOU WILL SOMEDAY RETURN," I DIDN'T THINK
I'D BE ALLOWED TO WRITE A WHOLE VOLUME.

THANK YOU!

PLEASE SEND LETTERS WITH YOUR COMMENTS HERE.

Satoru Takamiya
c/o VIZ Media
P.O. Box 77064
San Francisco,
CA 94107

I'M SLOW, BUT I WILL
TRY TO REPLY TO
EVERY LETTER. WELL
THEN, LATER!

Satoru Takamiya

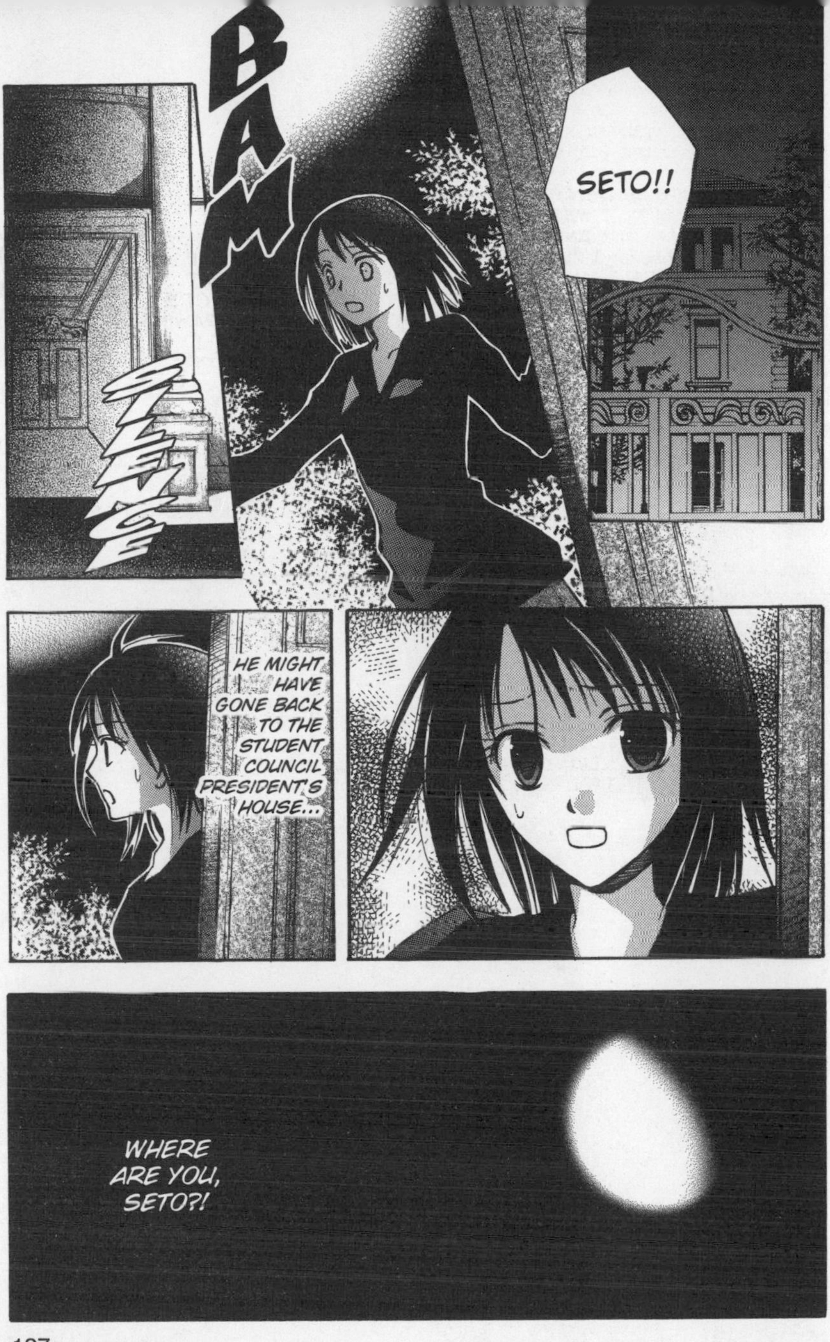
SETO!!
BAM
SILENCE
HE MIGHT HAVE GONE BACK TO THE STUDENT COUNCIL PRESIDENT'S HOUSE...
WHERE ARE YOU, SETO?!

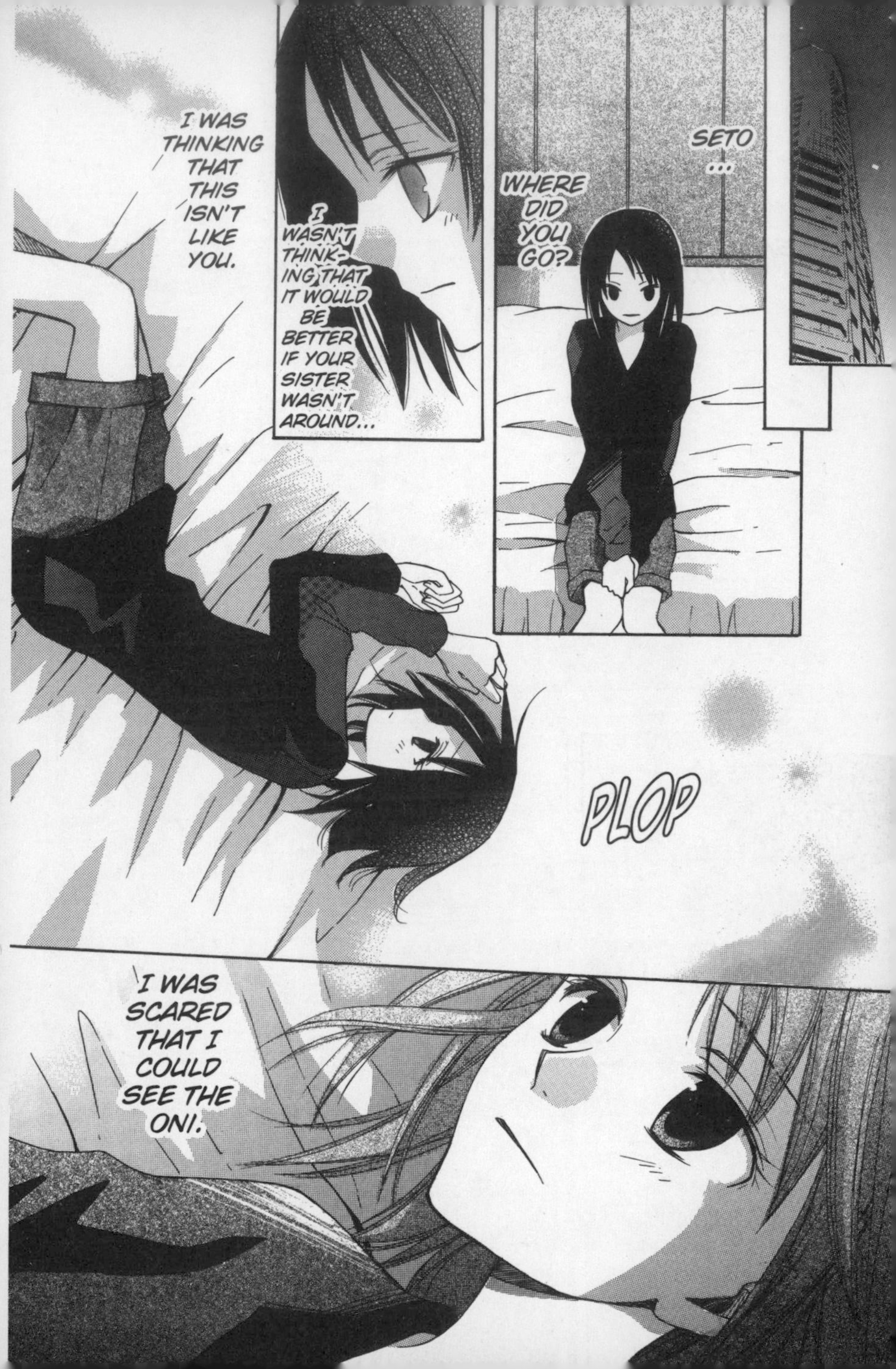
SETO ...
WHERE DID YOU GO?
I WASN'T THINKING THAT IT WOULD BE BETTER IF YOUR SISTER WASN'T AROUND...
I WAS THINKING THAT THIS ISN'T LIKE YOU.
PLOP
I WAS SCARED THAT I COULD SEE THE ONI.

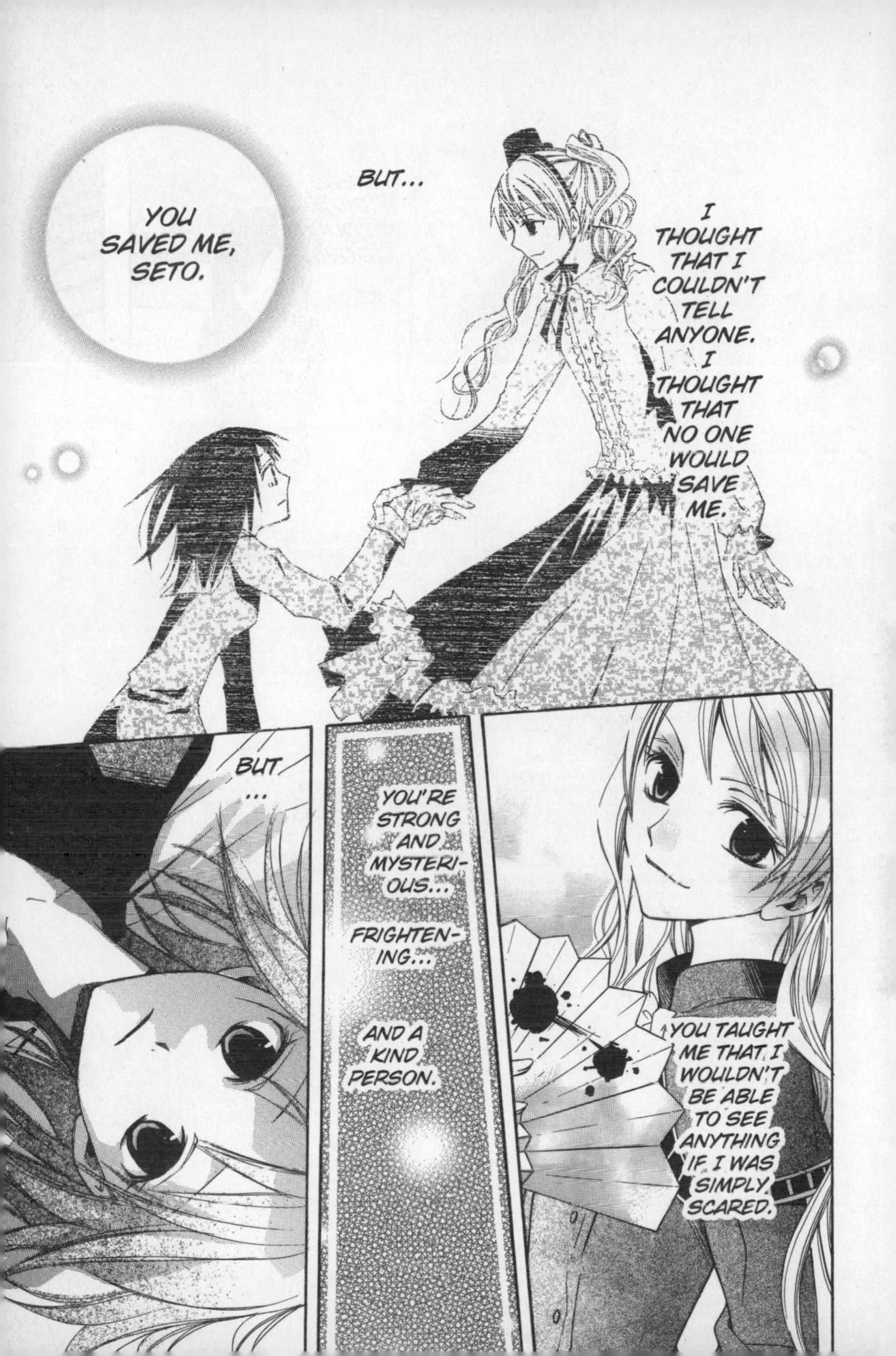
I THOUGHT THAT I COULDN'T TELL ANYONE.
I THOUGHT THAT NO ONE WOULD SAVE ME.
BUT...
YOU SAVED ME, SETO.
YOU TAUGHT ME THAT I WOULDN'T BE ABLE TO SEE ANYTHING IF I WAS SIMPLY SCARED.
YOU'RE STRONG AND MYSTERIOUS...
FRIGHTENING...
AND A KIND PERSON.
BUT ...

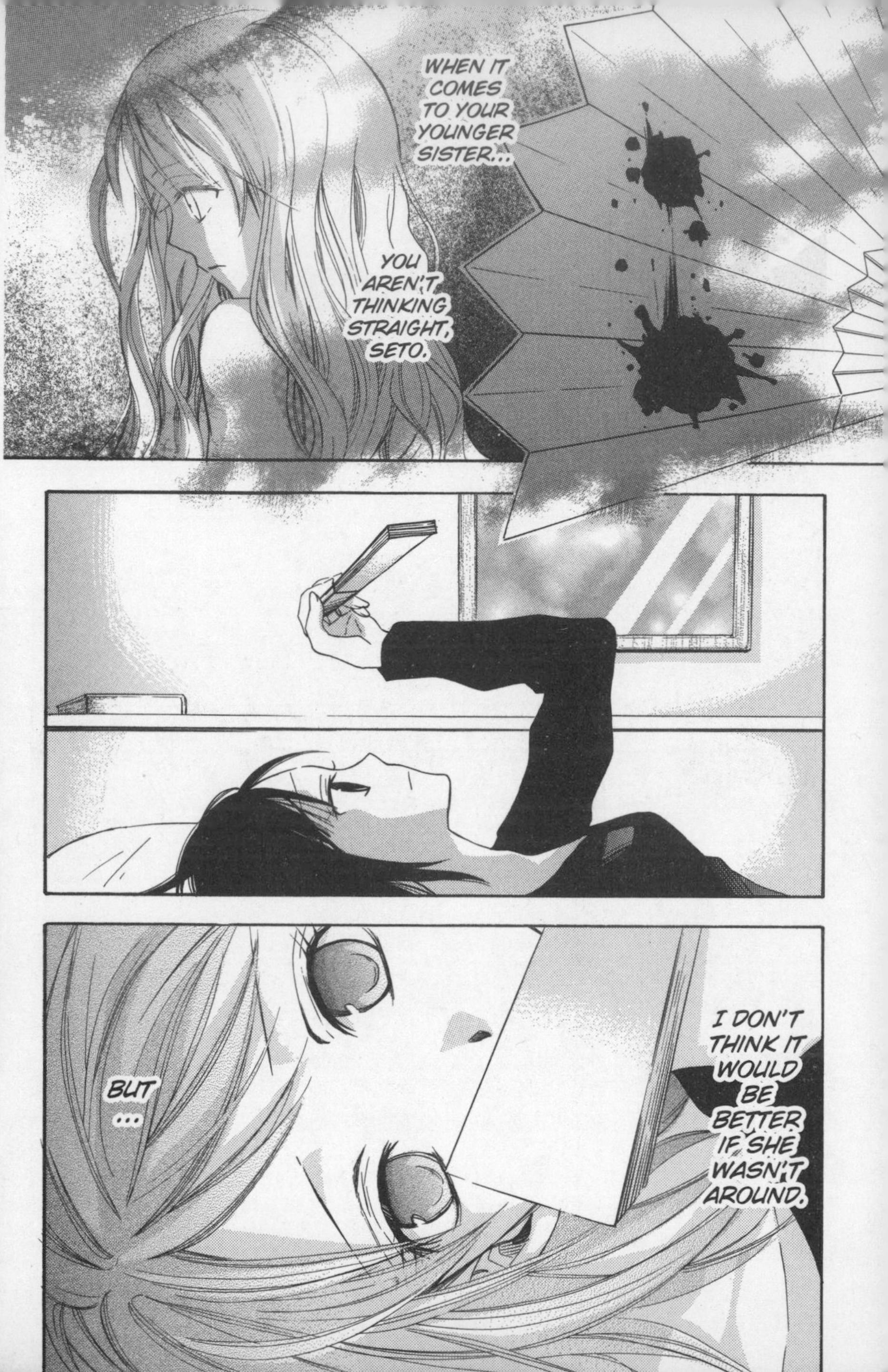
WHEN IT COMES TO YOUR YOUNGER SISTER...
YOU AREN'T THINKING STRAIGHT, SETO.
I DON'T THINK IT WOULD BE BETTER IF SHE WASN'T AROUND.
BUT ...

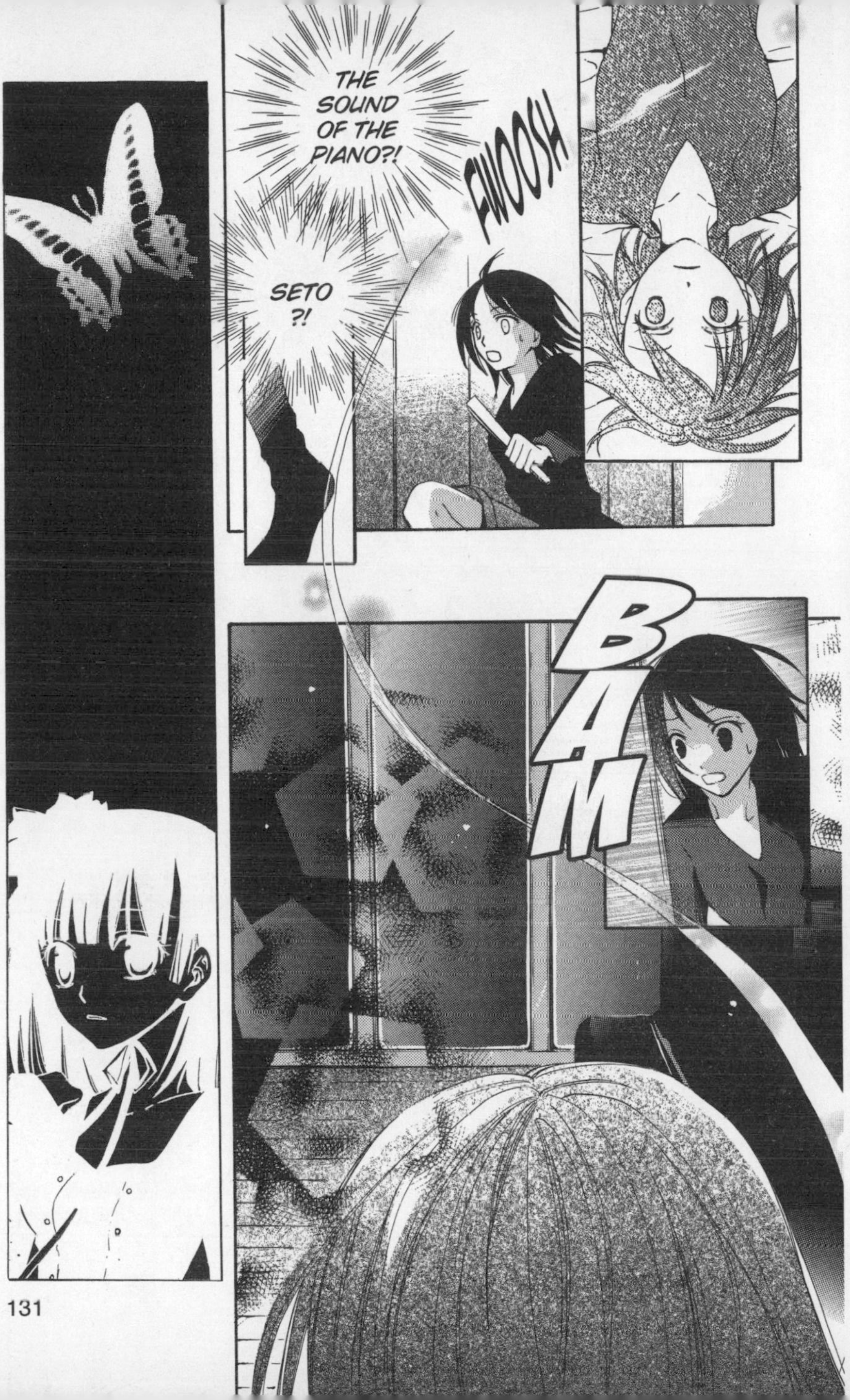
FWOOSH
THE SOUND OF THE PIANO?!
SETO ?!
BAM

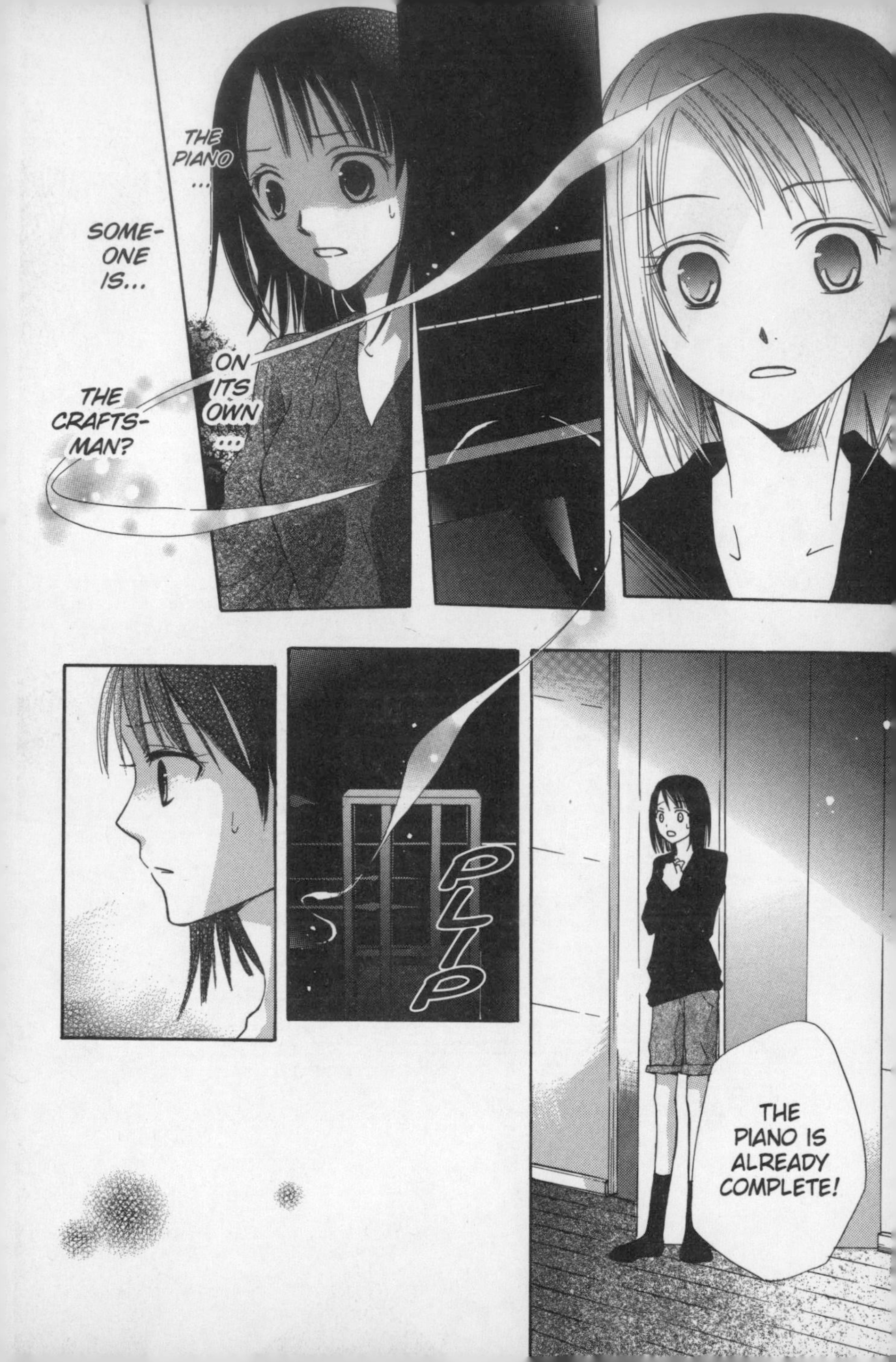
THE PIANO ...
SOME-ONE IS...
ON ITS OWN ...
THE CRAFTS-MAN?
THE PIANO IS ALREADY COMPLETE!
PLIP

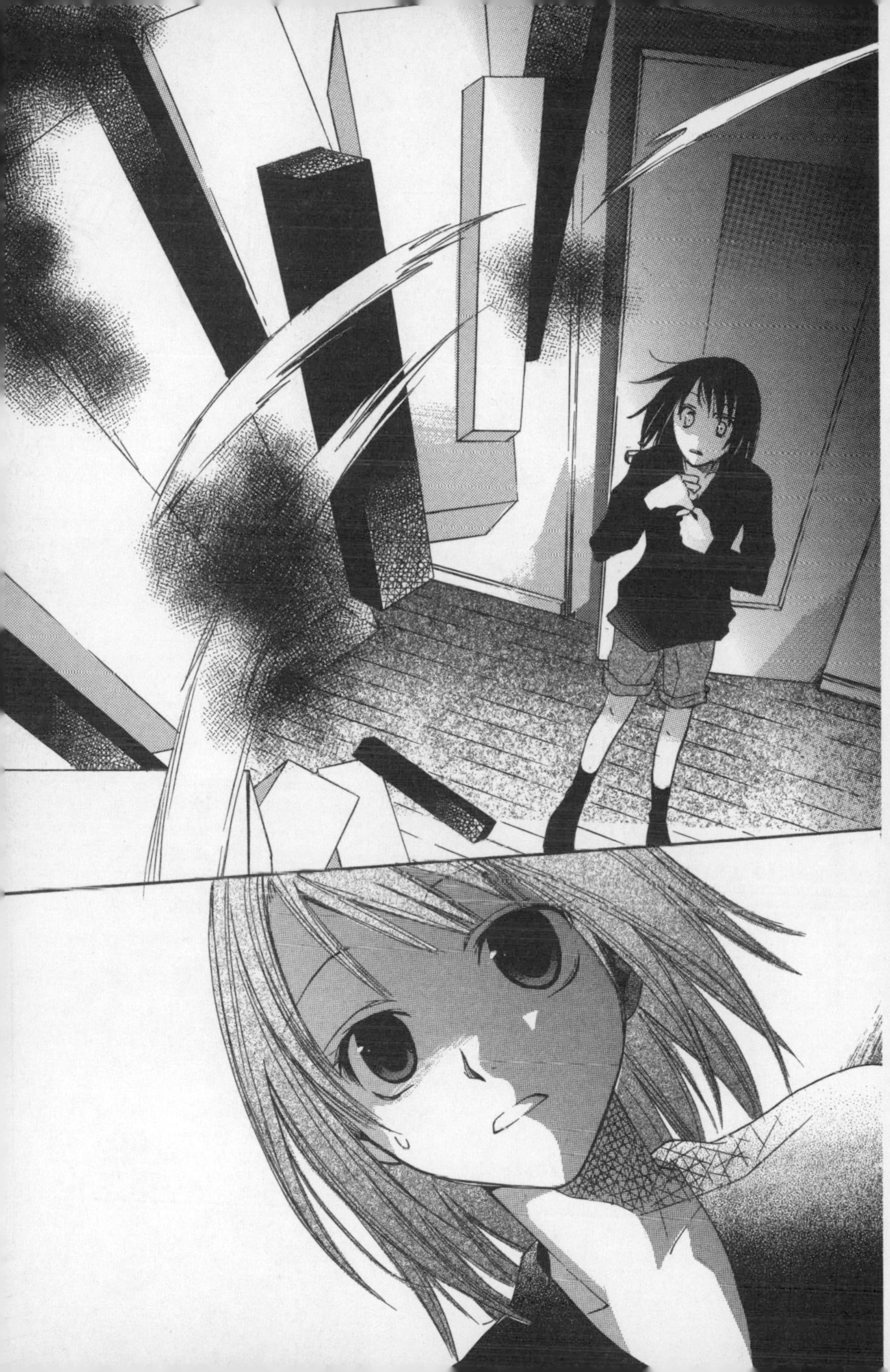

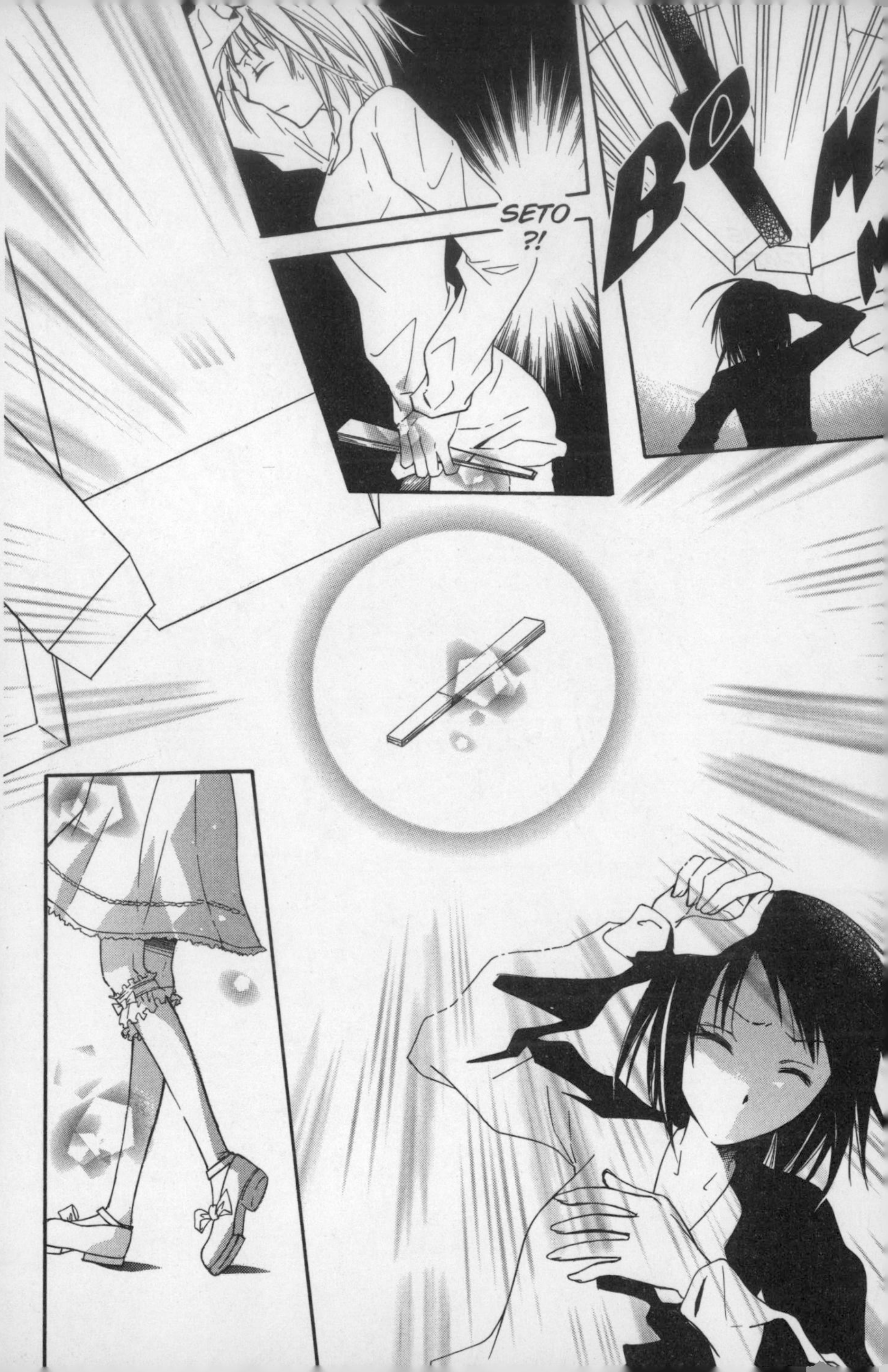
BOMM
SETO ?!

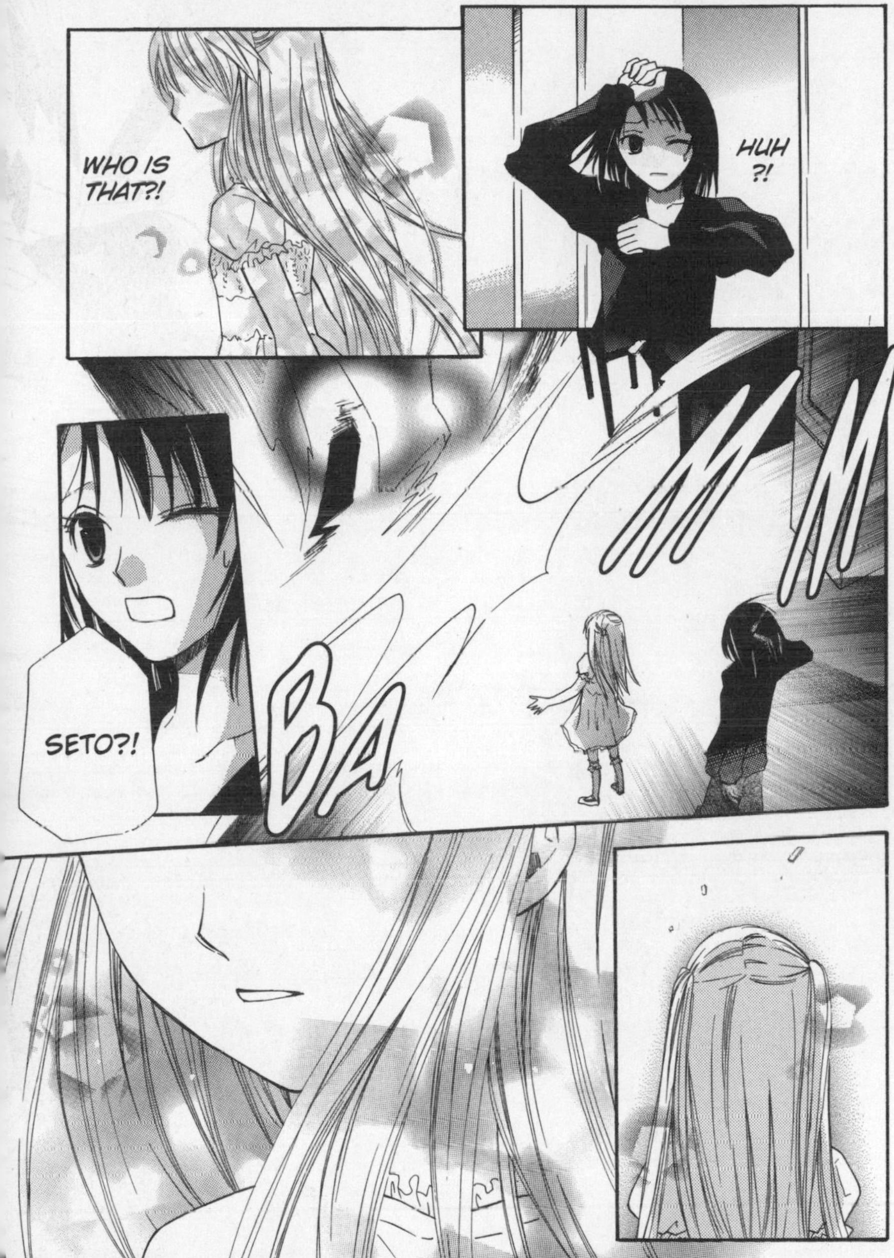
HUH?!
WHO IS THAT?!
BAMM
SETO?!

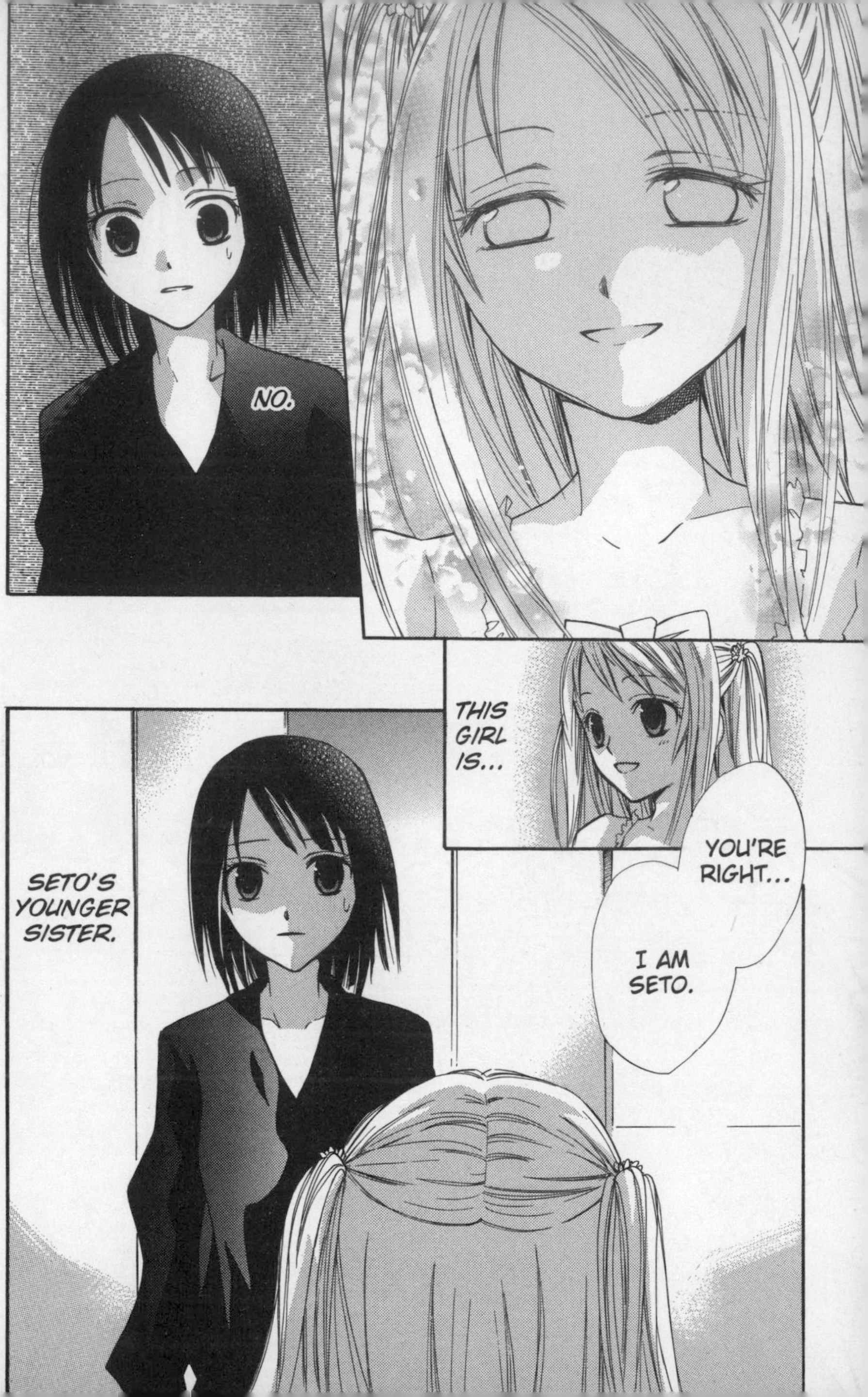
NO.
THIS GIRL IS...
YOU'RE RIGHT...
I AM SETO.
SETO'S YOUNGER SISTER.

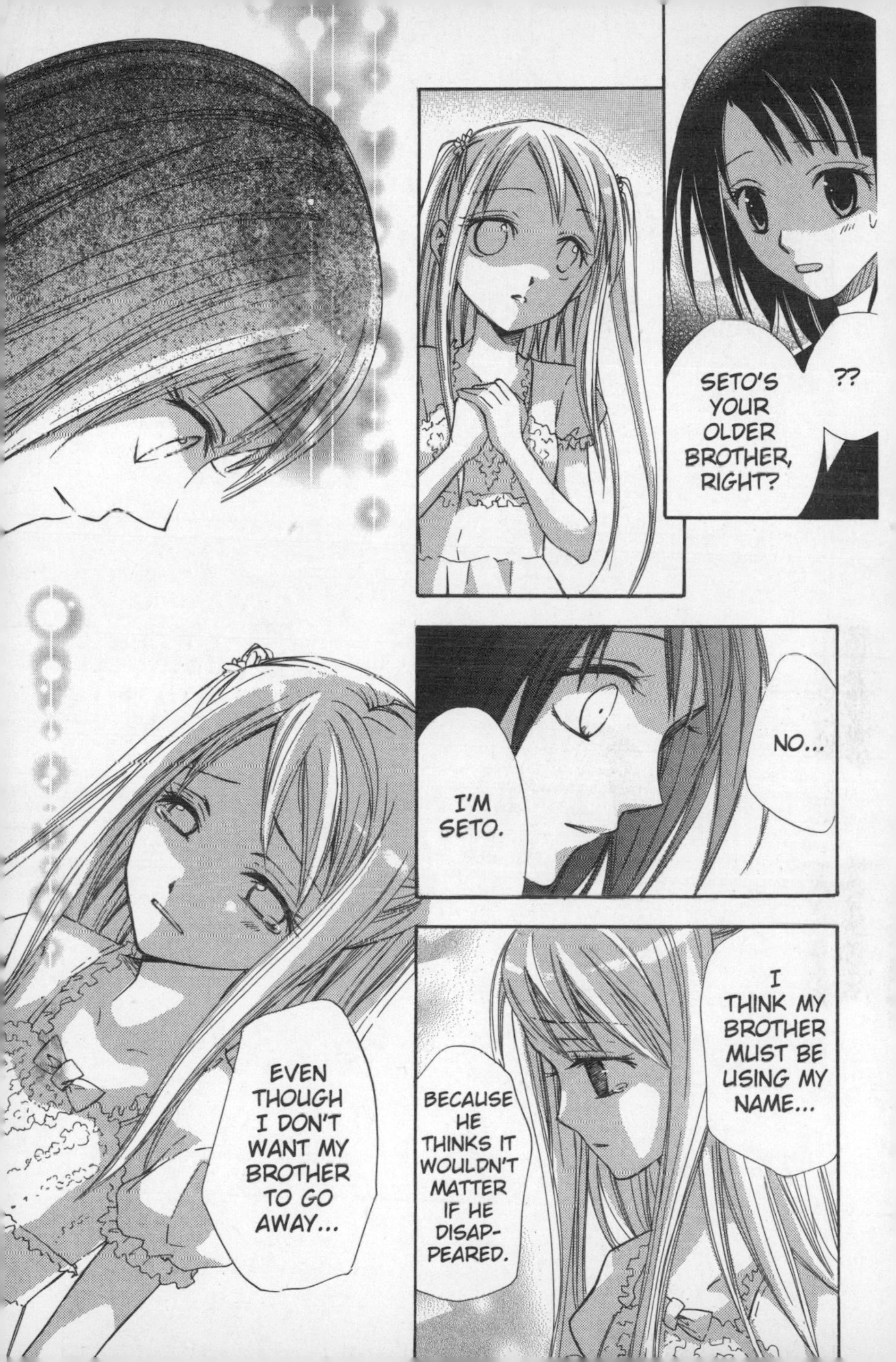
??
SETO'S YOUR OLDER BROTHER, RIGHT?
NO...
I'M SETO.
I THINK MY BROTHER MUST BE USING MY NAME...
BECAUSE HE THINKS IT WOULDN'T MATTER IF HE DISAPPEARED.
EVEN THOUGH I DON'T WANT MY BROTHER TO GO AWAY...

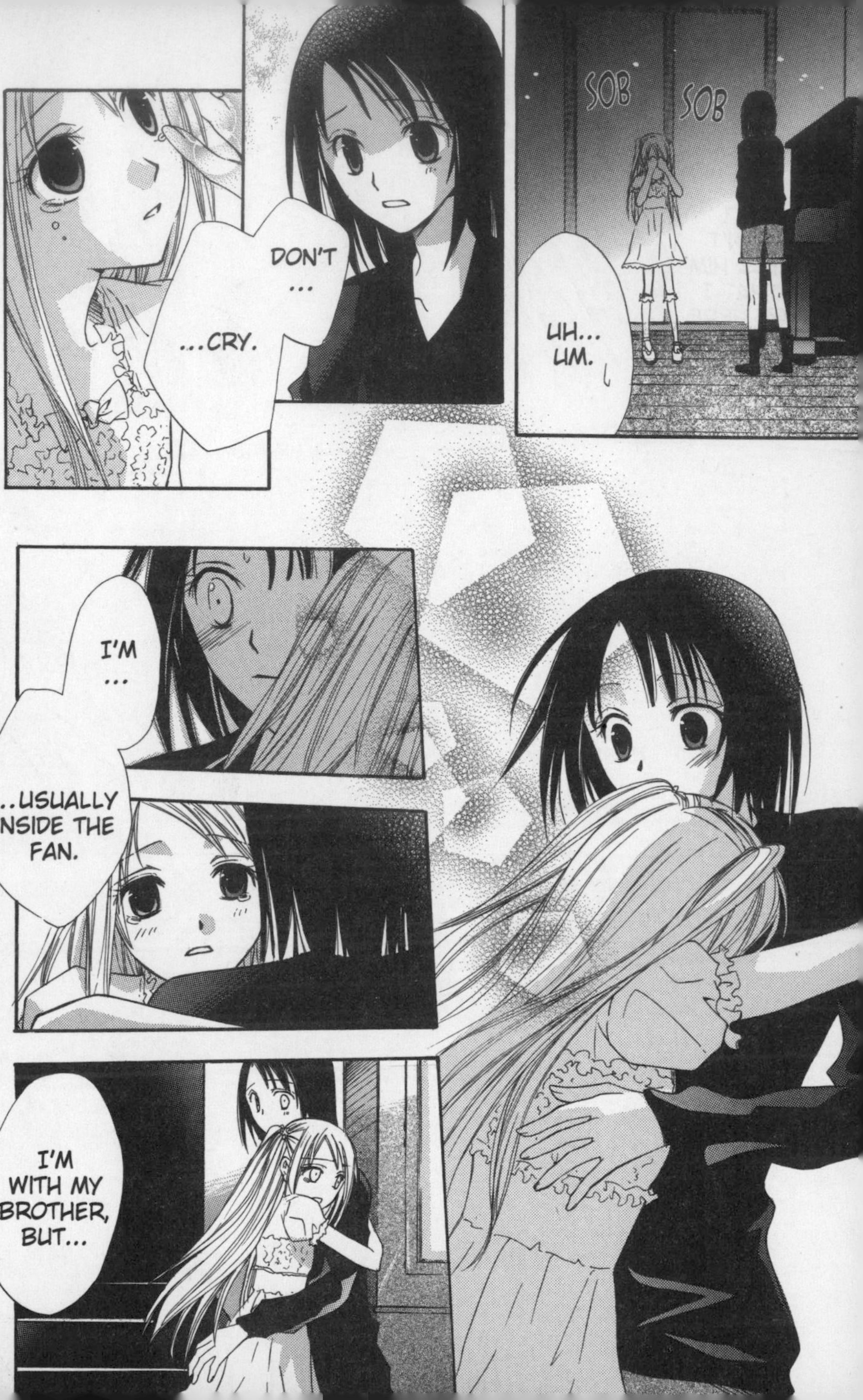
SOB
SOB
UH... UM.
DON'T ...
...CRY.
I'M ...
...USUALLY INSIDE THE FAN.
I'M WITH MY BROTHER, BUT...

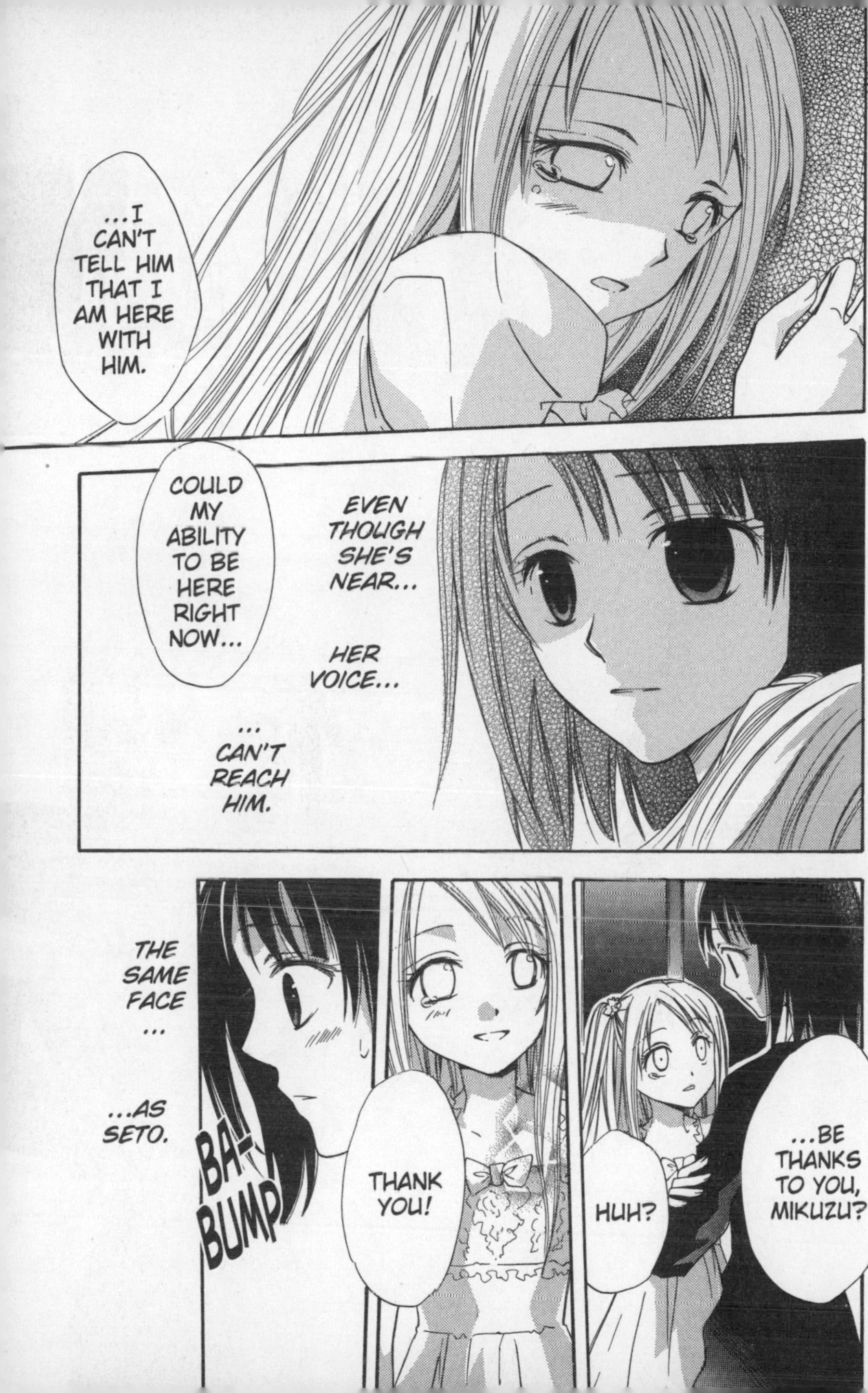
...I CAN'T TELL HIM THAT I AM HERE WITH HIM.
EVEN THOUGH SHE'S NEAR...
HER VOICE...
...CAN'T REACH HIM.
COULD MY ABILITY TO BE HERE RIGHT NOW...
...BE THANKS TO YOU, MIKUZU?
HUH?
THANK YOU!
BA-BUMP
THE SAME FACE ...
...AS SETO.

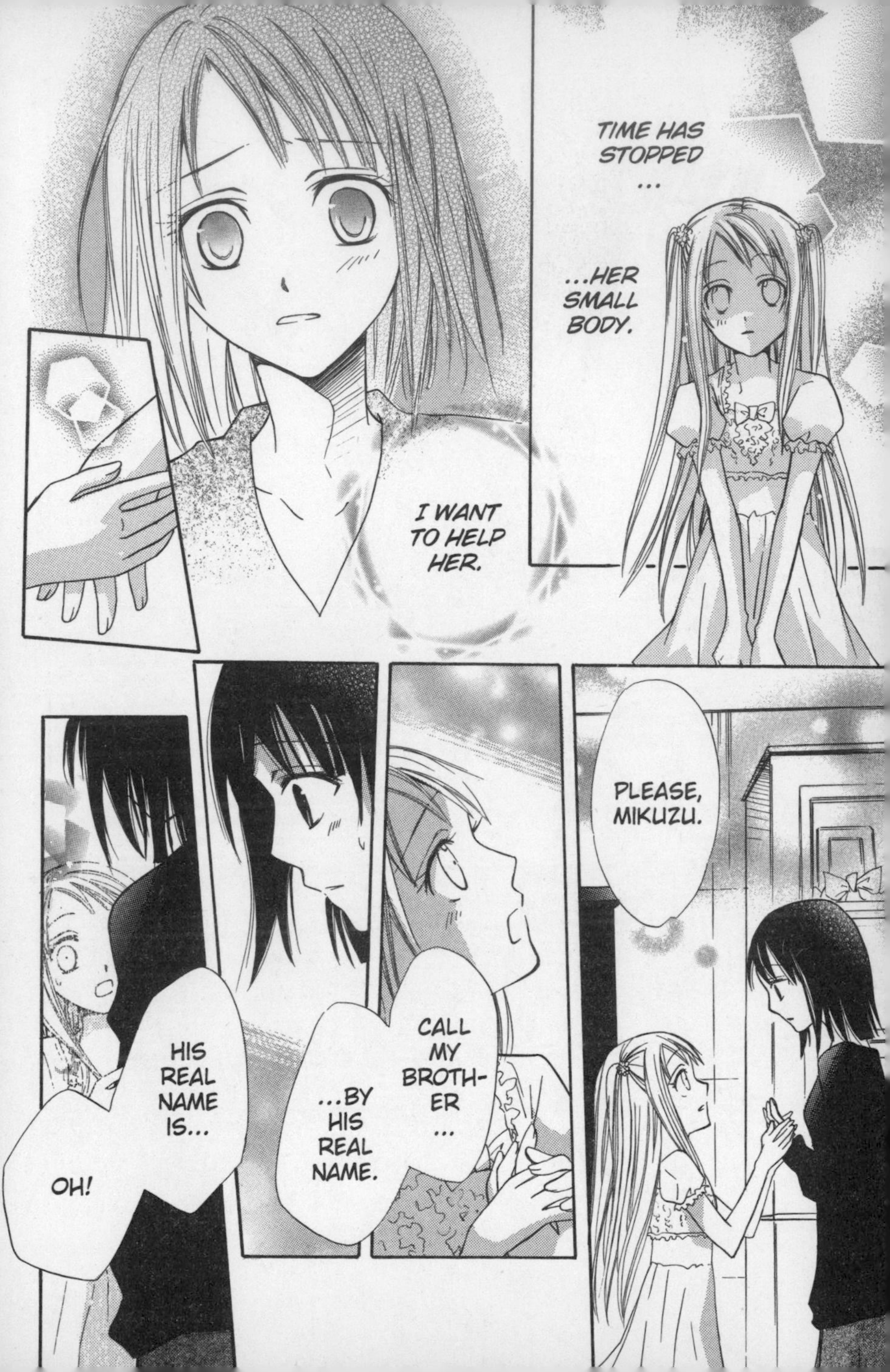
TIME HAS STOPPED ...
...HER SMALL BODY.
I WANT TO HELP HER.
PLEASE, MIKUZU.
CALL MY BROTH-ER ...
...BY HIS REAL NAME.
HIS REAL NAME IS...
OH!

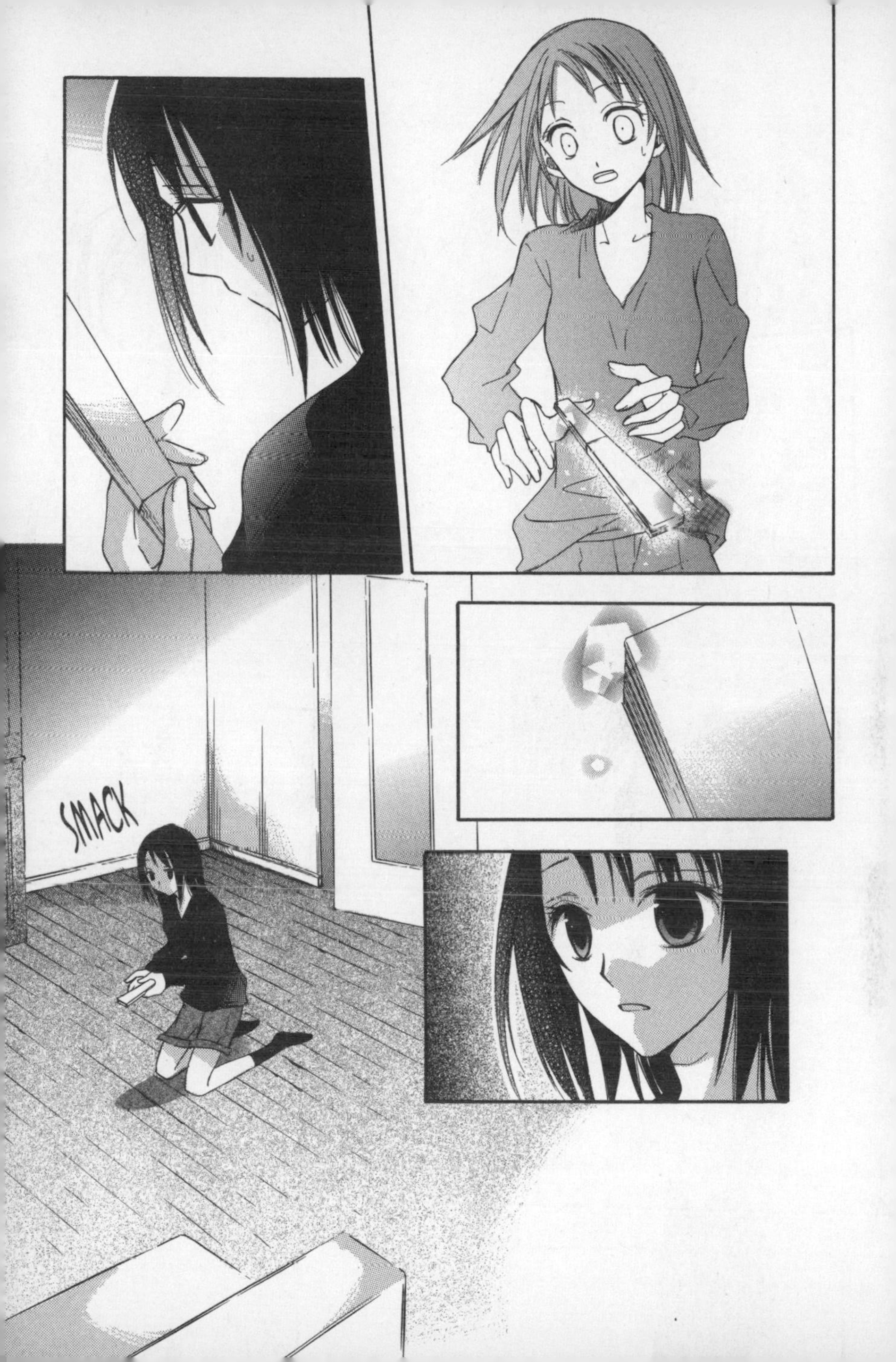
SMACK

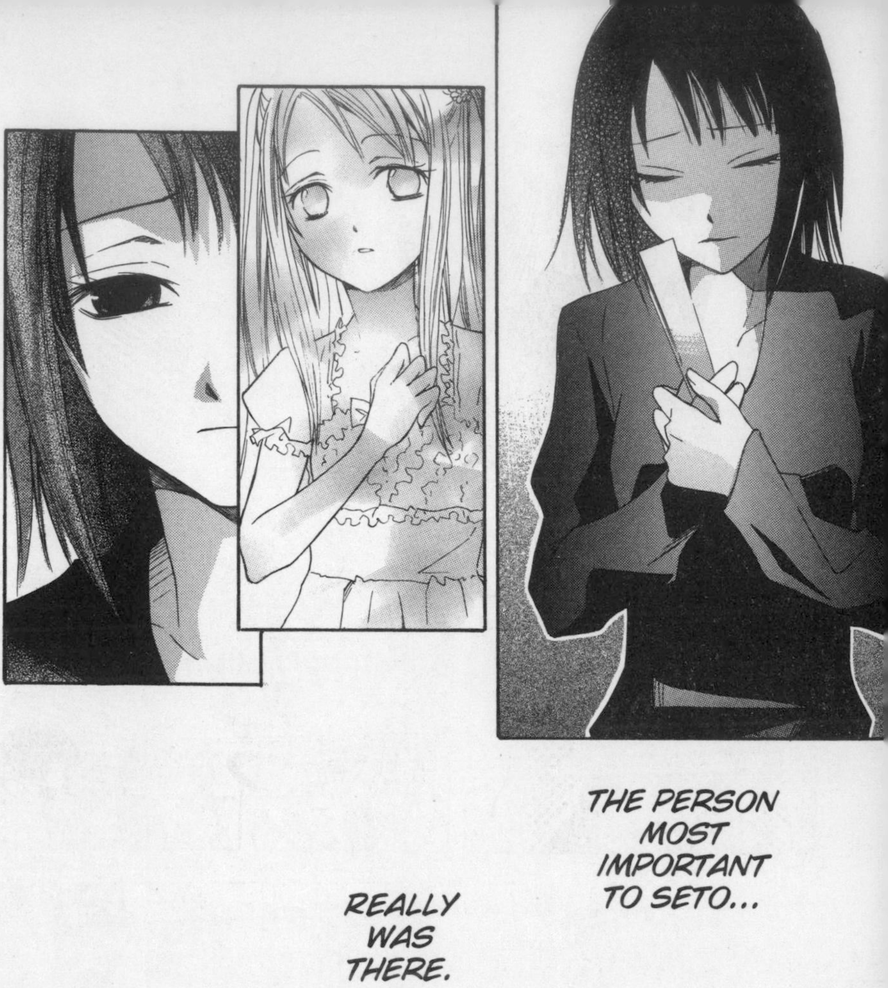
THE PERSON MOST IMPORTANT TO SETO...
REALLY WAS THERE.

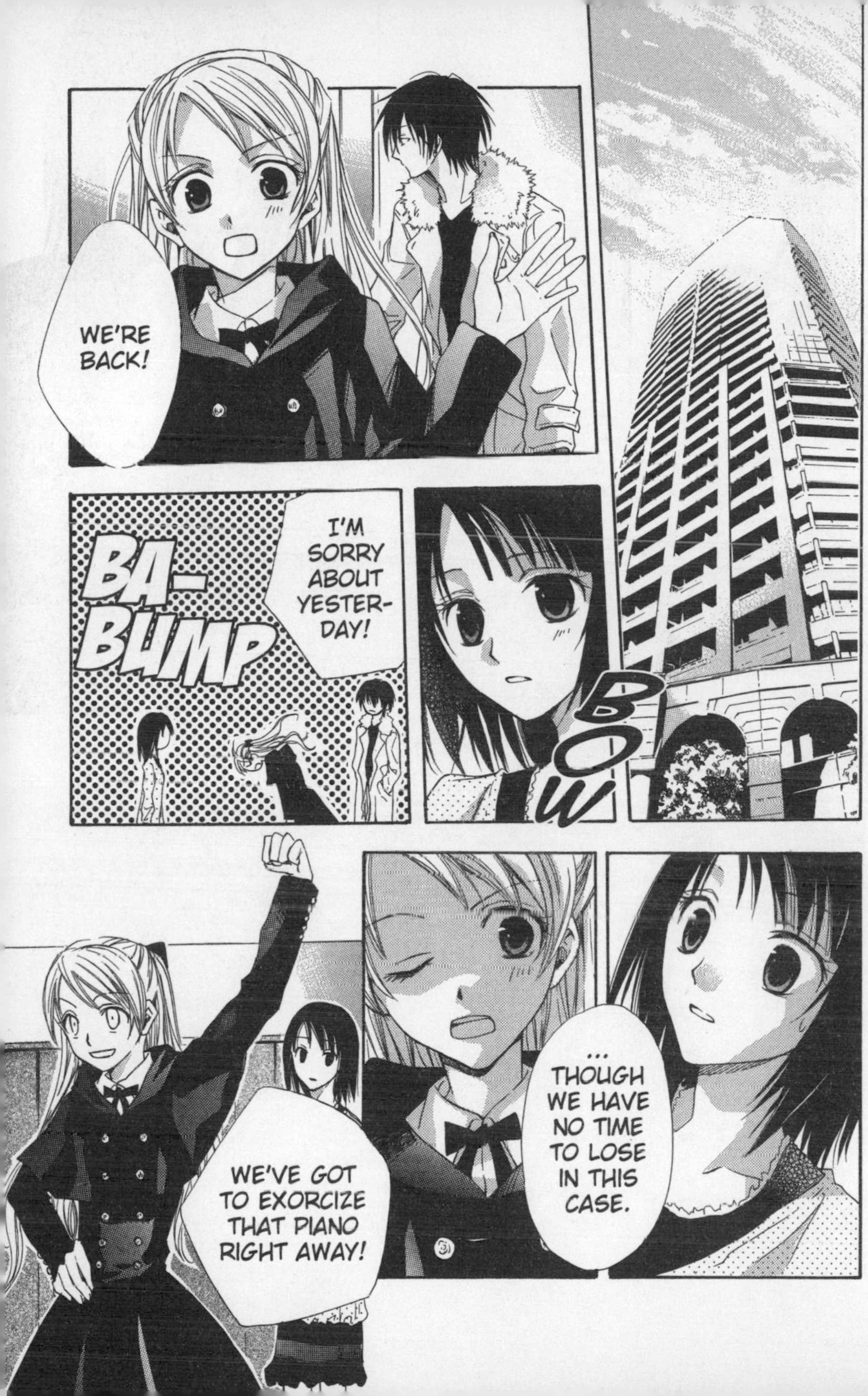
WE'RE BACK!
BOW
I'M SORRY ABOUT YESTER-DAY!
BA-BUMP
...THOUGH WE HAVE NO TIME TO LOSE IN THIS CASE.
WE'VE GOT TO EXORCIZE THAT PIANO RIGHT AWAY!

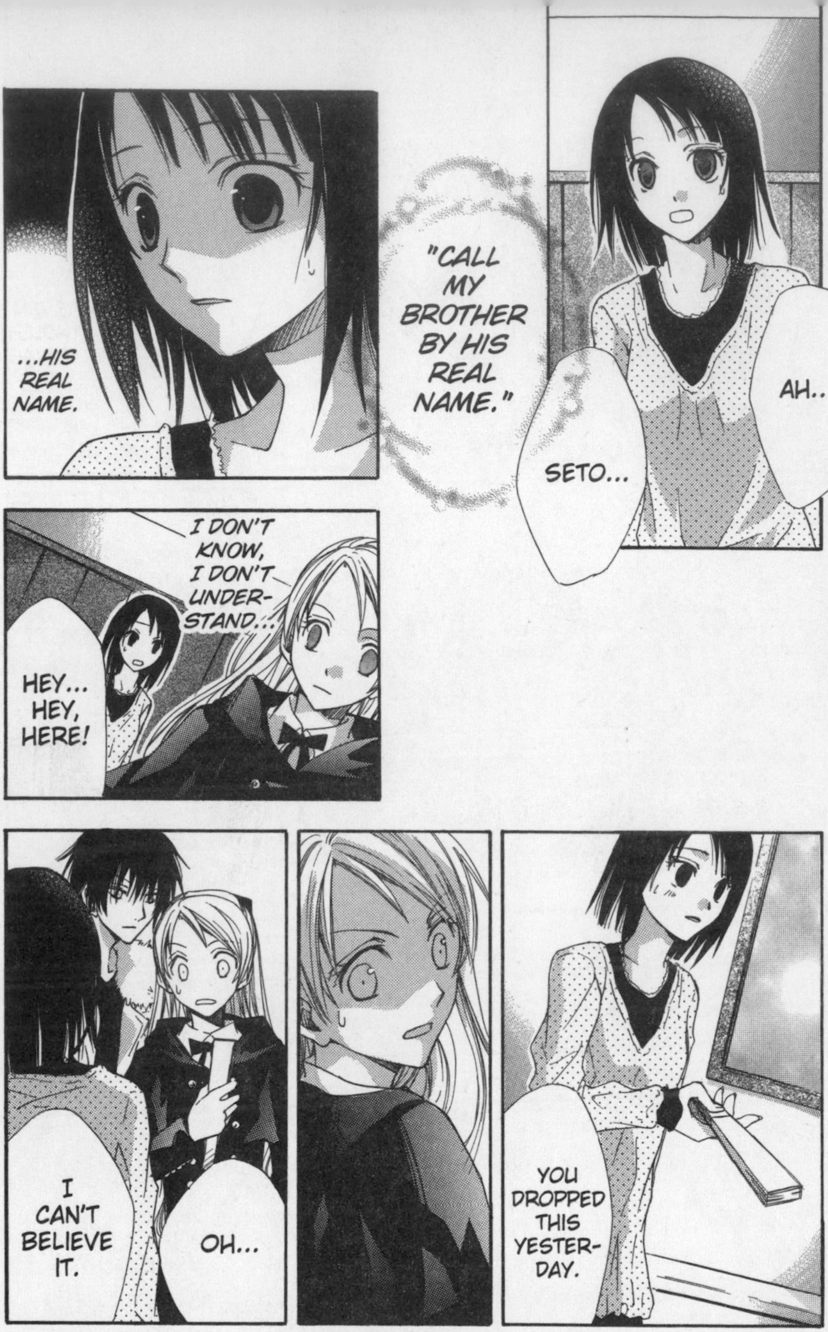
AH...
SETO...
"CALL MY BROTHER BY HIS REAL NAME."
...HIS REAL NAME.
I DON'T KNOW, I DON'T UNDERSTAND...
HEY... HEY, HERE!
YOU DROPPED THIS YESTERDAY.
OH...
I CAN'T BELIEVE IT.

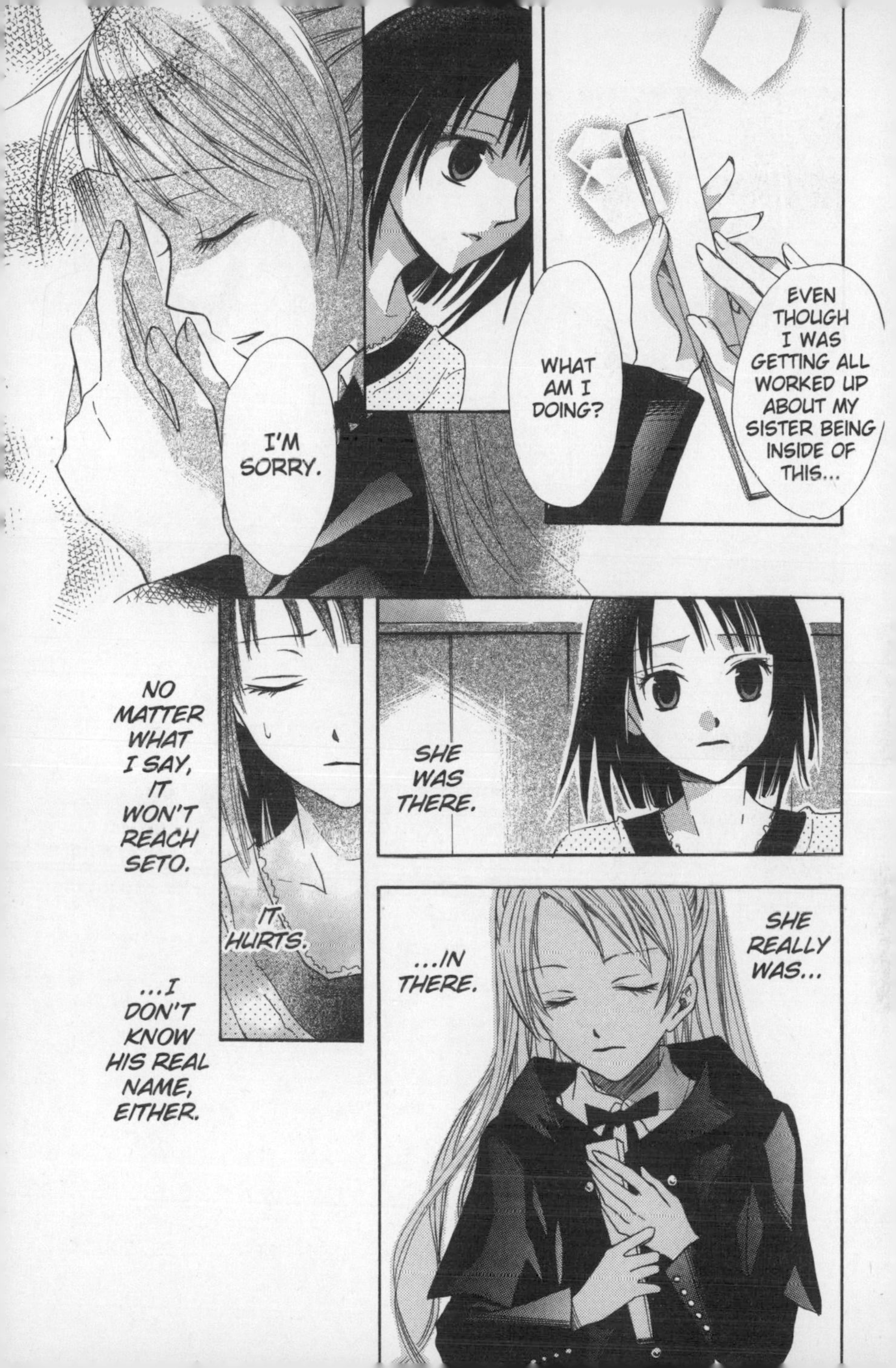
EVEN THOUGH I WAS GETTING ALL WORKED UP ABOUT MY SISTER BEING INSIDE OF THIS...
WHAT AM I DOING?
I'M SORRY.
SHE WAS THERE.
SHE REALLY WAS...
...IN THERE.
NO MATTER WHAT I SAY, IT WON'T REACH SETO.
IT HURTS.
...I DON'T KNOW HIS REAL NAME, EITHER.

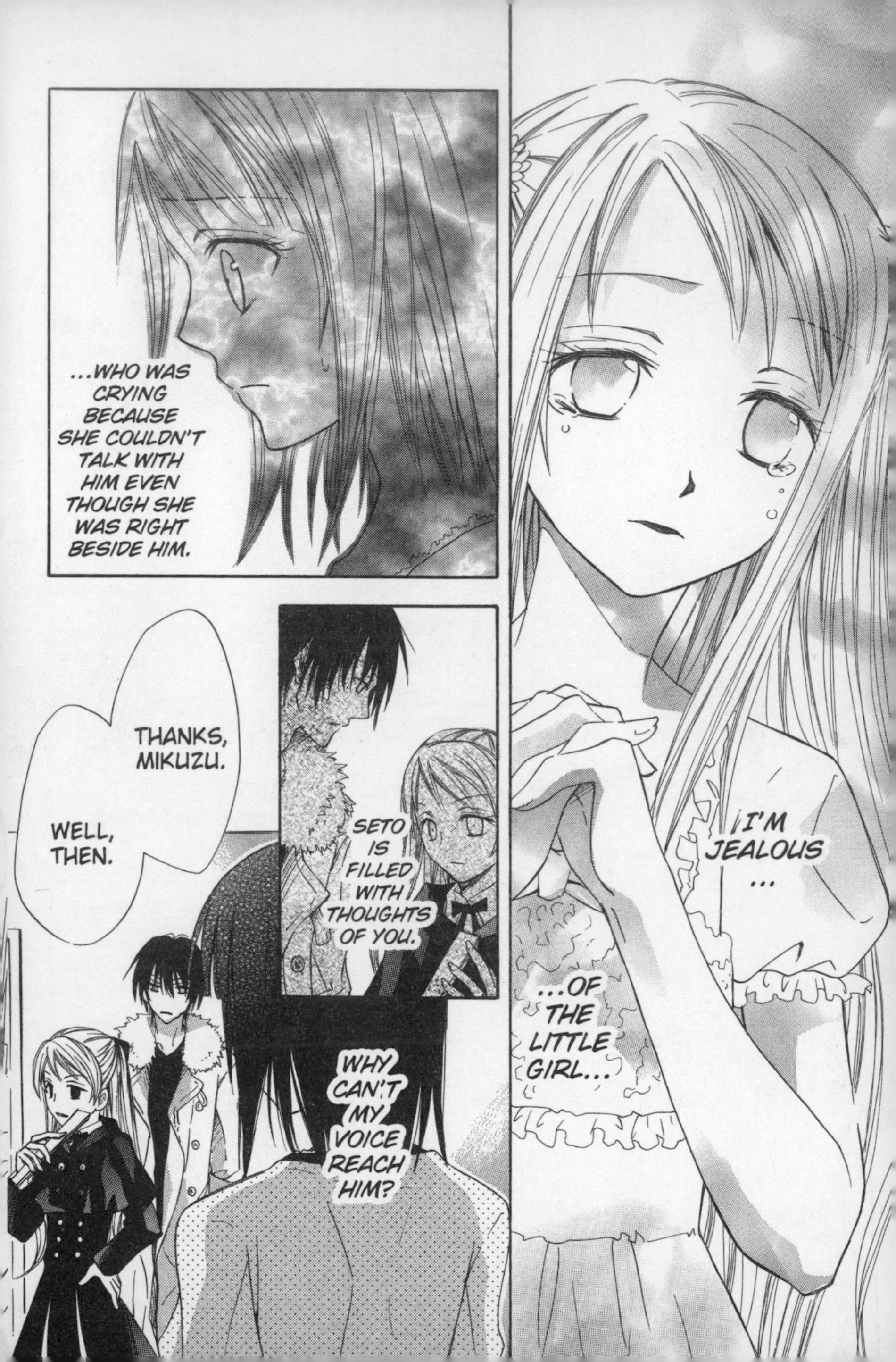
I'M JEALOUS...
...OF THE LITTLE GIRL...
...WHO WAS CRYING BECAUSE SHE COULDN'T TALK WITH HIM EVEN THOUGH SHE WAS RIGHT BESIDE HIM.
SETO IS FILLED WITH THOUGHTS OF YOU.
THANKS, MIKUZU.
WELL, THEN.
WHY CAN'T MY VOICE REACH HIM?

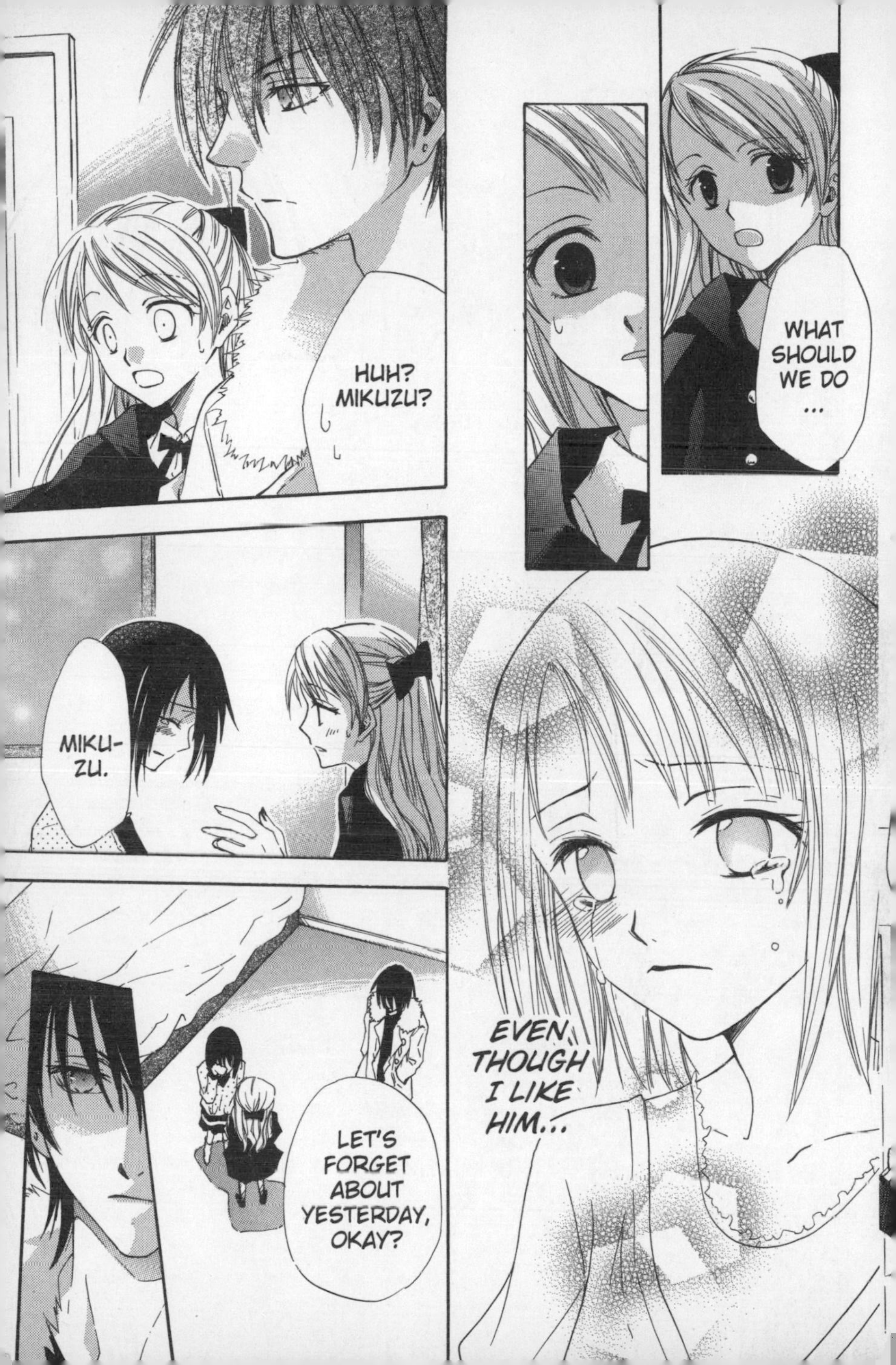
WHAT SHOULD WE DO ...
HUH? MIKUZU?
EVEN THOUGH I LIKE HIM...
MIKU-ZU.
LET'S FORGET ABOUT YESTERDAY, OKAY?

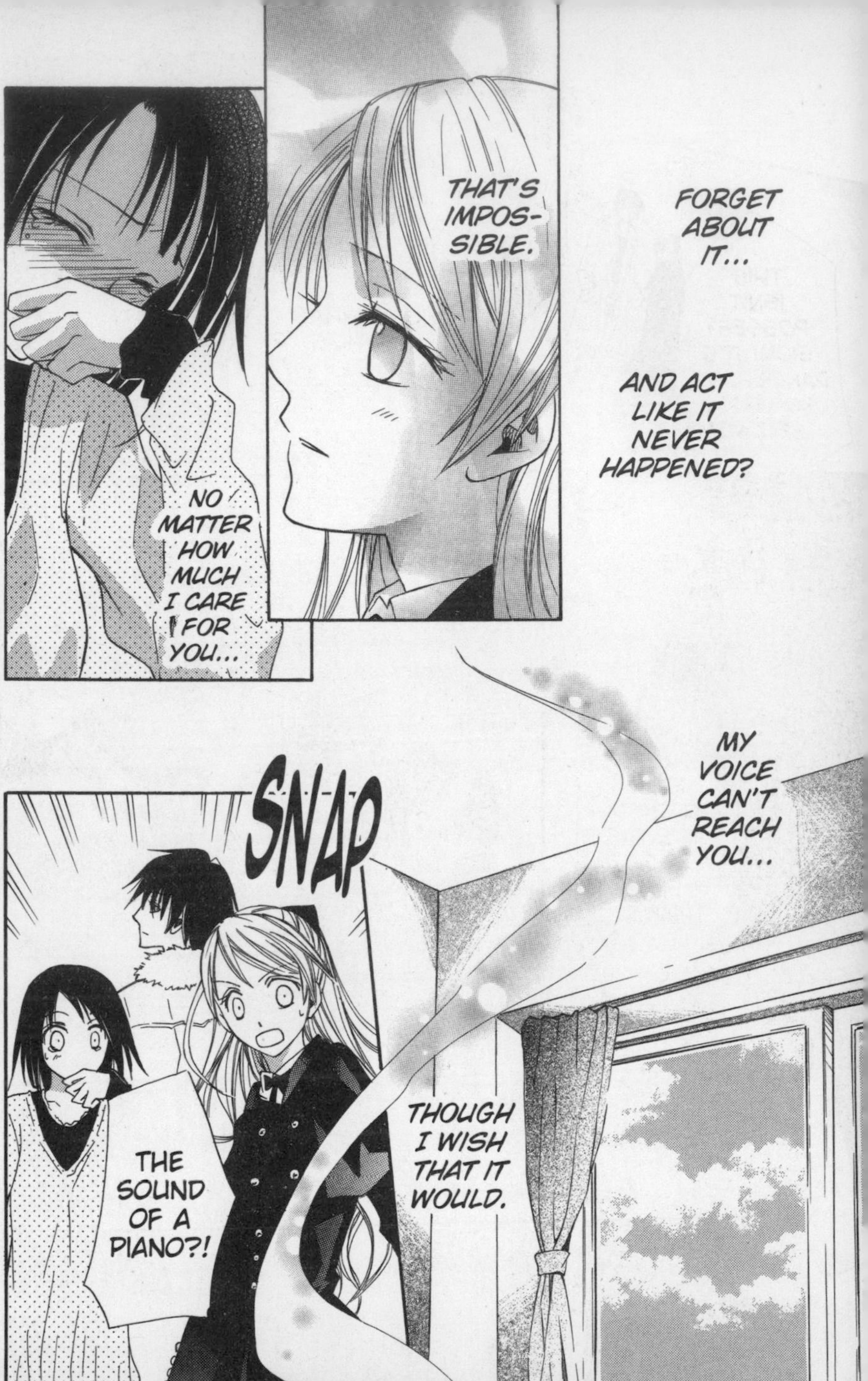
FORGET ABOUT IT...
AND ACT LIKE IT NEVER HAPPENED?
THAT'S IMPOS-SIBLE.
NO MATTER HOW MUCH I CARE FOR YOU...
MY VOICE CAN'T REACH YOU...
THOUGH I WISH THAT IT WOULD.
SNAP
THE SOUND OF A PIANO?!

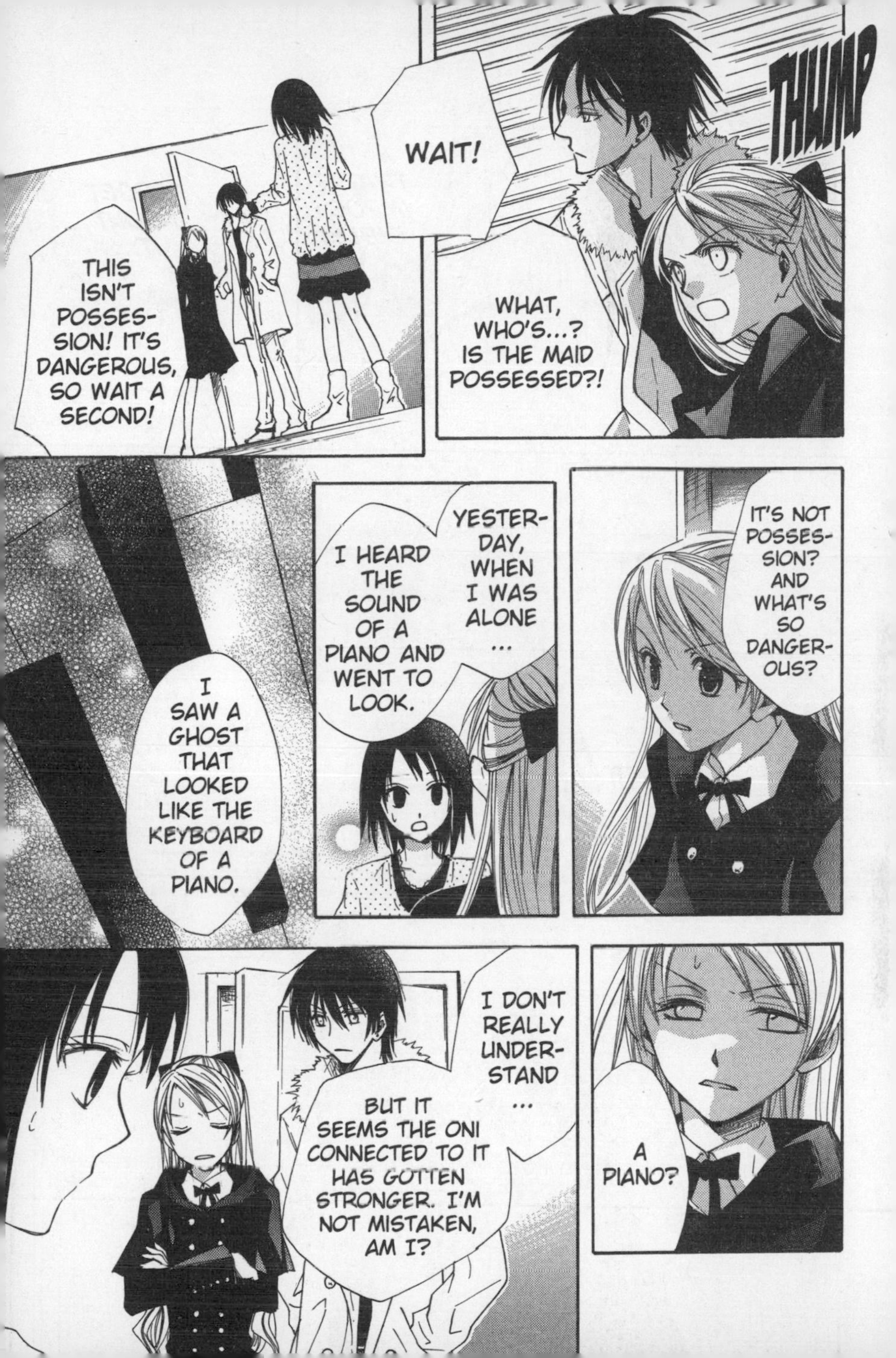
THUMP
WAIT!
WHAT, WHO'S...? IS THE MAID POSSESSED?!
THIS ISN'T POSSES-SION! IT'S DANGEROUS, SO WAIT A SECOND!
IT'S NOT POSSES-SION? AND WHAT'S SO DANGER-OUS?
YESTER-DAY, WHEN I WAS ALONE...
I HEARD THE SOUND OF A PIANO AND WENT TO LOOK.
I SAW A GHOST THAT LOOKED LIKE THE KEYBOARD OF A PIANO.
A PIANO?
I DON'T REALLY UNDER-STAND...
BUT IT SEEMS THE ONI CONNECTED TO IT HAS GOTTEN STRONGER. I'M NOT MISTAKEN, AM I?

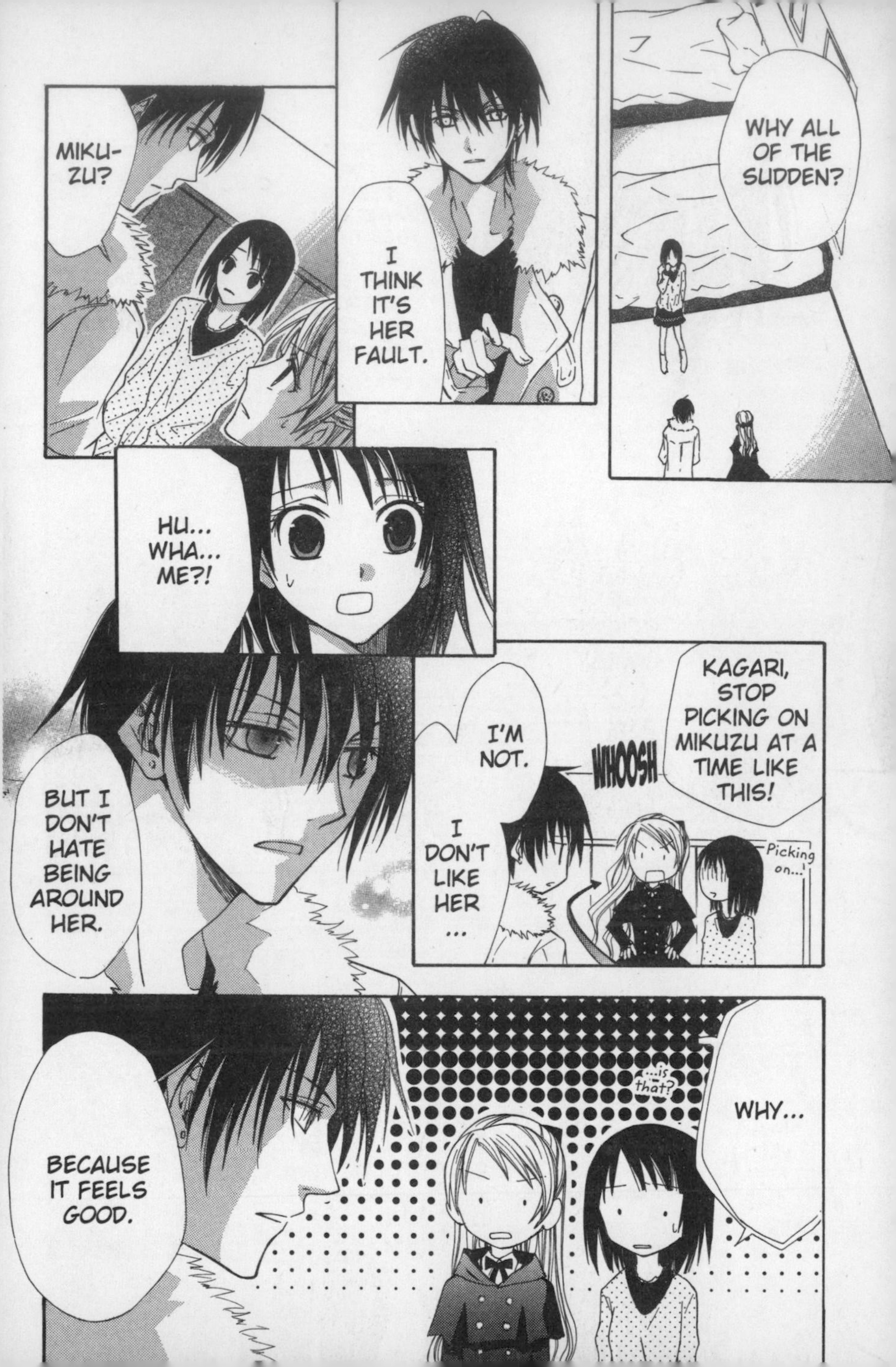
WHY ALL OF THE SUDDEN?
I THINK IT'S HER FAULT.
MIKU-ZU?
HU... WHA... ME?!
KAGARI, STOP PICKING ON MIKUZU AT A TIME LIKE THIS!
WHOOSH
I'M NOT.
Picking on...!
I DON'T LIKE HER ...
BUT I DON'T HATE BEING AROUND HER.
WHY...
...is that?
BECAUSE IT FEELS GOOD.

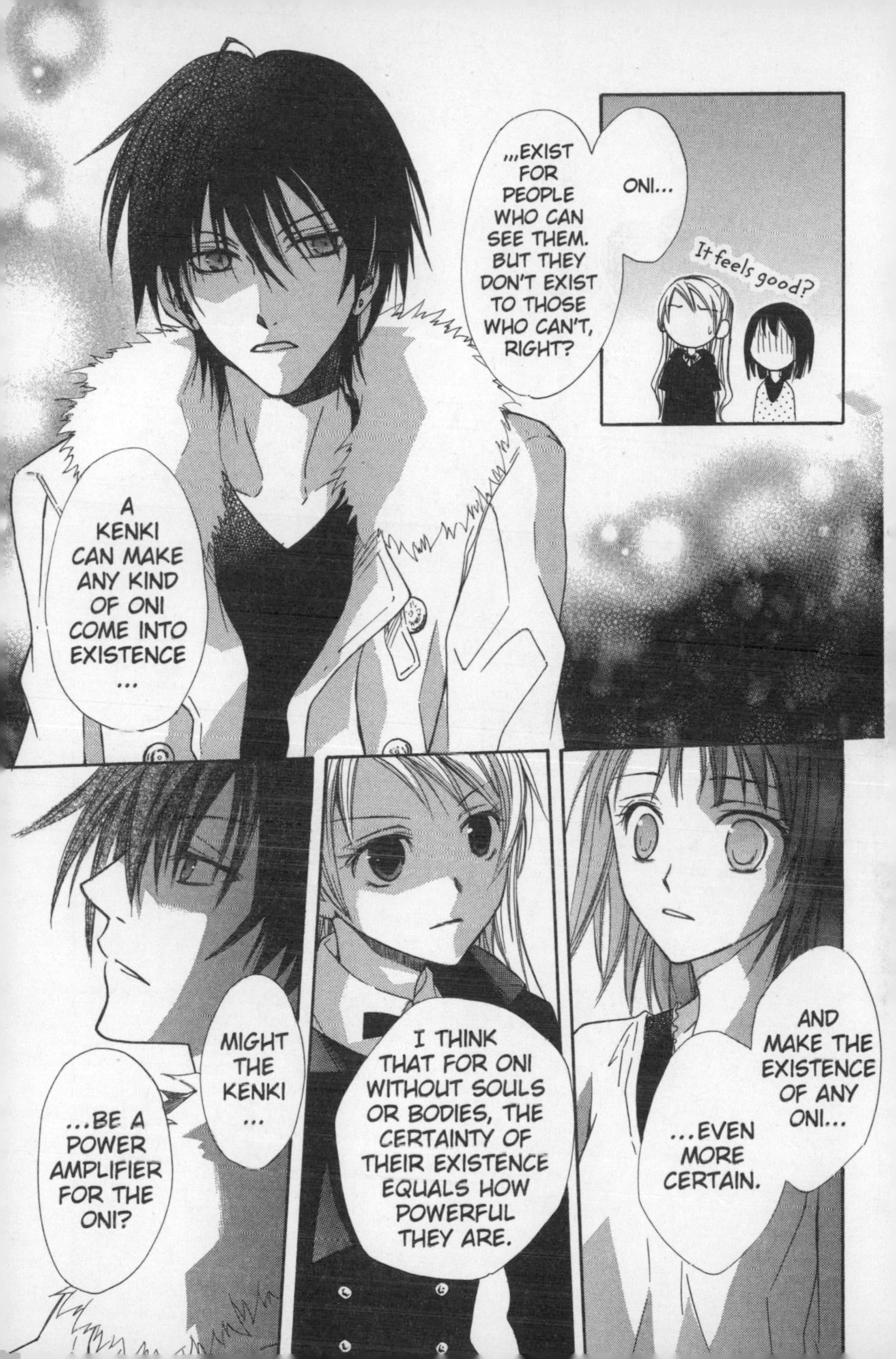
ONI...
...EXIST FOR PEOPLE WHO CAN SEE THEM. BUT THEY DON'T EXIST TO THOSE WHO CAN'T, RIGHT?
It feels good?
A KENKI CAN MAKE ANY KIND OF ONI COME INTO EXISTENCE ...
AND MAKE THE EXISTENCE OF ANY ONI...
...EVEN MORE CERTAIN.
I THINK THAT FOR ONI WITHOUT SOULS OR BODIES, THE CERTAINTY OF THEIR EXISTENCE EQUALS HOW POWERFUL THEY ARE.
MIGHT THE KENKI ...
...BE A POWER AMPLIFIER FOR THE ONI?

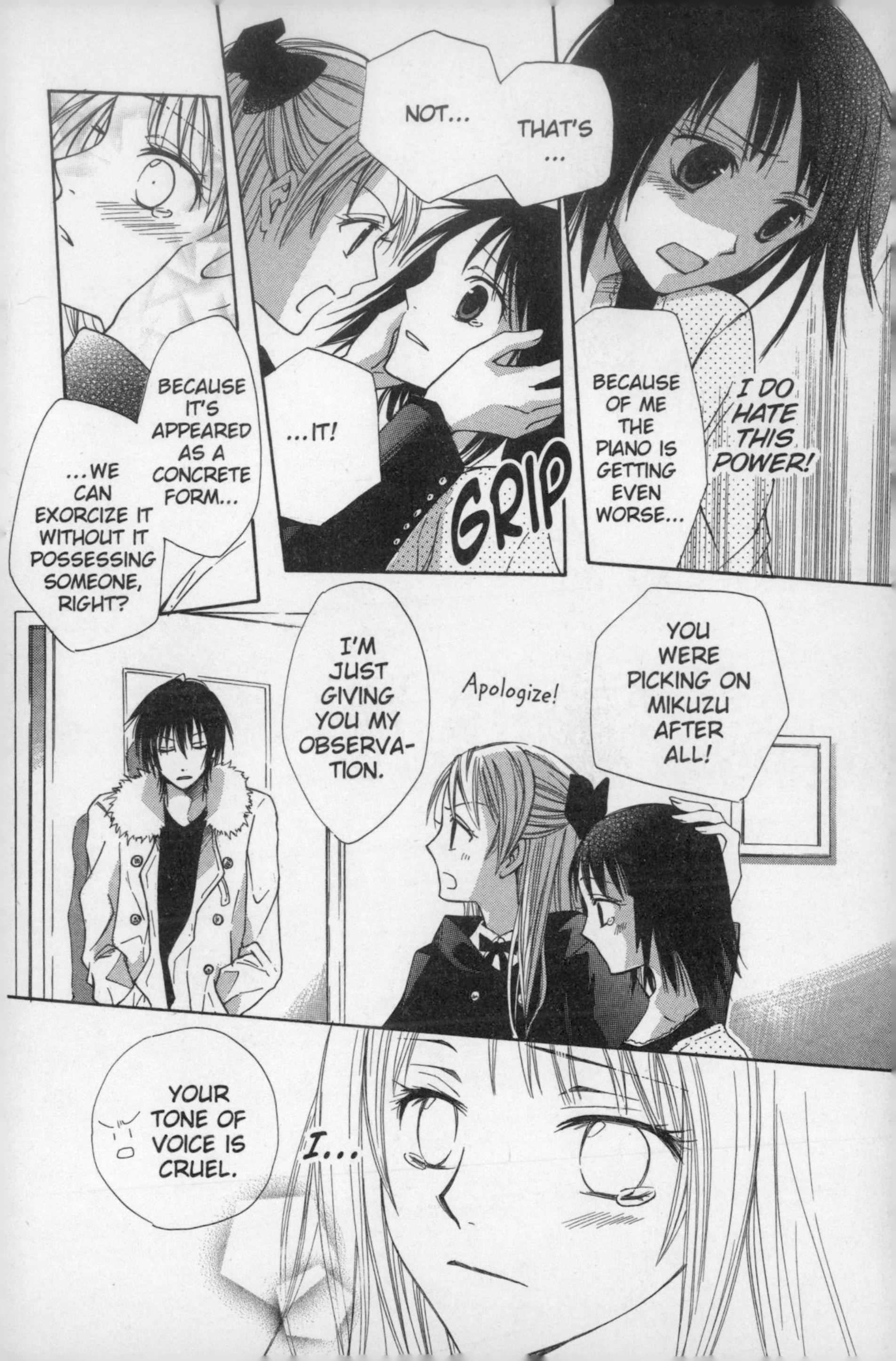
THAT'S ...
NOT...
BECAUSE OF ME THE PIANO IS GETTING EVEN WORSE...
I DO HATE THIS POWER!
...IT!
GRIP
BECAUSE IT'S APPEARED AS A CONCRETE FORM...
...WE CAN EXORCIZE IT WITHOUT IT POSSESSING SOMEONE, RIGHT?
YOU WERE PICKING ON MIKUZU AFTER ALL!
Apologize!
I'M JUST GIVING YOU MY OBSERVATION.
I...
YOUR TONE OF VOICE IS CRUEL.

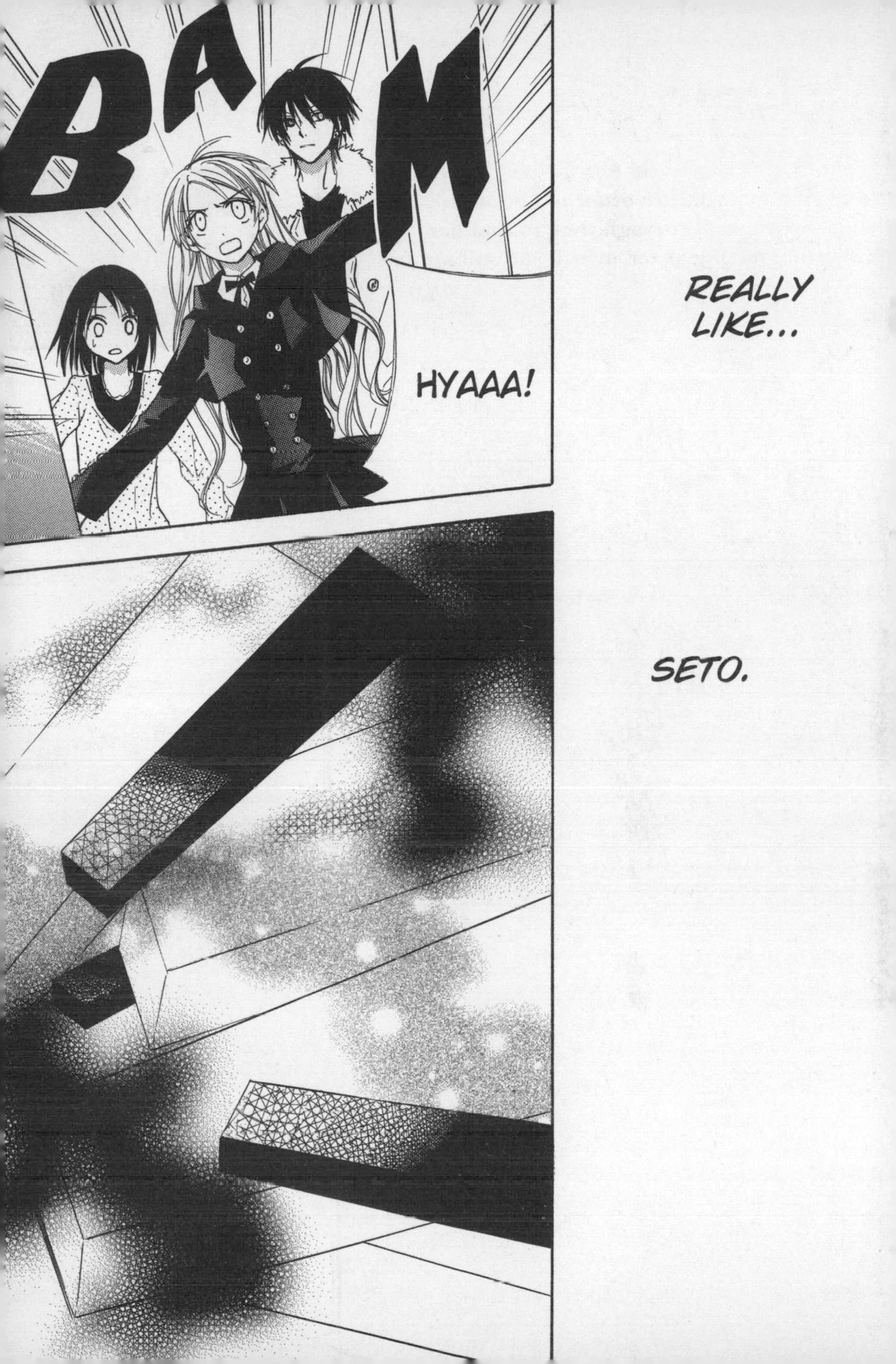
REALLY LIKE...
BAM
HYAAA!
SETO.

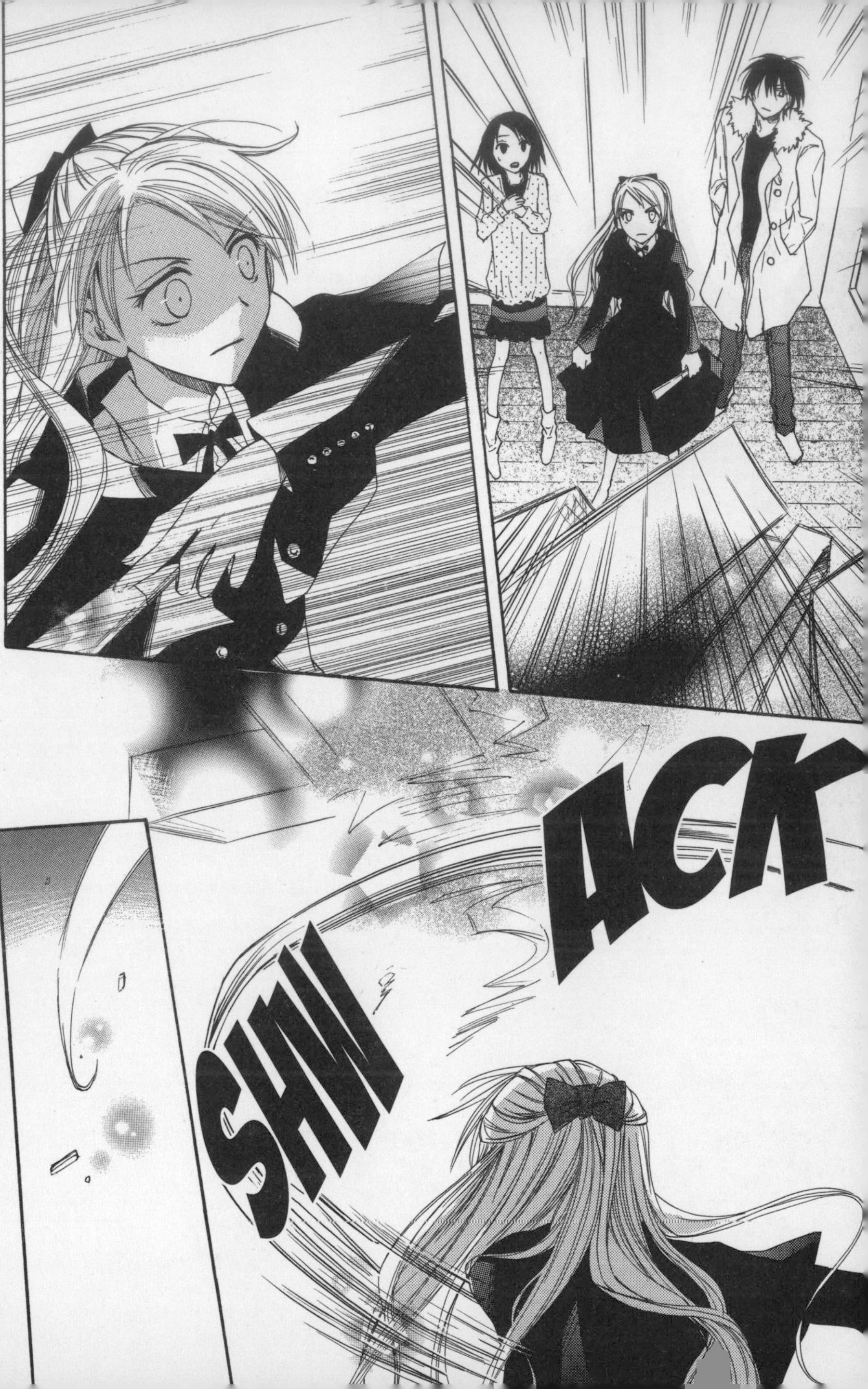
SHW
ACK

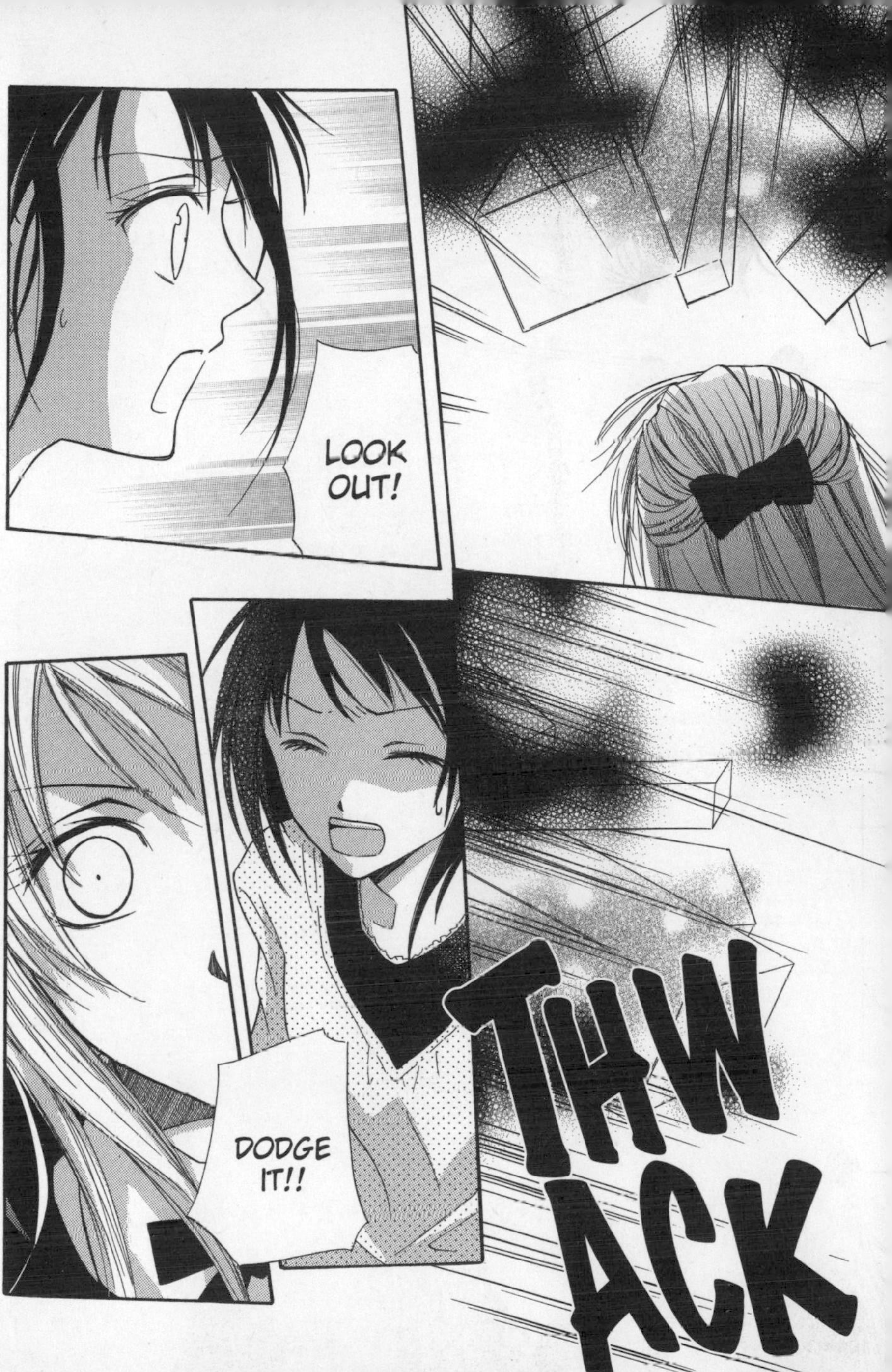
LOOK OUT!
THWACK
DODGE IT!!

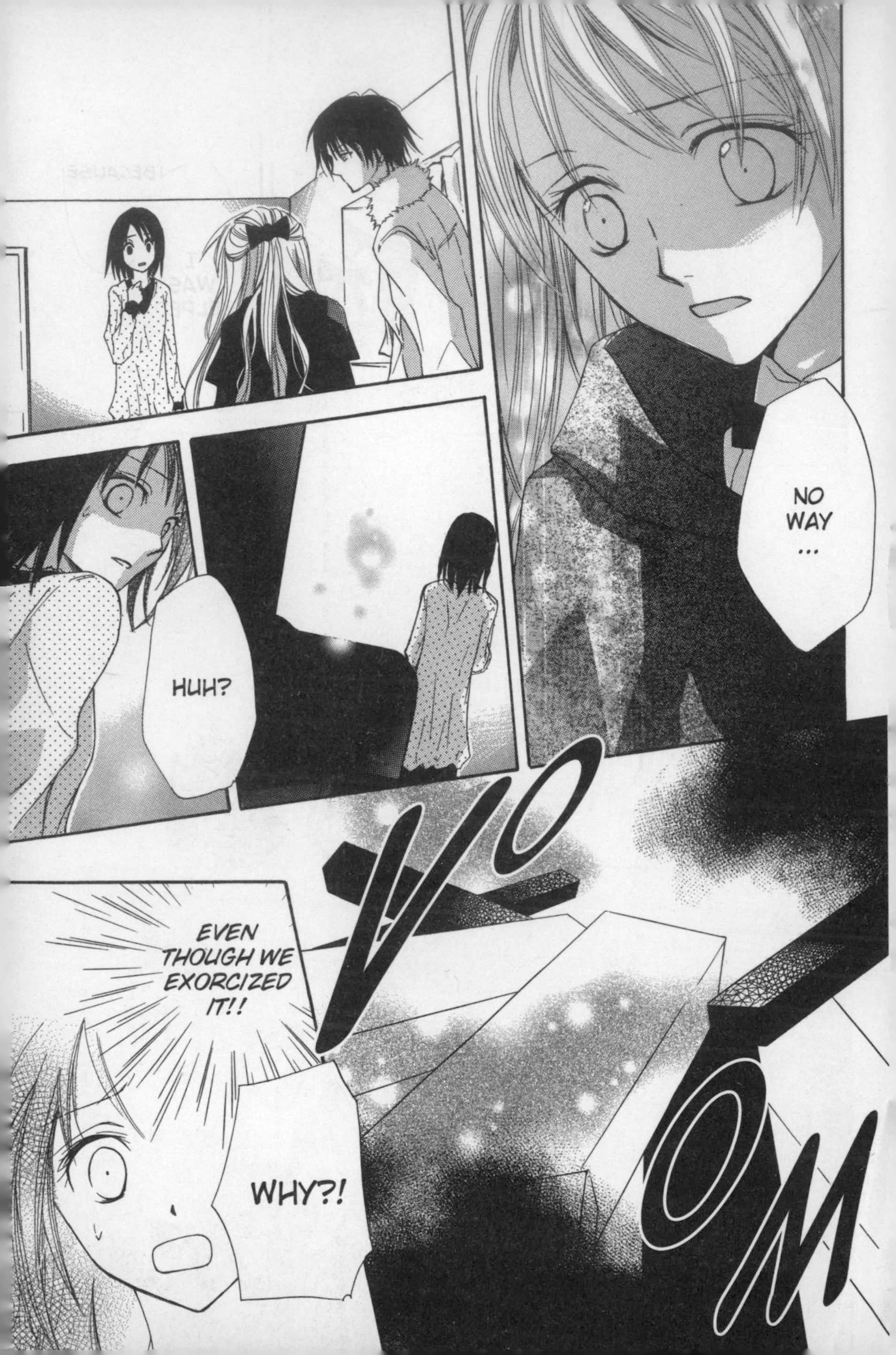
NO WAY ...
HUH?
VOOM
EVEN THOUGH WE EXORCIZED IT!!
WHY?!

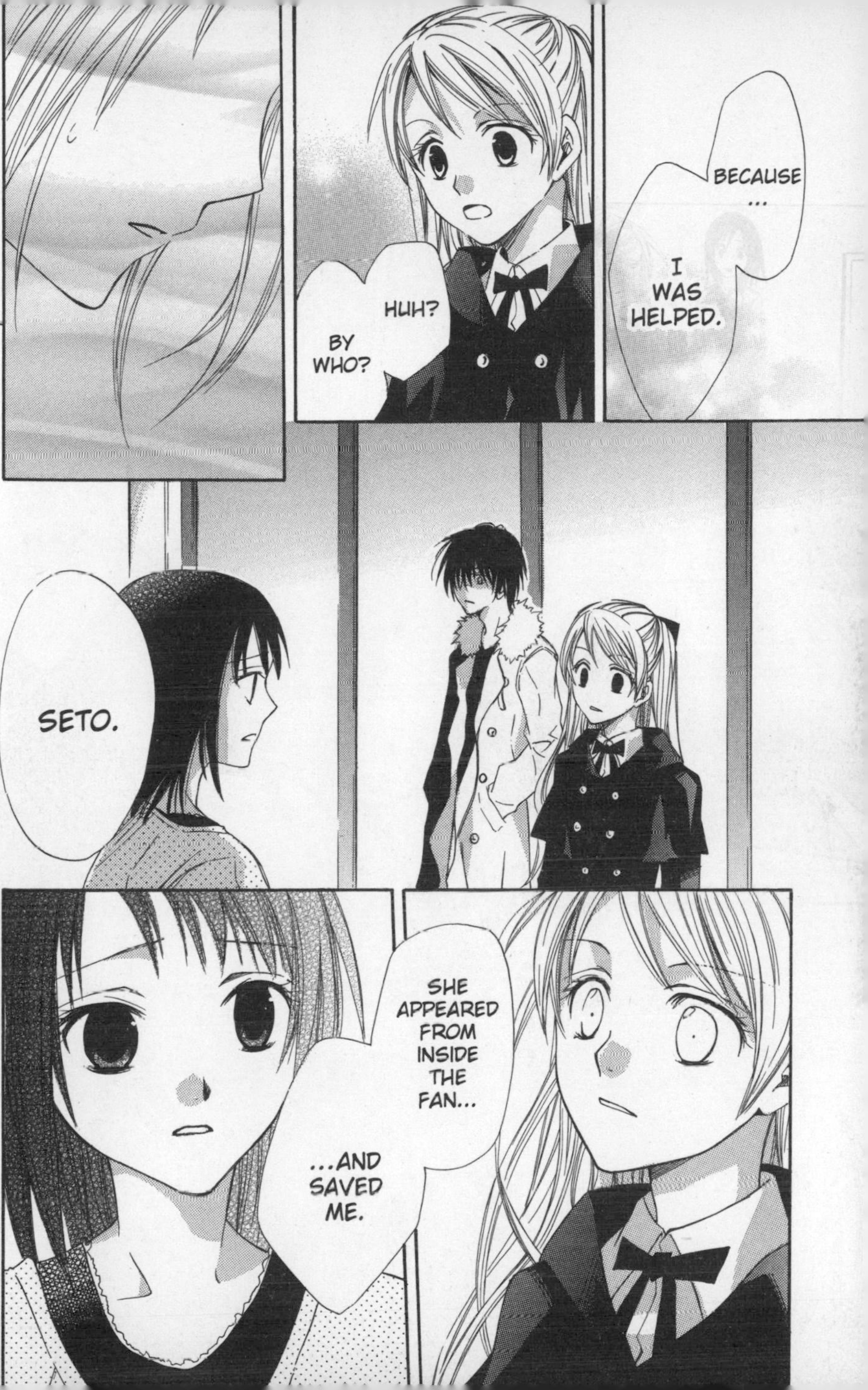
BECAUSE ...
I WAS HELPED.
HUH?
BY WHO?
SETO.
SHE APPEARED FROM INSIDE THE FAN...
...AND SAVED ME.

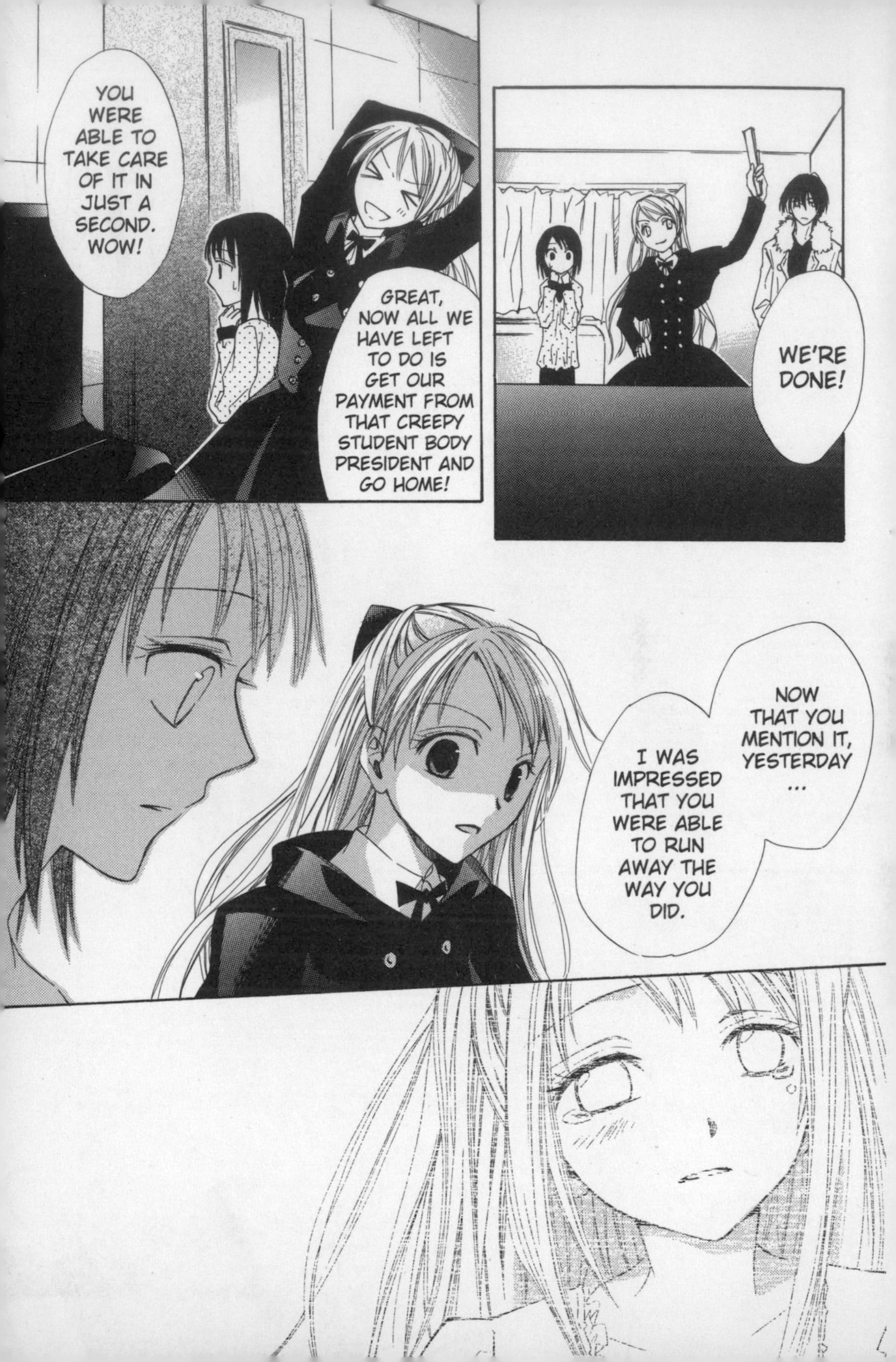
WE'RE DONE!
YOU WERE ABLE TO TAKE CARE OF IT IN JUST A SECOND. WOW!
GREAT, NOW ALL WE HAVE LEFT TO DO IS GET OUR PAYMENT FROM THAT CREEPY STUDENT BODY PRESIDENT AND GO HOME!
NOW THAT YOU MENTION IT, YESTERDAY ...
I WAS IMPRESSED THAT YOU WERE ABLE TO RUN AWAY THE WAY YOU DID.

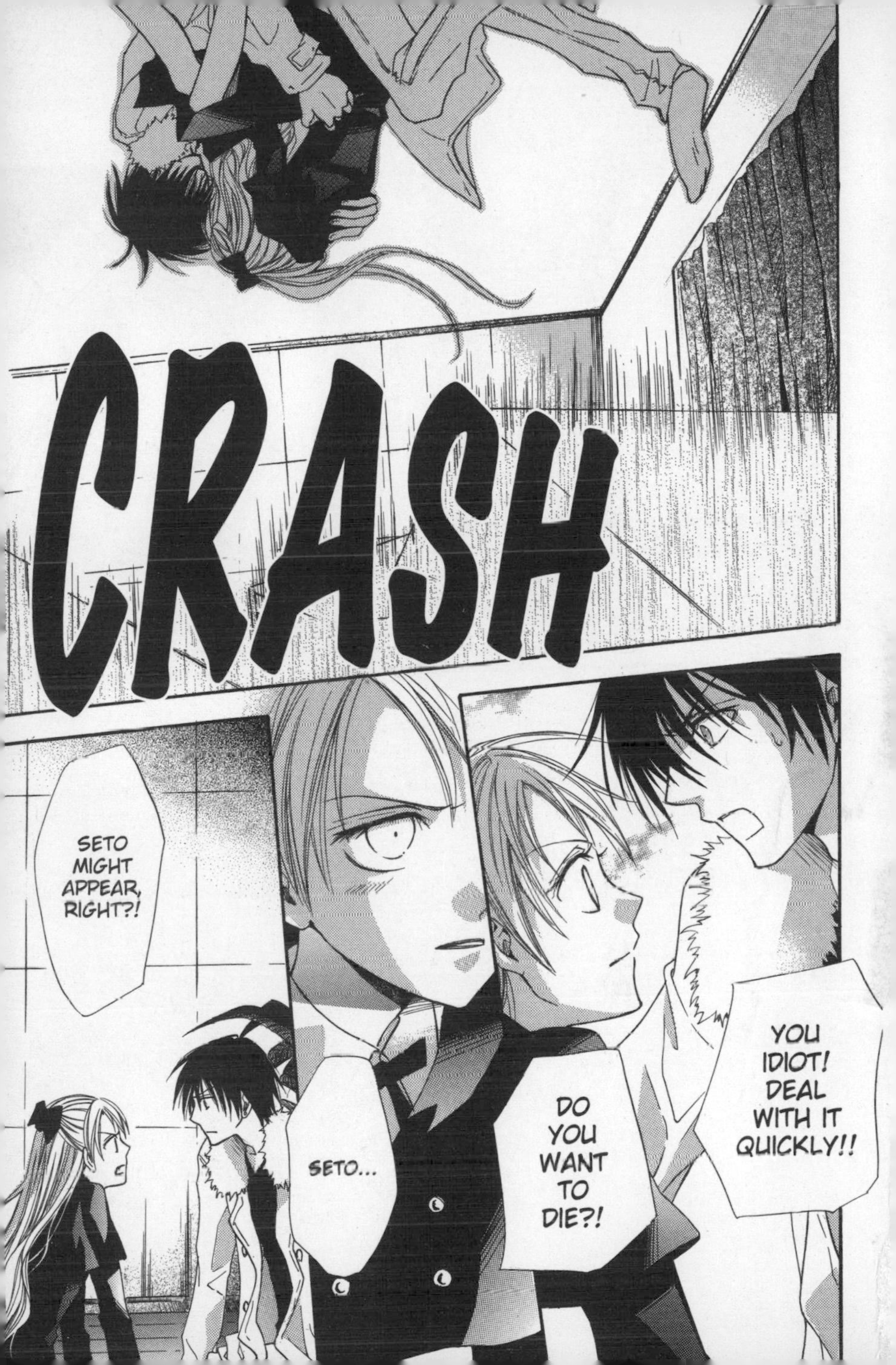
CRASH
YOU IDIOT! DEAL WITH IT QUICKLY!!
DO YOU WANT TO DIE?!
SETO...
SETO MIGHT APPEAR, RIGHT?!

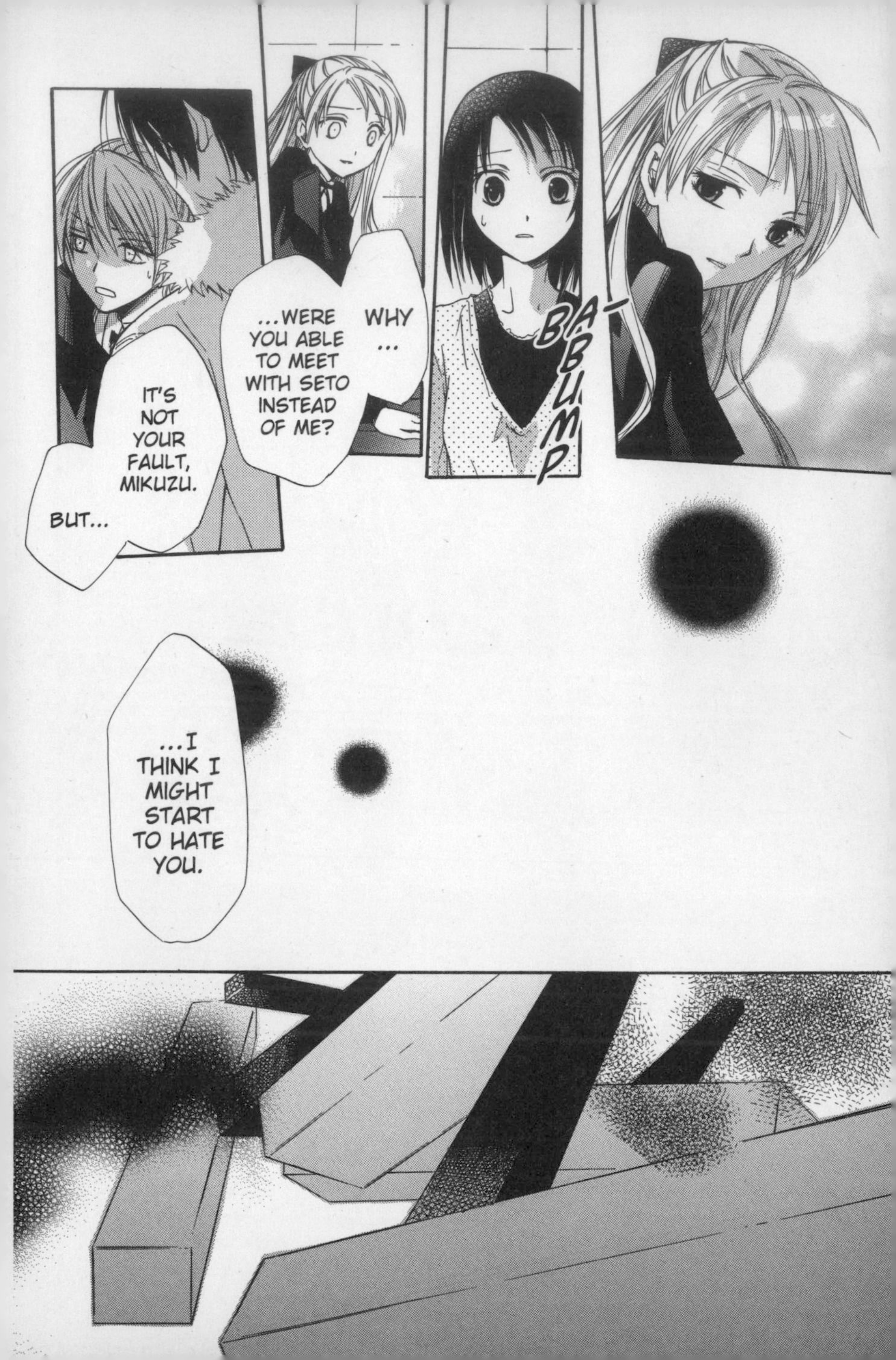
BA-BUMP
WHY...
...WERE YOU ABLE TO MEET WITH SETO INSTEAD OF ME?
IT'S NOT YOUR FAULT, MIKUZU.
BUT...
...I THINK I MIGHT START TO HATE YOU.

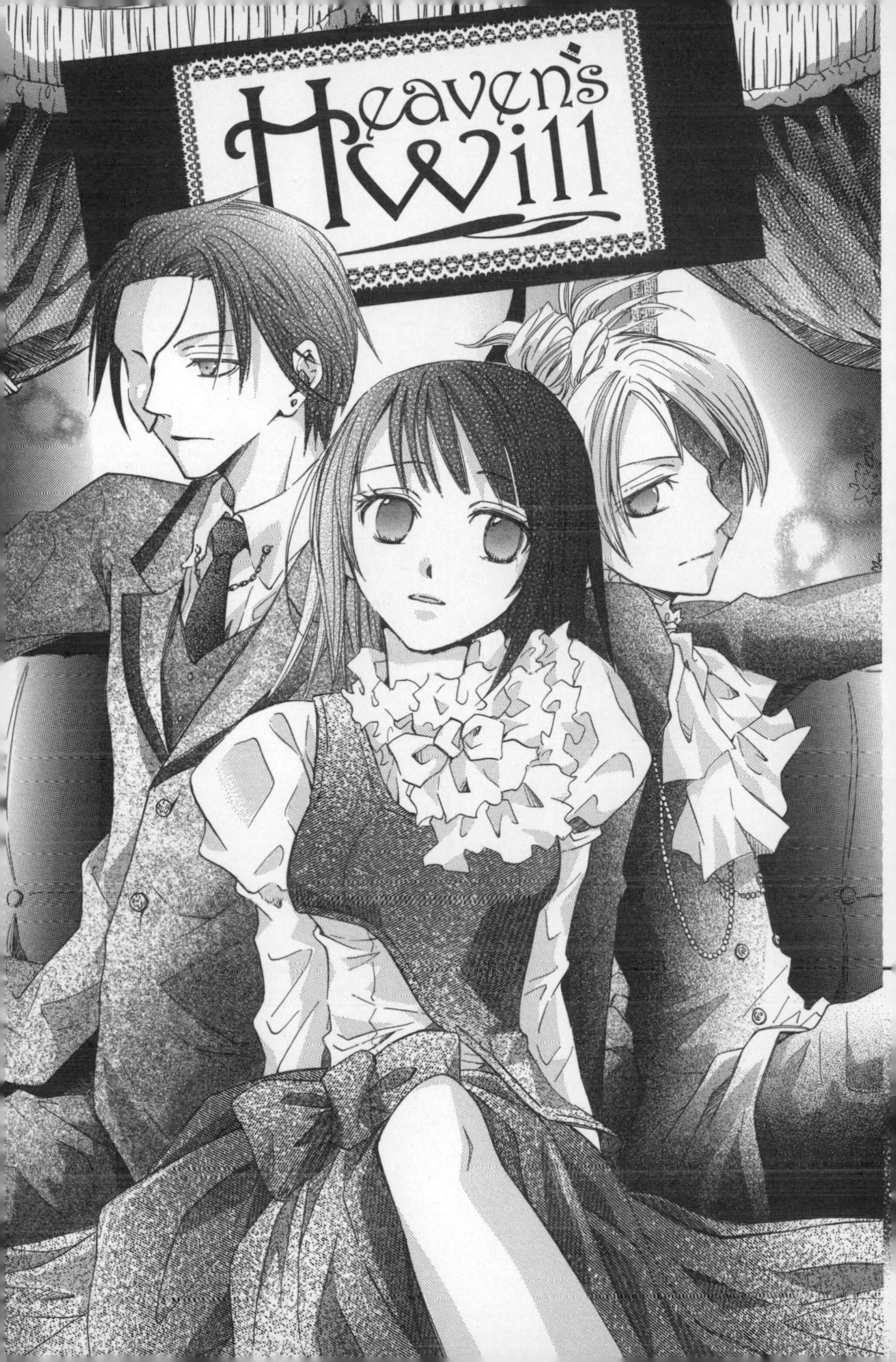
Heaven's Will

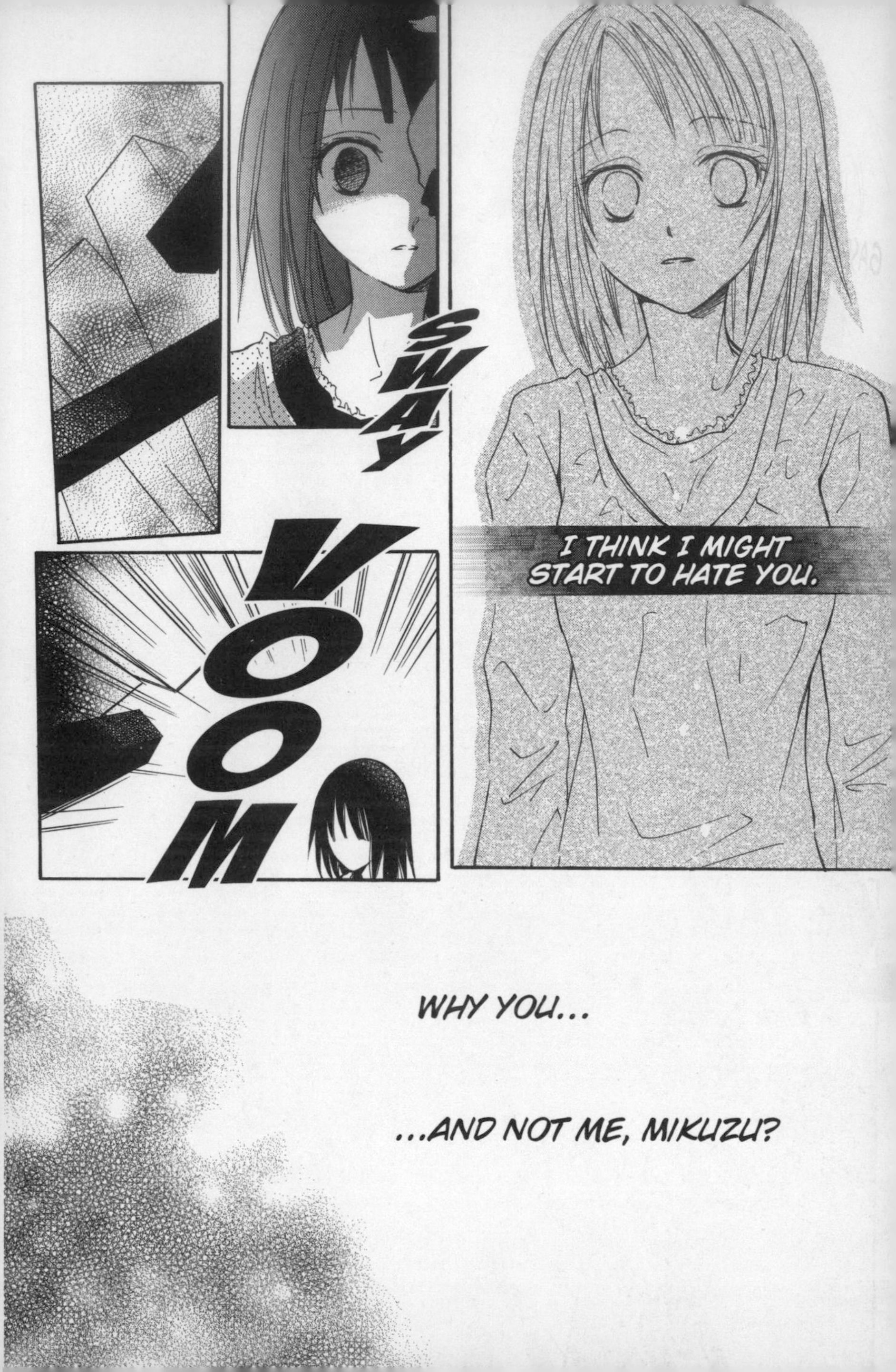
I THINK I MIGHT START TO HATE YOU.
SWAY
VOOM
WHY YOU...
...AND NOT ME, MIKUZU?

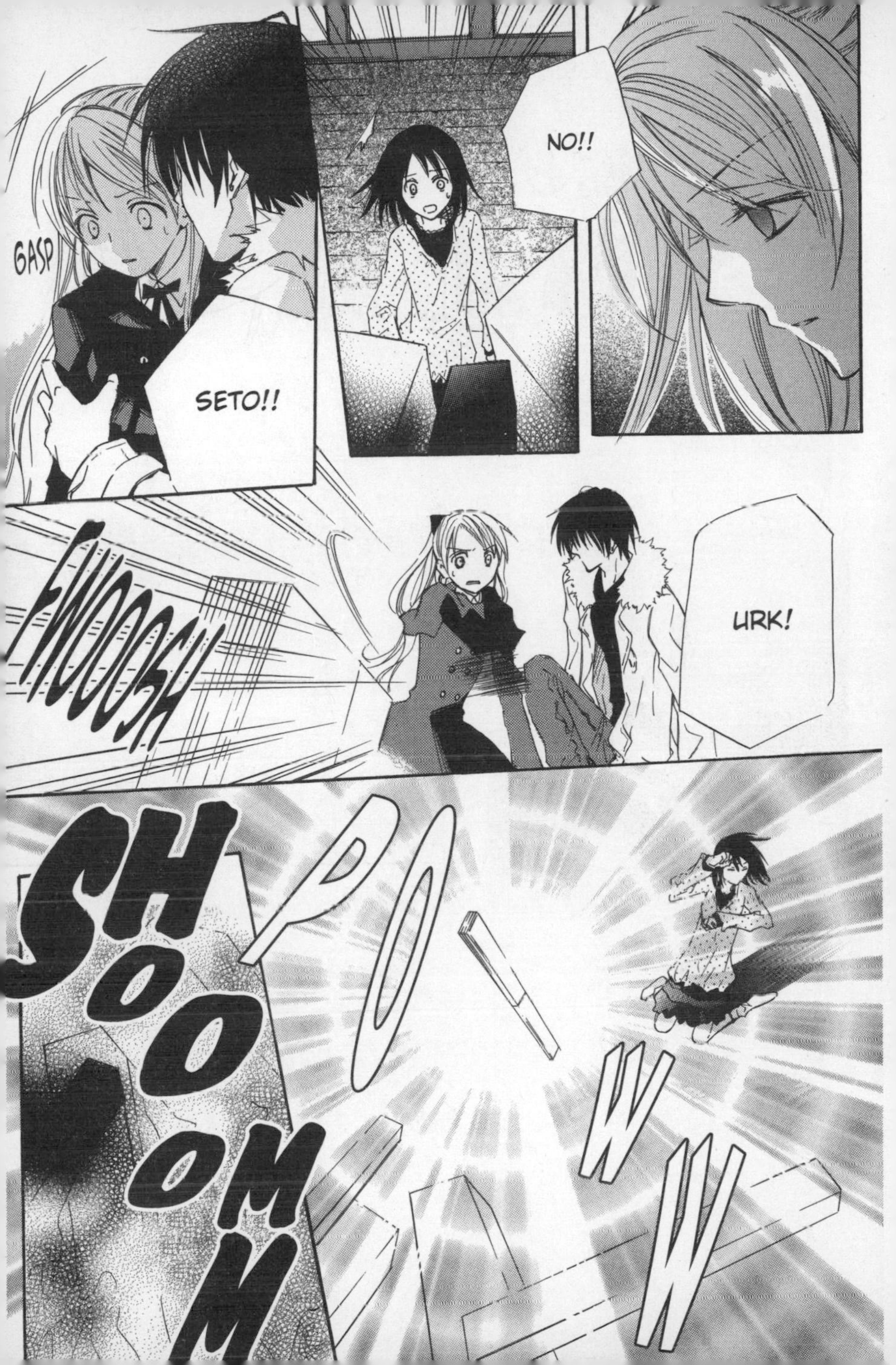
NO!!
SETO!!
GASP
URK!
FWOOSH
POWWW
SHOOOMM

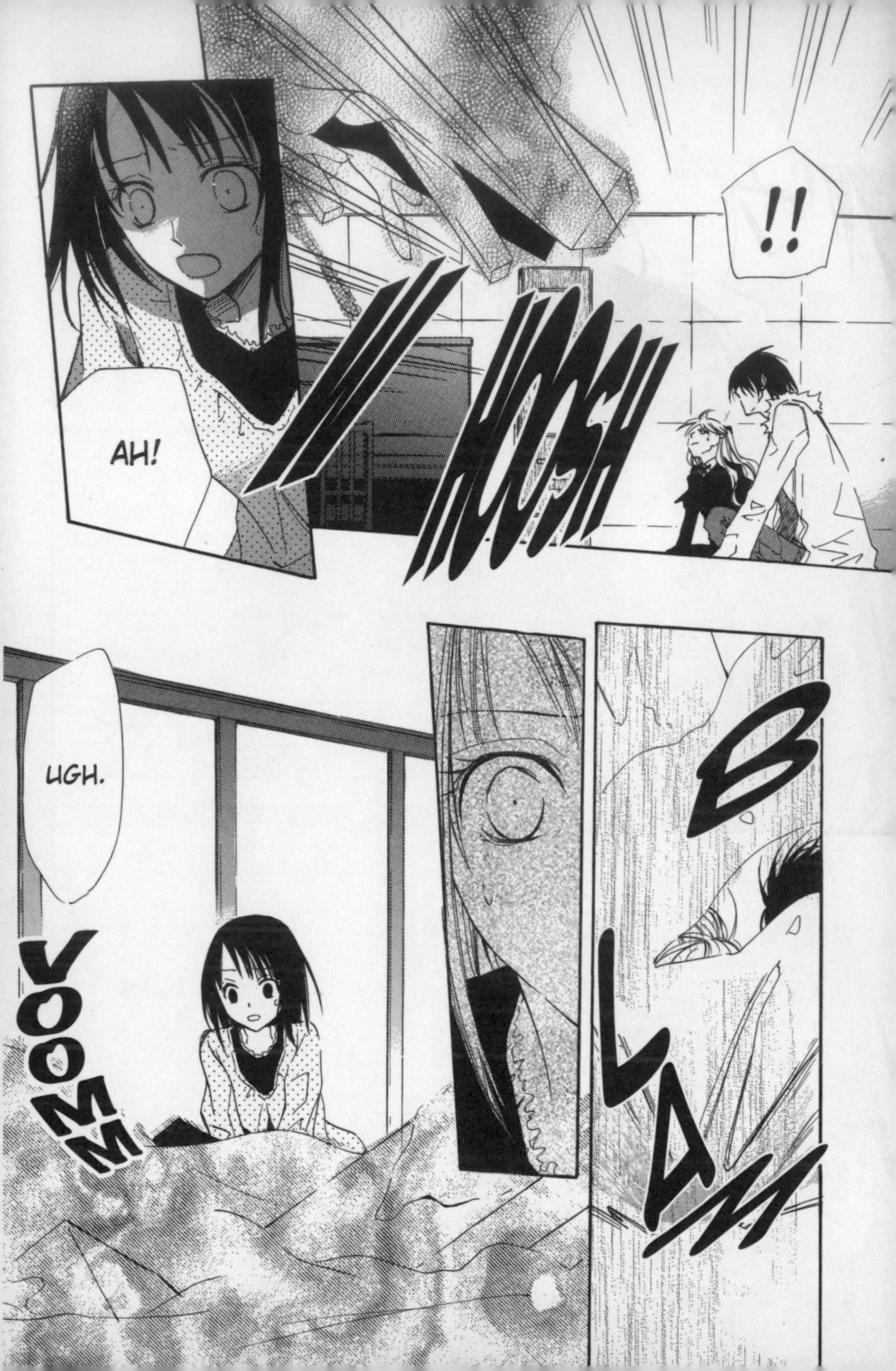
!!
WHOOSH
AH!
BLAM
UGH.
VOOMM

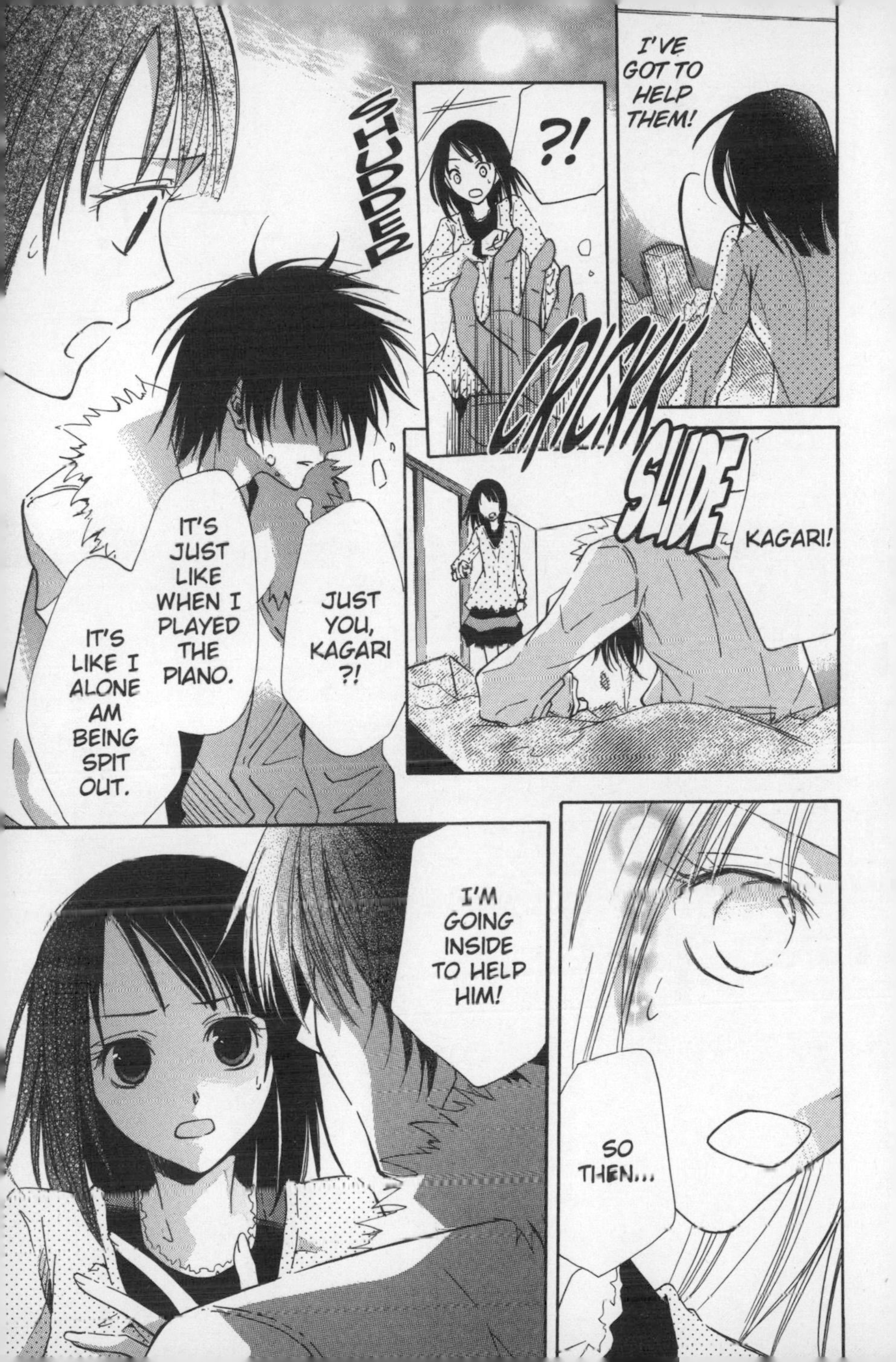
I'VE GOT TO HELP THEM!
?!
CRUNCH
SLIDE
KAGARI!
SHUDDER
JUST YOU, KAGARI ?!
IT'S JUST LIKE WHEN I PLAYED THE PIANO.
IT'S LIKE I ALONE AM BEING SPIT OUT.
SO THEN...
I'M GOING INSIDE TO HELP HIM!

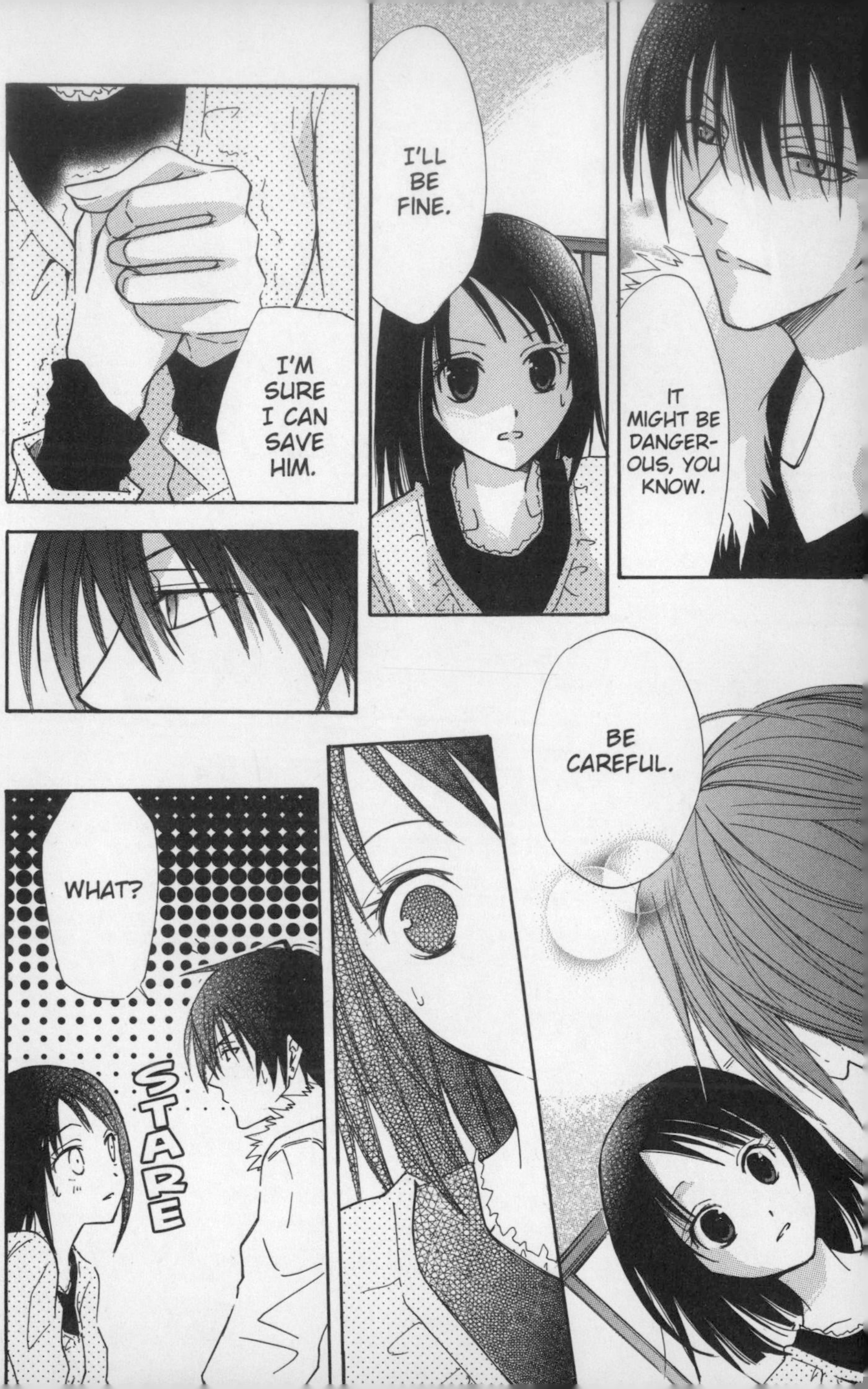
IT MIGHT BE DANGER-OUS, YOU KNOW.
I'LL BE FINE.
I'M SURE I CAN SAVE HIM.
BE CAREFUL.
WHAT?
STARE

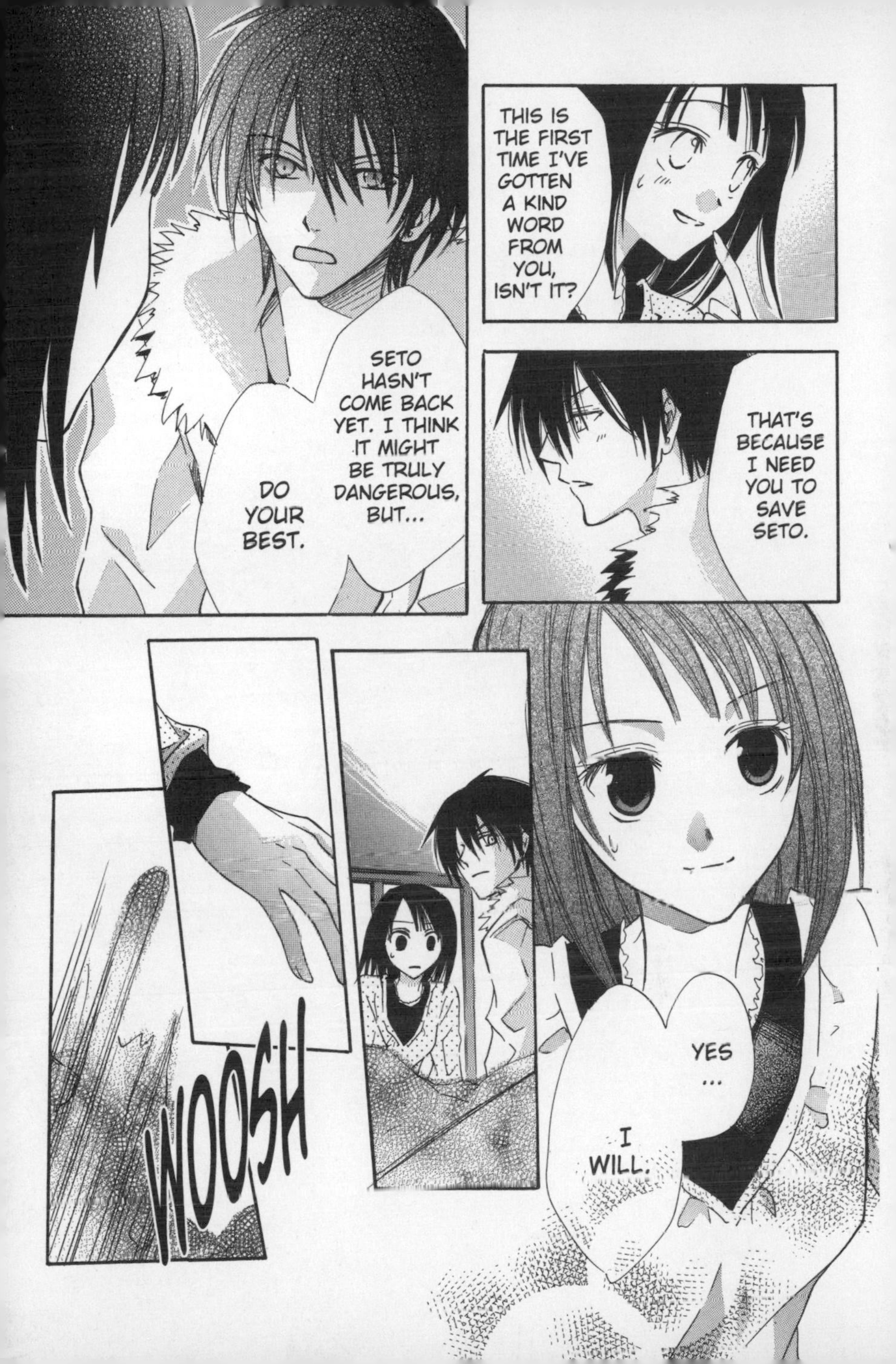
THIS IS THE FIRST TIME I'VE GOTTEN A KIND WORD FROM YOU, ISN'T IT?
THAT'S BECAUSE I NEED YOU TO SAVE SETO.
SETO HASN'T COME BACK YET. I THINK IT MIGHT BE TRULY DANGEROUS, BUT...
DO YOUR BEST.
YES ...
I WILL.
WOOSH

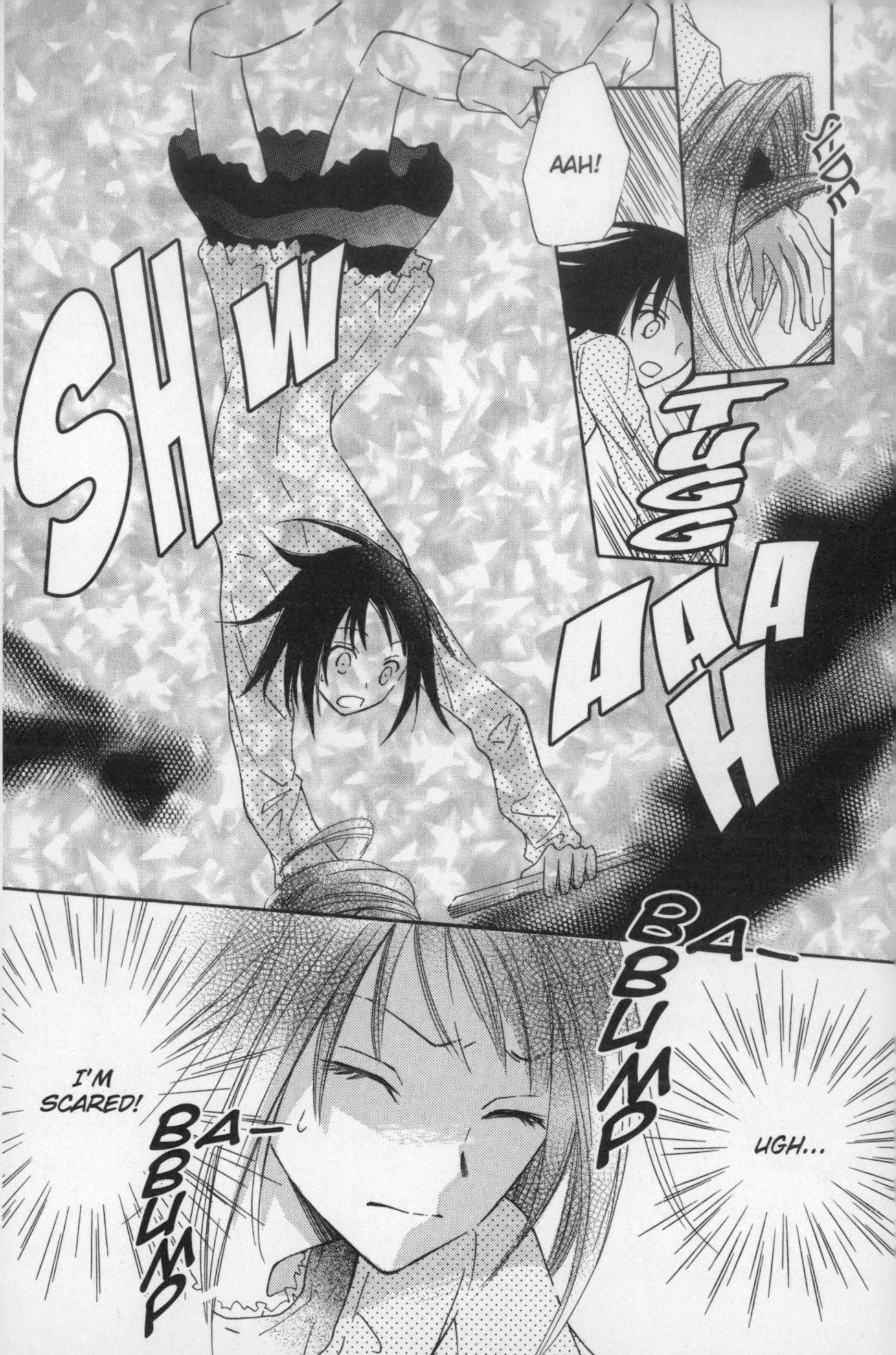

SLIDE
AAH!
TUG
SHW
AAAH
BA-BUMP
UGH...
I'M SCARED!
BA-BUMP

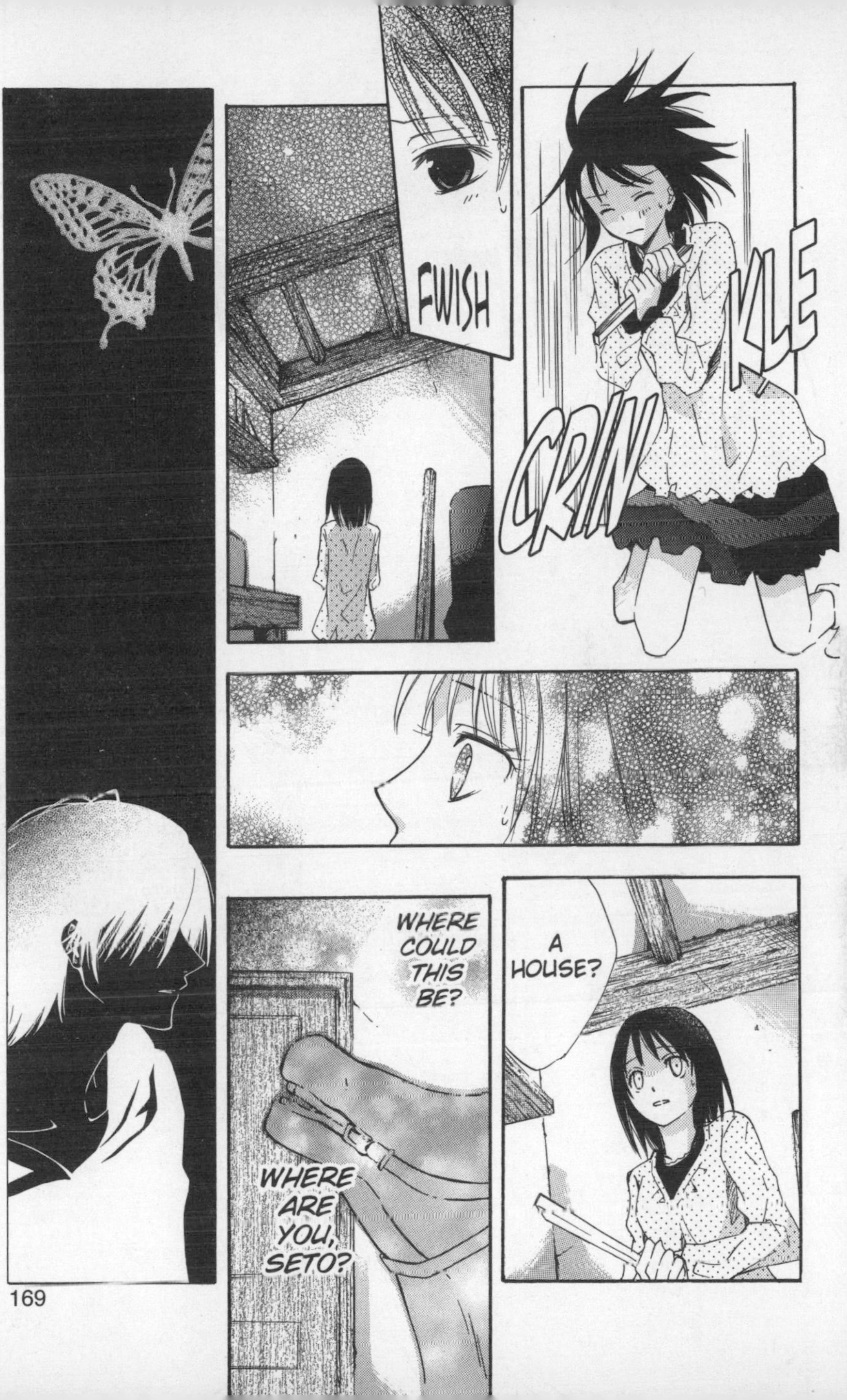
CRINKLE
FWISH
A HOUSE?
WHERE COULD THIS BE?
WHERE ARE YOU, SETO?

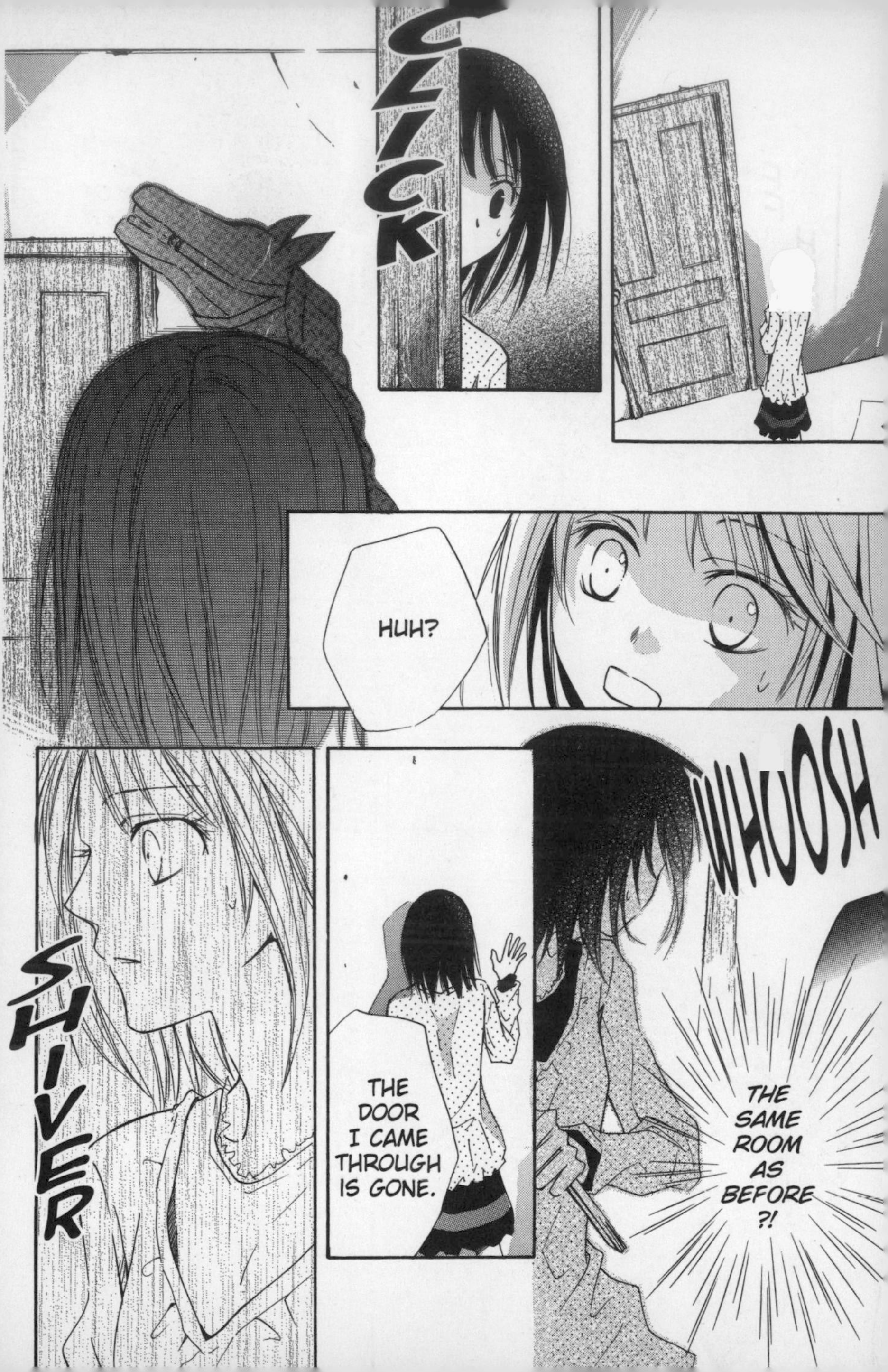
CLICK
HUH?
WHOOSH
THE SAME ROOM AS BEFORE?!
THE DOOR I CAME THROUGH IS GONE.
SHIVER

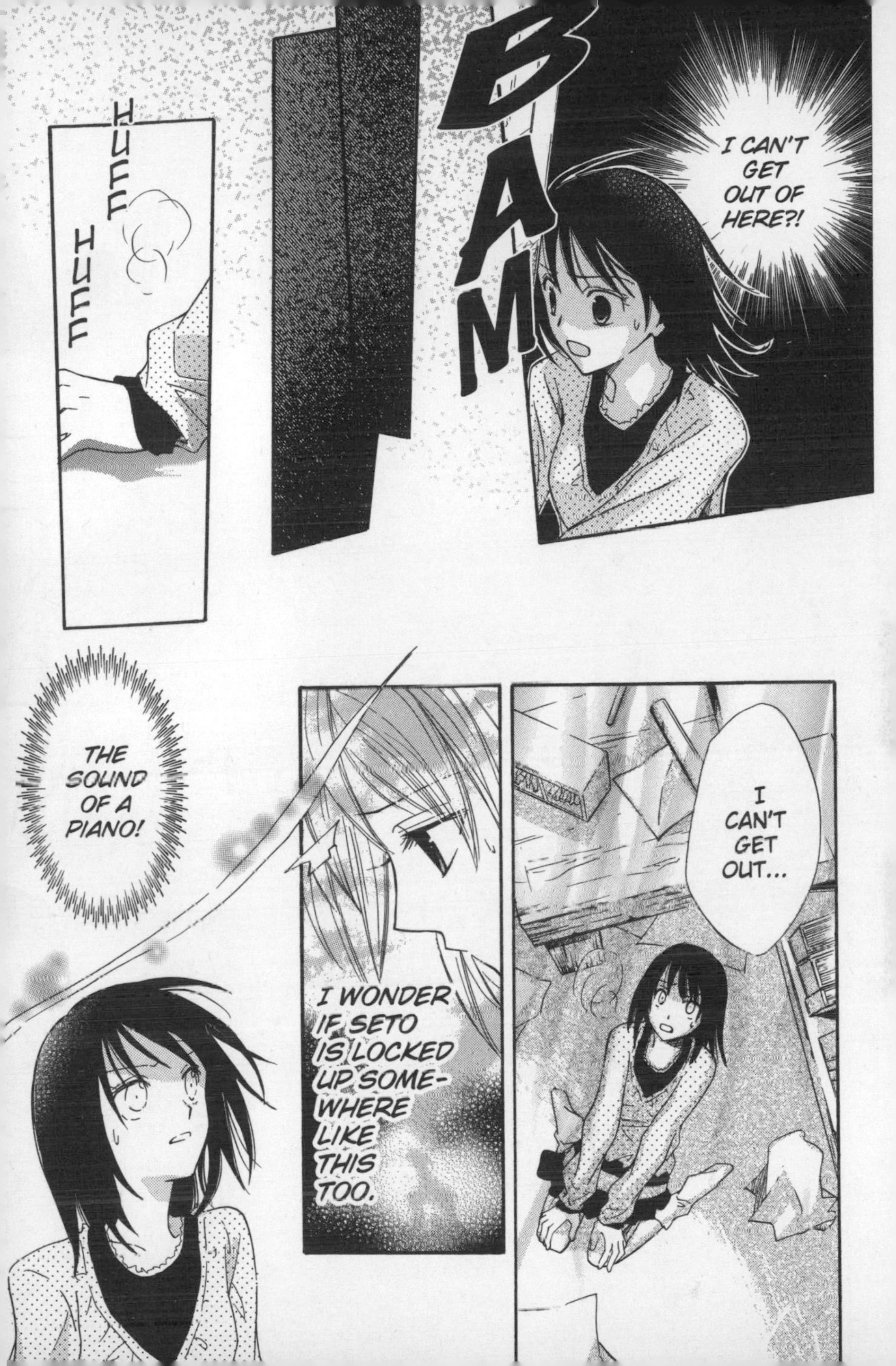
BAM
I CAN'T GET OUT OF HERE?!
HUFF HUFF
I CAN'T GET OUT...
I WONDER IF SETO IS LOCKED UP SOME-WHERE LIKE THIS TOO.
THE SOUND OF A PIANO!

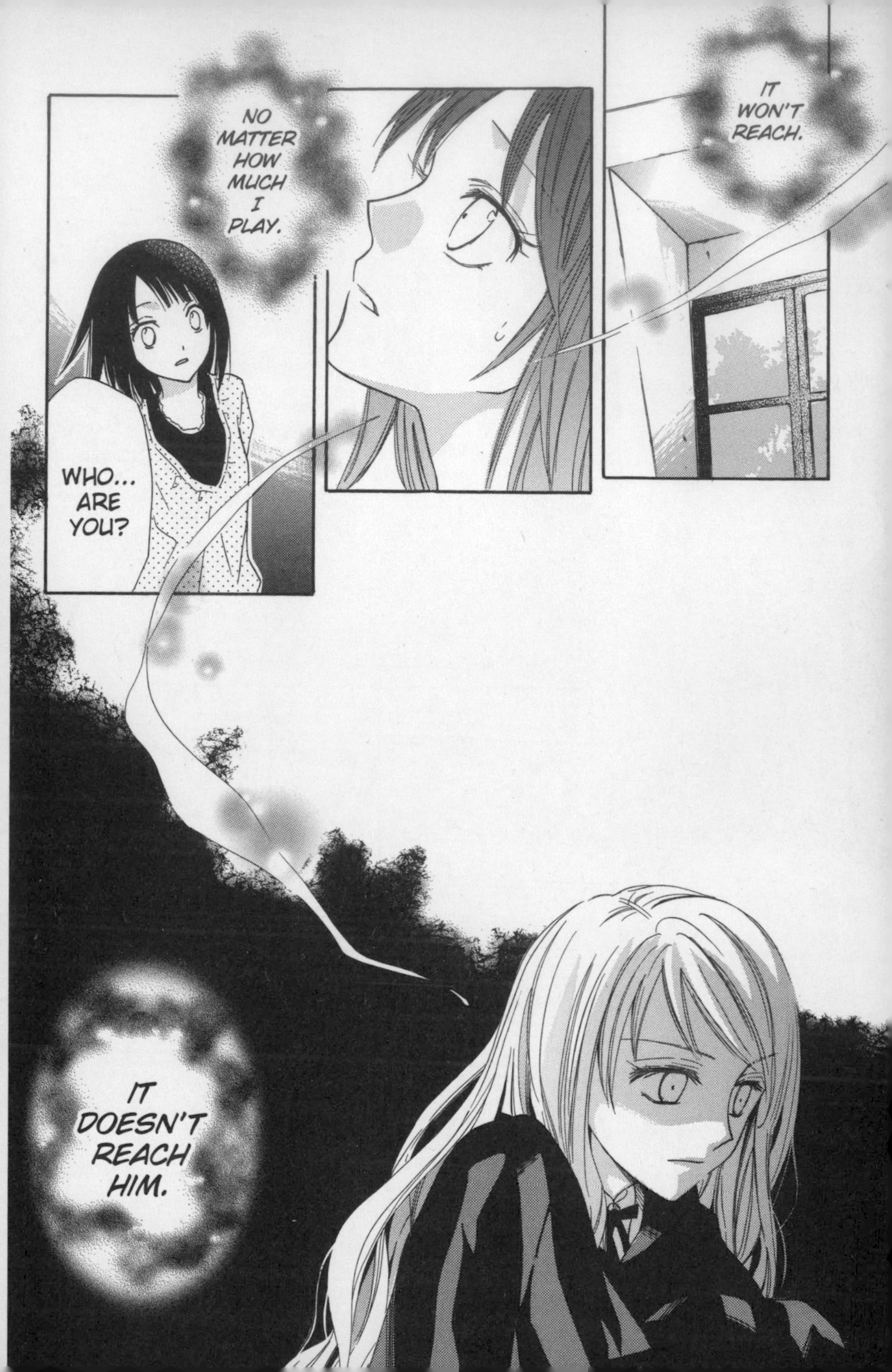
IT WON'T REACH.
NO MATTER HOW MUCH I PLAY.
WHO... ARE YOU?
IT DOESN'T REACH HIM.

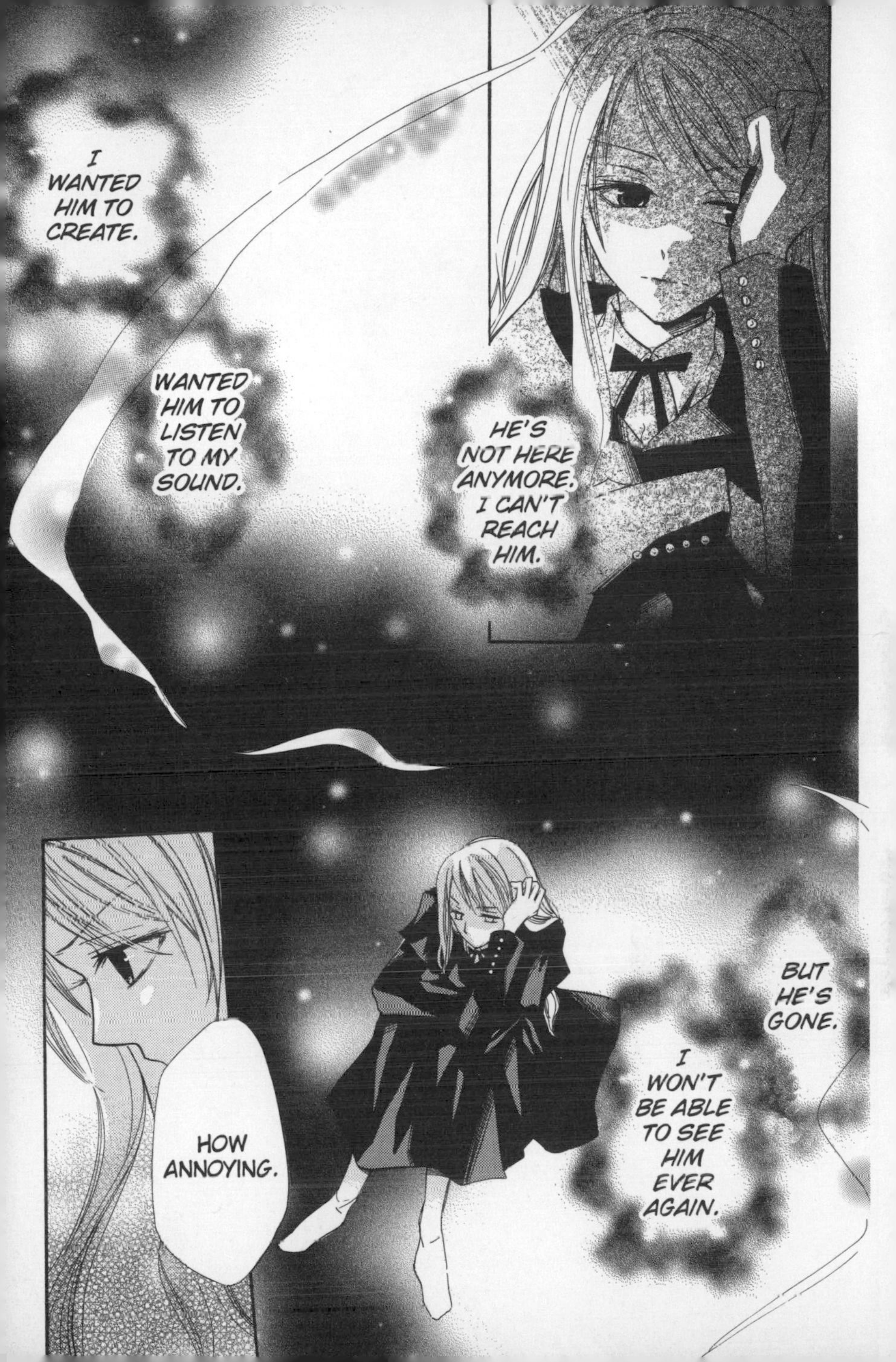
HE'S NOT HERE ANYMORE. I CAN'T REACH HIM.
I WANTED HIM TO CREATE.
WANTED HIM TO LISTEN TO MY SOUND.
BUT HE'S GONE.
I WON'T BE ABLE TO SEE HIM EVER AGAIN.
HOW ANNOYING.

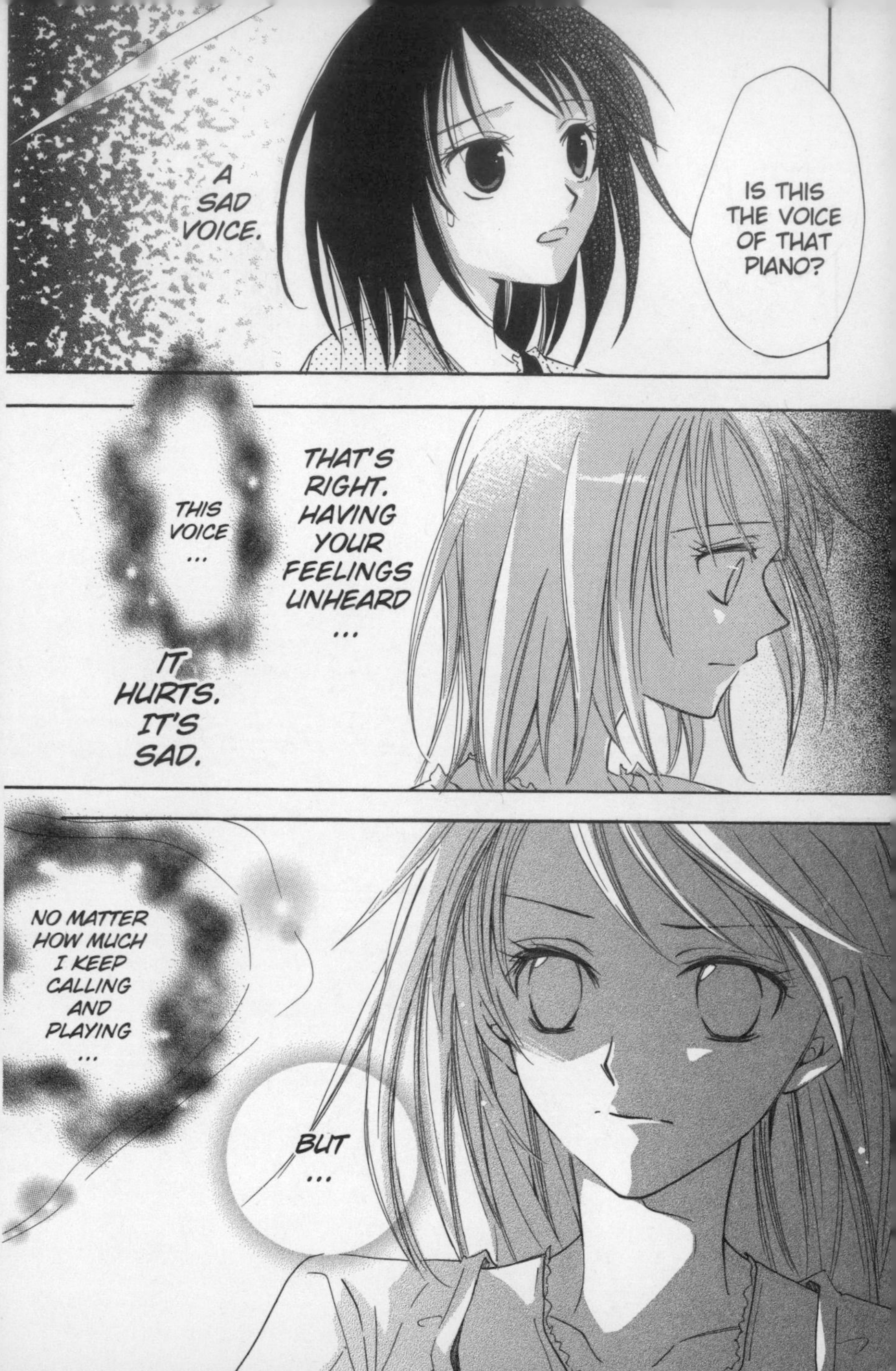
IS THIS THE VOICE OF THAT PIANO?
A SAD VOICE.
THAT'S RIGHT. HAVING YOUR FEELINGS UNHEARD ...
THIS VOICE ...
IT HURTS. IT'S SAD.
NO MATTER HOW MUCH I KEEP CALLING AND PLAYING ...
BUT ...

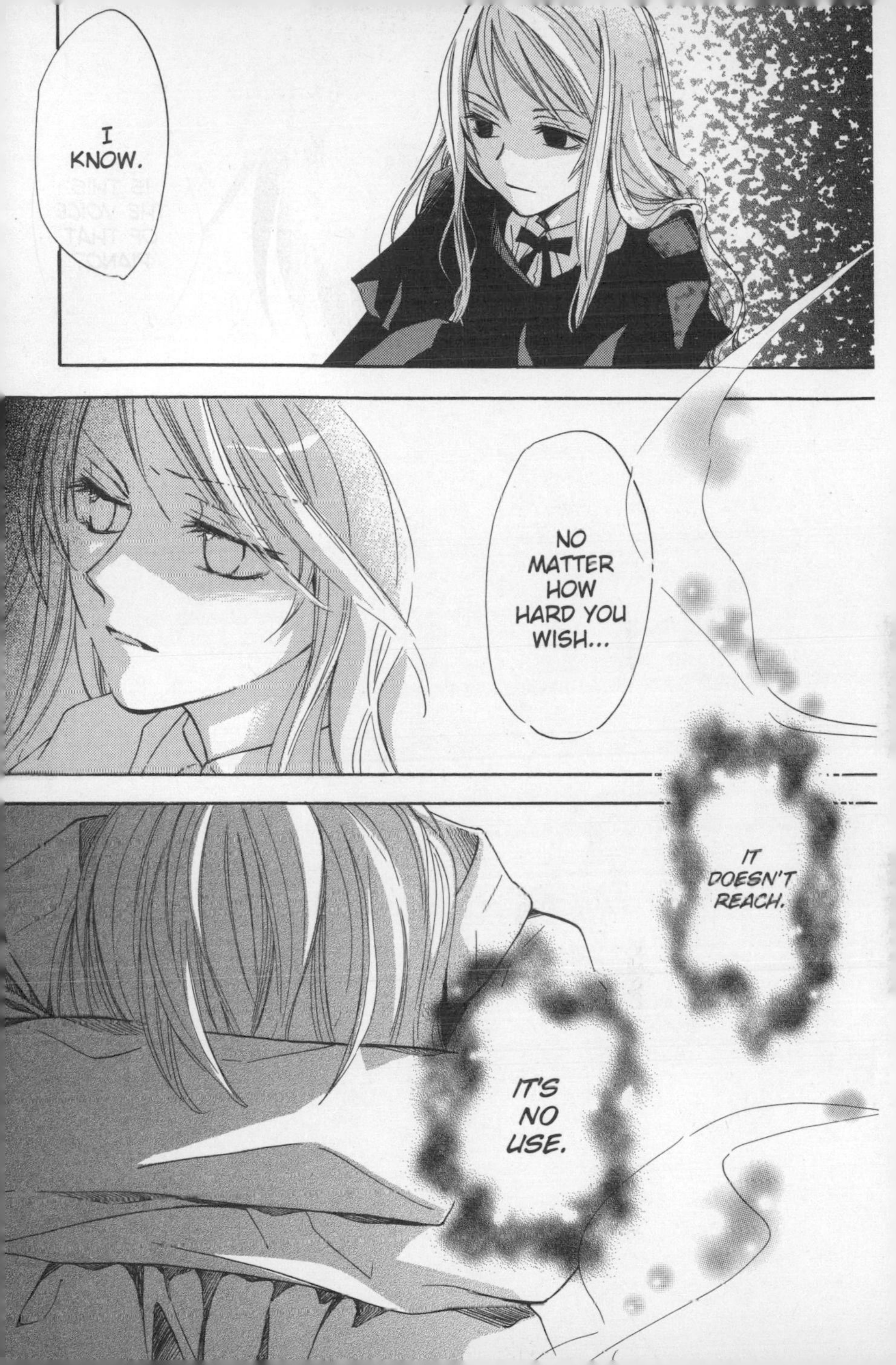
I KNOW.
NO MATTER HOW HARD YOU WISH...
IT DOESN'T REACH.
IT'S NO USE.

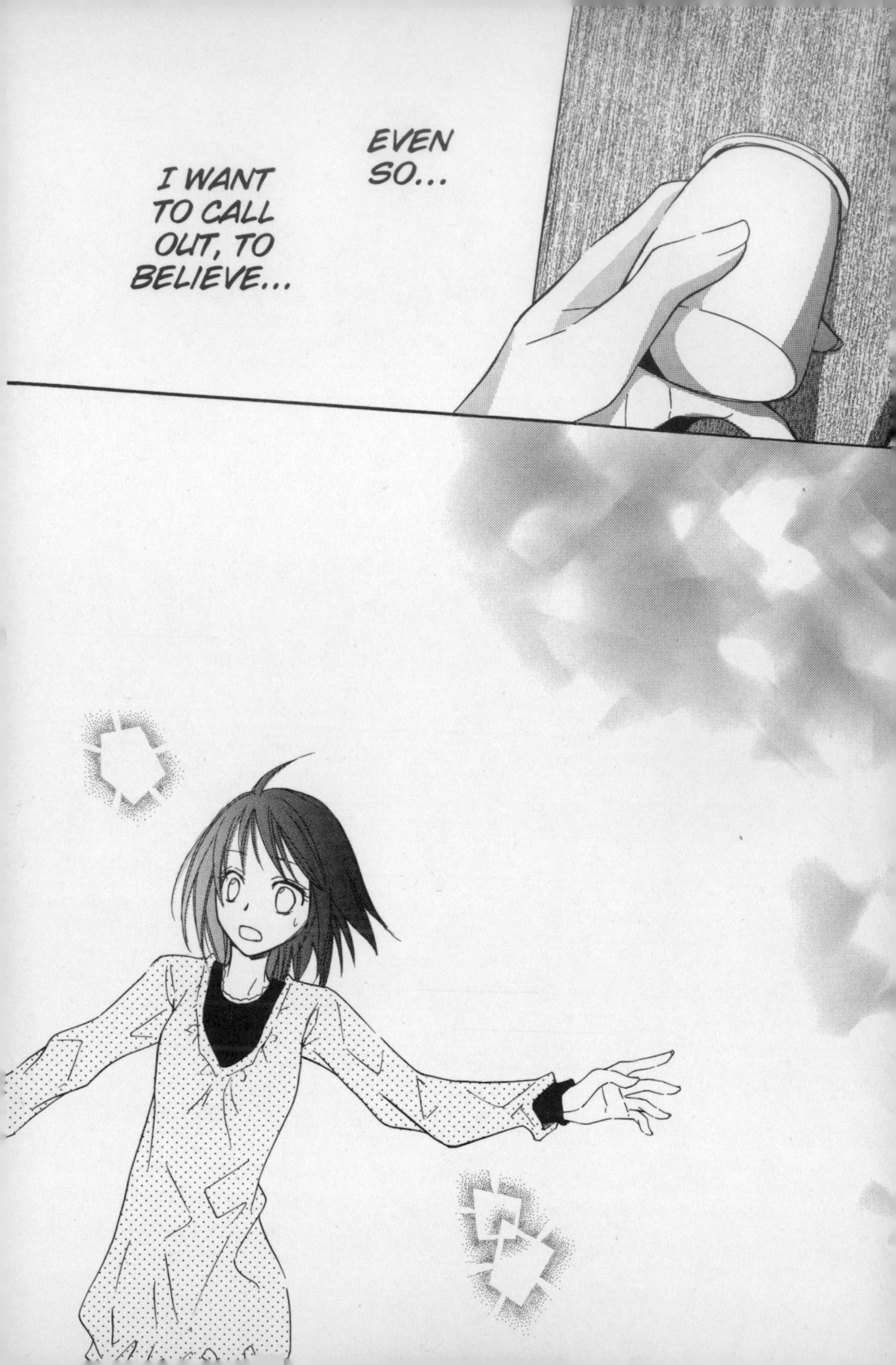
EVEN SO...
I WANT TO CALL OUT, TO BELIEVE...

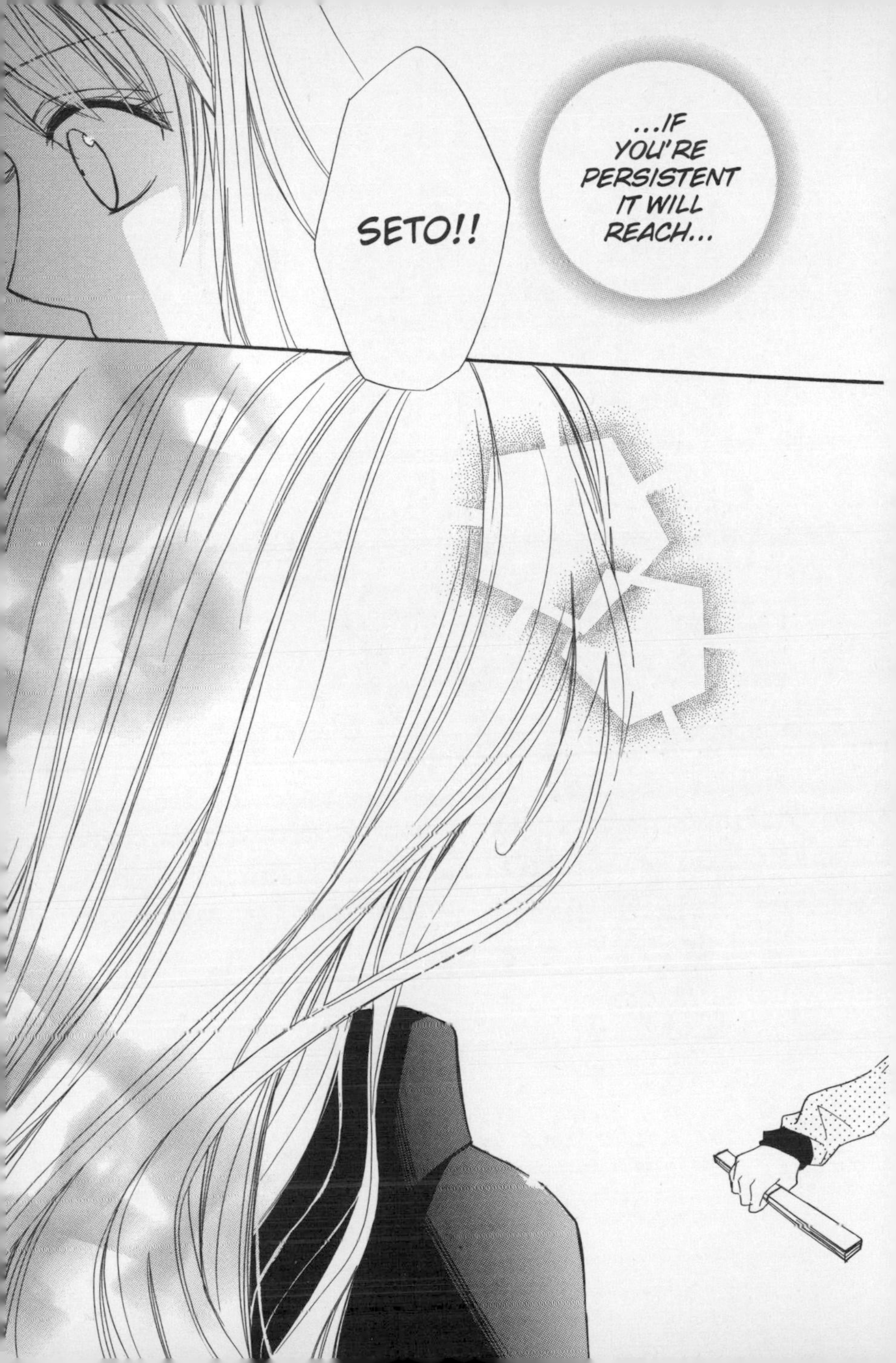
...IF YOU'RE PERSISTENT IT WILL REACH...
SETO!!

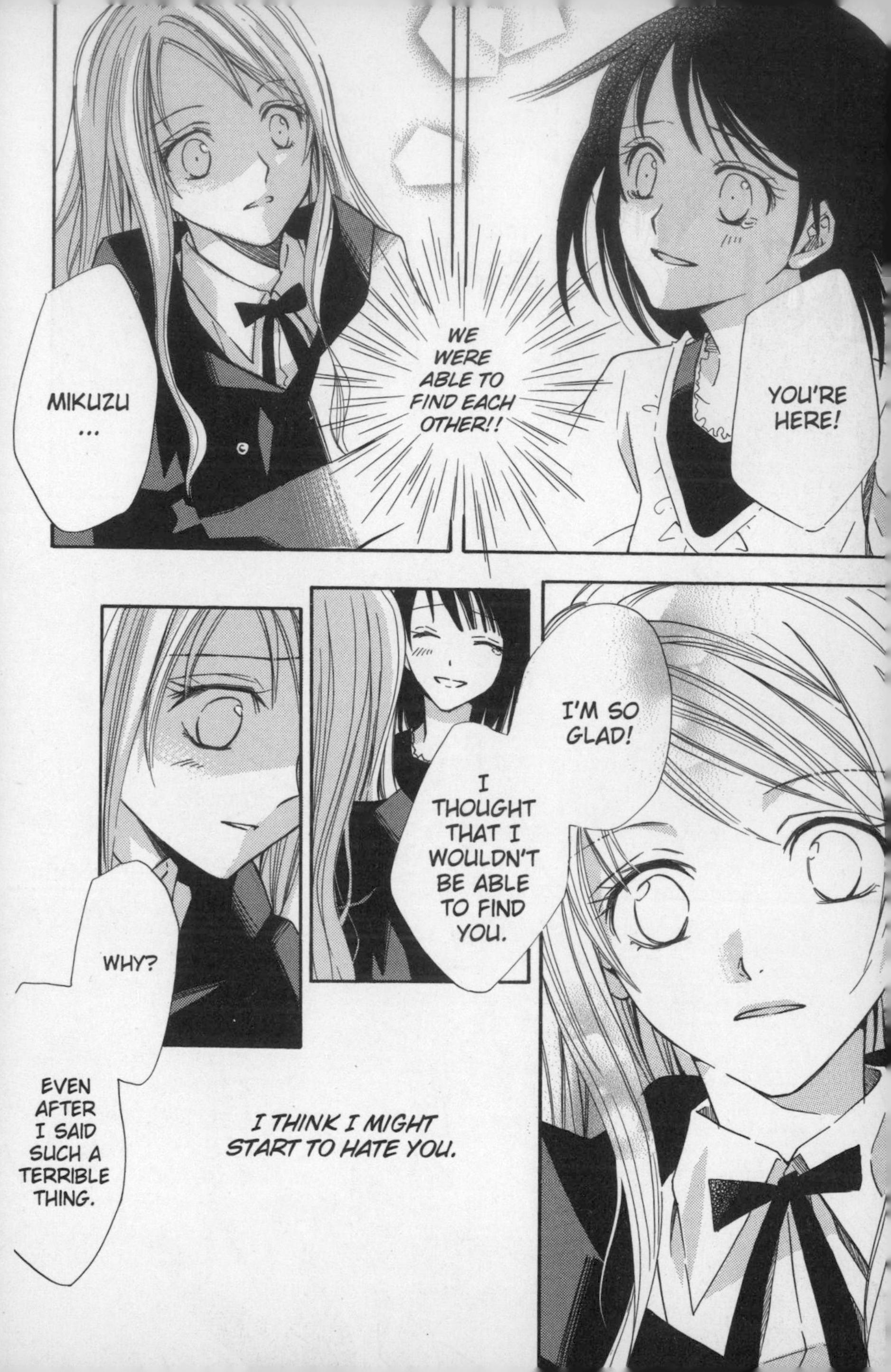
YOU'RE HERE!
WE WERE ABLE TO FIND EACH OTHER!!
MIKUZU ...
I'M SO GLAD!
I THOUGHT THAT I WOULDN'T BE ABLE TO FIND YOU.
WHY?
EVEN AFTER I SAID SUCH A TERRIBLE THING.
I THINK I MIGHT START TO HATE YOU.

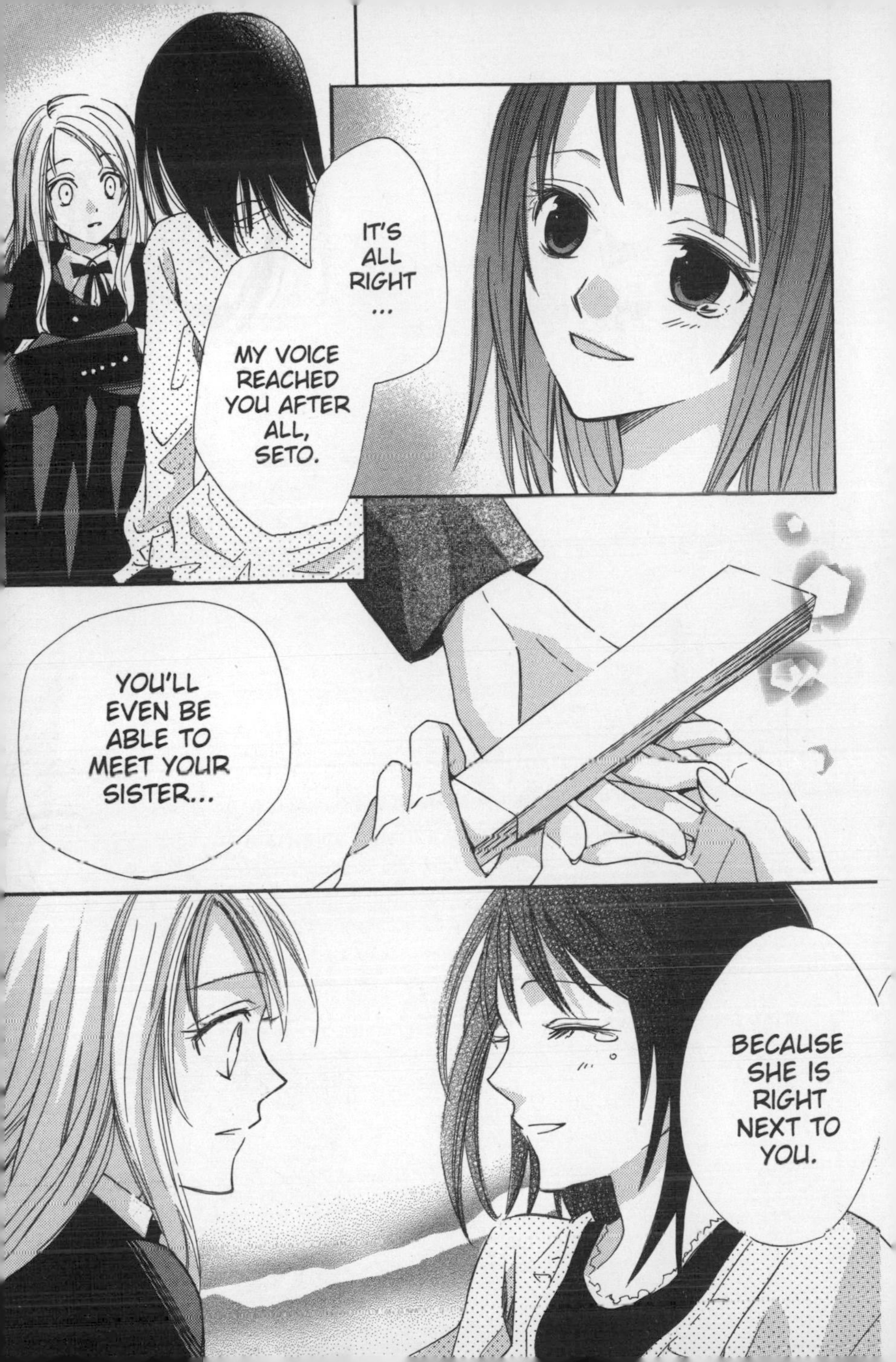
IT'S ALL RIGHT...
MY VOICE REACHED YOU AFTER ALL, SETO.
YOU'LL EVEN BE ABLE TO MEET YOUR SISTER...
BECAUSE SHE IS RIGHT NEXT TO YOU.

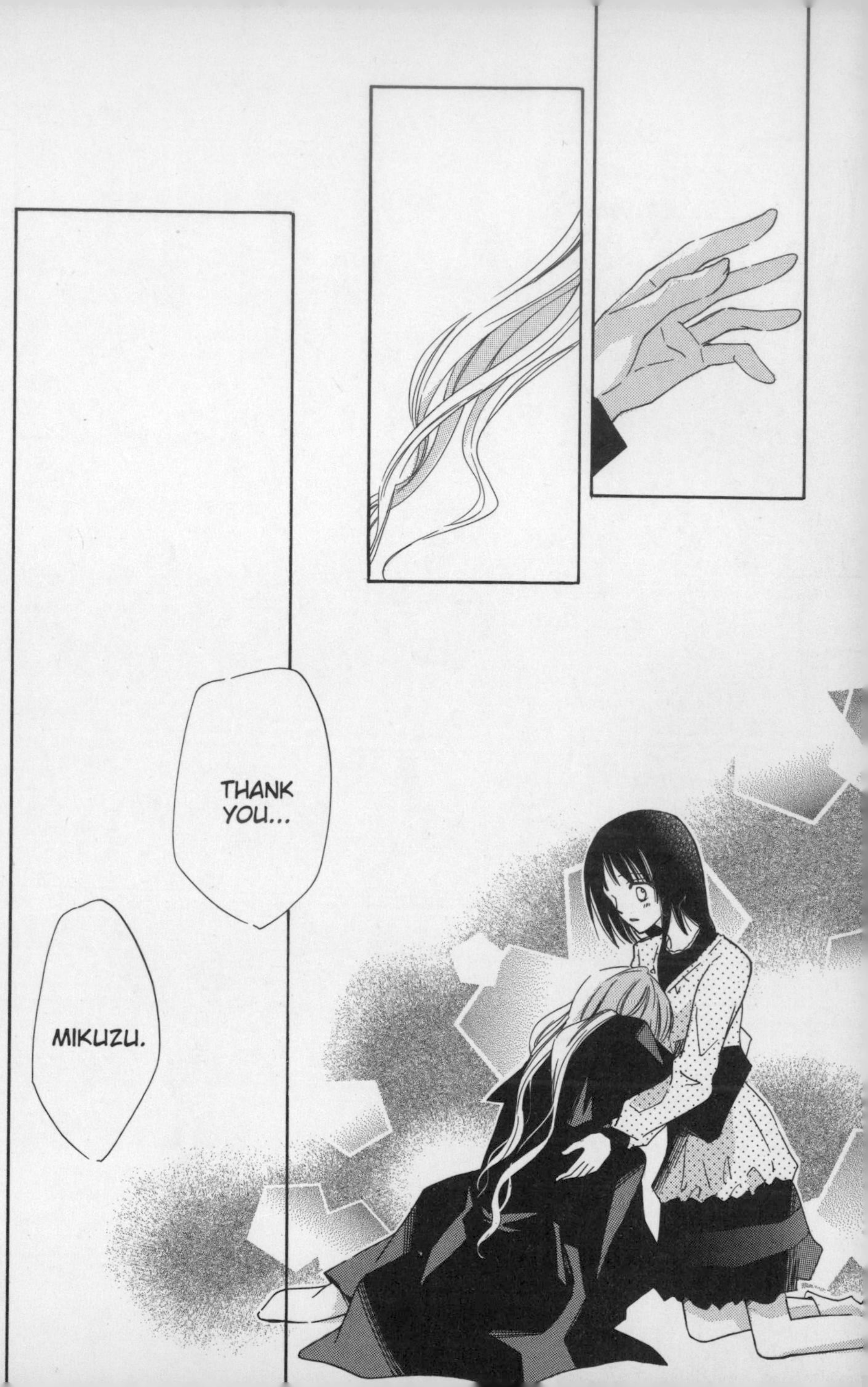
THANK YOU...
MIKUZU.

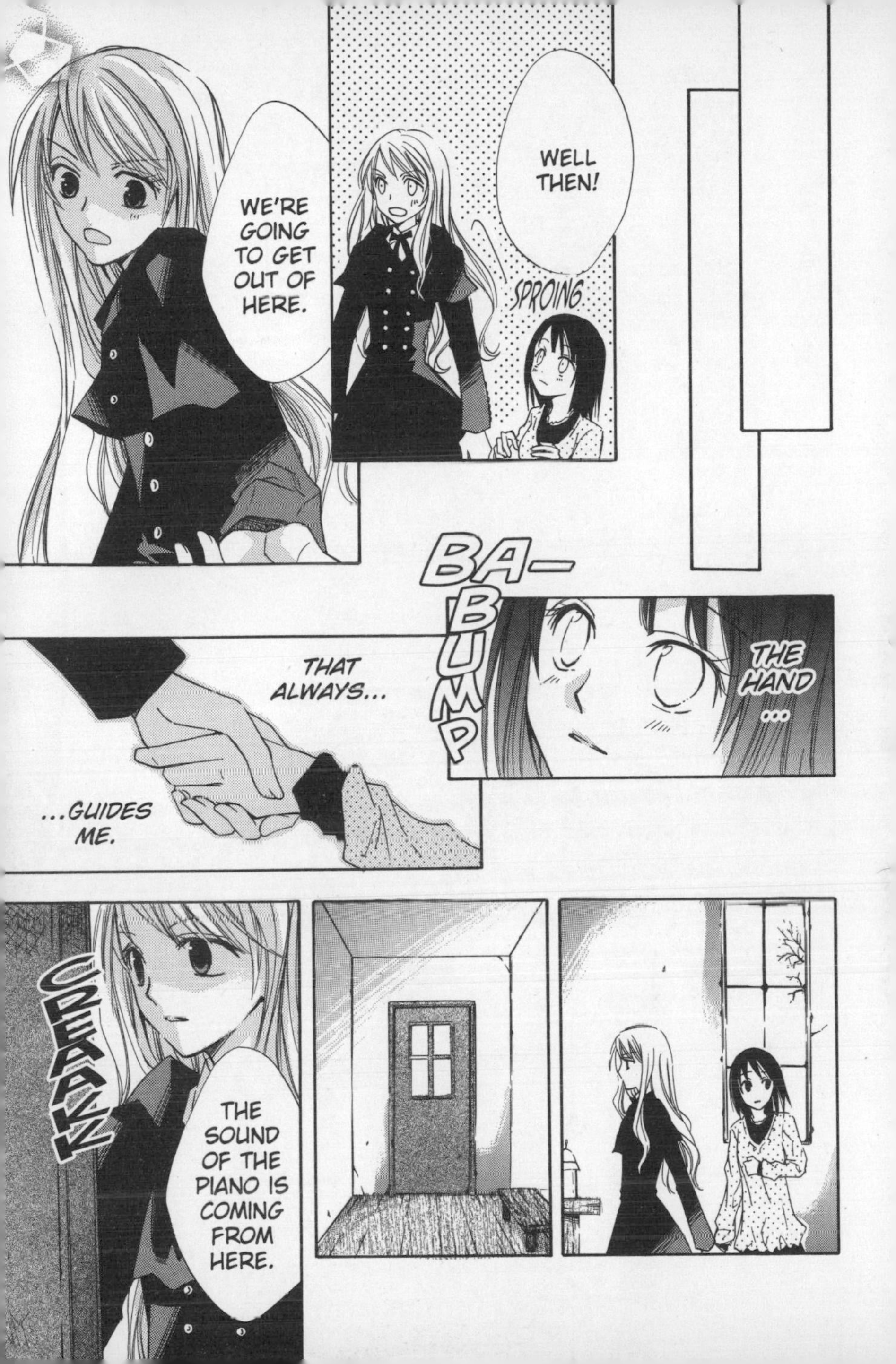
WELL THEN!
SPROING
WE'RE GOING TO GET OUT OF HERE.
BA-BUMP
THE HAND...
THAT ALWAYS...
...GUIDES ME.
CREAAK
THE SOUND OF THE PIANO IS COMING FROM HERE.

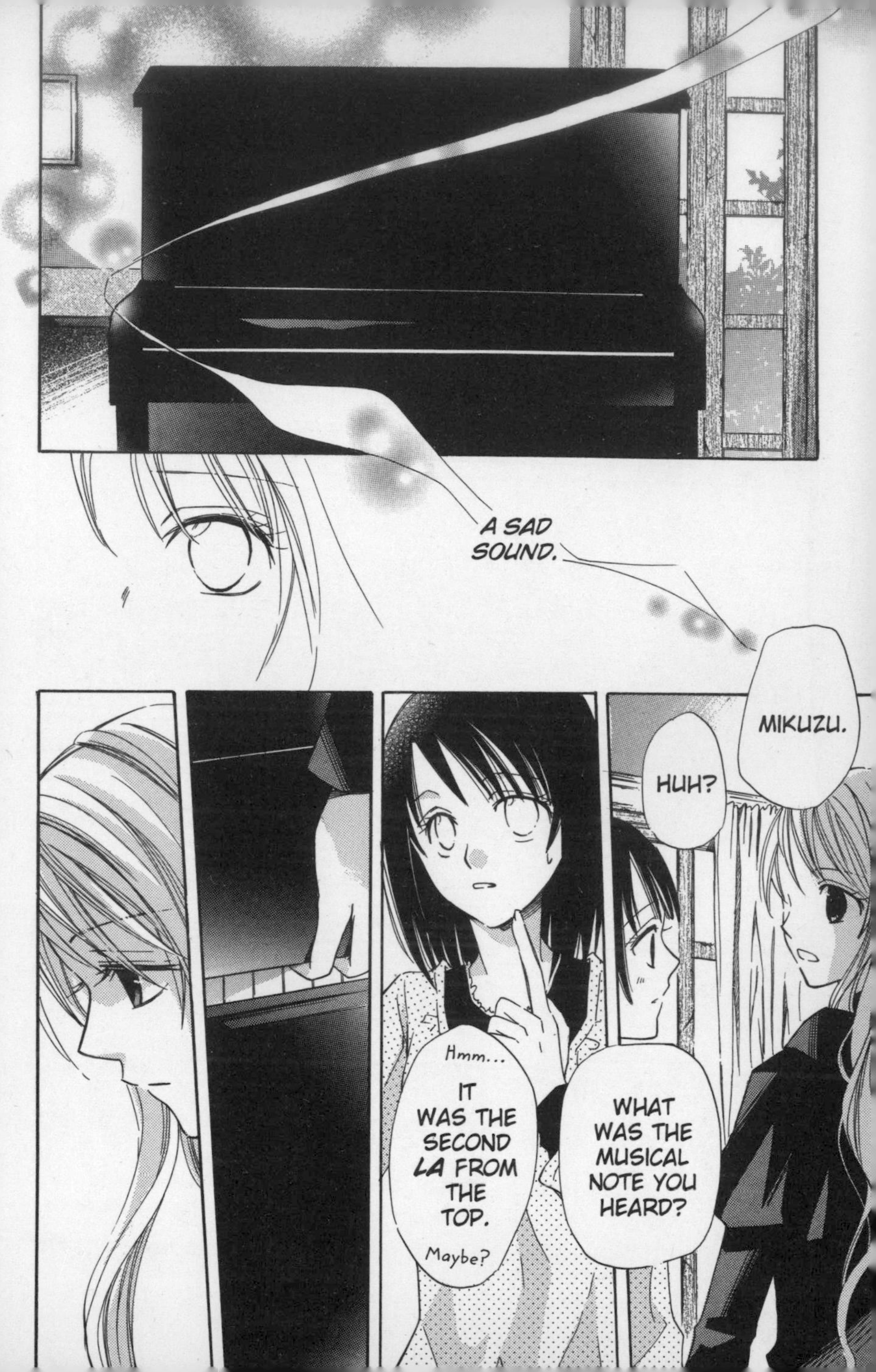
A SAD SOUND.
MIKUZU.
HUH?
WHAT WAS THE MUSICAL NOTE YOU HEARD?
Hmm...
IT WAS THE SECOND LA FROM THE TOP.
Maybe?

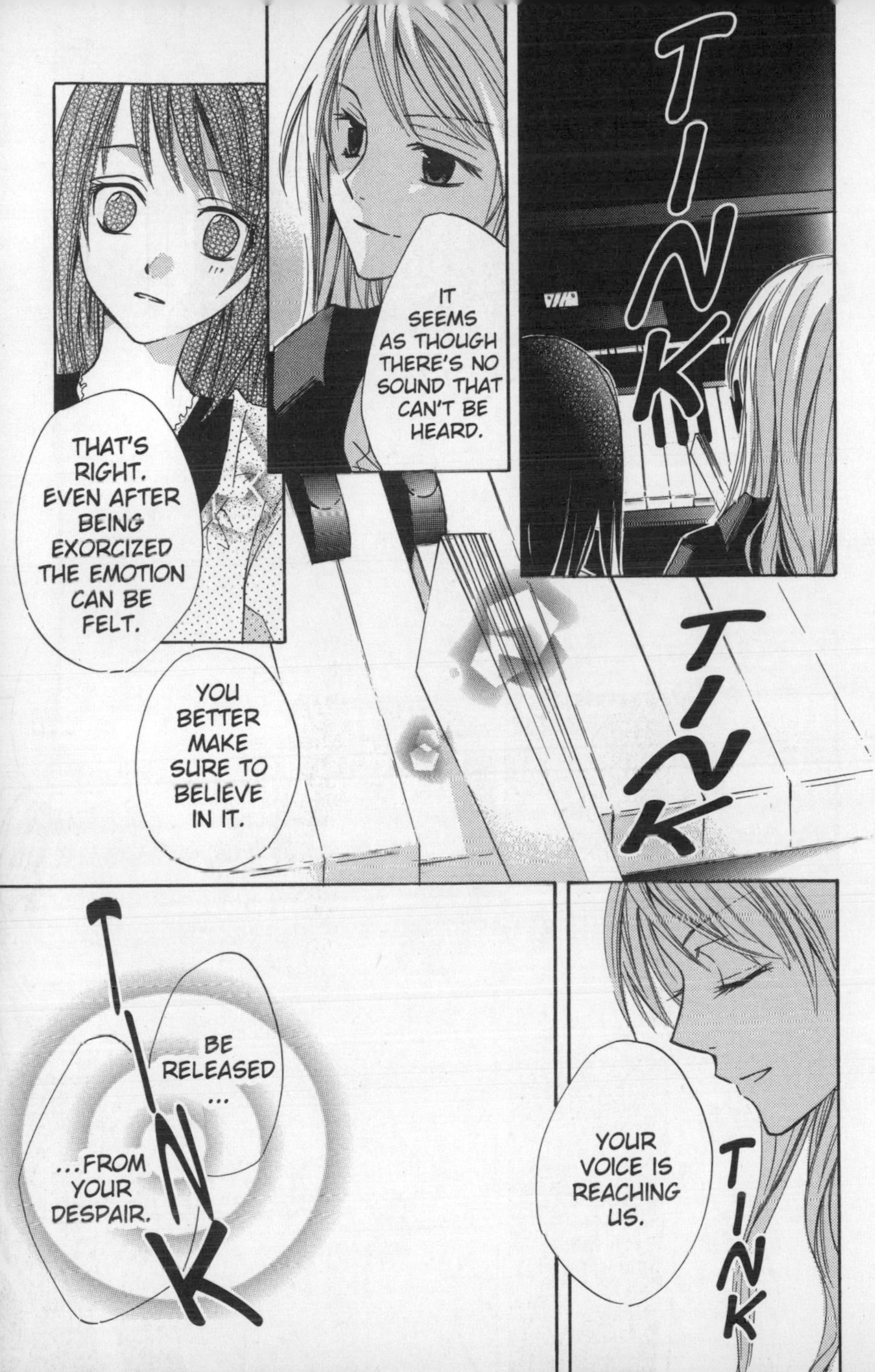
TINK
IT SEEMS AS THOUGH THERE'S NO SOUND THAT CAN'T BE HEARD.
THAT'S RIGHT. EVEN AFTER BEING EXORCIZED THE EMOTION CAN BE FELT.
TINK
YOU BETTER MAKE SURE TO BELIEVE IN IT.
TINK
YOUR VOICE IS REACHING US.
TINK
BE RELEASED ...
...FROM YOUR DESPAIR.

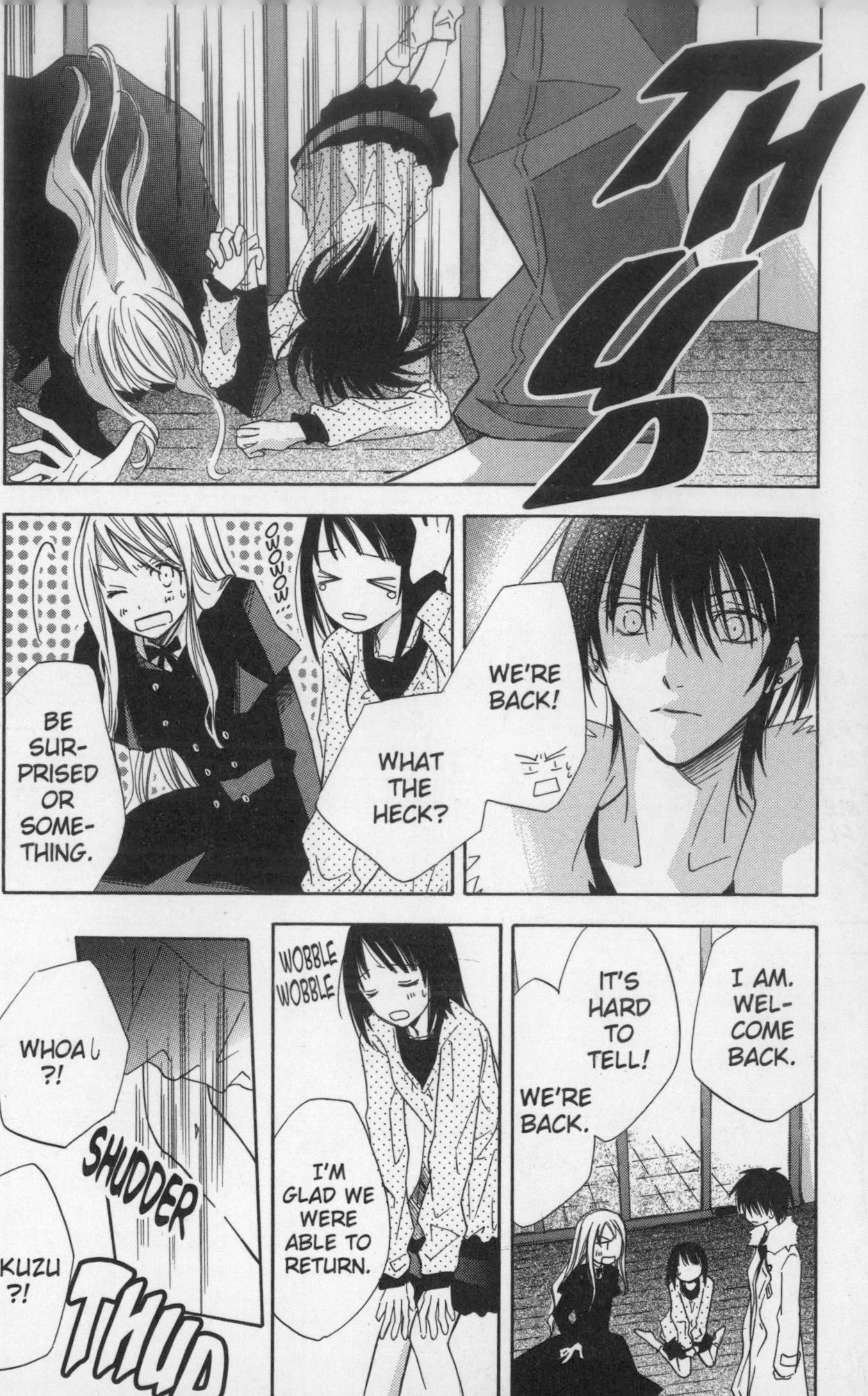
THUD
WE'RE BACK!
WHAT THE HECK?
OWOWOW!!
BE SUR-PRISED OR SOME-THING.
I AM. WEL-COME BACK.
IT'S HARD TO TELL!
WE'RE BACK.
WOBBLE WOBBLE
I'M GLAD WE WERE ABLE TO RETURN.
WHOA ?!
SHUDDER
MIKUZU ?!
THUD

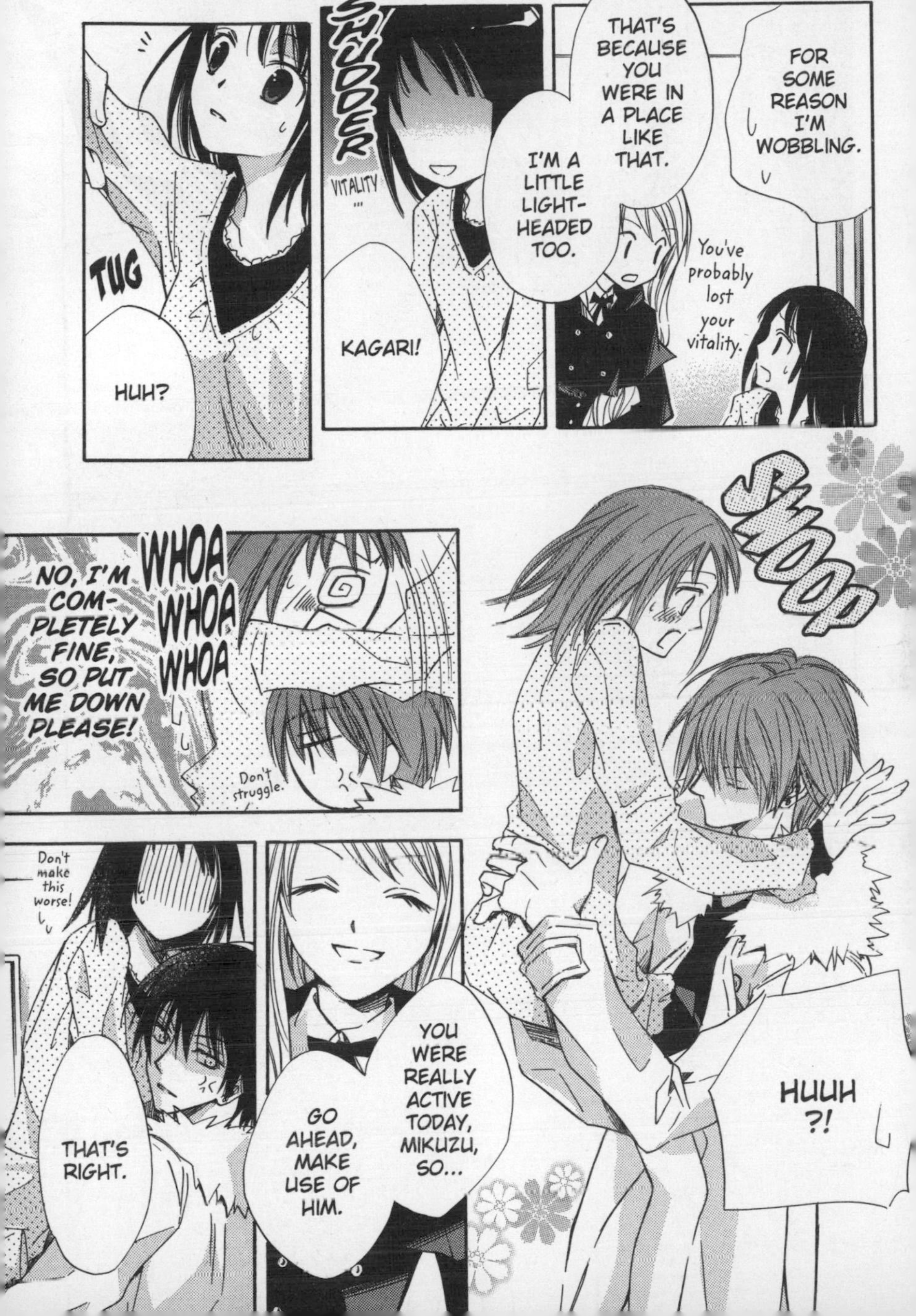
FOR SOME REASON I'M WOBBLING.
THAT'S BECAUSE YOU WERE IN A PLACE LIKE THAT.
You've probably lost your vitality.
I'M A LITTLE LIGHT-HEADED TOO.
SHUDDER
VITALITY ...
KAGARI!
TUG
HUH?
SWOOP
HUUH ?!
WHOA WHOA WHOA
NO, I'M COM-PLETELY FINE, SO PUT ME DOWN PLEASE!
Don't struggle.
YOU WERE REALLY ACTIVE TODAY, MIKUZU, SO...
GO AHEAD, MAKE USE OF HIM.
Don't make this worse!
THAT'S RIGHT.

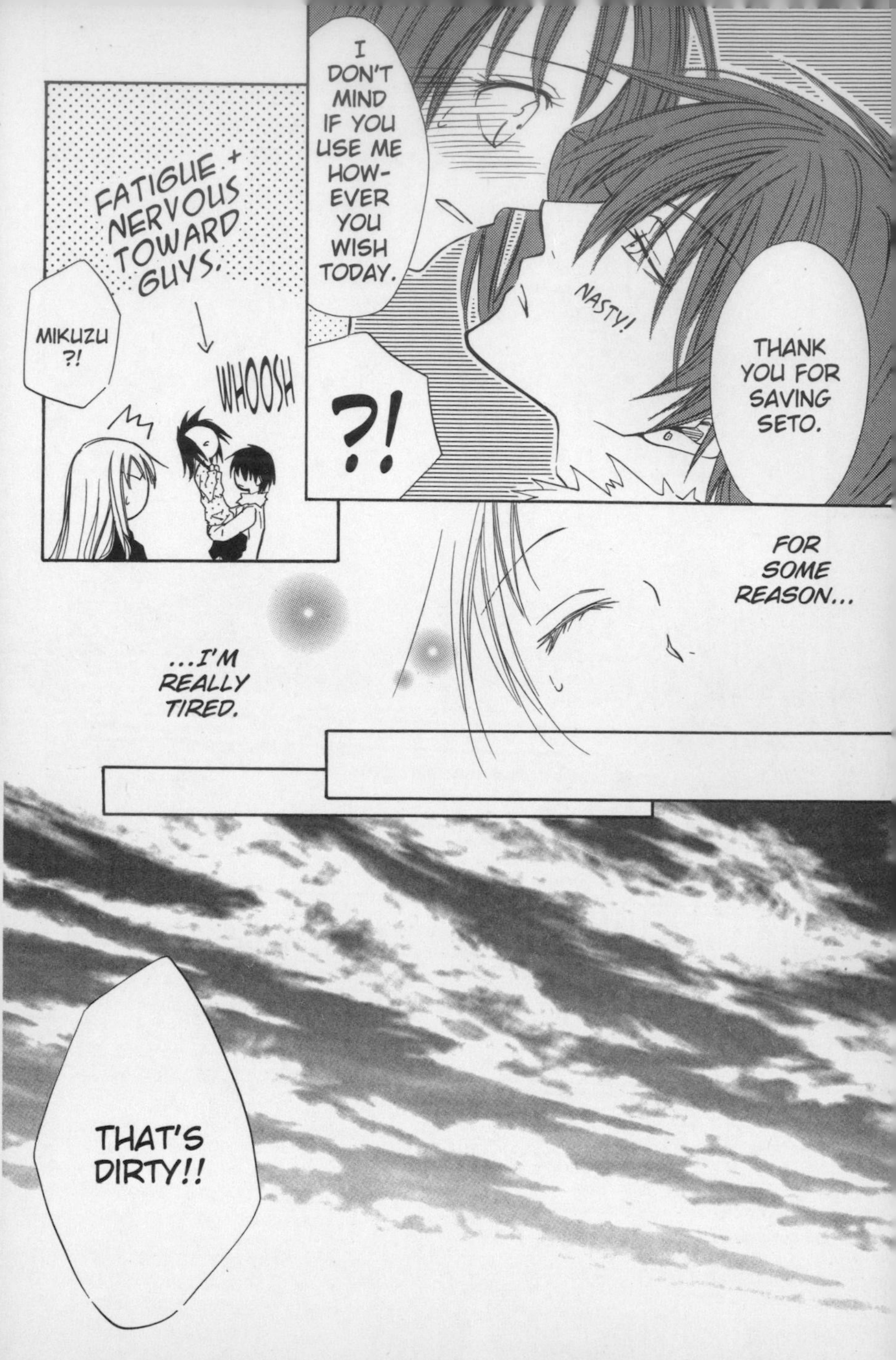
THANK YOU FOR SAVING SETO.
I DON'T MIND IF YOU USE ME HOW-EVER YOU WISH TODAY.
NASTY!
?!
FATIGUE + NERVOUS TOWARD GUYS.
WHOOSH
MIKUZU ?!
FOR SOME REASON...
...I'M REALLY TIRED.
THAT'S DIRTY!!

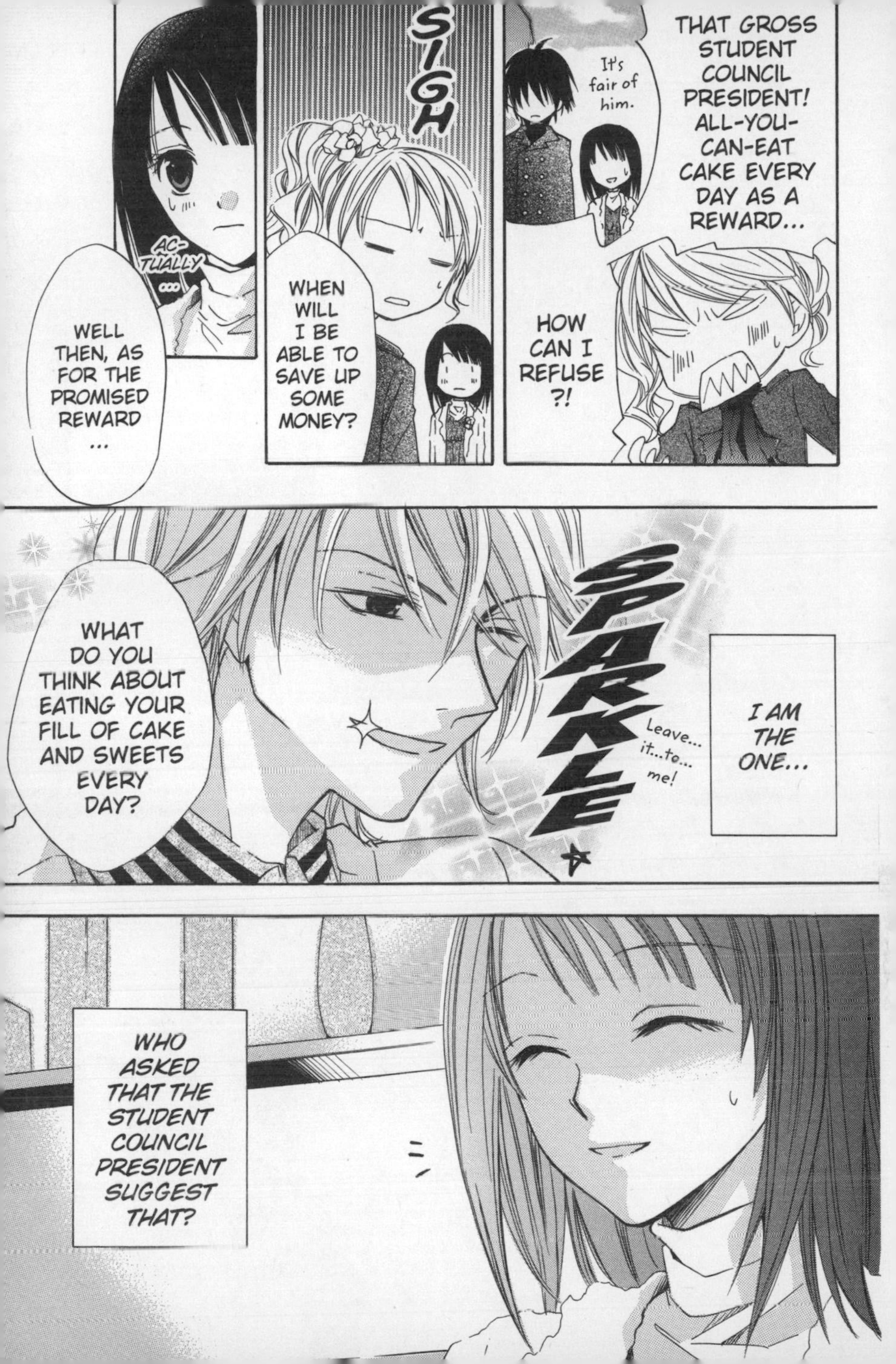
THAT GROSS STUDENT COUNCIL PRESIDENT! ALL-YOU-CAN-EAT CAKE EVERY DAY AS A REWARD...
It's fair of him.
HOW CAN I REFUSE?!
SIGH
WHEN WILL I BE ABLE TO SAVE UP SOME MONEY?
AC-TUALLY...
WELL THEN, AS FOR THE PROMISED REWARD...
I AM THE ONE...
Leave... it...to... me!
SPARKLE
WHAT DO YOU THINK ABOUT EATING YOUR FILL OF CAKE AND SWEETS EVERY DAY?
WHO ASKED THAT THE STUDENT COUNCIL PRESIDENT SUGGEST THAT?

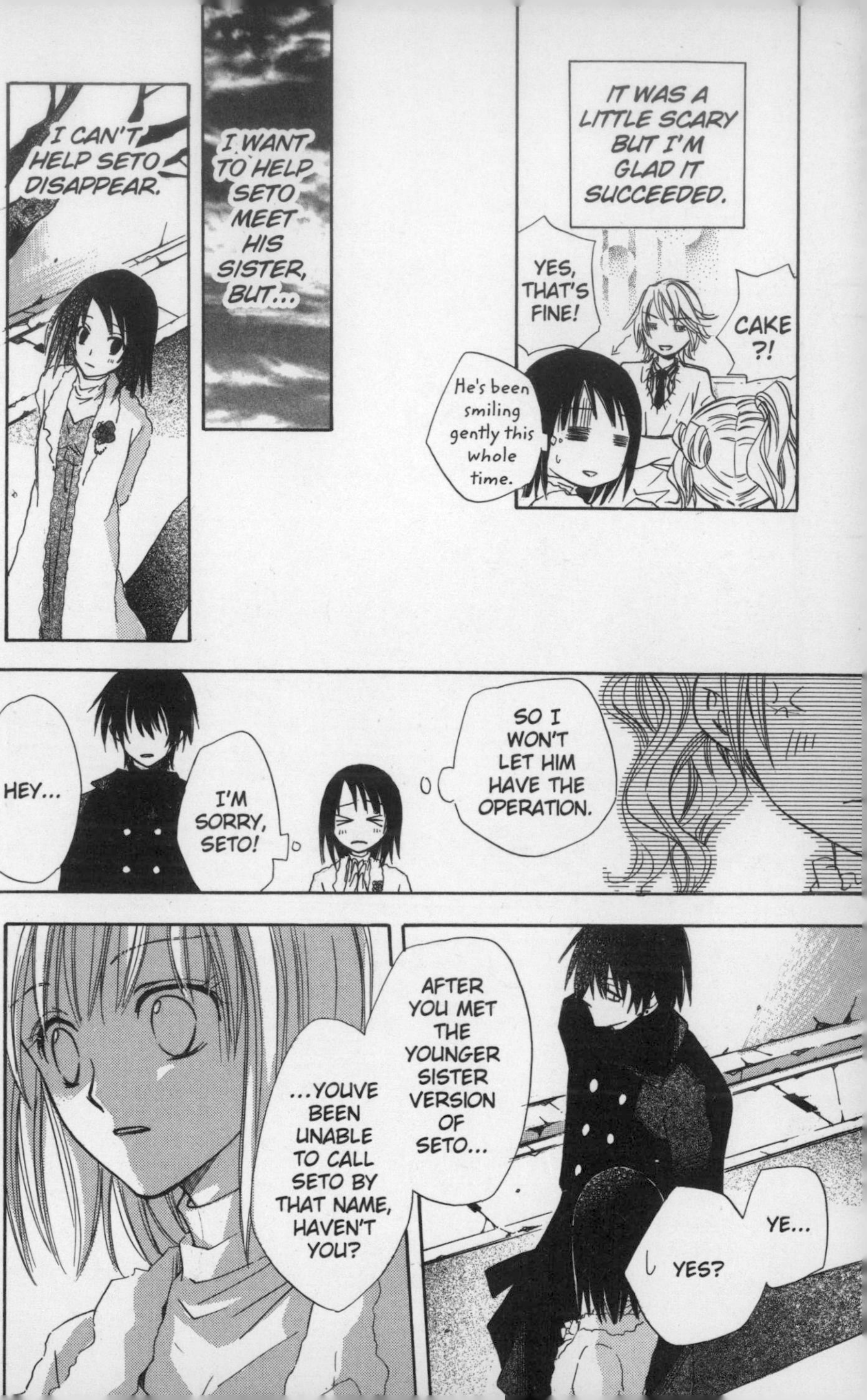
IT WAS A LITTLE SCARY BUT I'M GLAD IT SUCCEEDED.
CAKE ?!
YES, THAT'S FINE!
He's been smiling gently this whole time.
I WANT TO HELP SETO MEET HIS SISTER, BUT...
I CAN'T HELP SETO DISAPPEAR.
SO I WON'T LET HIM HAVE THE OPERATION.
I'M SORRY, SETO!
HEY...
YE...
YES?
AFTER YOU MET THE YOUNGER SISTER VERSION OF SETO...
...YOUVE BEEN UNABLE TO CALL SETO BY THAT NAME, HAVEN'T YOU?

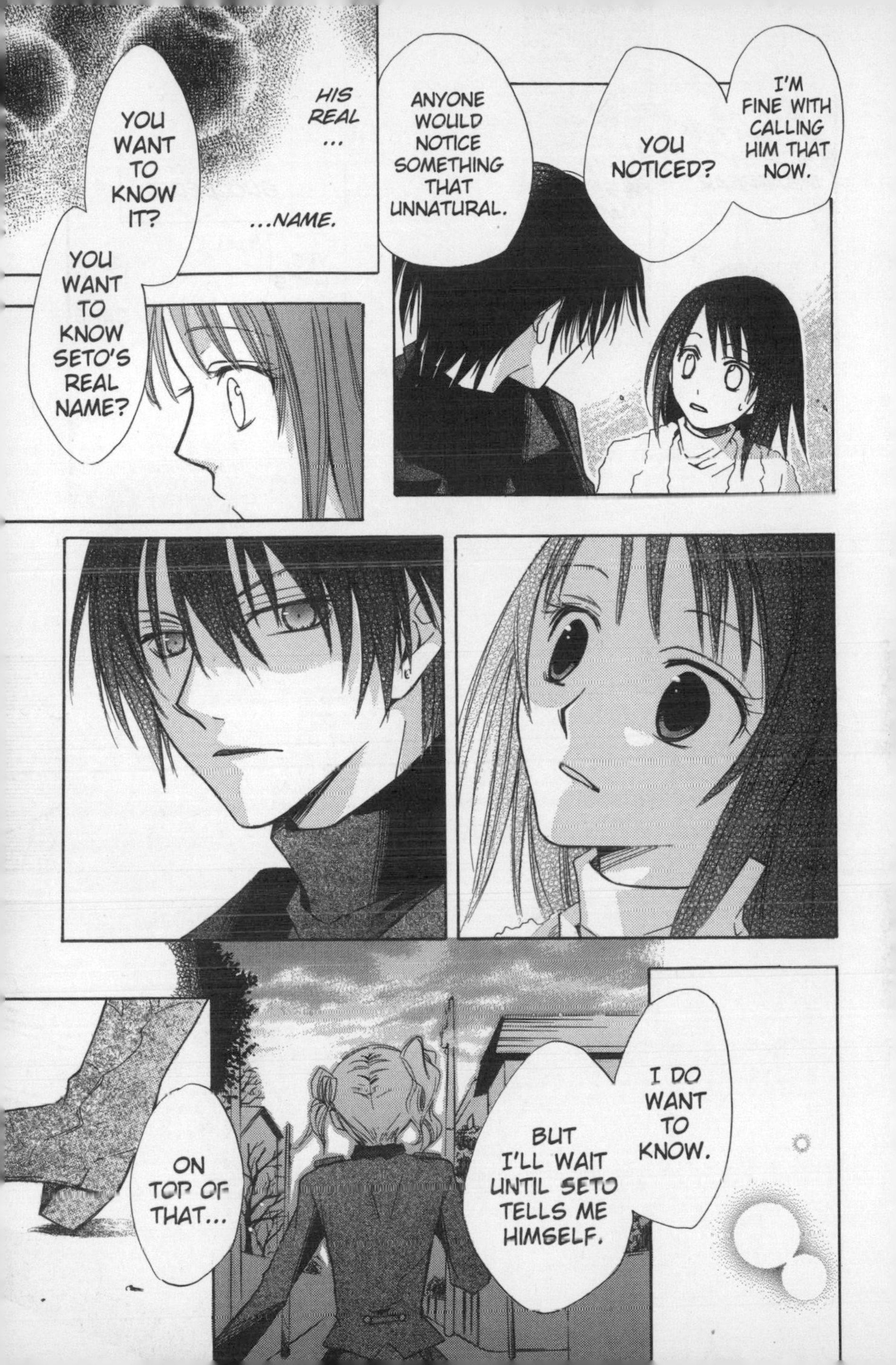
I'M FINE WITH CALLING HIM THAT NOW.
YOU NOTICED?
ANYONE WOULD NOTICE SOMETHING THAT UNNATURAL.
HIS REAL ...
...NAME.
YOU WANT TO KNOW IT?
YOU WANT TO KNOW SETO'S REAL NAME?
I DO WANT TO KNOW.
BUT I'LL WAIT UNTIL SETO TELLS ME HIMSELF.
ON TOP OF THAT...

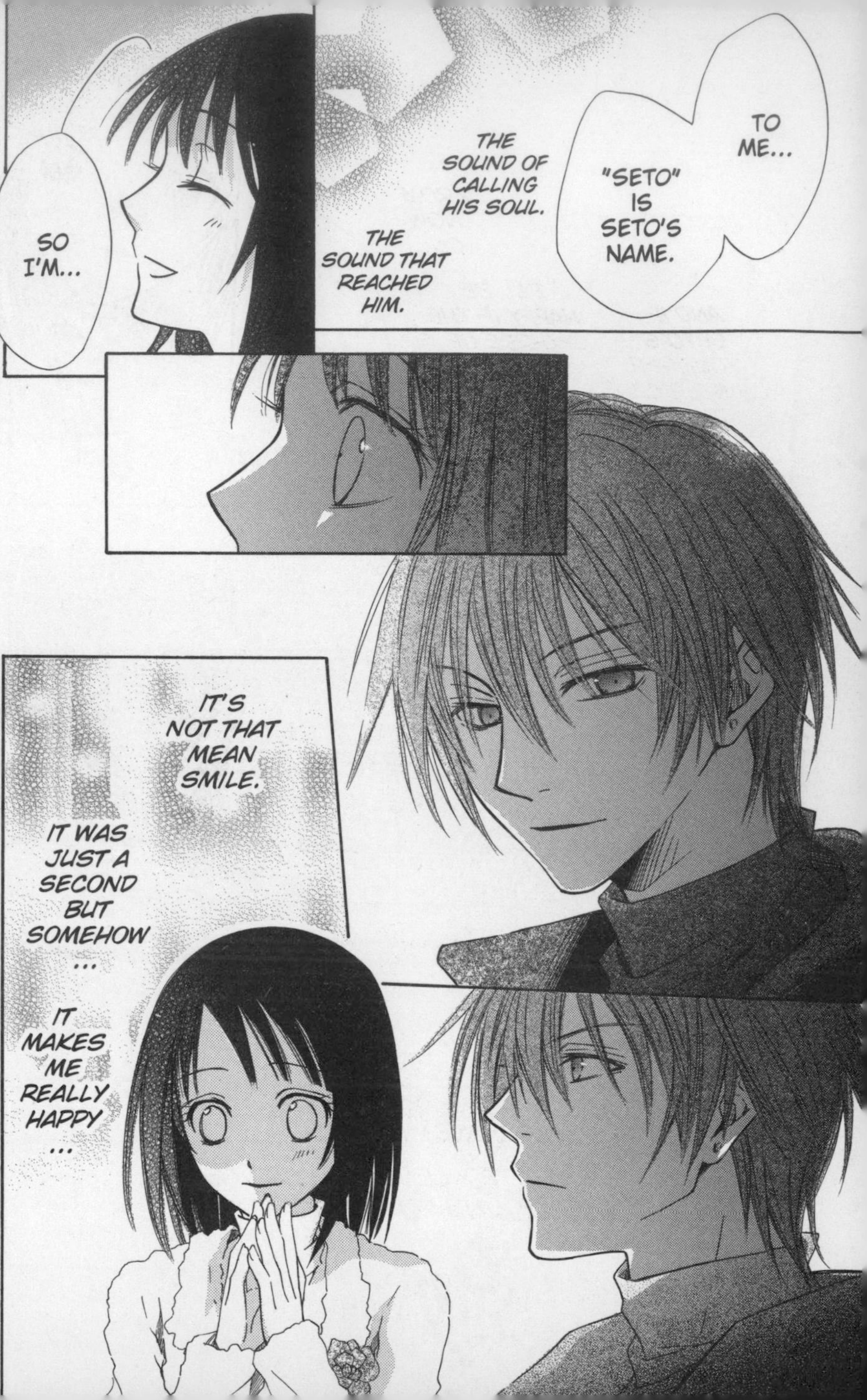
TO ME...
"SETO" IS SETO'S NAME.
THE SOUND OF CALLING HIS SOUL.
THE SOUND THAT REACHED HIM.
SO I'M...
IT'S NOT THAT MEAN SMILE.
IT WAS JUST A SECOND BUT SOMEHOW...
IT MAKES ME REALLY HAPPY...

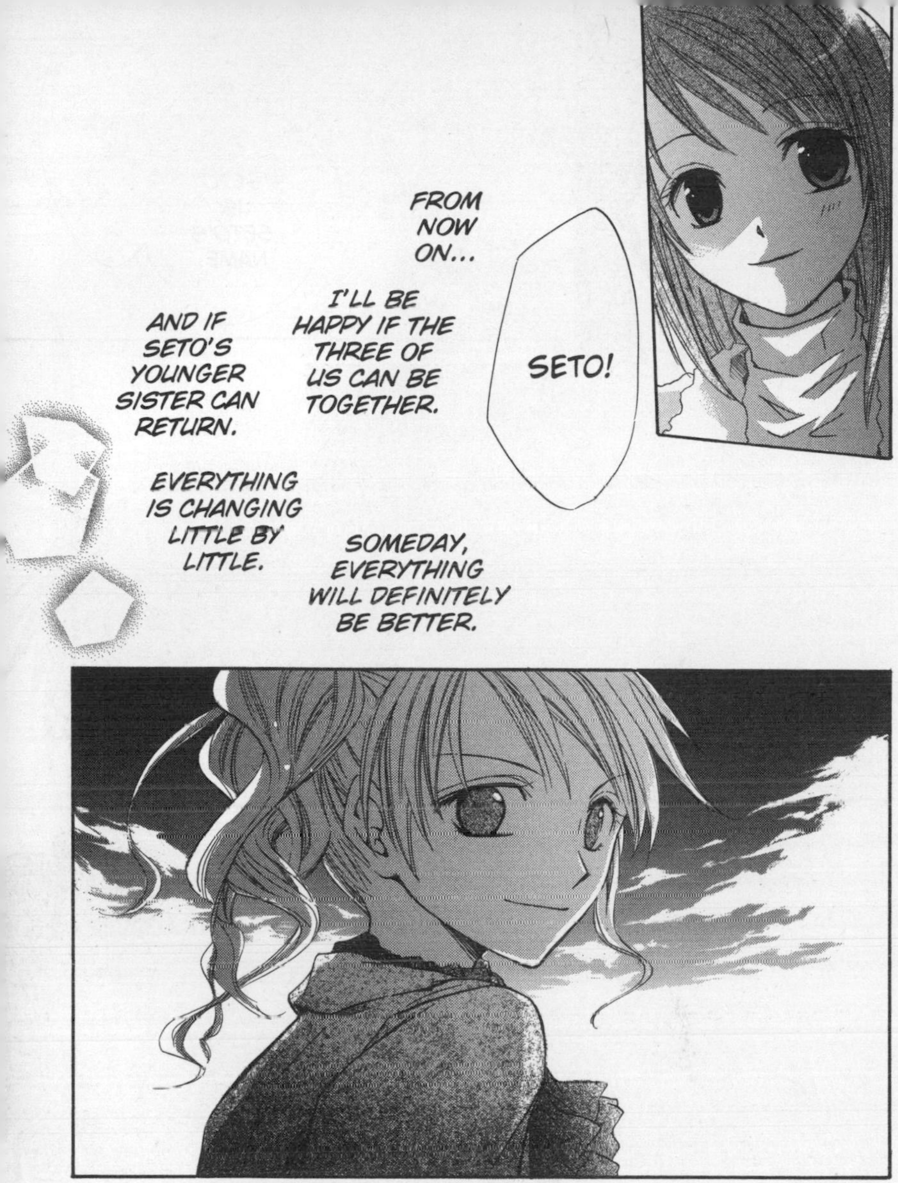
SETO!
FROM NOW ON...
I'LL BE HAPPY IF THE THREE OF US CAN BE TOGETHER.
AND IF SETO'S YOUNGER SISTER CAN RETURN.
EVERYTHING IS CHANGING LITTLE BY LITTLE.
SOMEDAY, EVERYTHING WILL DEFINITELY BE BETTER.

I WANT TO KEEP CALLING OUT THIS SOUND TO YOU FOREVER.

HEAVEN'S WILL *THE END*

DOPPELGANGER!

*S*atoru Takamiya was born in April and is a
Capricorn. She has been a professional manga creator
since 2001 when her series *Tenshi Tsuiraku* (An Angel
Falls Down) was first published. Since that time she
has drawn a variety of other titles such as *Otogibanashi
de Himitsu no Kisu* (Secret Fairytale Kiss), *Watashi no +
Okusuri* (My Medicine), *Kusuriyubi Hime* (Ring Finger
Princess), *Full Moon Joker*, and *Heaven's Will*. Currently
she contributes regularly to *Chu Chu* magazine. When
she's not drawing manga, reading books, watching
movies or playing video games, she likes to eat yummy
food. *Heaven's Will* is her first book to be published
since she moved to Kyoto. She moves around quite a
bit, but would like to stay put at least until her next
comic is complete. Her official website is
http://www.strangeparadise.fc2web.com.

HEAVEN'S WILL
The Shojo Beat Manga Edition

STORY AND ART BY SATORU TAKAMIYA

This manga volume contains material that was originally published in English in *Shojo Beat* magazine, December 2008 issue. Artwork in the magazine may have been altered slightly from what is presented in this volume.

English Translation & Adaptation/Lindsey Akashi
Touch-up Art & Lettering/Rina Mapa
Design/Julie Behn
Editor/Eric Searleman

Editor in Chief, Books/Alvin Lu
Editor in Chief, Magazines/Marc Weidenbaum
VP, Publishing Licensing/Rika Inouye
VP, Sales & Product Marketing/Gonzalo Ferreyra
VP, Creative/Linda Espinosa
Publisher/Hyoe Narita

Printed in Canada

Published by VIZ Media, LLC
P.O. Box 77010
San Francisco, CA 94107

Shojo Beat Manga Edition
10 9 8 7 6 5 4 3 2 1
First printing, January 2009

store.viz.com

The gripping story — in **manga** format

Get the complete *Be With You* collection— buy the manga and fiction today!

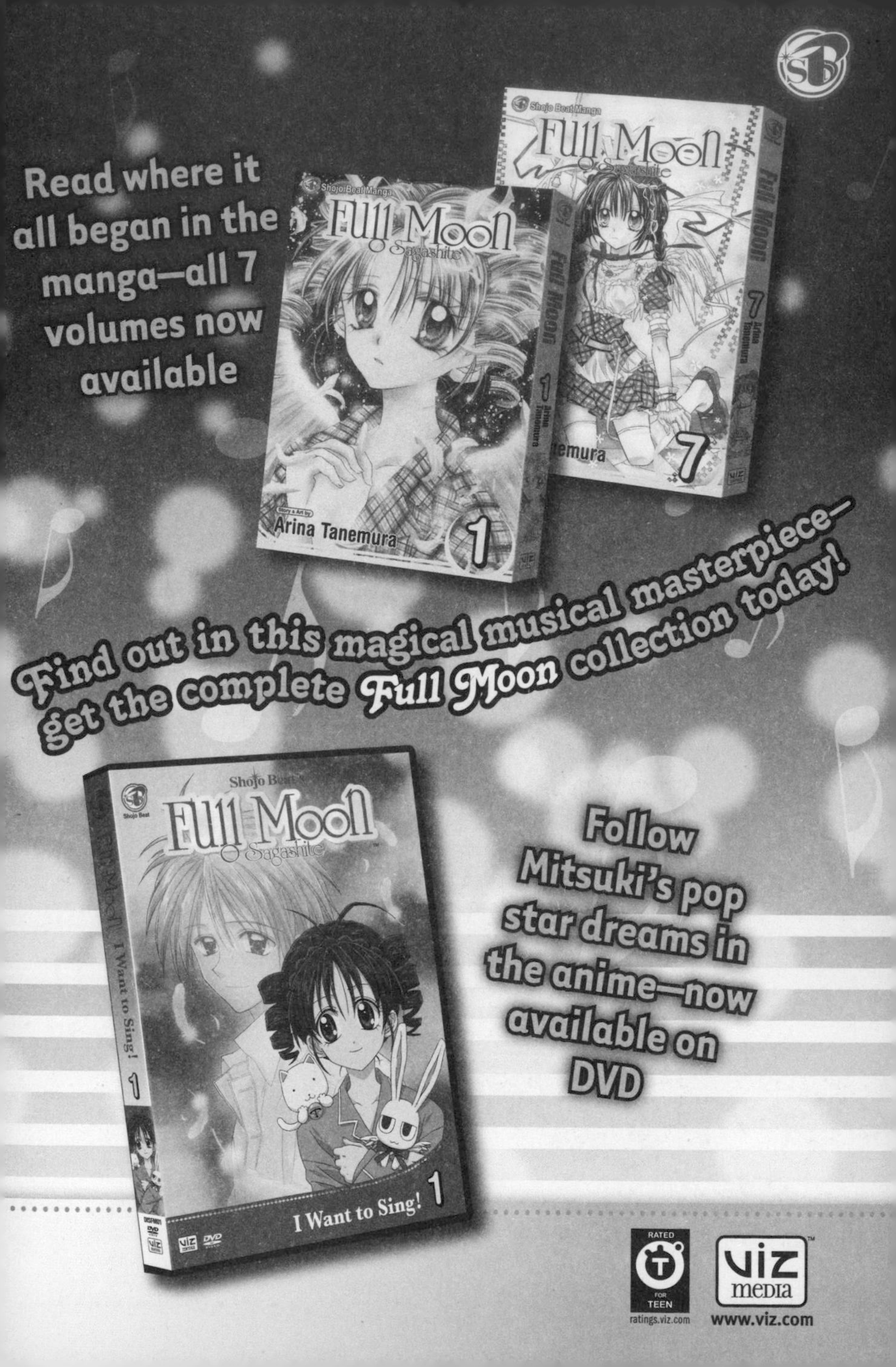
Shojo Beat Manga
Full Moon O Sagashite
Full Moon 7 Arina Tanemura
Tanemura 7
Shojo Beat Manga
Full Moon O Sagashite
Full Moon 1 Arina Tanemura
Story & Art by Arina Tanemura 1
Read where it all began in the manga—all 7 volumes now available
Find out in this magical musical masterpiece—
get the complete Full Moon collection today!
Shojo Beat
Full Moon O Sagashite
Full Moon I Want to Sing! 1
I Want to Sing! 1
Follow Mitsuki's pop star dreams in the anime—now available on DVD
RATED T FOR TEEN
ratings.viz.com
viz media
www.viz.com

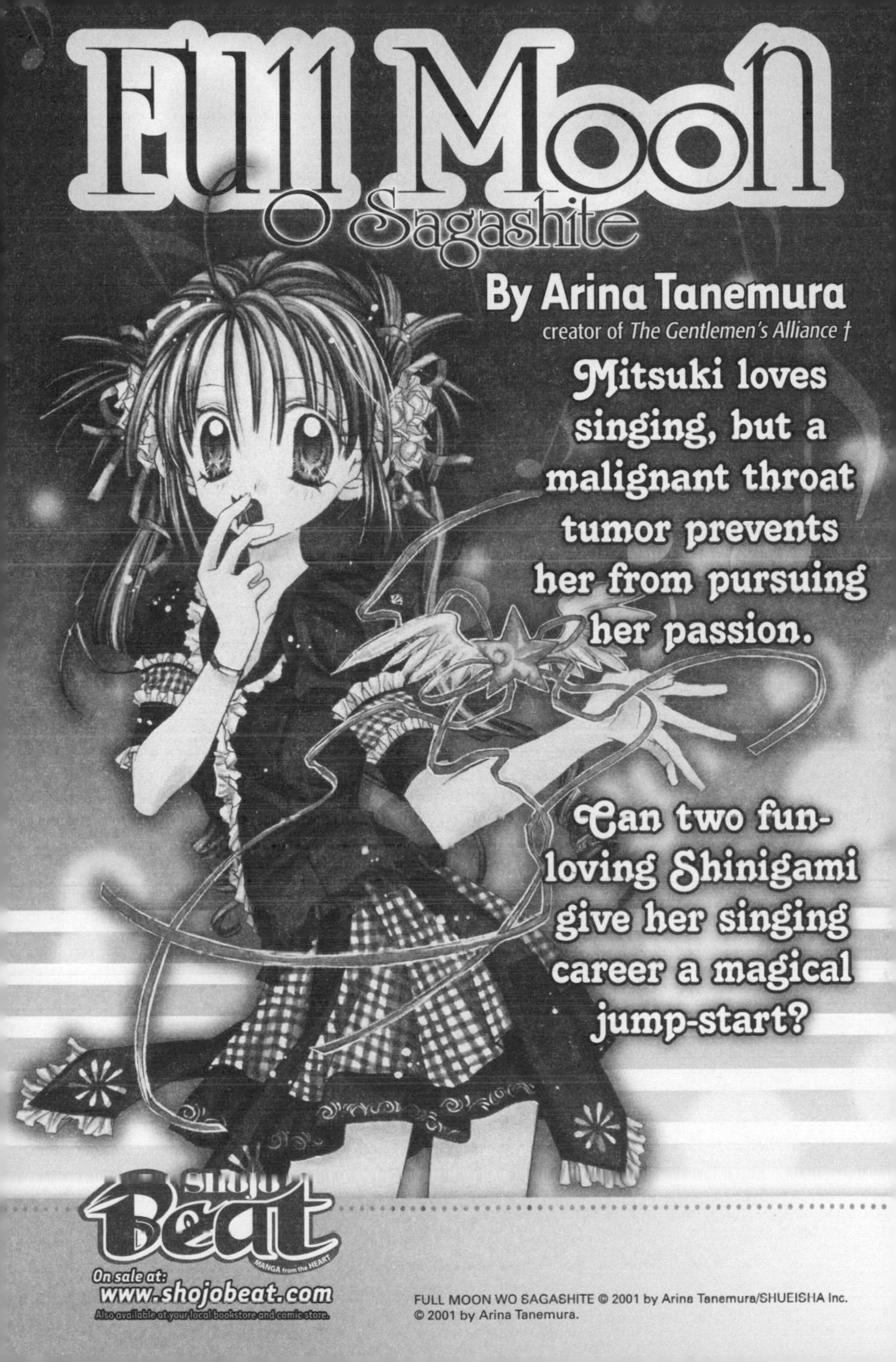
Full Moon
O Sagashite
By Arina Tanemura
creator of The Gentlemen's Alliance †
Mitsuki loves singing, but a malignant throat tumor prevents her from pursuing her passion.
Can two fun-loving Shinigami give her singing career a magical jump-start?
Shojo Beat
MANGA from the HEART
On sale at:
www.shojobeat.com
Also available at your local bookstore and comic store.
FULL MOON WO SAGASHITE © 2001 by Arina Tanemura/SHUEISHA Inc.
© 2001 by Arina Tanemura.

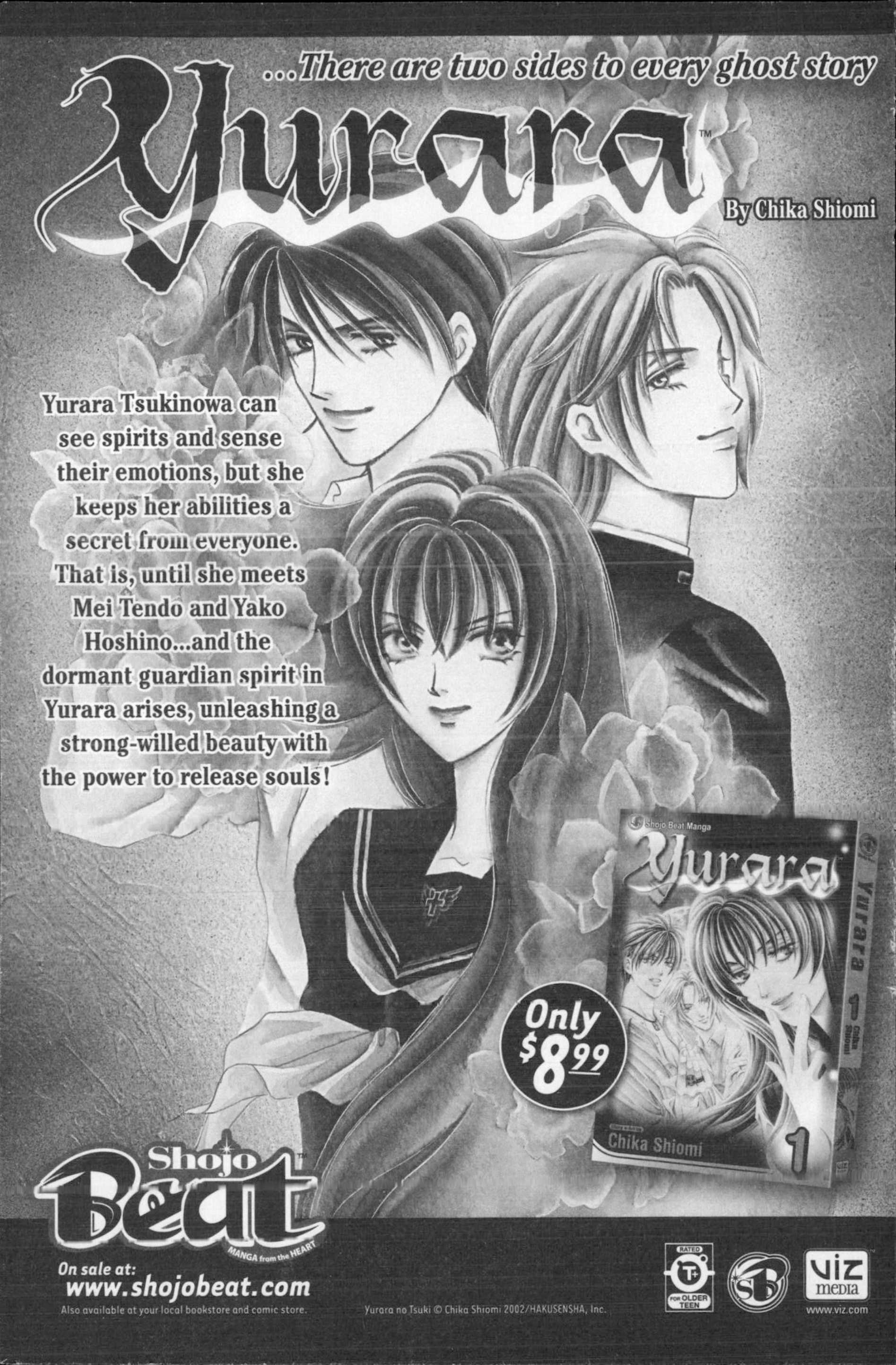
...There are two sides to every ghost story
Yurara™
By Chika Shiomi
Yurara Tsukinowa can see spirits and sense their emotions, but she keeps her abilities a secret from everyone. That is, until she meets Mei Tendo and Yako Hoshino...and the dormant guardian spirit in Yurara arises, unleashing a strong-willed beauty with the power to release souls!
Shojo Beat Manga
Yurara
Chika Shiomi
1
Only $8.99
Shojo Beat™
MANGA from the HEART
On sale at:
www.shojobeat.com
Also available at your local bookstore and comic store.
Yurara no Tsuki © Chika Shiomi 2002/HAKUSENSHA, Inc.
RATED T+ FOR OLDER TEEN
viz media
www.viz.com